God and Country?

Previously Published Works

Michael G. Long

2006

Billy Graham and the Beloved Community: America's Evangelist and the Dream of Martin Luther King Jr. New York: Palgrave Macmillan.

2004

Martin Luther King Jr. on Creative Living. St. Louis, MO: Chalice Press.

2002

Against Us, but for Us: Martin Luther King Jr. and the State. Macon, GA: Mercer University Press.

Tracy Wenger Sadd

2000

Close Encounters: New Testament Personalities. Scottdale, PA: Faith and Life Press.

1997

Who Is God? Scottdale, PA: Faith and Life Press.

God and Country?

Diverse Perspectives on Christianity and Patriotism

Edited by Michael G. Long and Tracy Wenger Sadd

First published in 2007 by
PALGRAVE MACMILLAN™
175 Fifth Avenue, New York, NY 10010 and
Houndmills, Basingstoke, Hampshire, England RG21 6XS.
Companies and representatives throughout the world.

PALGRAVE MACMILLAN is the global academic imprint of the Palgrave
Macmillan division of St. Martin's Press, LLC and of Palgrave Macmillan Ltd.
Macmillan® is a registered trademark in the United States, United Kingdom and
other countries. Palgrave is a registered trademark in the European Union and
other countries.

ISBN-13: 978–1–4039–7300–9
ISBN-10: 1–4039–7300–8

**Library of Congress Cataloging-in-Publication Data is available from the
Library of Congress.**

A catalogue record of the book is available from the British Library.

Design by Scribe Inc.

First edition: July 2007

10 9 8 7 6 5 4 3 2 1

Printed in the United States of America.

Chapter Three is adapted from *Honest Patriots: Loving a Country Enough to
Remember Its Misdeeds*, 263–286, chapter five, by Shriver, D. W. (2005). By permission of Oxford University Press, Inc.

Chapter Six originally appeared in *Kingdoms in Conflict*, pp. 243–251, 384–85,
by Charles Colson, Copyright © 1987 by Charles Colson. Reprinted by permission of HarperCollins Publishers, William Morrow.

Chapter Fifteen originally appeared in *Strength for the Journey*, pp. 116–25, by
Peter J. Gomes, Copyright © 2003 by Peter J. Gomes. Reprinted by permission
of HarperSanFrancisco, William Morrow.

Unless otherwise identified, Scripture quotations are taken from the *New
Revised Standard Version Bible*, Copyright © 1989 by the Division of Christian
Education of the National Council of the Churches of Christ in the United
States of America or the *Revised Standard Version of the Bible*, Copyright ©
1946, 1952, 1971 by the Division of Christian Education of the National
Council of the Churches of Christ in the USA.

Chapter Six uses Scripture quotations from *The Holy Bible: New International
Version*, Copyright © 1973, 1978, 1984 by International Bible Society.

Transferred to Digital Printing 2008

For Karin and Kevin

Contents

Acknowledgments

We must first acknowledge the encouragement and support of the Elizabethtown College Religious Studies Department, especially David Eller, chair, and Christina Bucher, former chair. Their administrative leadership made it possible for us to find the time and energy required to complete this project.

Our student assistant Brian Hess and friend Sharon Herr helped to prepare the chapters with their meticulous attention to the details of formatting and proofreading.

It has been a joy to bring together a collection of essays by such an eminent group of scholars. Each contributor has offered a thought-provoking, articulate, and accessible perspective on the topic. The chapters have exceeded our hopes and for this we are truly grateful.

We thank everyone at Palgrave MacMillan, especially our editor Amanda Johnson and her assistant Emily Leithauser, for seeing the potential in this project and for guiding us through the entire process. Thanks, too, to the anonymous reviewers who strengthened the book's themes and attention to context.

Finally, we are deeply grateful to our spouses, Karin and Kevin. While completing this project feels good, their love for us feels even better.

Contributors

Charles C. Colson is a former presidential aide to Richard Nixon and founder of Prison Fellowship. He is also the author, most recently, of *The Good Life: Seeking Purpose, Meaning, and Truth in Your Life* and *Lies That Go Unchallenged in Popular Culture*.

Peter R. Gathje is associate professor of Christian ethics and cross-cultural studies at Memphis Theological Seminary in Tennessee. He is also a coeditor of *Doing Right and Being Good: Catholic and Protestant Readings in Christian Ethics*, and author of *Sharing the Bread of Life: Hospitality and Resistance at the Open Door Community*.

Peter J. Gomes is minister in The Memorial Church and Plummer Professor of Christian Morals at Harvard University. His most recent books include *Strength for the Journey* and *The Good Life*.

Lee Griffith is a teacher and social activist working with a community mental health program in Elmira, New York. He has written *The War on Terrorism and the Terror of God* and *Fall of the Prison: Biblical Perspectives on Prison Abolition*.

Christine Firer Hinze is associate professor of theology at Marquette University in Milwaukee, Wisconsin. She is currently writing *Making a Living Together: Transforming the Catholic Living Wage Agenda for a New Century*, and has already authored *Comprehending Power in Christian Social Ethic*, as well as numerous articles on Christian social, economic, and feminist ethics.

Robert W. Jenson is (ret.) senior scholar for research at the Center for Theological Inquiry in Princeton, New Jersey, and professor emeritus of religion at St. Olaf College in Northfield, Minnesota. He has recently completed *Song of Songs, an Interpretation* commentary.

Thomas Massaro, S.J., is associate professor of moral theology at Weston Jesuit School of Theology in Cambridge, Massachusetts. His most recent books include *American Catholic Social Teaching* and *Catholic Perspectives on Peace and War*, each coauthored with Thomas A. Shannon.

Alyce M. McKenzie is associate professor of homiletics at Perkins School of Theology, Southern Methodist University, in Dallas, Texas. An ordained United Methodist minister, she has authored several books, including *Preaching Proverbs: Wisdom for the Pulpit*, *Hear and Be Wise: Becoming a Teacher and Preacher of Wisdom* and *Preaching Biblical Wisdom in a Self-Help Society*.

Keith Graber Miller is professor of religion and chair of the Bible and Religion Department at Goshen College in Indiana. He is also an ordained Mennonite minister and the author of *Wise as Serpents, Innocent as Doves: American Mennonites Engage Washington*.

Walter E. Pilgrim is professor emeritus of New Testament at Pacific Lutheran University in Tacoma, Washington. He has written *Uneasy Neighbors: Church and State in the New Testament* and *Good News to the Poor: Wealth and Poverty in Luke-Acts*.

Donald W. Shriver Jr. is president of the faculty and William E. Dodge Professor of Applied Christianity, emeritus, at Union Theological Seminary in New York City. His most recent books include *Honest Patriots: Loving a Country Enough to Remember Its Deeds* and *An Ethic for Enemies: Forgiveness in Politics*.

Mark Lewis Taylor is the Maxwell M. Upson Professor of Theology and Culture at Princeton Theological Seminary in New Jersey. He has recently authored *Religion, Politics, and the Christian Right: Post 9–11 Powers and American Empire* and *The Executed God: The Way of the Cross in Lockdown America*.

Theodore R. Weber is professor emeritus of social ethics at Candler School of Theology, Emory University, in Atlanta, Georgia. A past president of the Society of Christian Ethics in the United States and Canada, he has written *Politics in the Order of Salvation: Transforming Wesleyan Political Ethics*.

William H. Willimon is the bishop of the North Alabama Conference of the United Methodist Church. He is the author of many books, including *Conversation with Karl Barth on Preaching*.

Walter Wink is professor emeritus of biblical interpretation at Auburn Theological Seminary in New York City. His numerous books include *Jesus and Nonviolence: A Third Way* and *The Human Being: Jesus and the Enigma of the Son of Man*.

J. Philip Wogaman is professor emeritus of Christian social ethics at Wesley Theological Seminary in Washington, DC, and a leader in many denominational and ecumenical organizations. He has written many books, including *Christian Perspectives on Politics* and *Christian Ethics: A Historical Introduction*.

Why Rethink Christianity and Patriotism?

Michael G. Long and Tracy Wenger Sadd

To what extent, if any, should U.S. Christians embrace patriotism in this age of terror? This question is worth asking because a new wave of patriotism has just swept through our society and culture so completely that escaping it seems like an exercise in futility. Even where we live and work—Lancaster County, Pennsylvania, an area highly populated with Brethren, Mennonites, and Quakers—it has been impossible since September 11, 2001, to drive more than a few blocks without seeing one American flag after another, yellow ribbons galore, and bumper stickers demanding that we either love U.S. or leave it.

We teach at a college founded by individuals whose ancestors were persecuted by governing authorities for religious reasons, but there is no escaping patriotism here either, for every morning the American flag greets us in front of the main administrative building, located on the highest point of the center of campus. Since September 11, 2001, college administrators have invited high-level government officials, including the former head of Homeland Security, to share their grand patriotic visions with graduating seniors and the wider college community.

Unsurprisingly, we have also noticed that the bright flames of patriotism have scorched a few would-be dissenters along the way. Shortly following the collapse of the World Trade towers, for instance, the Mennonite owners of a local general store dared not to stock the flag on grounds that it might encourage jingoistic attitudes and actions. The public outcry at this "anti-Americanism" was so public—and threatening—that the owners quickly created shelf space for Old Glory.

Of course, this new wave of patriotism is far from unique to Lancaster County. It is an American phenomenon, and it comes as no surprise. Our national leaders, both Republican and Democrat, have always appealed to patriotism following national crises, and well-meaning citizens have always responded with generous public displays of their abiding love for America. For a recent example one need only recall the countless flags that appeared on cars and porches across the nation after George W. Bush's speech following the tragic explosion of the space shuttle Columbia on February 1, 2003.

But it is not just national crises that have fueled recent displays of love for America. U.S. patriotism has long been standard fare in times of victory and defeat, prosperity and poverty, war and peace, and it is a defining characteristic of our lives as individual citizens. Patriotism could be called the American way of life. From the first days of our public education—when we stand to pledge allegiance to the flag of the United States of America and to the Republic for which it stands—to the days following our death—when our bodily remains will most likely be squeezed between flags at the local cemetery—we move in and out of social roles, practices, and institutions that seek to inculcate in us the ways of patriotism, sanctify us as loyal patriots, and penalize, either by custom or law, those who would dare to betray our country. There is no virtue or practice that runs deeper in our collective conscience than patriotism.

At the same time, in spite of its omnipresence, U.S. patriotism has not always been defined clearly in public discourse, let alone in the practices of everyday citizens. Does American patriotism refer to love of our government or love of our country? Is it devotion to our fellow citizens or commitment to national ideals? Does it have anything to do with territory and resources or is it all about an intangible spirit, like the Spirit of 1776? Does patriotism involve obedience or only love? Is it ferreting out, labeling, and punishing all things anti-American? When does patriotism become nationalism? How does American Christian patriotism look different than, say, American Hindu patriotism or American atheist patriotism?

Like other organizing principles and values that typify the United States—freedom, democracy, and capitalism—patriotism often appears to have multiple meanings. The age of terror has only heightened our sense of competing, and sharply divergent, versions of U.S. patriotism. Shortly after September 11, 2001, a highly partisan tug-of-war over the meaning of true patriotism occupied center stage in U.S. politics, and it has steadfastly remained there ever since, making "patriotism" the most hotly contested word in public discourse since the 1960s, when the language of "revolution" was adopted by public figures as diverse as Billy Graham and Rap Brown.

The war on terrorism thus has renewed the battle over what U.S. patriotism is, and the two main belligerents—political conservatives and liberals—have set forth versions of patriotism that are so different, so opposed, so conflicted, that it is virtually impossible for either camp to see true American patriots among the opposition. Robert Reich has identified these two main versions as "negative" and "positive" patriotism, but we find it more exact to refer to them as conservative and liberal.[1] Simply put, conservative patriotism emphasizes traditional displays of American patriotism: pledging allegiance, waving the flag, and singing the national anthem. Its adherents believe in the "superior goodness of the American way of life," as Bill Bennett has put it, and are inclined to see international political enemies as part of an "axis of evil" that must be eliminated by physical force, even by unilateral military action, for the good of America and the world.[2] Unsurprisingly, conservative patriots favor President Bush's execution of the "war on terrorism"—largely unilateral military action in Afghanistan and Iraq—and believe that dissenters from the war only give comfort to the enemy. On the other hand, liberal patriots tend to be embarrassed by gratuitous displays of patriotism and avoid making any gesture that would hint at American exceptionalism. Liberal patriots are thus inclined to dismiss unilateral military action against an "axis of evil" in favor of "strong alliances with allies who share our basic values, of international cooperation backed by military strength when necessary, and of America's moral leadership in the world."[3] Consequently, they are also sharply critical of President Bush's execution of the war on terror and consider his policies to be ultimately anti-American.

There are variations on these main themes, but it seems that the major positions are well established and that our partisan politicians will continue to fight the raging battle over U.S. patriotism for years to come, especially if another security-related crisis explodes on the domestic scene. Reich, of course, encourages us to embrace his version of "positive patriotism," defeat President Bush's "negative patriotism," and thereby safeguard the liberal ideals set forth by John Adams, Thomas Jefferson, and James Madison. But how are we to choose? What criteria should we rely on when making the choice between conservative and liberal versions of patriotism? And do we have to choose only among these versions and their variations? Is there another type of patriotism that we can and should give expression to? More fundamentally, should we choose *any* version of U.S. patriotism in this age of terror?

Questions about patriotism become even more complicated for those of us who identify ourselves not merely as U.S. citizens but also as "resident aliens"—Christians who want to embrace community life without pledging ultimate allegiance to any political authority, civil society, or form of government, no matter how virtuous it may be.[4] As *resident* aliens, we can neither escape the recent wave of U.S. patriotism nor avoid hearing the rhetoric of the partisan strife between conservatives and liberals. Yet as resident *aliens*, we know that human authority sometimes conflicts with the divinity we experience in the life of Jesus and therefore we should not blindly follow the patriotic advice of any national leader or fellow citizen, conservative or liberal. While Reich is fun to read and President Bush fascinating to listen to, neither of these figures can ever be the primary source of political ethics for American Christians.

So where should we turn as we seek to answer the question of whether U.S. Christians should embrace patriotism in this age of terror? We believe that the proper sources for Christians engaged in thinking about patriotism are the same ones that should be used for the rest of everyday life—Christian scripture, tradition, reason, and experience. Reich's manifesto and President Bush's speeches may be important, but they are not the primary fonts of wisdom for Christians;

nor should Christians allow political liberals or conservatives to set the terms for our answers to questions that arise in political society. Our responsibility as Christians is not to turn to our political leaders for truth but to study the moral sources that define our character as Christians and lay out the practices that mark us as people who follow Jesus. Simply stated, U.S. Christians have an obligation to think and act like Christians—even when the subject is U.S. patriotism.

Our local Christian faith communities have provided neither sanctuary from the clarion call that fills the wider culture nor engagement with the kind of critical theology that creates the capacity for self-criticism. This past Independence Day saw several of our local churches advertising sermons touting the virtue of patriotism, the power of the American dream, and the responsibility of Christians to give to Caesar what is Caesar's. As William Sloane Coffin says, "Unfortunately, the churches now are pretty much down to therapy and management. There's very little prophetic fire in the churches. When I was growing up we had church leaders. . .who were full of passion, highly intelligent. They knew that love demands the utmost clear-sightedness. And they were not lazy about doing their homework."[5]

With this in mind, we want to challenge Christians to do their homework on U.S. patriotism. We have invited the best and brightest scholars of our various faith communities to mine the sources of Christianity and help us not only to think critically about the current battle over U.S. patriotism but also to answer a host of related questions. For example, should U.S. Christians be patriots in an age of terror? If not, how should we understand and deal with national leaders and fellow citizens who encourage us to love America first? If our moral sources do encourage us to be patriots—Billy Graham once said that "Christianity breeds patriotism"[6]—what form of patriotism should we embrace in this age of terror? Should we wave the flag, or should we refuse to display such "graven images"? Should we grab a gun in defense of our beloved country, or should we practice nonviolence and call upon our national leaders to overcome evil with good? Should we envision the United States as superior and divinely blessed, or should we adopt an internationalist perspective that sees America as equal in value to all other countries? Should we pinpoint terrorists and their support networks as "evil," or should we see them as redeemable, able to be brought into the international community? What should we do when our own governing authorities encourage us to adopt attitudes or undertake actions that undermine our core Christian beliefs?

The answers offered by our diverse contributors may surprise you, especially if you think that Christians in the United States are of one mind when thinking about patriotism in an age of terror. Nothing could be further from the truth, and the chapters of this book contain a multiplicity of Christian perspectives on American patriotism—arguments that range from the evangelical to the anarchist. What accounts for the wide variety? Social location certainly exerts influence on these Christian thinkers and, at the same time, the relative weight or primacy that the thinkers ascribe to the various moral sources of Christianity contributes to divergent views. For various reasons, some of them sociocultural, each Christian thinker operates with a bias toward certain sources of authority and then even gives preference to select parts within those sources.

Some readers might ask: Why present diverse perspectives on Christianity and patriotism? Why not just present one argument throughout the book? We have chosen to present various perspectives not because we believe that all are equally valid—we do not—but because we are convinced that the moral sources of Christianity can lead to various credible positions, not all of them complementary, and that deep familiarity with these various positions can only help us strengthen our understanding of the depth and diversity of Christian thought about patriotism, as well as our proper engagement in public debate. We believe that it is too simplistic, and even lazy, for U.S. Christians to hear only one side of the argument. "Really good conversation is about pretty deep things, and that's not what Americans engage in very often," says Coffin.[7] In this book, our goal is not rhetoric, but good conversation and informed debate. There are strengths and weaknesses in each of the positions presented in this book, and if we can draw from these various strengths while leaving behind their weaknesses, we will be better equipped to bear witness to the truth of our Christian beliefs about God and country.

Up to this point in the twenty-first century, U.S. Christians have not excelled in thinking theologically about patriotism in an age of terror. Some local churches have delved into patriotic themes on American holidays, but most of our faith communities, church leaders, and theologians have been painfully silent. While political leaders have raised their flags and demanded that we follow their version of American patriotism, many Christians have remained sheltered under steeples and ensconced in offices and pulpits. Perhaps we have been all too fearful of appearing unpatriotic or unsympathetic to the troops in Iraq and Afghanistan. Or perhaps we have just assumed, like Billy Graham, that Christianity breeds patriotism and that there is simply no question that the love of God demands love of country.

Whatever the case may be, we believe that the time has come for Christians to rethink U.S. patriotism on our own terms, to use our own moral sources for understanding the age of terror, to speak our own language in the raging public debate over the meaning and form of patriotism, and to do so while remaining true to our Christian convictions. We are already in the middle of the debate. Political leaders are currently fighting like mad for our souls and desperately trying to mold us into their patriotic images, and if we do not directly engage the debate swirling around us, we will soon discover that we have lost our souls to a patriotism that knows nothing of who we are, let alone the Jesus we claim to follow.

Notes

1. See Robert B. Reich, *Reason: Why Liberals Will Win the Battle for America* (New York: Vintage, 2004), 146–85.
2. Bennett is quoted in ibid., 150

3. Ibid., 151.

4. The descriptive terms "resident" and "aliens" occur in numerous places throughout the Christian scriptures, and the term "resident aliens" has been popularized most recently by Stanley Hauerwas and William H. Willimon, *Resident Aliens: Life in the Christian Colony* (Nashville, TN: Abingdon, 1989). We do not claim to use the term in the same way that Hauerwas and Willimon do.

5. Interview with William Sloane Coffin, *Religion and Ethics NewsWeekly*, episode 752, August 7, 2004, Public Broadcast System, available at http://www.pbs.org/wnet/religionandethics/week752/p-interview1.html.

6. News Release Transcript, Crusade Information Service, Billy Graham Team Office, November 17, 1965, Houston, collection 345, box 55, no. 5, p. 1, Billy Graham Center and Archives (BGCA).

7. Interview with Coffin, *Religion and Ethics NewsWeekly*, August 7, 2004.

Part I

Scripture and History

Chapter 1

Angels of the Nations?

Walter Wink

Nationalism is not, one could argue, an unmitigated evil. It provides a bonding force to unite highly diverse tribes and peoples. It furnishes a sense of collective identity capable of drawing people out of themselves and their family groupings into a larger whole. It is one of the sole forces capable of standing up against the economic onslaught of the transnational corporations. It prevents the great empires from imposing their wills without resistance. More might be said on its behalf, but what makes nationalism so pernicious, so death-dealing, and so blasphemous is its seemingly irresistible tendency toward idolatry. In the name of this idol whole generations are maimed, slaughtered, exiled, and made idolaters. More than one hundred million lives have been offered on the altar of this Moloch thus far in the twentieth century, and we are now watching in a kind of mesmerized horror as terrorism sweeps the world. Only a god could command such madness, carried out with such lucid rationality by some of the brightest minds of each nation, and that is where the irony begins: modern people do not believe in gods.

We believe in the existence of idols, true enough—things falsely worshiped as gods, but our worldview and our theologies forbid us to believe in the real existence of gods. To be sure, we know that when people idolize the nation-state, this idolatry serves to make that state a god, but surely the state is *not* a god, in any sense of the word. We do not understand the real dynamics of idolatry—that when a nation is made a god *it becomes a god*, not just as the inner conviction of individuals, but as the actual spirituality of the nation itself. We do not comprehend what is unleashed when millions of people worship the state as absolute; we do not discern the spiritual reality such idolatry actually creates. Because we do not believe, as all ancient peoples believed, that there are gods *behind* the states, we have nowhere to locate the center to which all this false devotion flows. We believe that idolatry is something idolaters do, but we deny that they do it toward anything real. Thus, we offer up countless new bodies to be sacrificed to the gods whose existence we deny, in order to make and keep the world safe for our nations and their interests.

Israel and the early Christians looked at the matter quite differently. Contrary to widespread misunderstanding, the ancient believers in Yahweh did not deny the existence of the gods. They merely denied their ultimacy. They perceived that "every nation and tribe and tongue and people"—the Book of Revelation's comprehensive way of cataloguing the diverse forms of collective life before the rise of the modern nation-state—was presided over by a spiritual power. Rome had its *genius*, Athens its goddess Athena, Ammon its god Chemosh, Babylon its Marduk, Israel its Yahweh. Gods were abundant and filled a multitude of functions, but they were nowhere experienced more ubiquitously than as the gods of great empires.

It is a modern misconception that these gods were the focus of the *religion* of a people. Both our distinction between church and state and our very use of the word "religion" are anachronistic for the period prior to the rise of Christendom. Worship was not the private choice of people who just happened to belong to a certain nation or people; it was to a very large extent the collective invocation of the spirit of that nation or people. Worship of the gods of a nation was the spiritual expression of what it meant to be a nation, tribe, tongue, or people. The gods of the nations—later weakened by being demoted to angelic rank by Jews and Christians—were conceived of in a projected way as possessing a separate existence as heavenly, transcendent beings. I hypothesize that *they were the actual inner spirituality of the social entity itself*. The gods or angels of the nations have a discernible personality and vocation; they too, though fallen, pernicious, and insatiable, are a part of the redemptive plan of God. Our role in this redemptive activity is to acknowledge their existence, love them as creatures of God, unmask their idolatries, and stir up in them their heavenly vocations.

Such an undertaking will not easily command assent; it has been quite some time since the angels of nations have been a regular feature of religious language. I will not request credulity, but only patience in understanding the notion in its original setting. Then we can assess whether it offers any clues for comprehending the self-annihilating madness of the nations and their neglected but holy vocation.

The Angel-Gods of the Nations

One of the earliest biblical references to the idea of angel-gods of the nations is Deuteronomy 32:8–9: "When the Most High gave to the nations their inheritance, when he separated the sons of men, he fixed the bounds of the people according to the number of the sons of God. For the Lord's portion is his people, Jacob his allotted heritage." Portrayed here are two levels of reality: heavenly and earthly. On earth, God separates humanity into its nations, traditionally fixed at seventy on the basis of Genesis 10. In heaven, God sets angels (called *bene elohim*, "sons of God" or "sons of gods") over each nation, to represent its interests and be accountable for its acts in the heavenly council, over which Yahweh alone presides. However, Yahweh appoints no angel over Israel; Yahweh alone will watch over it. It is only later tradition that assigns that task to the archangel Michael.

Daniel 10 provides the Bible's fullest picture of these angels of the nations in action. The scene is ostensibly set in the third year of Cyrus, King of Persia. In actuality, however, the passage appears to have been composed during 167–165 BCE in response to the attempt of Antiochus IV Epiphanes, the Seleucid ruler, to destroy the Jewish religion. According to the narrative, Daniel, a Babylonian Jew who has risen to a high post in the court of Nebuchadnezzar, and who enjoyed equal prominence under the conquering Persians, is moved by grief over the fate of the exiled Jews to fast and mourn for twenty-one days. On the twenty-first day an angel (which I will call the Messenger) appears to him in a dazzling vision, explaining that though Daniel's prayer had been heard on the first day of the fast, and the Messenger had been dispatched immediately, he had been withstood for twenty-one days by the "guardian angel" of the angel of the kingdom of Persia. Finally, Michael, one of the chief angels, came to help him, holding the angel of Persia at a standoff while the Messenger slipped through to carry a message to Daniel, and that message is the burden of Daniel 11–12. Then, the Messenger says, he has to return to "fight the guardian angel of Persia. After that the guardian angel of Greece will appear. There is no one to help me except Michael, Israel's guardian angel" (10:20–21, TEV).

This is remarkable: the angel of the Persian Empire withstanding for twenty-one days the angel of God sent to Daniel! This is not the sentimentalized image of angels of Sunday school art. The angel of Persia at the very least does not want foreign angels entering Persian air space. It has a will all its own; it has a right to contend for the best interests of the Persian Empire narrowly defined. It has a stake in censoring a message that foretells the destruction of the Persian Empire and the emigration of a talented and productive captive people. We are not presented with perfect angelic beings as the idealized personifications of nations. On the contrary, the angels of the nations, like the angels of any other corporate entity, represent the actual spirituality and vocation of visible and invisible Powers. The power of the angel-prince of Persia here reflects the political power of the Persian Empire, before which puny Judah, its temple destroyed, its land desolate, and its people captive in Babylon, must have appeared insignificant. Even God could not easily muscle this empire into compliance. Put less picturesquely, without the intercessions of Daniel, God could not intervene on Israel's behalf, since to do so would be to violate the Persian empire's freedom to resist the will of God.

Beneath the story of the Babylonian-Persian-Jewish "Daniel," however, lies a different story altogether, like a buried portrait on a reused canvas. However, this picture is not older but rather a representation of current events. The time is not 532 but 167 BCE. Antiochus IV Epiphanes, the Syrian ruler, has just proscribed the Jewish religion, declaring himself to be "the Manifest God." He has outlawed Sabbath observance and circumcision, had copies of the Torah burned, encouraged nude exercise in the gymnasia after the Greek fashion, and sacrificed a pig on an alter built for Zeus in the Jerusalem temple, all for the purpose of forcibly Hellenizing the Jewish people.

Against the background of those contemporary shocks, the author presents his hero as a stalwart Jew struggling to resist assimilation. Though Daniel has served as a high official for the Babylonian and the Persian courts, and has been given the name of a Babylonian god, Belteshazzar (meaning "may Bel protect his life?"), he has not compromised his faith in Yahweh. Daniel 10 finds him mounting a twenty-one-day fast out of grief for captive Israel and continuing to fast right through the Feast of Passover. Since Antiochus has prohibited celebration of Passover, this may be a covert call to defiance, as if to say: you can prevent our eating the Passover feast, but you have no power to prohibit our fasting.

One possibility for interpreting the meaning of his fast would be that the conflict between the Messenger and the guardian angel of Persia mirrors Daniel's own inner struggle to free his spirit from the last vestiges of internalized foreign ways. Daniel may then be made the model of the process demanded of Jews generally in the contest to save Judaism from enforced Hellenization. This interpretation founders on one point, however. The angel does not delay twenty-one days until Daniel has purged himself, nor is Daniel only heard after he has cleansed himself: "*for from the first day* that you set your mind to understand and humbled yourself before your God, *your words have been heard*, and I have come because of your words" (Dan. 10:12). Why then the delay?

The guardian angel of Persia blocked the Messenger. The scene answers the question on theodicy. To the usual reaction to calamity, "How could God have allowed this?" the text poses a radically different and new answer. God had no choice. The Powers are able to hold God's messenger at bay for twenty-one days and prevent the message from reaching Daniel. Israel normally factored only two elements into the equation of prayer—God and themselves. In that equation, if the petition requested of God was denied, only two alternatives survived. Either God said no, or the petitioners were at fault through sin or lack of faith, but here a third element was introduced into the equation: the Powers.

The angels of the nations have a will of their own and are capable of resisting the will of God. Perhaps God is omnipotent, but God certainly is not able to impose the divine will on recalcitrant Powers, due to God's own self-limitation: God will not violate the freedom of creatures.

What we have left out of the equation are the principalities and Powers. Prayer is not just a two-way transaction. It also involves the great sociospiritual forces that preside over much of reality. By this, I mean the massive institutions, social structures, and systems that dominate the world and the spirituality at their center. Daniel marks the moment when the role of the Powers in blocking answers to prayer was, for the first time, revealed to humanity.

The angel of Persia is able to block God's messenger from answering Daniel's prayer! For twenty-one days Daniel contends with unseen spiritual Powers. Perhaps he has to slough off internalized elements of Babylonian spirituality; he bore as his own a name compounded from the name of a Babylonian god,

Belteshazzar (Dan. 4:8). At the same time, whatever the changes in him that may have been necessary, it is not *after* he has purified himself that the angel is dispatched. He is heard on the *very first day*, as the words leave his lips. And the angel is sent the moment he prays, not after twenty-one days of purification. The real struggle is between the angels of two nations. The angel of Persia does not want the nation he guards to lose such a talented people. The Angel of Persia actively attempts to frustrate God's will and for twenty-one days he succeeds. The principalities and Powers are able to hold Yahweh at bay!

Daniel continues praying and fasting, God's angel continues to wrestle to get past the Angel of Persia, yet nothing apparent is happening. God *seems* not to have answered the prayer. Despite this apparent indifference, however, there is a fierce war being waged in heaven between contending Powers. Finally Michael, Israel's own guardian angel, intervenes and the Messenger-angel gets through.

This is an accurate depiction, in mythological terms, of the actual experience people have in prayer. We prayed for decades for the superpowers to reduce their arsenals, and for most of that time it seemed an exercise in abject futility. The "angel of the United States" and the "angel of the Soviet Union" were locked in a death struggle in which neither seemed prepared to relax its grip. Then, in the irony of God, the most vociferously anti-Communist president in American history, Ronald Reagan, negotiated a nuclear weapons reduction treaty with a Soviet leader Mikhail Gorbachev, whose new course of openness was not predicted by a single American Sovietologist. No doubt the economic deterioration and rising nationalism of the Soviet Union played a key part, but why then did the experts not anticipate the change? Would the cold war have ended without the demonstrations and prayers over the decades of the peace movement in the United States, Europe, and the Soviet Union? In any event, God found an opening, and was able to bring about a miraculous change of direction.

Notice that the Bible makes no attempt to justify the delay in God's response. It is simply a fact of experience. We do not know why God cannot do "better," or why, for example, Michael is not sent to the aid of the Messenger angel sooner. It is a deep mystery, but we are not appealing to mystery in order to paper over an intellectual problem. The Sovietologists are faced with mysteries as well. We just do not know why some things happen and others do not.

What does this say then about the omnipotence of God? About God's ability to redeem? God's sovereignty over history? The principalities and Powers are able to assert their will against the will of God, *and for a time they may prevail.* The wonder, then, is not that our prayers are sometimes unanswered, but that any are answered at all! We have long accepted that God is limited by our freedom. The new insight in Daniel is that God is limited by the freedom of institutions and systems as well. We have normally spoken of this as God's free choice to be self-limited. One may well ask whether God has any choice. In any case, whether by choice or not, God's ability to intervene, uninvited, is extremely circumscribed—as you may have noticed when you pray.

In short, prayer involves not just God and people, but God and people and Powers. What God is able to do in the world is hindered to a considerable extent by the rebelliousness, resistance, and self-interest of the Powers exercising their freedom under God.

God *is* powerful to heal. However, if corporations flush PCBs and dioxin into the water we drink, release radioactive gas into the atmosphere, or insist on spraying our fruit with known carcinogens, God's healing power is sharply reduced. Children, like a boy in my parish who lived on the edge of one of the largest petrochemical complexes in the world, die of leukemia. The situation is no different in kind from normal bodily healing. A clean cut will almost always wondrously mend; but if we rub infectious germs into it, God's capacity to heal is hindered or even halted.

God does want people to be free to become everything God created them to be. But when one race enslaves another to labor in its fields or dig its mines, when children's lives are stunted by sexual abuse or physical brutality, or when whole nations are forced to submit to the exploitation of other states that are more powerful, then what is God to do? We may pray for justice and liberation, as indeed we must, and *God hears us on the very first day*. But God's ability to intervene against the freedom of these rebellious creatures is sometimes tragically restricted in ways we cannot pretend to understand. It takes considerable spiritual maturity to live in the tension between these two facts: God has heard our prayer, and the Powers are blocking God's response.

In many cases, prayer is often regarded as merely autotransformative: the one who prays creates in himself or herself a more receptive frame of mind. In many cases, this may be a necessary component of effective prayer, but it is not the one stressed by the author of Daniel. The point here seems to be that Daniel's intercessions have made possible the intervention of God. Prayer changes us, but it also changes what is possible for God. Daniel's cry was heard on the first day; it opened an aperture for God to act in concert with human freedom. It inaugurated war in heaven. It opened a way through the impenetrable spirituality of foreign hegemony in order to declare a new and real divine possibility, and the message had the desired effect. Steeled by prophecies such as these, Jewish resistance mounted up against the policies of Antiochus, and in a shorter time than perhaps even the author himself envisaged, the temple was cleansed of pagan pollution and Jewish traditions were restored (the first Hanukkah, December 165 BCE).

Take the modern case of Somalia. Day and night, the media bombarded the world with heart-rending pictures of malnourished and starving Somalians. A great No! swelled up in people around the world. Money was raised. Governments pitched in. Ships filled with food were dispatched. Unfortunately, when they arrived opposite Mogadishu, they were forbidden to unload by the contending warlords, who found it to their advantage for their enemies to starve to death. The prayers of those starving people were heard on the very first day, but the Powers were able, for a time, to block God's answer.

If the Powers can thwart God so effectively, can we then speak of divine providence in the world? If our prayers are answered so sporadically, or with such great delays, can we really trust in God? Can God be relied on? Is a limited god really God at all? We have to face these questions, because our capacity to pray depends on some kind of working idea of God's providential care for us.

During the Nazi regime an entire nation was held hostage to an evil ideology. The Powers were holding God at bay. God appeared to be doing nothing. Meanwhile, unseen, there was war in heaven. When people not only submit to evil but also actively affirm it, malignant Powers are unleashed for which everyday life offers no preparation. The angel of Germany was being worshiped as an idol and acclaimed the Supreme Being. God, elbowed out of heaven, was out prowling every street at all hours, and could find few to help.

In such a time, God may appear to be impotent. Perhaps God is. God may be unable to intervene directly, but nevertheless, God showers the world with potential coincidences, which require only a human response to become miracles. When the miracle happens, we feel that God has intervened in a special way, but God does not intervene only occasionally. God is the constant possibility of transformation pressing on *every* occasion, even those that are lost for lack of a human response.

God is not mocked. The wheels of justice may turn slowly but they are inexorable. Look at the story spun around Daniel again. After fifty years of captivity, God had at last raised up Cyrus to deliver the Jews from Babylon, and God's people chose rather to remain in exile! Daniel, fasting and praying, creates a fresh opening for God. Into that breach God pours the vision of a new life in a restored Holy Land—an enticement and lure to coax Judah home.

The sobering news that the Powers can thwart God is more than matched by the knowledge that our intercessions will ultimately prevail. Whether we have to wait twenty-one days or twenty-one years or twenty-one centuries, we should find that this changes nothing for faith. It knows how massive and intractable the Powers and their system of domination are. We cannot stop praying for what is right because our prayers are seemingly unanswered. We know they are heard the very first day we pray, and we keep praying, for even one more day is too long to wait for justice.

That is why the delay of the kingdom was not fatal to Christian belief in the first century when, contrary to expectations, Jesus did not return. For the church could now see the Domination System for what it was, and could never wholly capitulate to it again. Once it had caught glimpses of God's domination-free order it could never give up the longing for its arrival.

Daniel had to wait twenty-one days to receive his vision of the restitution of the Jews to Palestine; it would be two centuries before any sizable number returned. Gandhi struggled with the angel of the British Empire for twenty-six years; the Aquino revolution in the Philippines unseated Marcos in only a matter of days. Whether the water rises drop by drop or through a flash flood, eventually the pressure bursts the dam of oppression and the Powers are swept away. They are but mortal creatures, and they are all the more vicious when they know their time is short (Rev. 12:12). Many innocent people may die, while the Powers appear to gain in invincibility with every death, but that is only an illusion. Their very brutality and desperation is evidence that their legitimacy is fast eroding. Their appeal to force is itself an admission that they can no longer command voluntary consent. Whenever sufficient numbers of people withdraw their consent, the Powers inevitably fall.

War in Heaven

If we conceive of heaven not as a super-terrestrial realm in the sky, but instead think of it as the interiority of earthly existence in all its potentialities, the image of war in heaven can be understood as the struggle between two contending spiritualities or national spirits for supremacy. Everyone knows that it is the spirit of a nation that determines its capacity to fight. One need only look to recent history for examples. The Thieu government of South Vietnam had eight to ten times the firepower in the field as its opponents; yet the final battle to bring down the Thieu regime never had to be launched. Instead, its soldiers just laid down their weapons—they did not even carry them along for self-defense or looting—and retreated to the sea. The government had simply lost legitimacy. The same thing happened to the army of the Shah of Iran. In both cases, the spirit of the nation—the tangible sense of its cohesiveness, stability and power—had simply evaporated.

Military superiority means nothing where there is no longer the will to fight. The angels of the nations, who have already exacted well over one hundred million human sacrifices in less than a single century, are not personifications. They are not "out there" or "up there" but within. They are the invisible spirituality that animates, sustains, and guides a nation. We reckon with them whether we acknowledge their reality or not.

The Personality and Vocation of Angels of Nations

The angel of an entity must be seen under two aspects: what it *is*, and what it is *called to be*. What it is might be called its personality, what it is called to be, its vocation. The personality of a nation-angel is discernable in the climate, light, moisture, quality of soil, availability and types, history, customs, religions, fears, guilt, and other factors. I have nothing to add to such analyses.

It is in the realm of vocation, however, that the concept of the angels of nations makes its most signal contribution. The social sciences or fine-tuned intuition can discern the contours of a nation's personality, but only God can reveal a nation's vocation. The angels of nations regularly abandon their vocations, falling into the utmost barbarism. Each considers itself superior to the others. People tend to laud the same egocentricity in nations that they find insufferable in their follow human beings. Nations almost inevitably define their interests in terms of immediate short-term gains rather than considering the larger whole. For a nation to act in accord with the synergy of the planet would require subordinating personality to vocation, "is" to "ought." The angels of nations are not static, changeless entities, nor are their vocations irrevocably fixed in their foundation. God's will for the nations is continually being modified, in accordance with God's primary objectives, in order to encompass the nation's latest infidelities and achievements. Nations, too, must repent. The somber refrain in the Book of Revelation, "They did not repent," even after the sun was allowed to scorch them and the kingdom of the Beast was thrown into darkness (Rev. 9:20–21, 16:9, 16:11), does not mean that nations *cannot* repent, but merely reflects the common experience that they generally *choose* not to repent.

To repent means to recover vocation. To recover a sense of call requires acknowledging the sovereignty of the One who calls. All the nations belong to God, and God is "King of the nations." God rules over the nations and judges them when they do injustice or forget God. God seeks to guide the nations in the ways of truth, so that finally all the nations might worship the Lord. God's revelation to Israel was to be extended to every nation. Israel was to be "a light to the nations," that God's "salvation may reach to the end of the earth" (Isa. 49:6, 42:6), and "nations shall come to your light" (Isa. 60:3). As the "messenger from God," the angel holds the vision of what a nation might become. When the angel of a nation defaults on its task, it is judged along with the nation. When the angel turns its back on its vocation, it becomes demonic, and a threat to the peace of the world. Nazi Germany says it all.

As Christianity took its gospel to the nations, it too largely failed to maintain the task of mediating the absoluteness of God to *this* world, and instead transferred the goal of redemption to another world in the beyond. This meant that the nations and their angel-gods were no longer the direct object of the church's evangelical task. Even though the church was occasionally able to exert a moderating influence on the nations during the Middle Ages, the practical consequence was that the nations and their guardian angels dropped out of the purview of redemptive concern altogether and became autonomous. The result was the secular state, which acknowledges no higher power than its own idolatrous aspirations, subverts religion to the role of legitimating its claims, and makes its own power the sole arbiter of morality. Whenever the state makes itself the highest value, then it is in an objective state of blasphemy. *This is the situation of the majority of the nations in the world today, our own included.*

The political and spiritual task of mediating the absoluteness of God to the nations has been largely abandoned by the churches. Yet it is unmistakably articulated in the New Testament. Christians are warned that they will be dragged before governors and kings for Jesus' sake, in order "to bear testimony before them and the Gentile nations" (Mt. 10:18). Jesus' own coming was prophesied, according to Matthew, as a coming to "proclaim justice to the Gentile nations. . .and in his name will the Gentile nations hope" (Mt. 12:18, 12:21). The gospel itself must "be preached throughout the whole world, as a testimony to all Gentile nations" (Mt. 24:14; see also Mk. 13:19). The very nations are called to repent, "that repentance and forgiveness of sins should be preached in his name to all Gentile nations" (Lk. 24:47; Rev. 14:6).

Alongside the motif of witness *to* the nations is the judgment *of* the nations. This point is emphasized in an unexpected way by Matthew's famous parable of the sheep and the goats (Mt. 25:31–46):

> When the Son of man comes in his glory, and all the angels with him [and if it is for judgment of the nations, these should probably be understood as including the angels of the nations]. . .Before him will be gathered all the nations [*ethne*, a neuter noun], and he will separate them [*autous*, a masculine pronoun] one from another. (Mt. 25:31–32)

A pronoun, you will recall, is supposed to agree in number and gender with the noun it modifies. The shift here from neuter to masculine means that not the nations as such, but individual *persons*, will be separated and judged ("and he will separate *people* one from another"). But the people are gathered *by their nations*: they will be individually held accountable for what they have done collectively as *nations* to provide food, clothing, shelter, health care, and justice: "I was hungry and you [plural] gave me food, I was thirsty and you [pl.] gave me drink, I was a stranger and you [pl.] welcomed me, I was naked and you [pl.] clothed me, I was sick and you [pl.] visited me, I was in prison and you [pl.] came to me" (Matt. 25:35–36). Each individual is responsible for the way her or his own nation has responded to the needs of the most powerless for food, clothing, shelter, medical care, hospitality, and fair treatment. The parable is not then simply an appeal for private charity, but for national righteousness, on the order of Psalm 82:1–8.

It is true that people are not judged solely on the basis of what their nations have done, quite apart from their own responses; but it is not just a matter of solitary judgment either, for Christ is also sovereign of the nations. Each one of us is responsible for the sins of our own nations, whether we condone them or not. No one is exempt, by virtue of her or his own goodness, from judgment of the nation. It was not, after all, one of the "German Christians" who had collaborated with Hitler, but the leader of the Christian resistance, Martin Niemöller, who spent eight years in a Nazi jail, who after the war was the first to say, "We all are guilty."

This witness to the judgment of the nations will ultimately issue in the redemption of the nations. The nations are not, in the biblical view, historical accidents or human contrivances. They are an integral aspect of the divine creation. Gerhard von Rad points out that the creation stories of Genesis do not end with the creation of humanity in chapters one and two, but with the creation of the nations in chapter ten. Human beings, that is to say, cannot exist in isolation from their larger social and political units. In the same way, the story of the exclusion of Adam and Eve from the garden in Genesis 3; it concludes in Genesis 11 with the confusion of tongues at the tower of Babel and the scattering of the nations. This "fall" of the nations is placed in parallelism with the "fall" of humanity. Their joint falls necessitate a divine-human drama of redemption played out on the stage of history, culminating in the salvation of both persons *and their nations*: "All nations shall come and worship thee, for thy judgments have been revealed" (Rev. 15:4). Even the redeemed nations will enter the holy city, New Jerusalem, bringing with them "the glory and the honor of the nations" (Rev. 21:26). Presumably, we are to think of the distinctive gifts and achievements, art and craft, music and letters, science and deeds of mercy and justice that they have wrought in history. One would have thought that the nations had been finished off once and for all at Armageddon (Rev. 16:16) or in the Great War of the Lamb (Rev. 19–20). However, the biblical view of the nations is more subtle than that. They are not demonized. They are not considered irremediably evil. Perhaps what we witness in the surrealistic violence of Revelation is their purgation from short-term views of their own self-interest and the destruction of the egoism of their collective personalities. In any case, these smitten nations, trod upon in the wine press of the fury of the wrath of God the Almighty and devoured by vultures (Rev. 19:15, 19:17), are integral to the Holy City. Even these shall be transformed at last by the tree of life whose leaves Ezekiel had said were "for healing" (Ezek. 47:12), to which the Seer of the Apocalypse has added, "of the nations" (Rev. 22:2). Our personal redemption cannot take place apart from the redemption of our social structures.

In the light of world history, this view can scarcely be regarded as too pessimistic. If anything, we are guilty of continually underestimating the capacity of the Powers to violate the public interest on behalf of private profits and the sheer lust for power. But the Powers are also no less the good creations of a good God than we are, and they are no more fallen than we. If we can experience redemption, so can they, though by virtue of their greater complexity, far less simply. In short, radical pessimism about the Powers needs to be balanced by a view of grace more radical still, but whether this redemption can take place in history is an open question, which only historical deeds themselves can answer. Perhaps the most we can say is that some nations can and have responded to demands for justice in specific situations, such as South Africa; yet even these acts of justice have been contaminated by overzealousness, revenge, greed, and pride. Nations cannot escape the effects of the Fall—that is the ax at the root of all visions of gradual human progress toward utopia or the Kingdom—but they can recover a sense of their divine vocation and manifest flashes of what will be when God is effectively sovereign over all creation.

Despite persecutions which cost his father's life and almost his own, the early Christian theologian Origen in the early third century CE believed that the angels of the nations could be converted: "If human beings can repent and pass from unbelief to faith, why should we hesitate to say the same of the Powers? For my part, I think that it has sometimes happened. . .some of the Powers were converted when Christ came, and that is why some towns and even whole nations accepted Christ more readily then others."[1] The "man of Macedonia" whom Paul saw in a vision beseeching him, "Come over to Macedonia and help us" (Acts 16:9) was, Origen suggests plausibly, the angel of Macedonia, responsible for the collective well-being of that entire people, appealing to Paul for help.

The nations are good, the nations are fallen, and the nations can be redeemed. They bear encoded within their very symbols, insignia, coins, and ideologies the memory that they are creatures, created in, through, and for the service of the Truly Human One (Col. 1:15–20). And yes, they are fallen. But "fallen" does not mean that they are irremediably *evil*; human beings are also fallen, and yet are capable of natural goodness. The tendency of nations is toward absolutism, but they are capable of responding to the revelation of their proper vocation. Their angels can be enjoined, like the angels of the church in Ephesus, to "remember then from what you have fallen," and repent (Rev. 2:5).

Ministering to the Spirituality of a Nation

If we equate the angel of a nation with its spirituality, how then might we go about ministering to the angel of a nation? What advantages, what gains, lie in resuscitating this antiquated notion, so uncongenial to the modern temperament? I have suggested that it can help us to *unmask* a nation's apostasy more ruthlessly, *discern* its vocation more perceptively, and *love it*, despite its evils, more faithfully. In nations, no less than in persons, divine calling can lead to inflation, megalomania, and self-idolization. So why reintroduce the notion? Has not secularism done us a favor by stripping us of the very grounds of these pretensions?

Not at all. Secularism has simply insured that, in the absence of any divine constraints whatever, nations are free to behave as if they had complete autonomy, as if they were indeed absolute, as if they were God deciding the fate of nations. Unmasking this power will oblige us to critique our nation in ways that will leave everyone uneasy. *We must entertain the terrible possibility that the salvation of humanity depends somehow on the decline, destruction, or transformation of the United States as a sign of God's sovereignty over the nations.* Rome, yes, but—America? Never! America the Righteous, the Chosen, the Destined, the Apple of God's Eye? The very suggestion of such a thing will strike many Americans as subversive, and that reaction itself is an index of our idolatry. A godly people would react to the threat of God's judgment with fear, awe, and consternation. They would *know* that no person and no nation are righteous before God. They would say, with Jefferson, "I tremble for my country when I remember that God is just." But Americans do not, on the whole, think that way. To the degree that they are religious at all, they actually believe that God is pleased with, beholden to, partial to, and identified with our land.

This is not to deny that, in many ways, our nation may be a more desirable place to live than some other countries, nor do I wish to ignore the many positive contributions it has made to human society. My point is simply that these contributions in no way mitigate the objective state of idolatry that has been the price we have paid for nationhood. The power imperative has co-opted every nation, and the tragedy is that what enhances power has proven to be suicidal for the species. The nations have reached the brink of an abyss that no additional gains in power can span. Indeed, the very momentum of our technological developments in warfare threatens to push us over the edge by accident even if not by choice. In all their history, the nations have not succeeded in realizing their vocations. The earthly city, as Augustine says in the preface to *The City of God*, has itself been ruled by its lust to rule. Will the last word on the nations be the terrifying pronouncement of judgment on the earthly city in Revelation 18:19: "In one hour she has been laid waste"?

Nothing in previous history prompts us to believe otherwise. One factor has emerged recently, however, that holds a thin margin of promise. The world has now shrunk to the communicative dimensions of a city. It may be, then, that the anarchy at the root of the power system may be checked at least by some loose federation of nations capable of enforcing armed conflict. It has now become clear to increasing numbers of people that the natural system will select us out of existence unless we learn to live synergistically with nature and each other, by our nations. Each nation will now turn to its angel and ask what it must do to be saved, or it will perish. Either the nations will submit themselves to the judgment of God, or they will submit to a never-ending nuclear night.

The act of discerning the spirit of a nation—its angel—and naming it must be accompanied by an equally difficult, and far more demanding response: objective love. The great prophets' hearts broke under the burden of predicting cataclysm for their people. When Jesus weeps over Jerusalem, or reaches out to it like a mother hen to her brood (Lk. 19:41–44, 13:34), what is this if not love pierced by grief over rejection by his people, now rendered desolate?

When people speak of loving their country, they mean—without having reflected on the matter—its spirit, its essence, what it stands for, its image in their minds and before the world. Naming this the angel makes it possible to distinguish the soul of the nation from the actions of any given administration, or leaders, or dominant class, race, or group. This distinction is crucial. It means we can censure, criticize, and oppose unjust policies without having to dissociate ourselves from our love and concern for the land, its history, traditions, and contributions to humanity. The angel makes it possible to relativize the psychic authority with which our leaders tend to become invested, and to recall people to the transcendent, spiritual vocation to which they are ordained and by which they—and their leaders—are judged. The angel, or spirituality, of America stands, as it were, before God; it bears the knowledge of that to which it is called. The angel of America is thus not identical with the present or past injustices of the nation. It always bears the divine judgment and calling to become what it is meant to be.

People do not change national attitudes and policies simply because they are told they are wrong. They change because of love for their country. Politicians have never forgotten this fact, and manipulate that love through misinformation and propaganda. Consequently, many have come to abhor patriotism altogether. Yet in the deepest sense, we must instill again a love for our nation and its angel. Patriotism in some form or another is indispensable for the survival of any state, and if it is not informed by the divine will and the divine judgment, it will become captive to demagogues and jingoists. A chastened patriotism that views the interests of our nation within the context of the well-being of the whole family of nations is required in order to counter the short sightedness of those who equate love for America with short-term economic gain or being "number one."

We cannot minister to the soul of America unless we love its soul. We cannot love its soul faithfully and truly, without sinking into idolatry, unless we have correctly discerned its true vocation under the God who holds the destiny of all the nations. We cannot discern that calling unless we know the angel who bears the message of what the nation might become. We must be international and transnational, but not antinational. The only cure for the evils of nationalism, paradoxically, is genuine love for one's nation as a creature of God.

The demonic spirit of nationalism has metastasized through the nations. It is a cancer that threatens to kill us all, but it is not enough to fight against each injustice piecemeal. The pattern of injustice perpetuated by the nations betrays a single spirit, a resolute momentum through time, a consolidated spirit of empire intent on gain at any cost. It is not just this policy or that which must be countered, but the very spirit of absolutism. It is not simply this leader or that administration which must be opposed, but the entire system of domination and the anarchic relationship between the nations that gives it rise.

The human race was ill-prepared for the contest for power into which it was thrown ten thousand years ago, with the rise of agrarian civilization. It is even less prepared, by dint of experience, for shaping a world of concord. At the same time, it is at least prepared by virtue of creation. We were made for harmony and synergism. The image of God, so near to extinction under the suffocating terrors of civilization, still holds out the possibility of change. We will never build a utopia on earth—but will we take that one gigantic, necessary step out of the domination system into God's domination-free order?

The whole creation is on tiptoe, waiting.

Note

1. On the potential conversion of satanic powers, see *De Principiis* 1.6.2; 1.8; and 3.6.5.

Chapter 2

God and/or Caesar?

Walter E. Pilgrim

It is a common assumption among interpreters that the New Testament has two contrasting positions toward the state: the attitude of subordination found in Paul and related texts, and the call to resistance in Revelation. The New Testament has, in addition, a third attitude toward the state found in the gospels and the memory of Jesus' life and teaching: the attitude of critical distancing from those in power. The purpose of this chapter is to examine the evidence in the New Testament for each of these positions. Then ways will be suggested, amid the diversity, for contemporary Christians to determine their faithful responses in their own times and places.[1]

Subordination in Pauline, Post-Pauline, and Related Texts

A letter written by Clement of Rome to the church in Corinth circa 96 CE preserves the earliest Christian prayer for those who govern:

> Grant that we may be obedient to thy almighty and glorious name and to our rulers and governors upon earth. Thou, Master, has given the power of sovereignty to them, through thy excellent and inexpressible might, so that we may know the glory and honor given them by thee and be subject to them, in no wise resisting thy will. To them, O Lord, give health, peace, concord, stability, so that they may administer without offense the governance which thou hast given them. For thou, heavenly Master, King of the ages, hast given the sons of men glory and honor and power over what is on earth; do thou, O Lord, direct their will according to what is good and pleasing before thee, so that with piety in peace and gentleness they may administer the power them by thee, and may find thee propitious (60:4–61:2).[2]

This prayer reflects the tradition of subordination to the state. Yet it also begins to go beyond it with its repeated affirmations of the power and honor and glory bestowed on the imperial authorities.

We will first look at those texts in the New Testament that regard governments as earthly institutions appointed by God and therefore advocate an attitude of subordination to those who rule. The primary sources are the Pauline and Deutero-Pauline epistles along with 1 Peter and Hebrews. These passages have been the most familiar to readers of the New Testament, and they have shaped the dominant attitude toward the state among Christians in the past and present.

Romans 13:1–7[3]

This text provides the fullest statement in the New Testament on the duty of Christians to be subordinate to civil rulers. The Greek word for subordination (*hypo-tassesthai*) refers to willing submission to persons worthy of respect—including God. Paul affirms without qualification that the authorities exist by divine appointment. Three times they are termed "servants of God" in promoting the good and punishing evil (13:4, 13:6). Accordingly, to resist them is to go against God and will result in judgment. Christians who do good as citizens have nothing to fear from those who rule. But if they do wrong, they can expect punishment and the sword (13:11). The "power of the sword" in classical Christian ethics derives from this Pauline verse. It clearly affirms that those in power have the right and duty to punish wrongdoing, but whether it affirms either capital punishment or war has been and is much debated.

Paul concludes his ethical instructions with some examples of civic duties: pay taxes, respect and honor rulers. The strong emphasis on payment of taxes might show this was a controversial issue both in Rome and Palestine. Jewish nationalists, such as the Zealots, fought against the Roman imperial tax to their death (66–70 CE). Jesus left the question open. In this passage, Paul sides against Christian resistance to the tax at least under the specific circumstances of Christians in Rome.

The Pastoral Epistles (1 Timothy, Titus)[4]

These epistles were written in Paul's name, but there is near-agreement on their composition by an anonymous author a generation after Paul. In the Pastorals, the lively expectation of Christ's return has subsided. There is a new concern for the survival of the church as an institution and the creation of ecclesiastic orders, creeds and canons. In general, there is a more cautious and conservative ethic. A vivid example is found in the "household codes." These codes are meant to order the domestic relations between husbands and wives, parents and children, and masters and slaves. In each case they become more hierarchical and patriarchal—especially so with the role of wives (1 Tim.2:8–11; Titus 2:3–10). One can therefore expect a similar attitude of caution with the government.

In 1 Timothy 2:1–2, the author seeks to encourage the practice of prayer (2:1–15). Note, however, how women are admonished only to modesty and good works and not to prayer (2:8–15). Prayer is urged for everyone, but those singled out for prayer are "kings and all in high positions" (2:2). This does include the emperor. While a special prayer for the emperor is not found in Paul, praying for the emperor does seem consistent with the spirit of Romans 13.

In 2:2, the author explains why Christians should pray for those who govern. It will lead to quiet and peaceable lives, and behind this is the hope that Christians will be viewed as model citizens, which will allow them to promote the cause of the gospel.

In Titus 3:1–2 we again hear the theme of Christian subordination. In chapter 3, the author begins an extended exhortation to good deeds with the admonition to be subject to rulers and authorities (3:1–8). The language contains a clear echo of Romans 13: the same verb for subordination (*hypotassein*) and the same noun for those who rule (*exousiai*) appear. Only the verb "obey" adds a new force to the encouragement. "Remind them" indicates that this behavior is thought to be typical conduct for Christians (3:1). In sum, both passages in the Pastorals affirm the tradition of loyalty and respect for the government found in Romans 13. Nowhere do we get a sense of potential conflict between believers and those who rule.

1 Peter 2:13–17[5]

While the letter is traditionally identified with Peter, most scholars identify the letter with an unknown author writing from Rome to Christians in Asia Minor (1:1, 5:13). The letter reflects a social milieu of growing tension between Christians and their non-Christian neighbors. They are mistrusted, and some are facing trial and prosecution from the civil authorities. As a result of their potential suffering, the author spends much effort emphasizing the way of Jesus as the way of innocent suffering and recalling and affirming the forgiving conduct of Jesus toward his enemies (2:21, 2:22–23, 3:9). What then should be the attitude of Christians toward those in power?

Whatever the debate, the author comes down forcefully on the side of submission. Like their Lord, Christians should be ready to suffer if need be. This entire passage on the government has close affinities to Romans 13. In 2:13, the same verb is used in reference to subjection to rulers (*hypotassein*); likewise in 2:14, a paraphrase occurs on the duty for rulers to punish or reward persons. For the Lord's sake, Christians are to be subordinate to both the emperor and governor.

Yet there are some points of difference from Romans 13. Nowhere does it say the authorities have been appointed by God nor are they called servants of God. Only Christians are called servants of God (2:16). More important, a new theme occurs when believers are told to be subject to their rulers as "free people"(2:16). As free people, the emperor is not their ultimate Lord. The final verse sums up the unique status of Christians. They honor the family of believers and the emperor, but they fear only God (2:17).

Hebrews[6]

This anonymous letter was written to Hellenistic Jewish Christians some decades after Paul. We include Hebrews because some passages describe a Christian community that has experienced some persecution yet responds without any apparent hostility or resistance.

One passage recalls occurrences of public abuse, imprisonment and loss of possessions, but one hears no call to struggle against their persecutors or pray for their downfall. Instead, Christians are exhorted to help one another and accept the plunder of their property knowing they have a greater reward awaiting them (10:32–39).

The heroic examples of faith in chapter 11 include Moses, who was unafraid of the Pharaoh's anger, and the Maccabean martyrs executed by the Seleucid ruler, Antiochus Epiphanes (11:24–27, 11:35–38). However, it is Jesus who is the supreme model of steadfast faith by his enduring the shame of the cross (12:2). Christians are challenged to possess the same kind of perseverance to the point of shedding one's blood, if necessary (12:4). Nowhere in this letter does one find any encouragement to resist the oppressors, however. Voluntary acceptance of suffering in imitation of Jesus' own suffering best describes the attitude of Hebrews. It thus stands within the tradition of loyalty and respect toward the governments we are exploring.

Critique of the Tradition of Subordination

We can affirm the understanding that governments have been instituted by God for the common good: to preserve order and to promote justice, peace, and earth's sustainability. What is troubling about Romans 13 is its apparent acceptance of all governments, no matter who or what, of fulfilling their divine purpose. We know from tragic experience, past and present, that this is not true. On the matter of the response of Christians toward authorities who abuse or misuse their power, there is a deafening silence in Paul and the tradition of subordination. How shall we understand this? When Paul claims all authorities have been instituted by God, is he calling for unquestioned obedience to those who rule? We think not and do so for these six important reasons:

1. A few interpreters argue that Romans 13:1–7 is a later addition by an author more favorable to Rome than Paul. However, the majority of interpreters look for explanations in the historical setting of the letter for Paul's positive view of Rome (54–68 CE). While the suggestions are helpful, no consensus has emerged.[7] Still others find exegetical reasons for Paul's affirming attitude. It is noted that in Romans 12–15 Paul sets forth the transformed life of the believer with love as the shape of the new life. Thus, 13:1–7 spells out the love ethic in the public realm, which includes respect and submission to authorities. Along with the love ethic, there is also the strong note of eschatological urgency in 13:11–14. This reflects Paul's

understanding that, in view of the nearness of the end, all human authorities are temporary at best. Beyond the attempt to interpret Paul's view of the state in Romans 13, other themes are also prominent in his thinking.

2. For Paul and the early church there is only one sovereign Lord (*kurios*) of the universe. Thus the Christological title "Lord" is most frequent in Paul. Despite the pseudo-claim of Caesar and other "lords and gods," there is only one Lord worthy of our ultimate trust and loyalty. In the "Lord Jesus Christ," Caesar has a new rival to the throne and the empire.

3. Likewise, there is the conviction that the believer's true citizenship belongs in the coming kingdom. In the present, they live as strangers and exiles as 1 Peter and Hebrews so movingly affirm. While governments as earthly institutions might serve in the interim as necessary for our public life together, they remain transient with no ultimate claim on believers.

4. The message of "Christ crucified" stands at the heart of Paul's message (1 Cor. 1:23; Gal. 2:1). Paul knows the one he proclaims as the crucified and risen Lord was executed by the Roman governor of Palestine. A crucified Messiah was a scandal to Jews and folly to Gentiles. The preaching of a "crucified Lord" would continually bring to mind the injustice of Roman power. Neither Paul nor the followers of Jesus could be naive about the empire that nailed their Lord to the cross.

5. Paul's own experience of suffering must also be a part of his grasp of Roman injustice. Paul's letters and the book of Acts show that Paul's mission outreach was characterized by continual conflict from both Jewish and Roman officials. Paul frequently urges fellow Christians to imitate his willingness to suffer with Christ (2 Cor.1:7). This means Paul does not expect peaceful relations with civil authorities. Neither he nor Jesus nor his followers experience it. Where believers confess only one Lord and live by that confession there will be inevitable clashes of loyalty.

6. In Romans 13 and the related texts there is only an ethic of submission to the political authorities, even if the result might be that Christians suffer unjustly. We hear only the counsel to accept one's suffering willingly for the sake of Christ. However, there are other voices in the New Testament that advocate quite different responses of resistance.

Summary of the Subordination Tradition

The tradition of subordination to the state has represented for the majority of Christians the primary view of the New Testament. As such, the government is God's gift to preserve and promote the common good of people and nations. In return, Christians owe it their respect, obedience and prayers. A kind of mutual partnership exists to benefit the public welfare.

How shall we respond to this tradition? It needs to be taken seriously as an expression of the divine intention for the state and the Christian conduct toward it, but is it the normative tradition as many have thought?

It is not, in light of both the state's troubled history of abuse and misuse of its powers and the reality of other responses to the government in the New Testament. Above all, it is a mistake to make absolute or nearly absolute the state's role as though all governments are ordained of God and Christians owe unquestioned patriotism and loyalty. Only Jesus Christ is Lord!

Critical Distancing: Jesus and the Gospels

Along with the response of subordination to the state, one finds a distinct attitude in the portrait of Jesus in the gospels: a posture of critical distancing from the religious and political authorities. While interpreters have recognized much of the evidence to be surveyed, few have grasped its significance for understanding the attitude of the New Testament toward those in power. Of course, we are keenly aware of the complexity of the topic and the problem of brevity. Yet it is our intent to demonstrate that the gospels present a different perspective neither of subordination nor of resistance in Revelation with regard to those who rule.

This inquiry will not be a study of the historical Jesus and the earliest sources. While this is legitimate and important, the purpose here is to study the gospels in their present form in the New Testament. Modern scholarship has taught us to distinguish between the synoptic gospels with their related narratives—Mark, Matthew, and Luke—and the gospel of John. We also accept the priority of Mark's gospel among the synoptics and the existence of Q, a source found only in Matthew and Luke. With these scholarly tools at our disposal, we now undertake a mini-survey of the evidence for Jesus' critical distancing from the holders of religious and political power.

Some have tried to argue that, in fact, Jesus was a Zealot, a member of the radical Jewish sect that advocated armed resistance to Roman occupation of Palestine and refusal to pay the imperial tax. There is little evidence in the Bible for a Zealot-like Jesus while no doubt Jesus was on the side of freedom from Rome.[8] Others have sought to interpret Jesus as an apocalyptic visionary whose life and teaching were focused on the coming reign of God with little concern for the present. However, the Jesus in the gospels is neither a militant Zealot ready to use the power of the sword nor one whose eyes were fixed only on the future. Jesus taught a way to live fully in the present doing the will of God while also awaiting the future when God's kingdom finds its fulfillment.

Gospel Traditions Prior to Passion History

Within the ministry of Jesus in the synoptic gospels there are multiple texts that underscore Jesus' opposition to the religious and civil authorities. The "conflict stories" depict Jesus on the attack against the tradition of scribes and Pharisees risking the charge of blasphemy and even death (Mk. 2:1–3:6 parallels). The imprisonment and beheading of John the Baptist by Herod Antipas, Jesus' own ruler in Galilee, must have heralded the same possible fate for Jesus, yet he persists with unabated courage. The passion predictions present a forceful picture of one who is unafraid to die despite the religious and political powers arrayed against him (Mk. 8:31, 9:31, 19:33 parallels). Two passages are of special importance for our topic.

Teaching on Authentic Greatness (Mk. 10:35–45; Mt. 20:20–28; Lk. 22:24–27)

This text offers a powerful critique of all civic and political structures in sharp contrast to the alternate vision of the new community founded by Jesus. The request of James and John for places of honor exposes their failure to understand this new community and the sacrifice it might require (Mk. 10:35–40). The teaching of Jesus on authentic greatness states with unmistakable clarity the profound and irreconcilable distinction between the two (Mk. 10:41–45). In the institutions of the world, their rulers exercise authority by being "lords and tyrants" (Greek: *katakyrieousin/kataexousiazousin*, 10:42). This is the world arranged hierarchically; between patron and client, strong and weak, master and slave, privileged and exploited. But in the countercommunity of Jesus the important words are "servant" and "slave" (Greek: *diakonos, doulos*) and the key values are its concomitant vision of shared authority and mutual leadership. Jesus is the model of authentic leadership by his life of selfless service to the end (10:45).

This passage is in reality an exposé of all human structures governed by control, dominance, and brute force. Behind it, one can recognize the abuse of authority, the oppression of the weak and vulnerable, and the disenfranchisement of so much of the human race caused by those who rule. The synoptic Jesus calls for a radically new way of exercising authority in the community of his followers where service and sacrifice are the norm.

On Paying Taxes to Caesar (Mk. 12:13–17; Mt. 22:15–22; Lk. 20:20–26, RSV)

One might expect this familiar text to provide a clear response to Jesus' attitude toward the political institutions. Unfortunately, it has proved surprisingly difficult to interpret. The gospels agree on its setting in the temple amid Jesus' debate with hostile Jewish leaders. They ask a question to trap him, "Is it lawful to pay taxes to Caesar or not?" (Mk. 12:14). Jewish groups in the first century were deeply divided on this question. Some said a violent "No!" (Zealots); others offered a grudging acceptance (Pharisees); some were openly cooperative (Sadducees, Herodians). Whatever answer Jesus gave would put him in jeopardy either as a rebel to Rome or a traitor to Israel's cause. Jesus responds by requesting a denarius, the silver coin by which the poll tax was levied and which bore the name and image of Caesar. This tax was highly unpopular both as the hated symbol of subjection to Rome and the blasphemous image of Caesar. The introduction of the tax in 6 CE led to a revolt in Galilee by the ultra-nationalists. Upon receiving the despised coin, Jesus makes his famous statement, "Render to Caesar the things that are Caesar's and to God the things that are God's." The statement is clever and provocative but ambiguous at best. What does it mean? We summarize three current responses along with our own brief evaluation of each.[9]

1. Two Kingdoms: God and Caesar. The traditional interpretation understood Jesus to accept two legitimate realms, that of God and of Caesar. Both have their distinct role to play in the human community. Persons owe respect and obedience toward those who rule, honor and worship toward God. Here Jesus takes a strong stance against the Zealots and those who refuse to pay the tax. This view also coheres with the Pauline attitude of subordination we discussed earlier.

This interpretation still has persuasive advocates and needs to be taken seriously. Where it falters has been in its tendency to equate the two realms as though both are deserving of our highest loyalty. History has shown all too often the tragic consequences. For Jesus and the evangelists, our prior obedience belongs to God alone.

2. One Kingdom: To God Alone. This position is the exact opposite of the first.[10] To the question, what belongs to Caesar? the answer comes loud and clear: absolutely nothing. Jesus' hearers would know it is a matter of obedience to the first commandment "to worship the Lord your God alone." It is also argued that Jesus took the stance of the Zealots and their followers by forbidding the payment of the tax—a charge leveled against Jesus at his trial (Lk. 23:2).

This view is attractive because it takes with greatest importance the prior obedience owed to God. Yet it is unlikely Jesus took the side of the nationalists with their call to violence and the refusal to pay the imperial tax.

3. Two Kingdoms: God Prior, then Caesar. This view accepts the reality of both realms, that of God and of Caesar, yet it insists on the absolute priority of God's kingdom. For disciples there can be no compromise between loyalty to God or to the emperor. This means there is in reality no peaceful coexistence between the two envisioned. Jesus' call "to give to God what is God's" opens up the possibility of conflict, disobedience, and even resistance to the emperors of the world as witnessed in Jesus' own life and death.

This interpretation is the most consistent with the memory of Jesus in the gospels. While acknowledging the role of those who govern, Jesus knows that obedience to Caesar has its limits for those who love God above all.

Jesus' Sermons in Matthew and Luke

We will now explore some key texts in Q, which is the common source used by Matthew and Luke. Each of the evangelists creates a sermon of Jesus early in each gospel. Although the sermons are quite different in content and length, two of the traditions are singularly helpful in determining Jesus' attitude toward those in authority.

1. Beatitudes. In the Matthean beatitudes, Jesus teaches a radical reversal of values for those in his kingdom community (5:3–12). Among the "blessed" (or "favored") are the poor in spirit, the meek, the merciful, the peacemakers, and the persecuted who do not retaliate. These distinct characteristics mark the disciples who put their trust in God for their reward.

The Lukan beatitudes draw a prophetic portrait of Jesus declaring divine blessings upon the poor and the hungry and declaring weeping and woes upon the rich, full, and well-esteemed (6:20–26). Luke is already pointing to other themes and texts in his gospel where Jesus makes powerful condemnations against the wealthy and promises God's coming reversal of justice.

2. *Matthean Antithesis of Non-retaliation and Love of Enemies.* The Q tradition preserves two of the most revolutionary teachings in the gospels. Here we find the love ethic of Jesus in its most radical form. We recognize, as well, the diversity of interpretations on these texts from that of the believer's personal response to that of Christian pacifism. We will limit our discussion to the Matthean antithesis in the Sermon on the Mount.

In this antithesis of non-retaliation in Matthew 5:38–42, the old way of limited revenge is contrasted with the new way: "do not resist an evildoer." Four examples are given of this changed response. In each, the disciple of Jesus: accepts the insult and turns the other cheek, gives both outer and inner garment to those who sue, carries the soldier's pack an extra mile, and gives freely to anyone who begs or borrows.

How shall we interpret these challenging words? Most persons have understood them as a counsel of passive submission. Disciples are not to retaliate in any way, even against those who do them harm. This view deserves our honor and respect. Yet its counsel of nonresistance does pose both ethical and practical problems. There may be other ways to interpret this passage. A recent commentator has argued persuasively that the Greek verb for "do not resist" should be translated as "do not resist violently" (5:39, *antistenai*). He then shows the creative ways Jesus demonstrates to resist evildoers without resort to violence.[11] This suggests a third way in the teaching of Jesus between the counsel of nonresistance and revenge: the way of nonviolent resistance. These subversive sayings on nonretaliation reject the path of violence, of hatred, and of getting even as the kingdom's way. Rather, they call disciples to the way of justice, peace, and reconciliation.

In Matthew 5:43–48, love of enemies constitutes the climactic antithesis of the sermon. This teaching embodies the heart of the love ethic of Jesus. The old command is said to be: Love your neighbor, but hate your enemy. In fact, Leviticus 19:18 has only "love your neighbor" and neither the Old Testament nor Rabbinic literature taught hatred toward others. Yet it was a kind of everyday morality to befriend your neighbor and despise your real or perceived enemies. Jesus envisions a radically new way in which love for the neighbor embraces the whole human family—even one's enemies. The source of Jesus' call to love without limits is his understanding of a compassionate and gracious God who cares for good and evil alike (5:38). Thus, disciples of Jesus pray for their persecutors and become perfect in love as their heavenly Father is perfect.

How does this ethic of nonretaliation and love of enemies become a reality for Christians today? For a few, it applies primarily to their personal relations with others. Still others hear it as a communal ethic that is required of all disciples. From this view has arisen Christian pacifism and its demand for a love that forbids any war or armed violence. Despite its deep attraction, the command of Jesus "to love the neighbor" has led to an acceptance of the need to protect communities and nations and "just war" traditions. As I have noted in a previous work, "Great caution is required in rejecting pacifism, given the predominant history of the church, co-opted by the temptations of earthly power and holy wars and crusades and church-state alliances, as well as the contemporary memories of the horrors of 'Christians' and 'churches' blindly pursuing the siren call of nationalism or racism or ethnicism or national security, all too often in the name of Christ."[12]

Special Passages in Matthew

Along with Mark and Q, Matthew draws from his own sources to tell the story of Jesus. Most interpreters regard Matthew as a Jewish-Christian gospel, in which the readers are engaged in an intense debate with the synagogue on the question of the Messiahship of Jesus as well as the Law.[13] These comments can look only briefly at certain texts that illustrate Jesus' conflict with those in power.

1. *Matthean Birth Narratives.* In chapter 1, Matthew identifies Jesus as the Messiah who comes to save humanity and is in truth "Emmanuel" ("God with us"). The cycle of infancy stories in chapter 2 sheds harsh light on the hostility between Jesus and the religious and political leaders. The visit of the magi from the East in search of the child born "king of the Jews" sets in motion the murderous plot of Herod the Great to destroy any rival to his throne (2:1–12). Divine protection results in the flight of the holy family to Egypt as refugees and in their return to Nazareth. In the midst of it all is the bloody massacre of the infants in Bethlehem, a vivid reminder of the cruel and vindictive deeds of the tyrants of the world. So at the beginning of Matthew's gospel we have a story of two contrasting kings: one born to bring God's peace and healing to the nations and the other who rules by the brute power of the sword.

2. *Jesus and the Temple/Roman Tax: "Free. . .but" (Mt.17:24–27).* Matthew alone preserves this provocative tradition about the payment of taxes. He also includes the debate over the payment of tax to Caesar. Here the question has to do with the Temple tax. In the pre-70 CE setting it was a tax levied annually on all male Jews twenty years and older living in Israel and the Diaspora. The tax consisted of a half-shekel (Greek: *didrachm*a), and it was paid faithfully by most Jews for the maintenance of the Temple.

This story occurs in Capernaum, the small fishing village located near the Sea of Galilee and the center of Jesus' ministry in Galilee. Each year on the fifteenth of the month, Ader, tables were set up in the villages to collect the tax. When Peter is asked whether the "teacher" pays the tax he answers "yes." Upon his return, Jesus inquires whether the "kings of the earth" collect tolls or tributes (Greek*: telos, kenson*) from their own children or from others? To the response, "from others," Jesus declares, "then the children are free."

But who are the free children, and what might it say in the post-70 CE setting of Jewish Christians living after the destruction of Jerusalem and the Temple? The emperor Vespasian levied the equivalent tax on all Jews to pay for the pagan Temple of Jupiter Capitolinus in Rome as both punishment and propaganda. Most likely, Jewish Christians also had to pay. The expression "kings of the earth" recalls a bitter history of exile and oppression by the succession of imperial tyrants, including Rome. Moreover, the reference to tolls and tributes of kings demonstrates that the topic of taxation has gone beyond the Temple tax. For readers of Matthew's gospel, the imperial Roman tax was real and relevant. Do we need to pay or not?

Most commentators have interpreted Jesus' words about the freedom of children to apply to Jesus, Peter, and to all subsequent disciples.[14] As children of God, the King above all earthly kings, they are free from obedience to all human rulers and free not to pay the tax. So understood, these are subversive words declaring with great force the freedom of God's people from every religious and political institution.

Yet freedom is not the only word. The miracle of the fish and coin enables Jesus to pay the tax. On this occasion he curbs his freedom for a greater good and not to cause offense. In so doing disciples of Jesus learn that they live between two worlds, those of freedom and submission. There may be times to claim this freedom when it is threatened or denied, but there are also times to submit and pay the tax.

Special Passages from Luke.
Creating his own story of Jesus from Mark and Q, Luke also uses some new sources. Again we can only make brief comments where we find Luke most helpful on Jesus' critical response to those who rule.

1. *Lukan Birth Narratives: Pax Romana vs. Pax Christi (Lk. 1–2).* Of all the evangelists, Luke is the most aware of the historical setting of imperial Rome and the provinces of Judea and Galilee. The formal literary introductions of his gospel and Acts claim to write a careful history aided by eyewitnesses and others (Lk. 1:1–4; Acts 1:1–5). Luke alone names and dates the key events: Herod the Great in Judea (1:5); emperors Augustus, Tiberius, and procurator Pontius Pilate (2:1, 3:1); Herod Antipas and High-Priests, Annas and Caiaphas (3:1). Against this imperial background, Luke tells his unique infancy stories of the birth of John and Jesus. Within its Jewish setting, Luke places the birth narratives among the hopes and promises of a Messiah from the house of David. However, Luke must revise the hopes, since the Messiah brings salvation to the nations and not to a restored Israel (2:11, 11:14, 24:47; Acts 1:6). Within the imperial setting there is the pseudo-claim of the empire to bring peace and justice to the world and the pseudo-claim of the emperor to be the savior of the world. The *Pax Romana* was in truth the story of peace through bloody and vindictive conquest and of prosperity for the elite few by victimizing or exploiting the masses. Luke's way is the *Pax Christi* where the disciples of Jesus learn another way to live from their Lord and Savior that brings liberation and hope to humanity.

2. *Lukan Hymn: Magnificat (1:46–55).* This familiar hymn, attributed to Mary, is a striking statement about a God who takes the side of the weak and vulnerable. At the beginning Mary expresses her surprise that God chose her, a humble servant (Greek: *doule, slave*). Yet the second half rings with the praise of the God who always puts down the proud, mighty, and rich and exalts the poor and lowly (1:51–53). The relevance of this subversive text to liberation

theologies in our time is obvious. It is also understandable that some governments have banned its reading in worship and study. All tyrannical structures here stand under divine judgment.

3. *Inaugural Address: Good News to the Poor (4:16–30).*[15] Drawing on a tradition from Mark (6:1–5), Luke begins the public ministry of Jesus with this inaugural address in his hometown synagogue at Nazareth. As a programmatic text it sets forth the main themes of Jesus' Messianic teaching and activity. As the Spirit-anointed servant of Yahweh promised in Isaiah (61:2, 58:6), Jesus brings good news to the poor, the captives, the blind, and the oppressed. In the gospel Jesus fulfills this mission. With respect to those in power, Jesus appears as the great liberator of humankind. His ministry will challenge the religious and political authorities until they put him to death.

4. *Go Tell That Fox: Lament over Jerusalem (Lk. 13:31–35) and The Things That Make for Peace (Lk. 19:41–44).* We will consider these texts together because they are distinct to Luke and shed surprising light on the Lukan Jesus' attitude toward his own ruler and his prophetic pathos for his own nation.

In the first passage, some friendly Pharisees warn Jesus to flee because Herod seeks his death. Herod Antipas, the son of Herod the Great, was given the minor title of "tetrarch" and ruled over Galilee and Perea for many years (4 BCE–37 CE). While Luke notes Herod's imprisonment of John and his desire to meet Jesus, this is the one time he records Herod's hostile intent. Luke also preserves the meeting between Herod and Jesus in Jerusalem and Jesus' daring refusal to speak or act (23:6–12).

Despite the warning, Jesus refuses to be cowed by fear or to stop his healing ministry, and he calls Herod by the unflattering epithet: fox. It means a sly or crafty person and implies a critical judgment on Herod and his rule. In fact, it might be a term of contempt, like skunk or rat. The portrait here is of one who acts boldly and courageously, even defiantly, toward his own ruler. Jesus lives in obedience to a higher authority and will not be swayed, even by the threat of death, from doing the will of God.

To this sharp rebuke of Herod, Luke adds the lament over Jerusalem (13:33–35; Mt.23:37–39). Like the prophets of old, Jesus' destiny will be to die in the holy city. While few prophets were actually stoned in Jerusalem, it was a proverbial saying about their fate. With the warm embrace of a brooding mother hen, this wise saying captures Jesus' profound sorrow over his imminent rejection and dying. With the coming judgments will be the destruction of the Temple.

The dramatic scene of Jesus weeping over Jerusalem comes immediately after the Entry (19:41–44). Luke thus contrasts the royal welcome with the city's coming demise. While Jesus comes as the messenger of peace—a repeated theme in the gospel (1:19, 2:14, 13:35, 19:38)—the people of Jerusalem do not recognize "the things that make for peace." This means, in part, their failure to recognize Jesus as the anointed Messiah and Savior of humankind. Yet it points with equal force to their refusal to adopt the path of nonviolence, love, and reconciliation, even for the enemy. Because Jerusalem rejects the way of peace, Jesus foresees its future end with grim detail (19:43–44). Luke writes after the city and

Temple's destruction in 70 CE. He is careful not to draw a direct link between Jesus' death and the brutal conquest by the Roman legions, but we do hear once more the gap between the *Pax Christi* (the things that make for peace) and the *Pax Romana* (the things that make for war and violence). Jesus weeps and the daughters of Jerusalem weep, knowing what is hidden from their eyes.

Passion History

Each gospel, including John, names the climactic events of Jesus' life as his suffering and death in Jerusalem followed by his resurrection. As the evangelists tell it, the suffering and crucifixion are the result of action against Jesus by the Temple hierarchy and the Roman governor in Judea.[16] It will be our purpose to examine briefly the response of Jesus toward the religious and political authorities. By so doing, this survey will support our thesis regarding Jesus' critical distancing from those who govern.

The two provocative actions, Entry and Cleansing, prepare the way for the passion history in the gospels, and they provide surprising evidence of Jesus' bold, if not defiant, attitude toward the civil and political rulers.

Entry into Jerusalem (Mk. 11:1–11, parallels).

In the synoptic gospels one gets the impression that Jesus has pre-arranged for the finding of the young colt or donkey, not yet ridden upon. The emphasis on its newness hints at its sacred significance. On mounting the donkey, Jesus begins the sharp descent from the Mount of Olives through the Kidron valley and enters by the city gate. As he does, the disciples and crowds spread their coats and branches on the path with great shouts of "Hosannah" (meaning "God saves"). While Mark has only "many people" present, Matthew has a "very large crowd" and John says "the whole world has gone after him." In Mark, the acclaim repeats the words of Psalm 118:26—the familiar cry of pilgrims entering the holy city. We find no direct Messianic claim for Jesus in Mark, only the hope for the coming kingdom of David. Yet Matthew and the other gospels view the entry as the fulfillment of Zechariah 9:9—the promise of the lowly king astride the donkey. Jesus is also named Son of David and King of Israel.

How shall one interpret Jesus' action? Two matters are of special importance for our topic. This is the one moment in the synoptics that Jesus solicits openly and eagerly the support of the people. Otherwise there is silence about his mission and identity; a kind of "Messianic secret." Now the silence is broken for all to see and in light of Jesus' knowledge of his imminent fate in Jerusalem, the Entry must be seen as nothing less than a courageous challenge to the religious and civil leaders. We also find significant the symbolic entry of Jesus on the donkey. We agree with those who understand it as a prophetic action rooted in Zechariah 9:9. The symbol of the humble king riding on a donkey, the lowly beast of burden, subverts all our notions of sovereignty. Here authority and kingship are reinterpreted in terms of lowliness, service and peacemaking. Here is kingship without violence, national ambition, or imperial dominance. In this sense, the entry provides a paradigm of authority that contravenes all the traditional images, then and now.[17]

Cleansing of the Temple (Mk. 11:15–19 parallels).
After the bold entry of Jesus into Jerusalem, the synoptics have the most provocative event in the gospels, the Cleansing of the Temple. This action associates Jesus with forceful, if not violent, protest against the religious leaders and leads to his arrest and final execution. Like the Entry, it seems preplanned and deliberate. When Jesus enters the Temple, he drives out the buyers and sellers of sacrificial animals and overturns the tables of the money changers and dove sellers. This involved aggressive physical force and John even has Jesus make a whip of cords (2:15). The action no doubt occurred in the Court of the Gentiles, the area on the Temple mount allowed for commercial activity and open to everyone. Despite the hatred of the Jews for Herod the Great, the rebuilt Temple was his magnificent gift and the cause of much pride.

Why this angry and deliberate protest in the Temple—the most sacred site for the worship of Yahweh, the God of Israel? Both the sacrificial animals and money changers were necessary for Temple worship. Therefore the activity in itself could not be the object of Jesus' disgust. Their presence on the Temple mount made it convenient for everyone. At the same time, we do not think Jesus' forceful action had to do with a Zealot-like plot to foment a rebellion (66–70 CE). Jesus' way is that of nonviolent and nonpolitical goals. Nowhere in the gospels do we find Jesus against sacrifice or speaking against the Temple itself, even though this becomes a charge of false witnesses at his trial.

Why the protest? The synoptics interpret it by two quotes: "My house shall be called a house of prayer for all the nations" (Isa. 56:7), "but you have made it a den of robbers" (Jer. 7:11). The first passage comes from Deutero-Isaiah's grand vision of a time when all nations will be saved and will worship on Mount Zion. The second arises out of Jeremiah's famous Temple speech, in which the prophet fearlessly denounces the Temple abuse and prophesies its destruction. Only friends save Jeremiah's life. So here the religious leaders are accused by Jesus of turning the "house of prayer" into a "den of robbers." What might lie behind the charge "den of robbers" and provoke the daring and fearless actions of Jesus?

While there was some dishonesty among the merchants and the commercial activity in the Temple was noisy and distracting, this does not seem sufficient to arouse Jesus' risky actions.

At the core of Jesus' protest was a profound and systemic corruption of the Temple system. The High-Priestly families and the other wealthy elite dominated the Temple both religiously and economically. They amassed great wealth, which was the source of their power and influence in Judea and even Galilee and was also influential with the Roman procurator. It is in this context that one can best understand the dramatic protest in the Temple. Jesus acts with prophetic courage against the corruption of the Temple hierarchy and their collaborators and pays the price. His actions threaten their control of Israel's central religious institution and cannot be tolerated. Here we have a Jesus resisting daringly, even defiantly, those in power.

Themes in the Passion Narratives.
Along with the two provocative events that introduce the passion history, we find four themes that reveal further the attitude of Jesus toward the religious and political leaders. One can only summarize them briefly, but they are consistent with the portrait of Jesus' critical response throughout the gospels.

1. *Silence.* In the synoptics Jesus speaks only when he is asked about his identity. Otherwise there is deliberate silence. In John, the silence is broken before the High-Priest, Annas, and the Roman governor, Pilate. Jesus explains the nature of his kingship and denies Pilate's authority over him.

2. *Nonviolent Suffering.* Jesus accepts his suffering and willingly takes the path of suffering love as the kingdom way. While he defends his innocence of the charge of blasphemy and insurrection, nowhere does he respond with hatred, bitterness, revenge, or contempt. Jesus is the model of nonviolent suffering to the tragic end. His teaching on love for the neighbor, prayer for the persecutors, nonretaliation and love of the enemy here finds its culmination.

3. *Nonpolitical Realm.* The enigma of Jesus' life and death is that he was crucified on the charge of political insurrection. Yet the evangelists and the early church insist the charge was false and the sentence a gross miscarriage of justice. Jesus did not seek to establish an earthly realm to replace Rome or any political structures, Jewish or Roman. We must be cautious, however, in that Jesus' ministry is political. He does seek to renew public life and to call into being new communities of disciples to do the same.

The passion history consistently uses the title "king" for Jesus and agrees on his Roman crucifixion as "King of the Jews," but it reinterprets the meaning of the Messianic hopes and royal claims in nonpolitical terms. While earthly realms exercise their authority by lording it over others, Jesus' realm or kingdom lays claim to another way to form human communities and renew the world.

4. *Sovereign Authority.* Here one notes those places where the evangelists show Jesus putting his accusers on the defense and making paramount claims for himself. Yet in each case he voluntarily submits in obedience to the Scriptures and God's predetermined plan for his death.

Each of the gospels heightens, in its own way, the sense of authority with the gospel of John interpreting the passion as the "hour" of Jesus' enthronement on the cross. Yet the profound paradox exists between Jesus' inherent authority and his voluntary submission to earthly powers.

Summary of Jesus' Attitude of Critical Distancing

Among the variety of texts in the gospels with respect to Jesus' response to the religious and political authorities we find some consistent themes that support our thesis of its distinctiveness. Jesus accepts the religious and civil structures, both Jewish and Roman, without seeking their removal. Unlike the Zealots, nowhere does he issue any call to rebellion or violent resistance nor is there any Messianic claim to a Davidic-like hope for Israel's national restoration. Moreover, Jesus and his disciples pay the tax to Caesar and to the Temple.

Nevertheless, the Jesus in the gospels stands as the constant critic of the religious and political institutions and their leaders. His life from beginning to end is a history of conflict with those in power. Jesus seeks to create new communities of disciples that are radically different from their contemporaries. The rulers of the earth are tyrants who lord it over others by the brute power of the sword. In the kingdom communities, the decisive realities are service and sacrifice modeled after Jesus' own life and death. These communities also exhibit the gifts of humbleness, mercy, peacemaking and innocent suffering. They also practice the audacious way of limitless love, in which nonviolence, nonretaliation, and love of enemies are taught and lived. The disciples may pay their tax to Caesar and the Temple but they do so knowing their obedience belongs to God alone.

The gospels also show that the God of Jesus is on the side of those most in need. The Magnificat proclaims the God who puts down the powerful and exalts the lowly. Jesus' ministry brings good news to the poor and oppressed, and in his communities the least and vulnerable find welcome. His words and deeds offer continued rebuke to those who misuse or abuse their power and wealth. Jesus refuses to be detoured from his mission even when he knows its violent end. His courageous, if not defiant, reply to his own ruler (fox) is typical of his fearless determination to put God's cause prior.

The conflict reaches its climax at the end of his life. Jesus' prophetic entry into Jerusalem and bold cleansing of the Temple deliberately provoke the religious and civil authorities to act, and they do. In the hearing before the Sanhedrin and trial before Pilate, the passion history tells the story of the Messiah who dies as the model of nonviolent suffering and ultimate trust in God. Jesus is crucified "under Pontius Pilate" as the innocent victim of Roman injustice.

As we have demonstrated at length, the response of Jesus in the gospels toward those in positions of power is not that of subordination. He continually challenges their authority and risks his life in doing so. We call this the attitude of critical distancing. Yet in the gospels, unlike in the book of Revelation, there is no sense that the state has become demonic or corrupt to the core and must be resisted accordingly.

Resistance in the Book of Revelation (The Apocalypse)

In Revelation, we find a response to the political structures that is neither subordination nor critical distancing. Here the state has become the mortal enemy of the church. There exists an irreconcilable conflict between Christ and Caesar that calls the church to resist heroically the temptation to compromise and idolatry.[18]

Why this radical change of attitude? Most interpreters agree that it has to do with the historical setting of Revelation. The Apocalypse was likely written near the end of the reign of the emperor Domitian (96 CE). While his early years were successful, in his remaining years he became increasingly cruel and vindictive leading to his assassination in Rome. Despite some claims to the contrary, there does not appear to be a widespread persecution of Christians under his reign. Yet there was deep fear of its imminent outbreak and clear evidence of trials and martyrdom in the neighboring province of Asia Minor (Letters of Pliny to Emperor Trajan, 98–117 CE).[19] The letters addressed by John to the seven churches in Asia Minor express deep concern for their vitality and faithfulness that extend beyond the threat of persecution (Rev. 2–3). However, there are explicit references to trials, imprisonment, and martyrdom, along with John's own exile on the island of Patmos. The entire Apocalypse has as its background the perceived coming clash between the church and the Roman imperium.

Of equal importance during the reign of Domitian is the cult of emperor worship. Archaeological evidence for the existence of the cult is found in five of the seven cities of Revelation. Civic leaders would vie for permission to build Temples in the emperor's honor and expect participation by all residents. In addition, Domitian had coins minted with the obverse side depicting Domitian in the form of the god Jupiter while on the reverse side Domitian sits enthroned in a palace like the god Jupiter. On all of his public documents and public appearances he insisted on the use of *dominus et deus noster* ("our Lord and God"). For many Christians and Jews, the worship of the emperor and claims to divinity were idolatrous blasphemy that could not be tolerated.

Perhaps enough has been said about the setting of Revelation to illumine its attitude toward the state. John perceives the threat of persecution and idolatry right around the corner. Like the author of Daniel who wrote to defy the Hellenizing tyrant, Antiochus Epiphanes IV (circa 175 BCE), John writes opposing the latest imperial tyrant centered in Rome. The Apocalypse offers Christian believers a message of encouragement, comfort, and protest in the face of political and religious oppression.

Understanding of the State

As interpreters have rightly noted, in Revelation the political authorities have become the enemy of God, the church, and humankind. The state in reality belongs to the kingdom of the world under the dominion of Satan and his rule. Three provocative images underscore this theme.

Beasts (Greek: to therion)

In Revelation 13, the apocalyptic image of the two beasts represents imperial Rome and its pseudo-claims to ultimate loyalty and obedience. The first beast arises out of the sea, the mythic symbol of chaos, and makes claim to rule the earth (13:1–8). Drawing upon Daniel 7, John creates his own symbol of human power that becomes demonic. The authority of the beast derives from the dragon (Satan) from whom it has received its absolute power and domination of the world. The seer notes with amazement that all the earth worships the beast ("Who is like the beast. . .?" 13:5, 13:8). Moreover, the beast in its arrogance becomes a parody of Christ by bearing blasphemous names upon its seven heads. The readers know the names are the divine titles claimed by the emperor. The beast also speaks blasphemy against God and makes war against the saints, but there are two challenges to the authority of the beast. The one is the divine limit placed on its time of rule (forty-two months, 13:5) and the other is the presence of the saints who are not seduced by earthly power and refuse to worship any other than God and the Lamb (13:8).

The second beast arises out of the earth and acts wholly under the authority of the first beast (13:11–18). It, too, is a parody of Christ with horns "like a Lamb" yet speaking "like a dragon." Its primary task is to create images of the first beast and to enforce its worship. Who is this second beast? There can be little doubt that John is describing the local religious and political leaders in Asia Minor who promote the cult of the emperor and its related practices. They enforce the worship of the images of the beast with the threat of death to those who refuse (13:15). John also alludes to magical practices and tricks that were used to prove the images' existence. More importantly, he points to social and economic pressures to conform. Without the "mark of the beast" on their right hand or forehead no one could buy or sell. Whatever the exact identity of the beast, 666 (Nero?), it is a person who is an emperor (13:18). Again, there are divine limits to the pseudo-authority of the beast. The "mark" has its counterpoint as the "seal" of the redeemed who bear the name of God and the Lamb on their foreheads. So, too, John contrasts those who receive the mark of the beast with the 144,000 sealed by God (14:1). In sum, the image of the two beasts reflects the deep conflict between Christ and Caesar. For the saints, their loyalty and worship belong to God and the Lamb alone. There is no room for compromise; hence the call for the "endurance and faith of the saints" (13:10).

Whore (Greek: he porne)
A second image of imperial Rome is that of the great whore in chapter 17 amid the vision of the seventh and final bowl of God's wrath upon the earth. It is the most grotesque of John's colorful symbols and needs careful interpretation in view of the long history of patriarchal insensitivity to biblical symbols. The image has its background in the prophetic portrayal of Israel or Jerusalem as God's bride or more often as a harlot gone whoring after other gods. The sin of idolatry is denounced repeatedly as fornication by the prophets (Isa. 1:21; Ezek. 16:15, 16:21). The same image is used against foreign nations and their capitols who are called "harlots and prostitutes" (Isa. 23:16–18). It was also common to employ female imagery for cities and nations.

Within Revelation there is a surprising diversity of female imagery. In the letter to the church at Thyatira we meet a prophetess, Jezebel, and her followers who are accused of advocating fornication and idolatrous practices (2:20–23). Yet the seer always makes use of counterimages. The woman in chapter 12, clothed with the sun, gives birth to the Messiah and then represents the persecuted mother church on earth. The counterpoint to the harlot and her followers is the bride of the Lamb, the New Jerusalem that comes down from heaven, "prepared as a bride adorned for her husband" (21:2). The church as the holy bride is the seer's response to the unholy company of the great whore. According to Elisabeth Schussler Fiorenza, "John thus uses the image of the woman to symbolize the present murderous reality of the imperial world power as well as the life-nurturing reality of the new world of God."[20]

The identification of the great whore with Rome is certain. She "sits upon many waters" and rules over the kings of the earth along with the seven mountains (17:1, 17:9, 17:18). Yet the images are fluid so that the whore and the beast are related and the judgment of the great whore becomes the fall of mighty Babylon. Although they remain distinct, the images together promote one human and demonic opposition to the followers of God and the Lamb.

For John, the imperial whore is the great seducer and corrupter of the earth. In his vivid imagination, he describes her royal appearance and all the wealth and power the kings of the earth have lavished upon her. Yet beyond the appearance is the reality of blasphemous names of Rome and her vassals who profit from their ill-gained wealth and of the idolatry of emperors and the goddess Roma. The scene culminates in the most repulsive imagery in the Apocalypse: the woman "drunk with the blood of the saints and the blood of the witnesses to Jesus" (17:6). John's sharp attack expresses his disgust at Rome and its way to rule in the world.

Rather than an institution to promote justice, peace, and good order, it governs with gross injustice and tyranny. The *Pax Romana* itself stands under divine judgment. Not only does it make idolatrous claims for itself and persecute the saints, but also it has become the center of the earth's lust for power and wealth as we will see in chapter 18. For the church of Jesus Christ there can be no attraction to this whore.

Babylon the Great (Greek: Babylon he megale)
The third image of imperial Rome in the Apocalypse is that of Babylon the Great. Babylon is the seer's pseudonym for Rome chosen because the conquest by Nebuchadnezzar and the resultant exile in Babylon marked the low point of Jewish history. The exile remained alive in their memory and caused both Jewish and Christian authors after the destruction of Jerusalem to identify Rome with Babylon.

In the literary structure of Revelation the fall of Babylon marks the completion of divine judgments upon all earthly kingdoms. John has carefully prepared the reader for its demise: in 14:8 an angel flying in mid-heaven cries out, "Fallen, fallen. . ."; in 16:19, violent earthquake destroys the great city and all cities in memory of Babylon; in 17:1, 17:5, Babylon is the great whore whose judgment is imminent. Only one verse describes her conquest by fire (17:16), but all of chapter 18 centers on the fall of Babylon the great and its significance.

John has written this chapter with dramatic, artistic skill and theological depth. We can only seek to highlight the main reasons for the judgment on Babylon and Rome. The opening announcement of Babylon's fall by an angel possessing great authority denounces her pretensions to unlimited power and wealth (18:1–8). One day mighty Babylon ruled the world secure in her economic, military, and political strength. "She glorified herself and lived luxuriously" confident that her prosperity and legions would keep her safe and secure (18:7). But then comes the fall and in a single day the great city becomes a haunt of demons and foul birds and beasts. The call for the saints "to come out of her" is a plea for God's people not to participate in Babylon's sins of gross injustice and idolatry (18:4).

In the heart of the chapter there are a series of three laments by those who have profited the most from Babylon's wealth and power (18:9–20). Each lament begins with a statement of how the rule of Babylon brought them rich rewards and why they now "weep and mourn" over its fall. Each lament concludes with the repeated refrain, "Alas, alas, the great city. . . in one hour your judgment has come" (18:10, 18:16, 18:19). The "alas" is typical of prophetic funeral laments and with the phrase "in one hour" one hears the finality of divine judgment. In the first lament, the kings of the earth are accused once more of committing fornication with Babylon and of living in luxury (18:9–10). No doubt the alliance with Rome brought the ruling elite extravagant wealth, but now they mourn their loss with the city's fiery destruction.

In the second lament by the merchants, we have extended comments on the commerce that created abundant wealth in the empire (18:11–17). In the first centuries CE the economic and political ties with Rome created a climate of stability and prosperity, and the merchants led the way with their commercial activity. Nevertheless, it was only a minority that prospered while the vast majority lived on the edge of hunger or were slaves. The lengthy list of the wares sold by the merchants is very instructive (18:12–13). John begins by naming all the luxury items only persons of wealth could buy—gold, silver, scented wood, ivory, costly wood, marble, and rare spices. He finally mentions the daily necessities of wine, olive oil, flour, wheat, cattle, sheep, and horses. It is important to note that this striking list ends with "slaves and human lives." Here the human cost of the Roman Empire is exposed. The fact that the majority lived near poverty or enslaved finds its strongest condemnation. In addition, the people bore the burden of excessive taxation. One can only conclude with the harsh reality that the status of Rome as a superpower was built on its ability to exploit the world's resources to feed the empire's insatiable appetite on the back of human slaves and persons. Nothing could be a more devastating critique of Rome and all subsequent superpowers, then or now.

The third lament comes from the ship owners and all those who benefited from their trade (18:17–19). Since the bulk of trade in the empire occurred by sea, the traffic was huge and immensely profitable. Mention is made once more of those who grew rich by her wealth and who now mourn her loss.

In the image of Babylon the Great, John depicts the Roman Empire as the evil power that dominates the earth and demands an idolatrous allegiance. Thus the fall of mighty Babylon is God's just judgment upon a human institution that has usurped its authority and become the enemy of God and humankind.

We find these three images—beast, whore, and Babylon—to express the seer's view of the state. In Revelation the government has become demonic, and it is the chief oppressor and exploiter of the world. This means, too, that evil has become institutionalized and personified in economic, political, and religious structures. Revelation's notion of ultimate evil is best understood today as systemic evil and/or structural sin," writes Schussler Fiorenza.[21] This makes evil all the more difficult to oppose and creates the necessity to trust in God to struggle with the saints against the demonic powers at work.

The Church's Response

In the Apocalypse, the church's response to the state is neither subordination nor critical distancing but is instead unyielding resistance.

"No!" to Compromise or Emperor Worship

Some letters to the seven churches suggest the prophet Jezebel advocated a kind of compromise with the pagan culture in Thyatira and other cities (2:20–23). Rather than the stance of "eating no meat sacrificed to idols," she argued it would be permissible since Christians already know idols do not exist. This view would make life easier for Christians and their heathen neighbors, but John is fearful this compromise would only blur the religious differences and lead toward more compromise.

On the question of emperor worship there could only be the one response of "No" for the saints. It is possible the prophetess even dared to suggest that Christians could offer a "pinch of incense" to the emperor and participate in temple worship since in reality they know the cult is only a matter of civic respect. At this point, John and the whole of Revelation insist that there can be neither worship of the emperor nor allegiance to anything other than to God and the Lamb. The Apocalypse proper begins with the magnificent vision of the throne room of God. In chapter 4, we are introduced to the *Pantokrator*, the Creator and Preserver of the cosmos. In chapter 5, the vision centers on the Lamb who was slain, the Redeemer of the world. In the remainder of Revelation, worship revolves around God and the Lamb and no other. In Revelation 13, as we have seen, the imperial beast succeeds in persuading all the kings and nations of the earth to worship him. Yet the saints refuse to worship any other than God and the Lamb. In the final vision of the new world, with the river and trees of life flowing from the throne of God, the faithful see God face to face and worship God and the Lamb (22:1–5).

Patient Endurance (Greek: hypomone)[22]

In Revelation, the primary struggle for the church has to do with its survival in the face of the oppressive and hostile state. In this context, the call to patient endurance becomes the primary ethic for Christians. Behind this dominant theme is the conviction that the future belongs to God despite all appearances to the contrary and that the victory over Satan has already been won both in heaven (12:7–12) and on earth by Christ's death on the cross (1:56, 5:9–10). Believers are challenged to wait with patient endurance since the end-time is near.

We can only touch briefly on the constant presence of patient endurance in the Apocalypse. In the opening scene, John announces his solidarity with the seven churches: "Your brother who shares with you in Jesus the persecution and the kingdom and the patient endurance" (1:9). In each letter there is the commendation of patient endurance and an admonition to faithfulness. Moreover, each letter concludes with the promise "to those who conquer" (Greek: *nikein*)—that is, those who remain steadfast to the end. This theme is found elsewhere and often in surprising texts. After John has depicted the imperial beast (Rome) in chapter 13, who makes war upon the saints and deceives all the earth to bow down and worship, the scene is interrupted by the words: "Here is a call for the endurance and faith of the saints" (13:10). Likewise in chapter 14, after the warning to those who worship the beast, the same refrain is repeated (14:12).

Along with the encouragement to endurance is John's certainty that the time is short. Like other apocalyptic visionaries both Jewish and Christian, he believes God's future is right around the corner (1:1, 1:3, 22:6, 22:10, 22:12, 22:20). What makes his assurance profoundly Christian is his conviction that the past victory of the Lamb on the cross is the guarantee of the final triumph of God and the Lamb. Thus, Revelation begins and ends with the promise of Christ, "I am coming soon" (1:1, 22:7, 22:12, 22:20). The saints pray with patient endurance and hope, "Amen, come Lord Jesus" (22:20).

Resistance and Martyrdom

In recent studies, there has been a revised understanding of apocalyptic literature. With its emphasis on the future and the demonic nature of evil, apocalyptic literature was viewed by many as teaching a flight from history—a kind of abandonment from the present world. A new view suggests quite the contrary. Rather than an escape from the present, this literature is written to encourage heroic resistance to the oppressive religious and political powers that are in control. The book of Revelation calls on the saints to resist the unjust and idolatrous claims of the Roman Empire even to the point of death. In this sense, it is subversive or underground literature written to create counterculture communities amid the evil empire's domain.

Such resistance is possible only with the conviction that the world ultimately belongs to God and that the victory over sin and evil has already been won by the Lamb who was slain. Of course, the struggle is not yet over since the Dragon and his earthly representative seek by all means to maintain their dominion. For Christians it is a bitter and costly fight.

What of the role of martyrs in Revelation? For John, Jesus Christ is the faithful witness (Greek: *martys*) par excellence by his courageous life and death. All his followers are called to imitate his life of service as members of the liberated community (1:5–6), but the Apocalypse also pays special attention to that group we identify as martyrs: those who die for the faith. Although there is little evidence of widespread persecution under Domitian, the threat was real and growing. Thus, we find repeated references to a martyr-church in Revelation: in the vision of the martyred under the altar (6:9–11); in the vision of the 144,000 sealed (7:9–17); and in the millennium where those who come to life and reign with Christ one thousand years are the martyred (20:4–6). Even the Christology with its central symbol of the Lamb who was slain evokes the image of the One who dies for our redemption and the invitation to follow in his steps. Nevertheless, the possibility of martyrdom lies in the future and does not dominate the seer's thinking. There is neither encouragement to become a martyr nor any assumption that most Christians will be martyrs. There is only the call to be ready as well as praise for those who endure to the end.

Throughout the Apocalypse one finds an active resistance to those in power. Christians pledge allegiance to only one Lord and not to Caesar. They dare to name the beast as imperial Rome and condemn its brutal exploitation of the people and resources of the earth. They both pray and work for Rome's collapse. They give fearless witness to the Lordship of Christ regardless of the cost. Yet their resistance is of a special kind. There is no call for rebellion or holy war, such as that which led to the tragic destruction of Jerusalem and the Temple (66–70 CE). There is no preaching of hatred, violence, or revenge against the enemy and oppressor. One passage in particular forbids the use of violence or the sword in retaliation (13:9–10). The way of victory over evil in Revelation is the Lamb's way of suffering love (1:5, 5:9–10). Here evil, hatred, and revenge are overcome by a love willing to absorb the hurt and suffer without retaliation. This, of course, is the ethic of love embodied in the life and teachings of Jesus and the profound mystery of the Lamb who was slain for the healing of the world.

Message of Hope or Judgment?

Among the troubling themes of Revelation are the visions of divine judgment upon the demonic powers and their earthly collaborators (chapters 5–21). Even more disquieting are those texts that seem to reflect a spirit of divine vengeance and vindictiveness against evildoers. A brief but necessary response may be helpful. In part, the theme of judgment is typical of apocalyptic literature. Moreover, its purpose is to demonstrate that God will have the last word in reclaiming the broken and fallen world. Of those disturbing texts that speak of divine retribution or eternal punishment with hellish or bloody delight we need to be even more cautious lest they are contrary to the spirit of Christ elsewhere in the New Testament (6:9, 14:9–11, 14:17–20, 16:5–7, 18:5–6, 19:1–4). In the end, we find these texts to be cries for justice, not vengeance. They ask God not to allow evil and injustice to have their way in the world or to be the final word. It is noteworthy that in Revelation it is God alone and not the saints who exercises judgment upon the world.

One further comment on the message of hope or judgment in the Apocalypse: there are some popular novels and commentaries today that appear to take secret (or not so secret) delight in God's destruction of this old world. With belief in the "rapture" of the saints before the final judgment, they provide what one interpreter rightly describes as "a violent biblical script" of the end time.[23] However, for most interpreters neither the "rapture" nor the violent scenario of the end is found in Scripture. The message of Revelation is the promise of a new or renewed world in which justice and peace will prevail and death and dying will be no more.

Summary of Resistance

In Revelation, there is a distinct change in attitude toward the state. Here the political structures are understood to be historical embodiments of demonic evil in the world. In response, the church is encouraged to adopt a stance of uncompromising resistance. As we noted, the historical setting of the Apocalypse has much to do with the attitude of resistance. Written during the time of the emperor Domitian, the churches in Asia Minor were experiencing increased hostility for their faith including the threat of persecution and demand for emperor worship. John writes to ensure loyalty to Christ above loyalty to Caesar.

Revelation employs three apocalyptic images to interpret the state as the historical representation of evil and injustice on earth: the two beasts, the whore, and Babylon the Great. While imperial Rome is the immediate context for the self-deifying and tyrannical government, John's images apply to all such political structures. Among the charges against the imperial authorities two are pre-eminent: idolatry (cult of the emperor) and abuse of power and wealth.

The response of the saints that John advocates is multiple. The response includes: a courageous "No!" to the cult of the emperor or any compromise; a call to patient endurance in the midst of suffering knowing the future belongs to God; active and daring resistance to the oppressive state but without hatred, revenge, or violence; willingness to put one's life on the line for Christ but not the seeking of martyrdom; and offering a message of hope and peace for the world but not its violent destruction.

How shall one interpret this attitude of resistance to the state in Revelation? Since it belongs to the New Testament, Christians must take its stance seriously and be open to its message for our time. We also find it significant because it declares so plainly that evil is not merely personal but also systemic—that is, evil is embedded in economic, political, and religious structures. For John, the government has become evil incarnate.

Obviously, many questions arise about Revelation's attitude toward the state. Has John's portrayal of the imperial government as demonic and unjust gone far beyond any realistic portrayal? Some think so while others argue the demonic potential is present in all authoritarian structures and especially governments. Others ask whether John's attitude of resistance is limited to special moments of demonic-like evil on the part of those in power. Or is the temptation to abuse a part of all human institutions?

It is time to articulate a way for the church to look with care and thought at the three possibilities in the New Testament with respect to our relationship to the state.

From the New Testament to the Present

We are now ready to make the giant leap from the New Testament to our twenty-first-century context as the church in North America. Of course we recognize the radical change from first-century to contemporary forms of democratic governments and the constitutional separation of church and state in our nations.

Beyond this we can now ask whether the New Testament provides us with a normative view of church-state relationships. For the majority, the priority has been given to the attitude of subordination we found in the Pauline and related literature. While we need to affirm this response and its continued importance in the church's understanding of the state, our study has shown that the New Testament itself has three differing perspectives: subordination, critical distancing, and resistance. In view of this, it is necessary we adopt a "contextual biblical ethic" toward the state. By this we mean an ethic in which all three responses are evaluated with regard to the present historical circumstances the church encounters from the government. To choose only one response as the norm would not be faithful to the New Testament witness as we have shown extensively.

We offer the following paradigm of church-state relationships proposed by Thomas Strieter, since it parallels closely with the results of our survey of the New Testament.[24]

- A *critical-constructive stance* is appropriate when the powers that be are attempting to achieve justice
- A *critical-transformative stance* when authority errs but can be realistically moved to salutary change
- A *critically resistive stance* when the powers are responsible for demonic injustice or idolatry and refuse to be responsible to change

Behind this paradigm are two basic assumptions with regard to the church's response to those who govern. One is the conviction that the divine mandate of the state is to serve the common good both nationally and globally. While there is room for debate about the "common good," it includes preservation of peace and justice and prevention of evil and lawlessness. The second assumption is the necessity of a "critical" posture toward all political authorities. We have shown this to be true even in the texts that encourage subordination to those in power. We will now look briefly at this helpful paradigm and its potential usefulness for contemporary Christians as they seek their fitting response in their own particular context.

The Critical-Constructive Stance

This view, appropriate when the powers that be are attempting to achieve justice, conforms to the attitude of subordination in the Pauline and related literature. It affirms the divine mandate of the state to preserve and promote the common good. Moreover, those who take this stance believe the present government is genuinely seeking the welfare of its citizens and seek to define the common good by the biblical principles of peace, justice, equality, freedom, concern for the poor, and the care of creation. Quite clearly, there is room for honest and healthy debate among Christians with respect to a particular government's understanding of and commitment to the greater good both locally and globally. In addition, this position both allows and encourages an openness to criticism and change. For many Christians in our democratic setting today, this constructive stance best represents their grasp of the role of governments and their critical but loyal response as citizens. However, there is present within this attitude of subordination the imminent danger of failing to distinguish with accuracy and precision between one's loyalty to God and allegiance to our nation. Love for God and love for nation are never one and the same.

The Critical-Transformative Stance

This view, necessary when authority errs but can be realistically moved to salutary change, coheres most fully with Jesus' attitude of critical distancing in the gospels. As we saw, Jesus accepted the religious and political authorities without seeking their removal by force or otherwise. Yet both his life and ministry to the bitter end were filled with continual conflict and uneasy tension with those in power. His life and death became the model of self-sacrifice and service for the countercommunity of his disciples both then and now. The transformative stance does not advocate a complete rejection of the political structures but finds them in need of serious correction on particular issues. Here we can recall certain ethical matters in our own nation's history that demanded urgent change: segregation, racial injustice, unjust war in Vietnam, and protection of the environment. To this we can add other ethical questions that confront us today: nuclear weapons, the spread of HIV/AIDS, local and global poverty and disease, gender inequality, divorce and family, homosexuality and gay marriage, abortion, euthanasia, war in Iraq, and genocide.

How do we deal with our disagreements, often profound and irreconcilable, as Christians and citizens? On the side of the Christian right, we have the more conservative churches that are deeply concerned with matters of personal morality (divorce, abortion, euthanasia, homosexuality). On the Christian left, the more liberal churches and advocacy groups center their priorities on social issues (hunger, war and peace, environment, homosexual rights). Of course, for many both personal morality and social responsibility can and do go hand in hand. Where differences remain that cannot be compromised or resolved Christians are called to respect the conscience of the other. This also requires continuing mutual conversation with each other even if there is no consensus on what the will of God or mind of Christ is on the matter. On ethical issues it is helpful to remember that the majority of Christians have not always been right on issues such as slavery, civil rights, and the equality of women. The voices of courageous prophets were all too often needed to act rightly and Christianly. As I have written previously, "Perhaps on this Christians can agree: Jesus' way is that of love and justice and service, with the good of the neighbor, concern for the least and the care of creation the goal."[25] How this works out in the political arena in the face of perceived failures of justice or morality remains the ongoing challenge for contemporary disciples. Again, for many this critical transformative response best represents their understanding of church and state relationships for our time.

The Critically Resistive Stance

This position, used when the powers are responsible for demonic injustice or idolatry and refuse to be responsible to change, finds near agreement with the attitude of resistance embedded in the book of Revelation. As we have shown in the Apocalypse, the state has become the enemy of God, the church, and humankind. The state's primary evils are its idolatrous claims to allegiance and its oppressive system of global injustice. When the government demands a loyalty Christians cannot give they may be perceived as enemies of the state and experience unjust suffering and persecution. In response, Revelation calls on the saints for a bold, daring, and uncompromising resistance to those in power. This includes a "no" to any allegiance to Caesar and not Christ and the willingness to accept suffering or even martyrdom. While the faithful resist courageously, they do so without resort to violence and in obedience to the love ethic of Jesus, which embraces even the enemy.[26]

When might this critical resistive stance be appropriate for the church? One can only point to crisis moments in the recent past and the tragic failure of both the Christian church and most Christians to practice resistance to a demonic state. With Hitler and Nazism in Germany from 1933–45, despite the ideology of nationalism and anti-Semitism, the vast majority of citizens and churches refused to question or combat its myths and propaganda. All too easily, love of nation (fatherland) and love of God became equated with each other, and the result was a global war of holocaust proportions. A second example is Marxist-Leninist Communism in the twentieth and twenty-first centuries when the church faced an aggressive ideology (atheistic materialism) and brutal regimes that sacrificed persons for the good of the nation such as Stalinism in Russia and Maoism in China. Presenting the promise of greater justice and prosperity, communism held a deep attraction for many. Yet its promises went largely unfulfilled and it became the bitter enemy of the church and sought deliberately to destroy religious faith and institutions. In response, the majority of Christians opted out of any public witness and adopted different strategies to survive. On the whole with the exception of some Catholic countries such as Poland and some religious leaders such as Pope John Paul II, the church under communist rule did not stand resolute and ready to resist. From 1950–1994 in South Africa there emerged a government that pursued a policy of racial segregation against black and colored people (apartheid) in favor of the white minority. Some white churches supported the policy of apartheid both biblically and ethically. After intense pressure worldwide from other countries and churches a new nation came into existence remarkably free of violence under the leadership of a black Christian resistance leader in 1990, Nelson Mandela.

No doubt other moments will arise often unexpectedly when the church must be ready and equipped to struggle against and defy tyrannical governments that refuse to change. Does this mean that the attitude of resistance to the state in Revelation is limited to the rare occasions of demonic-like governments? We have already seen in the twentieth century that the conflicts were both frequent and profound, and the churches were ill prepared or unwilling to respond. Like no other writer in the New Testament, John, the prophet and seer, recognizes most powerfully that governments, unlike any other human institution, can and do become evil and unjust and corrupt to the core. Thus we need his voice as a perennial reminder of governments who go astray and our need for Christian resistance when they do.

Some Christians today might find our present government involved in policies and practices that need bold and prophetic resistance. One can argue that our prosperity as both a nation and a global superpower is due largely to our systematic exploitation of the less developed world and its resources. The fact that one-sixth of the world goes to bed hungry each day, including 36 million in our own land who lack sufficient food and nutrition, and some 250,000 die daily of hunger and disease, presents a sinful reality that requires news ways to govern. An economic system that benefits primarily the richest nations and indebts the poorest and most vulnerable must be challenged and changed. The ecological crisis and our past and continued abuse of the earth and its finite resources along with the global warming that threatens our survival should challenge us to seek governments that understand the peril of what we humans face on planet earth. Perhaps only a few Christians will take a resistance stance against the government under which we live, but if they do, they deserve our honor and respect.

Conclusion

All three attitudes toward the state—subordination, critical distancing, and resistance—are Christian options found in the New Testament. Along with these three attitudes, several other themes have been prominent in our study.

One is the unique role of the government to serve the common welfare of its citizens both as a nation and globally. While the common good needs continual debate and definition the biblical mandates of peace, justice, human dignity, freedom, concern for the least, and the care of creation are fundamental.

A second theme is the idolatrous potential of the state. In Revelation, the state had become hostile to the church and humanity; in the gospels, Jesus is in constant opposition to the authorities; in the Pauline literature there is only one Lord that commands obedience and worship. In the New Testament as a whole the government is more a problematic than a beneficial human institution. Thus the church needs to remain alert and alive against the demands of the state for loyalty and allegiance that might compromise the church's ultimate loyalty to God and Christ. The church can best serve the state by acting as its "conscience"—that is, seeking to remind it of the biblical mandate for the public good. This might lead to confrontation, disagreement, and civil unease but is necessary for the church to remain faithful to its highest calling to serve God and the neighbor. Here again Christians become a counterculture community in their nation seeking to follow the way of the kingdom that Jesus taught and lived.

Finally, we learned in the last century how the church and Christians often failed, sometimes tragically, to place love and honor for God and Christ above love for country or how Christians collapsed in the encounter with other claims for allegiance. It is my hope that this study will provide both a warning and encouragement for Christians to be watchful amid the subtle temptations to confuse patriotism with the worship of God. This chapter has taught us there are times to say "yes" to good government, times to say "look out," and times to say a loud and fearless "No!" All three responses are rooted in the New Testament.

Notes

1. Walter E. Pilgrim, *Uneasy Neighbors: Church and State in the New Testament* (Minneapolis, MN: Fortress, 1999).

2. Robert M. Grant, *The Apostolic Fathers*, vol. 2 (New York: Thomas Nelson, 1964), 2:91.

3. Among the immense volume of scholarly literature on Romans 13 see James Dunn, *Romans 9–16* (Dallas: Word Books, 1988); B. Cranfield, *Romans: A Shorter Commentary* (Grand Rapids, MI: Eerdmans, 1985); Ernest Kasemann, *Commentary on Romans*, trans. and ed. Geoffrey Bromiley (Grand Rapids, MI: Eerdmans, 1980).

4. Arland J. Hultgren, *Augsburg Commentary on the New Testament: I–II Timothy, Titus* (Minneapolis, MN: Augsburg, 1984).

5. See John H. Elliott, *A Home for the Homeless* (Philadelphia: Fortress, 1981); David L. Balch, *Let Wives Be Submissive: The Domestic Code in 1 Peter* (Chico, CA: Scholar's, 1981).

6. Wolfgang Schrage, *The Ethics of the New Testament*, trans. D. Green (Philadelphia: Fortress, 1988), 323–50.

7. Neil Elliott also tries to explain the text from the historical circumstances of Christians in Rome. He argues that Paul is trying to protect the precarious position of Jewish Christians in Rome by encouraging respect and the payment of the tax. Other arguments are equally, if not more, persuasive. "Romans 13:1–7 in the Context of Imperial Propaganda," in *Paul and Empire: Religion and Power in Roman Imperial Society*, ed. Richard A. Horsley (Harrisburg, PA: Trinity, 1997), 184–204.

8. Martin Hengel, *Was Jesus a Revolutionary?* trans. William Klassen (Philadelphia: Fortress, 1971).

9. Joseph Fitzmyer, *The Gospel According to Luke X–XXIV* (Garden City, NJ: Doubleday, 1981), 1292–93; and Pilgrim, *Uneasy Neighbors*, 64–72.

10. R. A. Horsley, *Jesus and the Spiral of Violence* (San Francisco: Harper & Row, 1987), 306–17.

11. Walter Wink, *Engaging the Powers* (Minneapolis, MN: Fortress, 1992), 174–85. His discussion shows the colorful and creative way Jesus' responses are both courageous and yet uphold the dignity of the respondent without resort to violence.

12. Pilgrim, *Uneasy Neighbors*, 51.

13. Warren Carter, *Matthew and Empire* (Harrisburg, PA: Trinity, 2001). He argues differently about Matthew's readers. He accepts the insight of its Jewish-Christian audience but wants to supplement this with the reality of the Roman imperial world as the global context. While his knowledge of the Roman world sociologically is informative and encyclopedic, we find his interpretation of the texts often forced and unpersuasive.

14. Carter, *Matthew and Empire*, 130–44. Contrary to most scholars, he argues that Jesus and his disciples are not among the free so they pay the tax. The subversive nature of the text he finds in the miracle of the coin and the fish as representing God's sovereignty over the creation. His argument remains unpersuasive to us.

15. Pilgrim, *Good News to the Poor* (Minneapolis, MN: Augsburg, 1981).

16. Our concern is not with historical questions but with the evangelists' presentations. We are keenly aware of the debate over the role of the religious leaders in Jesus' trial and execution. While the Roman governor alone gave the order for crucifixion, it is plausible that the High-Priestly elite were also involved in handing Jesus over to Pilate.

17. See Marcus Borg, *Meeting Jesus Again for the First Time* (San Francisco: HarperCollins, 1995), 312. Borg calls it a "virtual parody of prevailing ideas of kingship."

18. On Revelation, see M. Eugene Boring, *Revelation* (Louisville: John Knox, 1989); and Gerhard A. Krodel, *Revelation* (Minneapolis, MN: Augsburg, 1989).

19. Pliny, *Epistles* 10:96–97, ca. 112 CE.

20. Elisabeth Schussler Fiorenza, *Revelation: Vision of a Just World* (Minneapolis, MN: Fortress, 1991), 95. A contrary position on gender is offered in Tina Pippin, *Death and Desire: The Rhetoric of Gender in the Apocalypse of John* (Louisville: Westminster/John Knox, 1992).

21. Fiorenza, *Revelation*, 307.

22. BAGD, *A Greek-English Lexicon of the New Testament and Other Early Christian Literature*, 2nd ed., ed. Rev. F. Danker (Chicago: University of Chicago Press, 1979), 846. Translates *hypomone*: 1. patience, endurance, fortitude, steadfastness, perseverance.

23. Tim LaHaye and Jerry Jenkins, *Left Behind* (Wheaton, IL: Tyndale House, 1994–2004). This series of twelve novels bases much of its plot on belief in the rapture and other questionable teachings. Barbara Rossing, *The Rapture Exposed: The Message of Hope in the Book of Revelation* (Boulder, CO: Westview, 2004), seeks to show the lack of "rapture" in the Bible and the "violent Biblical script of the End" the *Left Behind* novels and others falsely popularize.

24. Thomas W. Strieter, "Two Kingdoms and Governance Thinking for Today's World," unpublished Th.D. dissertation (Chicago: Lutheran School of Theology, 1986). Carter, *Matthew and Empire*, 174–75, draws on this same paradigm he calls the "Pilgrim-Strieter" paradigm and calls it a helpful one for Christians today.

25. Pilgrim, *Uneasy Neighbors*, 201.

26. We are aware that there is honest debate among ethicists and "theologies of liberation" about the potential use of violence in certain settings. Dietrich Bonhoeffer, the German Christian martyr under Hitler decided to join a plot against Hitler without binding the conscience of other Christians on his decision.

Chapter 3

Repentant Patriotism?

Donald W. Shriver Jr.

Perhaps the simplest definition of patriotism is "love of one's country." But there are empirical and moral-religious difficulties with this definition. Both "love" and "country" are deeply ambiguous. With or without a miserable childhood, associations with a home place are likely to endure for life. The smell of creosoted piles and salt water can still reduce me to a swirl of nostalgia about my port-city birthplace: Norfolk, Virginia. But then the leap from affection for birthplace to affection for the "rocks and rills, the woods and templed hills" of land bounded by the Atlantic and Pacific coasts is quite another stretch of geographical patriotism.[1] Finally, beyond both oceans are all the other places on this planet where humans live. Is there such a thing as global patriotism? For that matter, is there a love for America, an immigrant nation, uncomplicated by first generation nostalgia for the "old country"?

Affection for places, however, takes a back seat to affection for the history and ideology implied by a name like "The United States of America." Our politicians ring the changes on that fact every time they wind up a speech with a reference to the Declaration of Independence, the Constitution, or words spoken by Abraham Lincoln. Authoritative documents and persons sustain this patriotism. To love the United States of America is to love these authorities. If "love" is not the right word, "honor and respect" might do. One cannot get elected to any office in this country by openly dishonoring such authorities. Great ostracizing can follow from a public claim that something is wrong with one or more of these authorities as when abolitionists in nineteenth-century America attacked the racist flaw in the Constitution that politically identified nonvoting slaves as worth three-fifths each for counting a state's fair representation in Congress. Yet, the authority of this Constitution defined patriotism for numerous Southern whites who withdrew their states from the Union in the 1860s and went to war with the rest of it. When Confederates spoke of "our country" they meant the eleven states that had seceded. When Robert E. Lee refused the invitation to command the Federal armies, he did so from loyalty to Virginia, which transcended his loyalty to all other people and places of the American republic.

Thus, ever since 1776 patriotism in America has been a movable feast that spreads its tables in neighborhoods, states, regions, and from sea to shining sea. Given our legal way of dividing political authority between local, state, and national levels, a tension between love of locale and love of nation lies at the base of our political system. With every national election, the results raise questions among many voters about how "united," after all, is the United States. The side that loses the election will have members who ask, "Why should I love this country when a majority of its voters are so blind as to elect those guys to high office?" Yet both sides cast votes, allegedly, under the umbrella of a Constitution and laws that mandate elections and court trials rather than assassinations and secessions as the only legitimate methods of conflict settlement if the country is to remain a democracy. You lose an election in a democracy, and you love the country enough to wait until the next time. But your love has suffered assault. The people of your country include unfriendly neighbors. Some of them look like your enemies. Ambiguities permeate every honest love of a country.

Elections, in fact, do not solve underlying conflicts in how citizens understand the history, the ideology, and the authoritative legal documents behind any nation's existence. Majority votes are a necessary, practical but clumsy way to choose leaders carrying on the public business. Left over are diverse, divisive differences in how we interpret those roots of that existence. Post-election we may wonder if we really live in "one nation under God."

"God" is a second complication for defining and applauding patriotism, especially in America. The phrase "under God" entered the American Pledge of Allegiance in the 1950s under the urging of President Dwight Eisenhower as the cold war and the McCarthy hearings were heating up. To this day secularist Americans see this religious insertion as a violation of the principle of separation of church and state. They like to point out that there is no mention of God in the Constitution, which forbids any "religious test" for office and whose authority is not explicitly grounded in religion. True, reply the defenders of "Under God" but not true of the Declaration of Independence wherein Thomas Jefferson rooted "certain inalienable rights" of human beings in an endowment of "their Creator." Ever and again religious Americans have appealed to this language in the great Declaration to underscore the tension between the rights of all humans and constitutional restriction of those rights to some but not all citizens. The two most notorious original restrictions were on women and slaves whose full enjoyment of constitutional rights arrived in the twentieth century. Nudging, pushing, voting, demonstrating, and making war on behalf of this expansion of rights is no small stream of this history.

It swelled to a flood in the Civil War wherein two versions of constitutional rights clashed radically and impelled each side to justify its violence as defense of its version of patriotism. Rhetorically at least, God was very much present in the Civil War. Communication between generals routinely ended with hopes for divine guidance in battle. Soldiers on both sides attended church, prayer meetings, and revivals. Lincoln, above all, appreciated the irony here that "both read the same Bible and pray to the same God, and each invokes His aid against the other. . . . The prayers of both could not be answered. That of neither has been answered fully. The Almighty has His own purposes." As he uttered these words in his Second Inaugural of March 1865, he gave room to divine guidance to correct our fallible political judgments when he called the nation to discern "the right as God gives us to see the right." It was a religious opening, so to speak, in the canopy of constitution then being redefined to deny the right of state secession and to affirm the rights of slaves. From 1789 to 1860 opponents of slavery had protested against its constitutional status. As abolitionists like William Lloyd Garrison hammered at the authority of the Constitution in the name of human rights their allies, like Henry Ward Beecher, hammered in the name of God. The Constitution, they insisted, was a fallible human document. It ought not to be worshiped as an idol.

It is almost a cliché to note from this history that Americans have often resorted to "higher law" as a lever for change in lower law including the Constitution itself. In his simultaneous rhetoric drawn from the Declaration, the Bill of Rights and the Bible, Martin Luther King Jr. was a master of resorting to such levers. He punctured holes in the provincialism of racist patriotism and nationalistic parochial patriotism. He scored the latter in his eventual public opposition to the Vietnam War with its devastation of poor people in a country halfway around the globe. Critics of this move advised King to keep his focus on the rights of Americans. Refusing this advice, he promoted concern for human beings outside the American legal orbit and reinforced his obligation to do so by quoting universalistic passages from the Bible—for example, "Make a joyful noise to the Lord, all the lands!" (Ps. 100:1); "I will give you as a light to the nations, that my salvation may reach to the ends of the earth" (Isa. 49:6); "All authority in heaven and on earth has been given to me. Go therefore and make disciples of all nations" (Mt. 28:18–19); and "He made from one every nation of men" (Acts 17:26).

Whatever qualification and sense of danger might attend an American citizen's reception or rejection of the claims inherent in such language there is no denying certain compatibility between the notion of God's creation of "all nations" and the "inalienable rights" of all human beings. In scope, at least, the concepts are akin.

To be sure, the hard work of politics with its compromises to high ideals always leaves the participants aware of how every law and policy falls short of ideals. But the ideals have a way of remaining in the minds if not on the books of some members of a democratic electorate. Having room for reappeal to them can keep election losers from cynicism and despair. In 2005 an American president may assert that neither our Bill of Rights nor American signature on the Universal Declaration of Human Rights should hinder an American government's protections of its citizens from imprisoning alleged terrorists and denying them right to *habeas corpus*. But grounds for argument over the matter were laid long ago in the history of the republic and in and beyond that history lie appeals to older norms rooted in universalistic ethics and religion. Political philosopher Ronald Dworkin has stated that the "central doctrine" of a liberal democratic society is "the thesis that questions about the good life for man. . .[is] to be regarded from the public standpoint as systematically unsettleable."[2] The phrase "good life for man" is so general that political policymakers may regard it as useless for the concrete tasks of their profession. But the phrase will mean something to groups of citizens who want to open up narrow political vision to subject it to judgments about the good life for "man"—that is, all humanity including some portion of humanity currently being denied its human rights, for example, accused terrorists held incommunicado in American military prisons. In reply to their critics, citizens who cry injustice over government treatment of accused terrorists have some American law on their side. Lacking its clear support the religious among them can call for respect for the humanity of terrorists in the name of that Creator who "made from one every nation of men to live on all the face of the earth" (Acts 17:26). When, currently, they stand on the authority of Christian texts like this, of course, they confront the irony that another world religion is the alleged authority by which some terrorists may legitimate their terrorism.

If there is no "systematic" settling of how universalistic standards are to be translated into concrete political policy and behavior, resorting to other measures for a settlement is inevitable. An election is one measure. War is another. Proposals for going to war almost always include appeals to patriotism and the idea of dying for one's country is endemic to national cultures. That some wars, in retrospect, were worth the deaths of patriots but that another war was not is a recurring theme in many domestic political debates. Invoking moral and religious judgment on the decisions of another country's leaders to go to war might be easy, but invoking the same on the history of one's own country is likely to be harder especially if one sympathizes with that first half of the famous toast of Stephen Decatur, "To my country: may she always be right." Deciding that the leaders one trusted were not to be trusted is hard unless one sees all political leaders as untrustworthy. Even though the right to change one's mind about a great policy issue ought to be counted a democratic and religious virtue, the turnaround can be uncomfortable and unpopular. On no level, personal or collective, does repentance come easily to human beings.[3] Public accusations of being unpatriotic lie at hand for those who change their minds about what is and what is not patriotic. They have public work cut out for them as they invoke contrary interpretations of patriotism.

The key persuasion in this change for many is likely to be their rumination on the agonizing questions: "How much suffering must we endure for a cause we once thought to be good? And how much evil must we inflict on others before our cause is not good for them or for us?" Only those who have never had their patriotism rewarded with unbearable grief will shun such a question. Among our American ancestors perhaps none asked it in greater numbers or with deeper grief than those who lost the Civil War. Shelby Foote narrates an incident that sums up the ambiguous patriotism of many Southerners fighting a war in the name of their country.

> One of [General] Longstreet's Deep South veterans put it strongest, dropping back toward the tail of the column as he struggled to keep up, tattered and barefoot, yet still with some vestige of the raucous sense of humor that had brought him this far along the four-year road he had traveled. "My shoes are gone; my clothes are almost gone, I'm weary, I'm sick, I'm hungry. My family has been killed or scattered, and may now be wandering helpless and unprotected." He shook his head. "I would die; yes, I would die willingly," he said, "because I love my country. But if this war is ever over, I'll be damned if I ever love another country."[4]

Another version of this story has the last line, "Ah hopes to God ah never loves another country." Both versions emerge from that hardest of educators: the school of suffering. Whether as fruit of experience, democratic dialogue, or new divine wisdom, some past decisions turn out to have been poor, bad, and wrong. Not to come to that conclusion is to ignore how to think and act the next time old versions of patriotism call the citizen to battle.

Below is an array of incidents in which some American citizens and even their governments have concluded that some of their collective past deeds were misdeeds not to be repeated in the future. In every incident clashing versions of patriotism are at issue and clashing norms for judgment. Most of the incidents are international. Altogether they suggest that there is such a thing as public repentance in public politics. Without appeal to humanity-wide standards of justice and human rights plus appeal to religious regard for the humanity of world neighbors some of the incidents might never have occurred. Debate over mixes of international right and wrong and good and evil afflicts them all. Some are far enough in the past to have yielded relative unanimity of judgment among Americans of our current generation, and others are still the stuff of anger in living room conversation and in Op-Ed pages of newspapers. The stress in these accounts is on people and agencies who have given public expression to their new awareness of moral blame belonging to something done internationally in the name of America that should not have been done or something undone that should have been done. Public repentance for public misdeeds is rare in national histories ancient and modern. Rare or not, as Kenneth Boulding once said, "If it has happened just once, it must be possible."

Vietnam: The My Lai Massacre

Like forgiveness, the human potential for belated acknowledgment of wrongdoing is a hopeful virtue. Its exercise is most constructive when it portends a new level of commitment to a more humane future. There is encouragement, for example, in the contemporary phenomenon that Elazar Barkan calls "a new threshold of morality in international politics": victims in numerous locales entering into intense negotiations with perpetrators of atrocity and their descendants over how to remember, memorialize, and remedy the lingering damages of that atrocity.[5]

Disentangling justified, unjustified, heroic, and atrocious actions on the American side of war remains a permanent challenge to this country's historians, public leaders, and citizens. We Americans have scarcely begun a morally mature public debate on the assaults of terrorists on us on September 11, 2001, or on our assault on Iraq in 2003. But we are forty years into the debate over the Vietnam War. That we have not come to the end of that debate was on exhibition in our 2004 presidential campaign.

Civilians like me must not forget that it is to the soldiers and veterans that we owe some of our most convincing persuasion that Vietnam was the wrong war for Americans to have undertaken. Whether or not we shall ever have public consensus on reasons for the war, soldiers know that much wrong was committed by all sides. Some explicit governmental testimony to that knowledge came on March 6, 1998, in a ceremony undertaken by the Pentagon in one of the quasi-sacred sites of our national capital: the Vietnam Memorial. There, in antithesis to the Medals of Honor granted members of the Seventh Calvary for "heroism" at Wounded Knee in 1890, the Pentagon awarded its Soldier's Medal to three helicopter crewmen who turned their guns against their fellow soldiers to halt the slaughter of My Lai villagers in 1968.

Almost every critic of the war remembers My Lai as a symbol of American military power run amok[6] in the heat of war. The West Point curriculum now includes analysis of this incident as a warning to future army officers against violating the "rules of engagement." In May 2004, Lt. Colonel Dave Grossman, a West Point instructor, said that the army now requires annual troop review of these rules, which include definitions of orders not to be obeyed. "It's the first time in history when an army is instructed in disobedience of orders." (This is not true, however. The Bundeswehr of Germany has had such instruction for over forty years.[7]) In retrospect, the killing of approximately 200 villagers in this assault was to many, inside and outside of the U.S. Army, a gross violation of the "just war" principle of discrimination between military and civilian targets. One did not need to appeal to universal human rights; the Army Manual would do. (Vietnam now has a local memorial to the massacre in My Lai and, to my knowledge its government has no memorials to atrocities committed by its own soldiers in the war.) The 1998 Pentagon citations to three helicopter crew members read:

> For heroism above and beyond the call of duty on 16 March 1968, saving the lives of at least 10 Vietnamese civilians during the unlawful massacre of noncombatants by American forces at My Lai, Quang Ngai province, South Vietnam, Warrant Officer Thompson landed his helicopter in the line of fire between fleeing Vietnamese civilians and pursuing ground troops to prevent their murder. He then personally confronted the leader of the American ground troops [Lt. William Calley] and was prepared to open fire on those American troops should they fire upon the civilians.

The tributes further described how Thompson and his two fellow soldiers—Specialists Lawrence Colborn and Glenn U. Andreotta—coaxed villagers out of bunkers and assisted them to flee. In a pile of ditched dead bodies they found a wounded child whom they flew to a hospital in Quang Ngai. Together, the citations concluded, the behavior of each exemplified "the highest standards of personal courage and ethical conduct, reflecting distinct credit on himself and the United States Army."[8]

The Soldiers Medal event is rare in the annals of countries. One could skeptically assess the ceremony as part of a belated Pentagon program for keeping American troops from getting involved ever again in a war with Vietnam-like ambiguities. Given the court martial of Lt. William Calley, his short imprisonment, and the clean bill of military health granted almost every one of his superiors, explicit repentance for My Lai seems superficial among high-level military and political leaders. But a new generation of leaders may now realize how damaging to America's international reputation is even one My Lai. In May 2004 some were ruefully remembering My Lai as they grappled with the damages to the United States in the abuses of prisoners in Iraq.

So far as we know, no one present that March day in Washington voiced the excusing view, "Atrocities by the Vietcong were greater. And what about all those massacres by the Russians in Chechnya, the Hutus in Rwanda, the Khmer Rouge in Cambodia, and the Bosnian Serbs?" Memorials, medals, and occasions signifying political repentance are best conceived case by case and in one major dimension. Better to leave to other occasions synoptic comparisons between virtues and vices on various sides of terrible conflicts. In the psychology of apology, "We're sorry" gets undercut by the additional clause, "but we had our reasons and besides, others were worse." One Vietnam veteran, once a helicopter pilot and now a Presbyterian minister, said to his New York congregation in 2003 that in his experience all war is "the Devil's work." He wonders if the rules of "just war" can ever overcome the fundamental injustice of organized killing.[9] He is deeply aware of the hazard in lesser-and-greater evil calculations with their propensity for leading the calculator into moral comfort with the lesser. Lesser evils are still evil. Moral innocence vanishes on a battlefield, which is why Reinhold Niebuhr once cautioned fellow Christians, "We may find it possible to carry a gun, but we must carry it with a heavy heart."

In the fall of 2001 and the spring of 2003 the U.S. military portrayed its new weapons in Afghanistan and Iraq as inflicting only unintended, "collateral" damage on civilians. It thereby reaffirmed the old rule of a "just war"—target-discrimination. It was also implying that the carpet and nuclear bombing of cities in World War II no longer has military justification.[10] Was it justified then? American memory of 9/11 should revive the question. On that day we enrolled anew in a world consensus that unprovoked attack on civilians is wrong. The March 6, 1998, award to that helicopter crew was a military application of a rule that historian Gordon Craig coins for his own profession: "The duty of the historian is to restore to the past the options it once had."[11]

Doubtless, if the whole history of good and evil done by all parties in any war were ever to be told, all their descendants would have large resources for a complex experience of pride and shame. Those of us who did not fight in Vietnam and who opposed the war can look back with our own form of chastened pride when we remember how close many in the antiwar movement came to treating American veterans of the war as scapegoats. "My country sent me to do evil and then hid from me because I reminded them of it. I was a victim of America's arrogance, and I was being blamed for it," lamented one hospitalized veteran.[12] Vietnam veterans have much reason to resent some of the treatment accorded them when they returned to a country whose civilians were blaming them either for losing the war or for fighting it in the first place. This is to acknowledge that America's domestic processing of the Vietnam War is far from over. The awards to Thompson, Colborn, and Andreotta embodied a central principle for political ethics: next to refraining from collective evildoing, the best thing to do is to collectively repent. Righteous persons and righteous peoples are those who follow Psalm 15:4 by "swearing to their own hurt."

Agenda for an American Future: Mourning, Apology, and Responsibility

Will the people of the twenty-second century say that Americans of the twenty-first were unafraid of facing their own evil or, like those Virginians later in the 1830s, will we be seen as falling back into the same old sins? Political repentance is sluggish work; there is always the chance that we will tire of it with a dismissive "stuff happens" or "it's history" or an imitation of Germans who say, "We have had it up to here with public remorse for the Holocaust." To tire of repentance can be to retire from moral reflection. It might also be to throw off the protection against repetitions of evil, which memory can offer.

"As human beings we have learned, as human beings we remain endangered. Yet we always have the strength to overcome dangers afresh."[13] When President Richard von Weizsaecker said this before a hushed German Bundestag in 1985, the gassing of Kurds, two Iraq wars, the genocides in Bosnia, and Rwanda were oncoming history. We shall overcome? Memory might be a slim source of hope that we shall, and no realist who has lived through the twentieth century can avoid wondering if "we" do have the strength to overcome our catastrophic addictions to unjust killing. But, like forgiveness, repentance is an optimist among the virtues. The first step to repentance is memory. The second is mourning.

The Scope of Public Mourning

Along with numerous colleagues across the United States, Haskel Simonowitz protests the implication voiced loudly by various American officials after 9/11 that to oppose any policy of a government's response to that terrible event is unpatriotic, even treasonable:

> I stated that in times of national stress governments often do bad things and, our government being no exception, that we should try and stop them from doing these bad things in our name, rather than lament them in later years, but that often such belated lamentation may be centuries in

coming, e.g., recognizing that killing Native Americans was not such a good thing after all and that Columbus murdered many, many people. Accordingly, it will probably not be until the year 2500 that we will recognize as a nation the millions of Vietnamese, Cambodian and Laotian civilians American bombs killed during the period we know as the Vietnam War. So, by comparison, a few thousand dead Afghan civilians is probably not too big a deal for American sensibilities.[14]

Leaving aside for the moment this defiance of democratic principle one has to applaud his plea for shortening the time interval between collective wrongdoing and its retrospective collective acknowledgment. Publics and their leaders will always turn quickly to observe the wrongs of others, but political prudence might put a damper on that tendency, too. In the year 2000 the U.S. Congress was about to pass a resolution labeling the 1915 deaths of one and a half million Armenians a "genocide" inflicted by the Turkish government of the time. The resolution "was tabled in the face of Turkish threats to cut [American] access to military bases."[15] Turkey's adamant official resistance to admitting the Armenian genocide continues now in its prosecution of its own citizens who "insult Turkish identity" by referring in public to 1915.[16]

Ordinarily, in any conflict, we get around to compassion for the enemy side much later than to compassion for our own side. On a space in a memorial garden in Berlin in the 1990s there appeared a memorial "To All Our War Dead." Some local group then covered over this inscription with a banner that inserted a German possessive: "To All the Dead of Our Wars,"—that is, all fifty million humans killed in the war of 1939–1945 of which Germany was a chief instigator. To mourn this expanded version of "our war dead" requires supra-nationalist moral imagination. It assumes that enemy war dead are worth mourning as well as those of one's fellow citizens. In general modern Germany is far ahead of the rest of us in its public recognition of this principle. In the cathedral of Bad Doberan on the north German coast, for example, the usual plaque for mourning national war dead from two world wars has a perimeter with the names of twelve sites of mass wartime killings in the 1930s and 1940s: "Guernica, Rotterdam, Coventry, Lidice, Stalingrad, Monte Cassino, Auschwitz, Oradour, Hamburg, Dresden, Ravensbruck, Hiroshima."

Most nations, including the United States, have a long way to go before their citizens enter into this widened scope of public mourning. In company with Simonowitz, I wonder when, if ever, there will be:

- a marker on the site of the Washington Vietnam Memorial noting the one to three million Vietnamese killed in their disastrous civil war,[17]
- a similar marker on the nearby Korean War Memorial noting the one million Koreans, North and South, killed in that war,
- a plaque, paralleling the U.S. military's public regret for the My Lai Massacre, expressing similar regret for the 1950 deaths of some 200 Korean civilians from American gunfire at the bridge of No Gun Ri,[18]

- a tablet located somewhere in the now-completed Washington memorial to World War II, which expresses grief for the millions of civilians killed by air power on both sides of that war, and
- a global symbol in the midst of the future World Trade Center memorial, which details the foreign countries represented among the 2,982 deaths there, in Washington, and in Pennsylvania. The number of countries would come to at least eighty.

Counting and Remembering Enemy Dead

The mourning of foreigners requires courage and moral imagination not popular in any nation. One can dismiss the idea as simply beyond the capacity of citizens and leaders who understandably have reason to attend first of all to next-door neighbors. But there is a deep moral flaw in exclusive domestic grief. In post-1989 Berlin one could have understood a gathering of public pressure for destroying the huge Soviet war memorial in the Pankow district. In the final battle for Berlin 300,000 Soviet soldiers perished. The East German government erected giant heroic statues and stone-inscribed Stalinist rhetoric to commemorate the event, in which thousands of Berliners died, too. In spite of bitter local memories of how Soviet troops treated Germans (especially German women) in the final months of the war, it is unlikely that the city government will ever obliterate this remnant of a Soviet invasion, which helped defeat Nazi Germany at terrible cost of human life.[19] One hopes that Germans will increasingly see the Pankow park through eyes filled with grief for "all the dead of our wars." The imagination of many Germans is better equipped than that of Americans to understand what it meant for the Soviet Union to lose twenty million soldiers and civilians in the war.

In stark contradiction to a principle of "just war," 90 percent of deaths in recent wars are civilian. To the contemporary credit of the American military, it has recently adopted a policy in Iraq of offering compensations between $1,000 and $6,000 to Iraqi civilians who could make valid claims for family deaths or injuries from misdirected American bombs and bullets. "While occasional payments were made to families wrongly bombed in Afghanistan, there was nothing this formalized before." Inadequate and symbolic as this gesture is and as little combined with apology or empathy, it sets a new precedent of overt military affirmation of the target-discrimination rule along with reparations to the unjustly killed and injured.[20] As this is written reparatory awards to abused prisoners in Iraq seem also to be intended by the U.S. government.

American presidents on the other hand, among other representatives of the body politic, have shown little inclination in recent years even to mention the cost of "our wars" to other peoples. In his victory speech to the U.S. Congress in March of 1991 President George H. W. Bush expressed no empathy for the Iraqi military killed in the Gulf War and ever since no official estimate of the number dead has emanated from the Pentagon. For years after the war, Beth Daponte, a demographer employed by the Department of Commerce, researched the question, publicized her findings, and then lost her job. She concluded that Iraqi deaths in the war from all causes, including deteriorated health care, totaled 158,000 almost half of whom were women and children. Other researchers came to lower estimates and debate continues mostly in nongovernmental quarters.

Twelve years later, in 2003, one journalist wrote of the Iraq invasion that "the Pentagon said it wasn't possible to estimate Iraqi civilian casualties and was unhappy that anyone else in government attempted to do so."[21] The principle in this policy is: keep the public eye focused on war costs to our own people, and forget about the cost to the enemy. Mainstream news media have largely accepted this principle. "The result is a war in which apparently only 'we' suffer and only 'we' die."[22] More ethically scandalous as Luc Sante recognized is the impression left by this policy: "If civilian deaths are not recorded, let alone published, it must be because they do not matter, and if they do not matter it must be because the Iraqis are beneath notice."[23]

Soon after the formal end of that short 2003 invasion the surviving Iraqi Ministry of Health proposed investigating the number of Iraqi dead, but on December 10, 2003, the American authority in Baghdad ordered a stop to the investigation in spite of the fact that, with some justification, British and American military leaders had "talked a lot about smart, precision bombs" that limit civilian casualties. One private agency now estimates Iraqi civilian dead as 30,000 or fourteen times American dead who in late 2005 had totaled 2, 175. To that total, seldom mentioned in media, should be added the hundred "coalition" dead.

In the meantime, photos of U.S. soldiers killed weekly in Iraq appear regularly on American television screens and in newspapers. We read their names, ages, hometowns, and ranks. No such data appears under a headline, "Two Iraqis killed." To the credit of modern journalists, their most striking recent attention to the personal tragedies of mass violence has been the series of portraits and short biographies, month after month, in the *New York Times* memorializing every identifiable person killed on 9/11. This journalistic memorialization reflects the wisdom of many Holocaust survivors who insist, "It's not that 'six million died,' but that a person died, one by one, six million times." Like the names of over 58,000 on the Vietnam War Memorial, this individualization of mass violence adds to public culture an accretion of moral realism. It rebuts Joseph Stalin's famous cynical remark, "The death of one person is a tragedy, the death of a million a statistic," as well as Hitler's equally famous, "Who remembers the Armenians?" Again, Germans have set a high modern standard for taking public account of the individual deaths that comprise the numbing totals. In one below-ground room of the new Memorial to the Murdered Jews of Europe in Berlin, a camera projects the recovered names of the victims onto a wall with about thirty seconds of known biographical detail. A side inscription notes that time for devoting thirty seconds each to all six million victims would come to some six years and eight months.

Were Americans ever to try to reckon with analogies to mass murder in our own history, we would have to give more detailed public attention to the deaths of Native Americans and African Americans at the hands of European explorers, merchants, and settlers. One could begin with Columbus Day, October 12th. That holiday in 1992 marking the 500th anniversary of his famous landing in the Caribbean fell under a muffling public cloak when Native Americans protested that Columbus was the villain of their histories. Can Columbus Day be reformed for the purpose of mourning as well as celebration? Americans like their holidays pure and undefiled with negative history.

Germans, in their January 27th Remembrance Day, invented a secular form of the Jewish *shoa*. Repentance for all forms of mass murder in the history of the United States needs a national day. Perhaps October 12th can be reformed to become that day. It could be renamed "All America Day" with implicit permission of descendants of Indians to make the holiday a memorial to the deaths of their ancestors at the hands of Columbus as well as a monument to his courage as "Admiral of the Ocean Seas."[24]

Expanding the Scope of Public Mourning: 9/11 as a Test Case

On a day in the 1990s a twelve-year-old African American elementary school student joined her class on a visit to the Holocaust Museum in Washington, DC. After viewing one exhibit she turned to her companion and said, "See, other people have suffered, too."

The death of people closest to us will always assault our emotions more radically than the deaths of people far away in time or space. Yet to rest content with this fact is to cut off the possibility that one's own immediate suffering can be a door opener, not a door closer, to empathy with the suffering of others. One Manhattan psychotherapist reported that out of the 9/11 event the American "empathy bar has been raised. We no longer say, 'Why me?' but 'Why not me?'" It is the survivor syndrome. From counseling with people in his downtown Presbyterian congregation after 9/11 Rev. Jon Walton reported, "We are so aware of every life that ten more deaths in our city add to the loss that we've already borne."[25]

Unforgettable for most Americans will always be how, in the immediate aftermath of 9/11, many doors to our losses opened around the human world. Did doors open in new American reciprocation? Four months after 9/11 Claudia Rosett wrote in *The Wall Street Journal*:

> Here, we might look to countries that know far more, firsthand, of the kind of horror we witnessed on September 11. In the week following the attack, [Mayor] Guiliani compared the bravery of New Yorkers to that of Londoners during the blitz. The bravery I would not contest. But—heretical though it feels to say this right now—the blitz was worse. For months, from 1940–1941, German warplanes bombed not only London, but a slew of British cities, burying people in the rubble of their own homes and setting off firestorms in the streets. More than 40,000 civilians died.[26]

Amid hundreds of deaths in New York on 9/11 and many thousands in the bombed cities of World War II physical remains often disappeared beneath the rubble leaving statistics of deaths uncertain. And those 40,000 Londoners were only a fragment of British and German deaths in the war. The Germans would lose an estimated 100,000 lives each in Hamburg and Dresden. Chinese and Japanese historians argue even today over the toll of the Nanjing Massacre—300,000 or 20,000?—but for the Japanese there is no doubt that they lost 900,000 lives from aerial bombing of their sixty-seven cities of whom "only" 200,000 were in Hiroshima and Nagasaki. We Americans are likely to remember, first of all, that our 1941–1945 war deaths approached 400,000, and we are as likely to be shocked when people of other countries minimize that number with the remark, "It was nothing compared to our loss of millions."[27]

Numbers can numb. That is why we will forever need the recorded personal experience of an Anne Frank, a Dietrich Bonhoeffer, and a single Iraqi widow as narrow door openers into glimpses of massive historical evils. Mayor Giuliani deserves a moral-political salute: he stood on a growing edge of public leadership for expanding New Yorkers' necessarily immediate grievances toward similar, larger grievances of neighbors worldwide. It is better, after 9/11, to remember the Blitz, Dresden, and Tokyo than to draw tight the perimeters of moral imagination and indignation. Empathy for the "far off" as well as for "the near"[28] belongs to the calling of democratic leaders. It belongs most of all to citizens whose religious faith impels them toward a humanity-wide ethic.

Democracy notwithstanding it is a difficult ethic to translate into political act. When psychologist G.H. Moore said once that democracy depends upon voters who vote for the interests of somebody else as well as their own interest, he echoed Edmund Burke. Conservative Burke reminded his Bristol electors that his representation of their local interests in parliament required the reciprocal of representing the national interests back to them.[29] Americans in particular now need leaders who will adapt and expand the Burkean theory to an interdependent global human community. Even if domestic acknowledgment of far-off sufferers is accorded only a public token, that token is a supremely important increment of public moral education. There would be no Holocaust memorial in Washington, DC if a U.S. president had asserted, "The Jews that the Germans killed were not Americans. Let the Germans memorialize them. It is none of our business." As members of a world religious community American Jews would have protested this claim out of deep religious conviction. John Donne would have protested it out of a similar Christian conviction. His metaphor of Europe and his sexist language might need our updating; but it is time in the sad aftermath of the twentieth century to adapt his famous words to our globalized twenty-first:

No man is an Island, entire of it self; every man is a piece of the Continent, a part of the main; if a clod be washed away by the sea, Europe is the less, as well as if a promontory were, as well as if a manor of thy friends or of thine own were; any man's death diminishes me, because I am involved in

Mankind; And therefore never send to know for whom the bell tolls; it tolls for thee.[30]

The American politician who best exemplified this rigorous moral perspective was Abraham Lincoln in his Second Inaugural Address. On a March day in 1865 Lincoln addressed a war-weary Northern audience expecting a speech that would blow the trumpets of victory and scourge the South for bringing on a war in which more men-in-blue died than men-in-gray.[31] Instead, with great solemnity and an undertone of grief mixed with hope, Lincoln promised "charity for all" for "him who shall have borne the battle" on both sides "and for his widow, and his orphan." The injection of compassion for the defeated into a victory speech set a new precedent in presidential rhetoric. His openness to divine judgment on the prayers of both sides also had little precedent. Lincoln knew that this address would not be popular. "Men are not flattered by being shown that there is a difference of purpose between the Almighty and them."[32] Such speech has had few imitators, Democratic or Republican, in Lincoln's successors.

The Scope of Apology

In March 1947 President Truman visited Mexico City. On an unscheduled stop at Chapultepec Castle he laid a wreath on the monument to six army cadets who killed themselves rather than surrender to the American army that conquered the city one hundred years before. Numerous local Mexicans rejoiced in the presidential gesture. A newspaper headline proclaimed: "Rendering Homage to the Heroes of '47, Truman Heals an Old National Wound Forever." A cab driver exclaimed, "To think that the most powerful man in the world would come and apologize." Back home Truman avoided the word "apology," saying simply, "Brave men don't belong to any one country. I respect bravery wherever I see it."[33]

We do not know what combination of justice and injustice Truman saw in the Mexican War. We do know that Lincoln opposed it as a congressman and failed to be reelected as a result. Many Americans have viewed the Spanish American War of 1898, the Philippine War of 1899–1901, Vietnam of 1962–1975, and Iraq of 2003 as national power aspirations rather than "just wars." Truman may not have intended to apologize, but as an avid reader of history he knew that wars are great occasions for "sins of omission and sins of commission" as he put it, echoing a phrase he surely learned as a member of the Southern Baptist Church. For years after his ascent to the presidency in 1945 various critics challenged him to consider the atomic bombing of Japan as among our recent national sins, but he refused to repent of that decision. Significant for any relevance of religion and moral law to affairs of state, however, was his theological move from sins of individuals to sins of the American nation. Truman's reference to the sins of his country, as Martin Marty commented wryly in 2003, was "not the favored form of discourse in these imperial times."[34]

Some will say that a mere apology for ancient collective wrongs has little political impact. The Chapultepec illustration speaks eloquently to the contrary.

When, in the second half of the twentieth century, Protestant and Roman Catholic leaders openly confessed the wrongs done to Jewish people from early centuries into the present, they took a step toward new relationships with the descendants of an abused people.

Perhaps the most dramatic illustration of a thoroughgoing political apology in recent American history was that to Japanese Americans. In 1976 President Gerald Ford revoked the presidential order of 1942 that confined 120,000 Japanese Americans in desert camps in the West. In 1980 Congress convened a commission for confirming the history and for interviews with camp survivors resulting in a comprehensive 1982 official report. Finally, in 1990 the first Bush administration wrote checks of $20,000 each to all still-living camp survivors. But there remain on the agenda of American history other candidates for apology to descendants of those who once suffered unjustly at the hands of governmental power either by the latter's "commission" or "omission":

The Tories of 1775–1983
Lest the focus be only very recent history Americans might start with our Revolutionary War and how Patriots treated Loyalists. The people of modern Nova Scotia number many descendants of the latter. Their memories are vivid with murders, burning of farms, tar and feathers, and expropriations. It is a side of revolutionary fervor about which Americans have little reason to be proud. To my knowledge, no government of the United States has ever offered a representative apology to either Canadians or British for patriot mistreatment of the Tories.[35]

West European, American and African Collaborations in Slavery
In retrospective moral judgment, slavery always was an international crime. It is now legally so in the 1948 United Nations Universal Declaration of Human Rights and in the founding statute of the International Criminal Court under the official label "crime against humanity." It would behoove a three-continent coalition of leaders someday to make a collective confession of this wrong as part of a new international commitment to human development on the African continent. Africa lost an estimated fifty million people to the slave trade.[36] Like the stalled proposal for an apology for slavery by the U.S. Congress,[37] opponents of an apology the world over fear that demands for reparations will follow soon after a verbal apology. Were the Western world to mount an African version of the 1947 Marshall Plan along with confession that African slaves helped furnish no small part of Western wealth over several centuries, descendants of both perpetrators and victims of slavery on all three continents might then look each other in the eye with overdue historical honesty.

Presidential Apologies
On February 14, 1995, General John Shalikashvili, chairman of the joint Chiefs of Staff of the U.S. military, "stood before thousands in the Kreuzkirche in Dresden and apologized for the senseless firebombing of the city fifty years ago

to the day."[38] As readers of Kurt Vonnegut's *Slaughterhouse Five* know well, Dresden was a museum city with little military significance. Not profoundly different from current terrorist strategies, civilians were the intended targets of the British and American bombs that killed "at least 35,000 people and perhaps 135,000."[39] The General's apology fitted the reaffirmation of just war doctrine of target-discrimination in the 1990s in the face of its massive violation during World War II. His words carried weight. But generals are responsible to presidents and prime ministers whose words carry greater weight. Commenting on belated, ambiguous public expressions of regret for Vietnam by former Secretary of Defense Robert McNamara—never quite rising to the level of apology—Samantha Power says:

> Reexamining our reasoning is not something that has come naturally to American statesmen. In fact, Mr. McNamara is one of the very few senior American government officials *ever* to admit major error without being forced to do so. . . . On those rare occasions when American officials have expressed remorse for previous policies, they have tended to do so offhandedly. And while on these shores, such utterances were ignored or derided as insincere, in the countries grievously affected, many victims and survivors welcomed the gesture with surprising grace.[40]

One thinks of the "surprising grace" of audience response that greeted many perpetrator confessions before the South African Truth and Reconciliation Commission (TRC). A striking illustration of an admission of American political policy mistakes came in late 2003 from an American president not noted for this practice in his first three years of office. An Arab advocate of democracy for his region, Saad Eddin Ibrahim, expressed his astonishment that in a speech George W. Bush "admitted past foreign policy mistakes and vowed not to condone dictatorial regimes, even among close traditional allies." Among obvious examples would be the military help that the Reagan and Bush administrations supplied Saddam Hussein's war against Iran in the 1980s. Journalists like Power keep remembering that no less than Donald Rumsfeld negotiated U.S. military aid to Saddam Hussein in 1988 as that dictator was gassing thousands of Kurds.

It is easy, perhaps, to apologize for mistakes of previous administrations and easier, too, when years have dimmed memory of the events. In the 1990s President Bill Clinton apologized in Guatemala for the CIA's help to General Rios Montt in his coup that overturned the 1954 election there. Tens of thousands of Native Guatemalans died in the subsequent war of Rios Montt against his own people. The faults and defaults of Western powers in response to the two outstanding genocides of the 1990s—Bosnia and Rwanda—prompted apologies from Clinton that marked him as a president more open to this verbal gesture than were many of his predecessors. But even he shied away from humanitarian missions by American soldiers. As Power writes about his 1998 visit to Rwanda:

With the grace of one grown practiced at public remorse, he issued something of an apology. 'We in the United States and the world community did not do as much as [we] could have and should have done to try to limit what occurred,' Clinton said. 'It may sound strange to you here,' he continued, 'but all over the world there were people like me sitting in offices, day after day after day, who did not fully appreciate the depth and the speed with which you were being engulfed by this unimaginable terror.' Clinton's remorse came too late to save the 800,000 Rwandans who died, and he pretended to be ignorant of the impending genocide in face of the fact that UN General Delaire had persistently predicted it.[41]

An ounce of prevention is worth pounds of apology. But apologies can still be anticipations of "better next time." In late 1999 UN Secretary General Kofi Annan undertook a pair of apologies in his introductions to two long UN studies of the Srebrenica Massacre and the Rwanda genocide. His language had the ring of genuine personal contrition on behalf of UN-related governments who failed to act to arrest these horrors.

> Both Reports—my own on Srebrenica and that of the Independent Inquiry on Rwanda—reflect a profound determination to present the truth about these calamities. Of all my aims as Secretary-General, there is none to which I feel more deeply committed than that of enabling the United Nations never again to fail in protecting a civilian population from genocide or mass slaughter. . . . All of us must bitterly regret that we did not do more to prevent [the Rwandan genocide]. . . . I fully accept [the Inquiry's] conclusions, including those which reflect on officials of the UN Secretariat, of whom I myself am one. I also welcome the emphasis which the Inquiry has put on the lessons to be learnt from this tragedy. . .with the aim of ensuring that the United Nations can and will act to prevent or halt any other such catastrophe in the future.
>
> [Annan introduces his Srebrenica report with a quotation from Judge Riad of the International Tribunal for the Former Yugoslavia:]
>
> The evidence tendered by the Prosecutor describes scenes of unimaginable savagery: thousands of men buried alive, men and women mutilated and slaughtered, children killed before their mothers' eyes, a grandfather forced to eat the liver of his own grandson. These are truly scenes from hell, written on the darkest pages of human history. . . . In reviewing these events, I have in no way sought to deflect criticism directed at the United National Secretariat. . . . There is an issue of responsibility, and we in the United Nations share in that responsibility. . . . All of [the] exceptional measures that I have taken in preparing this report reflect the importance which I attach to shedding light on what Judge Riad described as the "darkest pages of human history."[42]

Simultaneously with these UN reports, President Clinton spoke to an audience of Kosovars gaining much applause as he celebrated their liberation from attack by Serbs via NATO bombing. Then he added a caution against seeking revenge on the Serbs: "You will never forget what you suffered. . . . No one can force you to forgive, but you must try." To that there was no applause.[43]

Repentant apologies if not reconciling forgiveness popped up in astonishing number in various world places in the 1990s as nations seemed about to recover from the cold war. September 11, 2001, provoked new depths of American resistance to such gestures. It might be years before public empathy for civilian deaths in the 2003–2006 Iraq war creeps into official words from the American government. In the meantime one has to agree with sociologist Nicholas Tavuchis that public leaders must be careful not to apologize so often that the gesture loses credibility. "The consummate collective apology is a diplomatic accomplishment of no mean order," because leaders' constituents may not yet believe there is anything to apologize for and the victims may find the apology casual, cheap, and premature. If it is to be an event and not only a gesture its practice must not be too frequent lest its limited healing power be squandered. Indeed apologies for great political harms will soon drown in public cynicism if unaccompanied by tangible reparations and other measures that credibly promise "never again."[44]

As upsurges of terror and genocide continue to rampage across the world of the twenty-first century, how much preventive action, including risk to American lives, will national leaders and publics be willing to undertake? What costs will we be willing to pay for protecting our world neighbors from mass deaths imposed, not by volcanoes, earthquakes, and hurricanes, but by organized human hands? It is a last, general question that I want to pose in the context of what it means to be an American patriot in the twenty-first century.

The Scope and Limit of American Responsibility for World Neighbors

"Ah! As our commerce spreads, the flag of liberty will circle the globe, and the highways of the ocean—carrying trade of all mankind, be guarded by the guns of the republic. . .Fellow Americans, we are God's chosen people."

—Albert Beveridge, Indiana Republican, calling for
annexation of the Philippines in September of 1898.[45]

"Expansion and imperialism are a grand onslaught on democracy."

—William Graham Sumner, later in 1899

These pages come to print in months of raging debate worldwide over the degree to which Americans—our soldiers, businesses, NGOs, and national governments —are responsible for intervening in the lives of other people. Though many world conditions have changed, the debate between the Beveridge and the

Sumner views is not over. In 1899 the Beveridge speech went to 300,000 copies and helped propel its author into the U.S. Senate.[46] A hundred years later the speech had an astonishing echo in the opening words of Representative Henry Hyde to a 2004 meeting of the House Committee on International Relations. Our unilateral pursuit of war in Iraq he said, "is all to the good, for it is unambiguous proof that absolutely nothing will deter us, that the entire world arrayed against us cannot stop us."[47]

On 9/11, Americans experienced a new, unprecedented vulnerability to the harms that some other humans mean to inflict upon us, and it is understandable that national political leaders should respond to aggression with counter-aggression. But few seemed alert to William Graham Sumner's cautions about power in a democracy. How shall we as citizens of a "superpower" resolve the dilemma between expecting too much from our power to influence the world and expecting too little? With our ideals, economic strength, and military power are Americans now able to control the rest of the world to the benefit of its interests and our own? To this end a 2002 publication of the U.S. Department of Defense envisions American power in year 2020 under the rubric of "full spectrum dominance": ". . .[G]iven the global nature of our interests and obligations, the United States must maintain its overseas presence and the ability to rapidly project power worldwide in order to achieve full spectrum dominance."[48] A "good" nation like the United States, say supporters of this "vision," will build a good empire.

Whatever our diverse citizen attitudes toward America's current official stances worldwide we have to acknowledge that with power always comes responsibility and that power always has both scope and limits. Hyde's claim that "the entire world. . .cannot stop us" rings with historical ignorance and with no regard for the choices that all wielders of power must make. Consistency in those choices is hard to find in recent American history. Moral realists have to ask how, if military intervention in famine-wasted Somalia in 1993 was justified, was not intervention in Serb-invaded Bosnia even more justified—most of all in genocide-ravaged Rwanda? Realists also have to add: once military force acquires a cloak of justice, does the precedent make easier the disguise of unjust interests under cover of the same cloak? It is one thing to say that America had to strike back at terrorists in Afghanistan. It is another to ask, where, in the name of just interests, American power must halt before the just interests of others? And it is still another to ask, what sacrifices of life and wealth should Americans consider for serving the life and well-being of non-American peoples? What restrictions are we willing to put on the pursuit of our interests in service to those others? And what changes of intention are called for when our best intentions go awry?

In her passionate conclusion to her landmark study of "the age of genocide" Samantha Power summarizes the history of American inaction in response to this "problem from hell." No American government saw fit to risk even a few American lives on behalf of halting the mass killing of Armenians, Cambodians, Kurds, Shiites, Bosnians, or Rwandans while time for a halt was still open.

Rallying the nation to attack Iraq in 2003 depended most of all on government claims that weapons of mass destruction and terrorist havens directly threatened America. Those claims gave way eventually to the humanitarian argument of liberating the Iraqi people from tyranny. If that argument is worth the lives of 2,175 American soldiers (as of January 1, 2006), why was not saving a million Muslims and Tutsis in Bosnia and Rwanda worth the same risk? Power's indictment of our government's sins of omission brings the shamed conclusion that across many administrations, Democratic and Republican, Washington has taught citizens that the United States will go to war for oil but not to halt mass murder.

> American leaders have been able to persist in turning away because genocide in distant lands has not captivated senators, congressional caucuses, Washington lobbyists, elite opinion shapers, grassroots groups, or individual citizens. The battle to stop genocide has thus been repeatedly lost in the realm of domestic politics. . . . In the end, however, the inertia of the governed can not be disentangled from the indifference of the government.[49]

It is easy to doubt the willingness of citizens to support costly humanitarian intervention abroad by their government. We are more likely to tolerate inhuman domestic policies like slavery and the destruction of Native Americans when they serve powerful interests of our own. And in a democracy, what citizens tolerate they are in part responsible for. "If democracy is about the right to choose one's leaders," wrote one South African recently, "it is also about taking responsibility for their leadership."[50] When Americans traveled abroad in 2005 we were apt to find ourselves roundly criticized for the current nationalistic aggressiveness of our government. The excuse, "I didn't vote for that government" did not have much weight as a reply especially when few of us have spent large energies criticizing that government or entertaining the thought that it has more power than its leaders know how to use in the service of good for this or that foreign people. Ideologically we like to disguise power-to-dominate as power-to-serve. As ethicist Edward LeRoy Long Jr. says in his 2004 book, *Facing Terrorism*, there is little suggestion in the above quoted document that "full spectrum dominance" equals a "servanthood" definition of power: "One is a form of playing God; the other is an acknowledgment of being human. The temptation to take on the world and make it into the images of our own ideals, especially by the use of power, is a form of idolatry, even in morally plausible versions."[51]

Power and Humility: A Conclusion

The world jury is out on the mixture of good and evil in America's current exercise of power on the world stage, but there is one aspect of that exercise on which the wise among the religious and the seculars might agree. As that worldly-wise *Proverbs* puts it: "Pride goeth before destruction, and a haughty spirit before a fall" (16:18).

One does not have to be sure of the ultimately good or bad outcome of a war to know that arrogance and self-righteousness are unbecoming to both interpersonal and international relations. The terrorists who destroyed life and property on 9/11 were guilty of this vice, and unfortunately all religions have sometimes nourished it. Paradoxically, religion can provoke both super-certainty and modesty in human claims about right and wrong. Its "views of the Absolute" often morph into "absolute views."[52] Edward Long quotes journalist Joe Klein of *Time* on the religious stances of the 2003 White House: "George W. Bush's faith offers no speed bumps on the road to Baghdad; it does not give him pause or force him to reflect. It is a source of comfort and strength but not of wisdom. . . . The world might have more confidence in the judgment of this President if he weren't always bathed in the blinding glare of his own certainty."[53]

Reinhold Niebuhr was acutely conscious of this wisdom as he wrote about Soviet-American hostility in the 1950s. He could have written much the same about the post 9/11 reactions of the White House to the challenge of terrorism:

> The cure for a pretentious idealism, which claims to know more about the future and about other men than is given mortal man to know, is not egotism. It is a concern for both the self and the other in which the self, whether individual or collective, preserves a "decent respect of the opinions of mankind," derived from a modest awareness of the limits of its own knowledge and power.[54]

Two very different relations between religious-moral conviction and political policy-justification are at conflict here; two different spirits in American devotion to our most cherished word for democracy: freedom. Said President Bush to Congress in January 2003, "The advance of human freedom—the great achievement and the great hope of every time—now depends on us. . . . We go forward with confidence, because the call of history has come to the right country."[55] Such rhetoric parallels that of the Beveridges and the Strongs of American history, but it is far distant from Judge Learned Hand's definition of freedom: "The spirit of liberty is the spirit that is not too sure it is right." Lincoln would have liked that.

In the immediacies of 2006 the right and wrong of America's current role in world affairs has to be subject to the judgment of future generations. Who knows for what contributions to the world the United States might yet be thanked; for what injustices our descendants might need to apologize? The caution of historians about writing any history of events less than twenty-five years old comes to mind here providing a convenient exit for the end of this essay from judgments about the uses of American power in 2006. As citizens we cannot claim that luxury.

If cases of national, local, and personal repentance in our time offer any precedented political wisdom, however, a first resource for human *metanoia* is listening to one's critics. The Learned Hand version of "liberty" implies freedom to learn about the "right" from the perspectives of other human beings if not from Lincoln's "as God gives us to know the right." That is one of the hopes inherent in constitutional freedoms of citizen protest against government power whether long ago in the 1735 free-press case of John Peter Zenger or the 2005 case of civil rights for foreign prisoners taken in a "war" against terrorism.

How then should Americans respond to our contemporary world neighbors who think ill of us? Should we reject or accept their judgments *in toto*? To answer we need a nuanced concept of responsibility such as H. Richard Niebuhr crafted when he wrote:

> An agent's action is like a statement in a dialogue. Such a statement. . .is made in anticipation of reply. It looks forward as well as backward; it anticipates objections, confirmations, and corrections. It is made as part of a total conversation that leads forward and is to have meaning as a whole. Thus a political action, in this sense, is responsible not only when it is responsive to a prior deed but when it is so made that the agent antic-ipates the reactions to his action. . . . Responsibility lies in the agent who stays with his action, who accepts the consequences in the form of reac-tions and looks forward in the present deed to the continued interaction.[56]

In short, responsibility has to be learned. We learn it first by listening. Thomas Jefferson's "decent respect for the opinions of mankind" still holds. It requires of Americans a rigorous, patient discipline for the rest of the twenty-first century. Whether this dialogue issues in proud rejection or in contrite acceptance of the critics' points of view future debate among us will have to determine. Meantime when a former mayor of Berlin writes that "above all we need to listen to each other" he remembers how important it was for Germans to listen to Americans in the post-1945 world. Even about the "unilateralism" to which he objects in current American foreign policy he feels bound to remember that he is a citizen of a country that had to learn lessons of political repentance from its enemy, the United States.

> As a German I know by instinct that I have to be very careful when mak-ing judgments on German-American relations. After all, they were hostile for the first half of the past century. During those decades, America was basically right and Germany wrong. But didn't Germany learn, at least [the Western] half of our country, how to live and behave in an alliance which is based on international law? Didn't German society learn from the American way of life?. . .Germans have no moral right to lecture Americans on the dangers of unilateralism. But I believe that American democracy itself will find out those dangers through its deep-rooted checks and balances.[57]

These words come from a person who has spent years in the United States and whose hope for change in its worldwide relationships rises from close personal acquaintance with numerous Americans. Another eminent German statesman, also a former mayor of Berlin, echoes a similar mixture of admiration and alarm when he reflects on his eighty years of learning and relearning how to combine repentance and pride in the history of his country and how to shift the national ideals of Germany from domination of other countries to collaboration with them.

> America's self-reliant political and moral guidelines are based on a general American idealism which aspires to make the world a better place. Yet they appear as a kind of missionary work which in its core will not make a dialogue of civilizations around the globe easier. In the long run the world is not prepared to accept a unipolar globe.
>
> American patriotism and idealism are admirable. But in the long run America will not be able to go it alone. The most important tasks around the globe are not solvable by military means. . . . Germans believe that partnership will be needed on both sides of the Atlantic. Neither side will find anywhere else a better fitting partner. Neither side will serve its own interests and indeed its mission without that partnership.[58]

Repentance and forgiveness are optimists among the virtues because they oppose tragedy with hopes for healing. Symbolic and practical healing of politically enacted hurts suffuse the illustrations in this essay and as one patriotic American by a definition implied in the foregoing pages, I hope for the healing of contemporary, widespread, hostile rifts in my country's relations to the world of nations during the year 2006. Friends of mine in two countries, Germany and South Africa, have helped nourish that hope as will be evident below in some concluding quotations from their recent thoughtful communications to me.

Against the background of his own country's historic need of help from abroad for combating the evils of the apartheid regime, Alex Boraine, South African deputy chairman of the TRC, writes:

> I recall vividly the bleakness of South Africa during the 1980s. . . . It was during that time that I turned to the U.S. Congress for moral support and for statements of opposition from members of the House and Senate. I went to Washington on a number of occasions and was greatly encouraged by the response I received from leading congress people. This experience, coupled with my time in America during the civil rights movement, has always filled me with admiration for the United States as a leader in democracy and human rights. . . . But now, if South Africa were in crisis, I'm not sure I would turn to the U.S.A. For me and so many others around the world, this is tragic. Everywhere I travel, people look to America, not for freedom and justice and human rights, but rather for the abuse of power. America must find itself again and use its enormous resources so that it is seen to be strong, but also fair and compassionate. If it does so, its leadership will be rewarded; but if fails, the whole world will fail with it.[59]

Coming from a man who experienced 9/11 a few blocks from the World Trade Center and who since has visited hundreds of political leaders on six continents this is painful testimony. A like mixture of pain and hope came in early 2004 from Peter Storey, a South African Methodist minister and pioneer church opponent of apartheid:

> Ever since 1966 I have traveled to the United States at least once a year. Most of those journeys were about seeking help in our struggle against apartheid in South Africa, and through it all you never failed us. The story of your nation itself was an inspiration. But it may be our turn to challenge you now, because of the great *disconnect* between the kindness, compassion and caring of most American people, and the way American power is experienced across the world. . . . Perhaps there are two Americas. This week in Duke University Chapel, we commissioned a fine group of young American students to go out and serve the struggling people of Costa Rica, and spent time with some remarkable ex-students working in the mountains of Haiti. These are people who have voluntarily left their "bubble of comfort" to care and listen and serve. They are the other America, and there are many thousands of them. 'Alienation of Empire' does not have to be the last word on this great enterprise called the United States. It could be reversed, if only enough good Americans came to see that the national interest of the wealthiest, most powerful nation on earth might be better served if it translated its power into different, more compassionate ways of relating to the rest of our troubled planet.[60]

No one can predict the mix of justice and injustice, benefit and harm that a future generation of Americans may need to remember from our relation to the rest of humanity. We must hope that the justice and benefit will outweigh the injustice and harm just as we must hope that we can learn to practice a chastened form of patriotism that combines pride in the best and shame for the worst in our national history.

Among theologians who embodied that combination in both life and writing none is more memorable than Dietrich Bonhoeffer. Tempted to remain in New York as war was gathering in Europe in the summer of 1939 he cut short his three-week American visit to board the last ship back to Germany convinced, he said, that love of his own German people required him to share with them the sufferings of the war and to oppose the Nazi government about to start that war. In prison four years later for his role in the plot to assassinate Hitler, he wrote to a friend that "in gratitude and contrition my present life and my past are united." He had much in his German past to be grateful for and much in the German present to be contrite about. In 2004 a new generation of Germans was seeking to practice that combination in their own "love of country." Two of them remembering Bonhoeffer and their anxieties about America's past and present wrote to me at the end of 2003:

America will achieve leadership in self-restraint and critical self-reflection. The problems ahead of us in the global village are too big even for the strongest nation to handle. Gratitude and contrition make honest patriots, and such patriots are best qualified to be responsible World Citizens.[61]

Notes

1. Samuel Francis Smith, "America, My Country Tis of Thee," 1861.
2. As paraphrased by Alasdair MacIntyre, *After Virtue*, 2nd. ed. (Notre Dame, IN: University of Notre Dame Press, 1984), 119.
3. *Metanoia*, the New Testament Greek word for "repentance," means literally "a change of mind," and the Hebrew Bible's word is "turn" (*tshuvah*). Both are applied first of all to a comprehensive moral change in both inward disposition and outward behavior; but, especially in the Hebrew prophets, "repent" is often a call to an entire nation.
4. Shelby Foote, *The Civil War*, vol. 3 of *Red River to Appomattox* (New York: Random House), 913.
5. Elazar Barkan, *The Guilt of Nations: Restitution and Negotiating Historical Injustices* (New York: W. W. Norton, 2000), xviii.
6. There is irony in the fact that the word "amok" comes from Southeast Asia. Webster's third definition is "a murderous frenzy that occurs chiefly among Malays."
7. *NewsHour*, PBS, May 11, 2004. In the early 1990s I asked the German minister of defense, Volker Ruhe, if all NATO forces had such rules. He answered, "No, it was we Germans who needed those rules." Some Americans in the discussion were prompt to disagree. Americans can be glad that on this issue our military has caught up with the Germans.
8. Quotations taken from the official program of the event, March 6, 1998, provided by the Pentagon. Andreotta subsequently died in combat. His name is on The Wall. In April 2004 Thompson was inducted into the Army Aviation Hall of Fame in ceremonies in Nashville. It meant more to him than the Pentagon award, he said, "because they were my peers" (Interview, see note 6).
9. Rev. Fred Anderson addressing a congregational study group in the spring of 2003. He says that he participated in so much unjust killing in Vietnam that he lost confidence in the just war theory and is sure that Christians should never take unambiguous comfort in that theory for support of any war.
10. Few American military or political leaders have voiced much criticism in the past fifty years about the strategy of city-bombing that escalated in the final months of World War II. Invented by the Germans early in the war, developed by the British and the Americans as the war in Europe went on, and climaxed in the atomic bombing of Hiroshima and Nagasaki, the strategy has often been justified as the only way to have brought that war to an end. Debate over this issue flared up in 1995 over how Hiroshima was to be remembered publicly at the Smithsonian Institution in Washington. That debate would have been sobered on both sides if each had conceded that discrimination of military and civilian targets had been routinely abandoned by 1945. More Japanese civilians perished from "conventional," mostly incendiary, bombs than from the two atomic bombs. For two accounts, see Robert J. Lifton and Greg Mitchell, *Hiroshima in America* (New York: Avon Books, 1995), 245–97; and John Dower, *War without Mercy* (New York: Pantheon, 1987), 300–301.
11. James W. Loewen, *Lies My Teacher Told Me: Everything Your American History Textbook Got Wrong* (New York: Simon and Schuster, 1995), 126; Gordon Craig,

"History as a Humanistic Discipline," in *Historical Literacy, ed. Paul Gagnon* (New York: Macmillan, 1989), 134. Craig goes on to observe that to teach history with the options actors faced would be to make history-teaching more vivid, human, and memorable for students.

12. Walter Davis, *Shattered Dream: America's Search for Its Soul* (Valley Forge, PA: Trinity, 1994), 106. Davis based this book on interviews with some two hundred veterans in California Veterans Affairs hospitals.

13. See Donald W. Shriver Jr., *An Ethic for Enemies: Forgiveness in Politics* (New York: Oxford University Press, 1995), 111.

14. Haskel Simonowitz, "Tattletales for an Open Society," *The Nation*, January 10, 2002, http://www.the nation.com/doc.mhtml?i=20020121&tattle20020110.

15. Belinda Cooper, review of *The Armenian Genocide and America's Response* by Peter Balakian, *New York Times Book Review*, October 19, 2003, p. 35.

16. That was the criminal accusation in 2005 against Hrant Dink, editor of the Turkish-Armenian bilingual weekly *Agos* and against novelist Orhan Pamuk. Both faced jail terms for saying that the genocide actually happened. For lack of legal freedom of speech for its citizens, Turkey's case for admission to the European Union is the weaker. "Turkey Brings Another Case against an Ethnic Armenian," *New York Times*, December 26, 2005, p. A5.

17. In interviews done for the making of the 2003 film *The Fog of War*, Robert McNamara uses the figure 3.4 million for the dead of the Vietnam War. No one knows the exact figure, but this one is the highest that any public figure has advanced. Others have said "between one and two million." Stephen Holden, "Revisiting McNamara and the War He Headed," *New York Times*, October 11, 2003, p. B9.

18. In July 1950, as inexperienced American troops were attempting to stop the advance of the North Korean army, a group of Korean civilians sought protection under this bridge. Thinking that many of them were North Korean infiltrators, Americans opened fire. In the late 1990s, South Korean scholars and officials presented data on this tragedy to the Pentagon, which, after its own belated investigation, responded with the indefinite conclusion that in the confusion of those early weeks of the war, no blame could be clearly assigned. In 2003, a film on the incident was underway at the direction of a Korean director captured by North Korea in the 1980s and forced to make films for that government. The experience left him with little admiration for that society. For a thorough recent study of the incident, see Charles J. Hanley, Sang-Hun Choe and Martha Mendoza, *The Bridge at No Gun Ri* (New York: Henry Holt, 2001).

19. From interviews in July 2003, I know that elderly contemporary residents of the former East Germany have bitter memories of the systematic looting and raping that Soviet troops undertook in the final months of the war, quite often under the direction and approval of their officers.

20. Jeffrey Gettleman, "For Iraqis in Harm's Way, $5,000 and 'I'm Sorry,'" *New York Times*, March 17, 2004, pp. A1, A9. The payments come under the U.S. Foreign Claims Act for compensation to civilians in noncombat situations. So far, payments are unaccompanied by "a formal apology or claim of responsibility." Upon accepting $6,000 in compensation for the death of his wife and three children, Said Abbas Ahmed commented bitterly: "this war of yours cost billions. Are we not worth more than a few thousand?" (A9).

21. Jack Kelly, *Pittsburgh Post-Gazette*, February 16, 2003, (accessed October 18, 2003). The official Pentagon tally of American combat deaths was 148 and 145 of noncombat deaths. In 1993, Daponte concluded that 56,000 Iraqi soldiers and 3,500 civilians

died, noting that the rest of deaths came from "adverse health effects" and subsequent slaughter of Kurds and Shiites by Saddam Hussein's army. A National Defense University study puts the soldier deaths between 20,000 and 25,000 and the civilian deaths between 1,000 and 3,000, which is close to the Iraqi government's claim of 2,278 civilian deaths.

22. Yvonne Klein, letter to editor, *New York Times*, November 15, 2003, p. A12. Ms. Klein is Canadian.

23. Luc Sante, Op-Ed, *New York Times*, May 11, 2004, p. A23. He teaches creative writing and photography at Bard College.

24. Howard Zinn, *A People's History of the United States*, 7. Howard Zinn quotes Samuel Eliot Morison of Harvard who celebrates the contribution of the Columbus voyages to world history but who concedes that "the cruel policy initiated by Columbus and pursued by his successors resulted in complete genocide." Zinn insists that the details of this genocide need to enter American history texts, for example, "in two years, through murder, mutilation, or suicide, half of the 250,000 Indians on Haiti were dead" (5).

25. Clyde Haberman, "As Opposed to Numbness, Pain Is Good," *New York Times*, October 21, 2003, p. B1. The therapist was Dr. Lauren Howard.

26. Claudia Rosett, "Letter from America," *Wall Street Journal*, January 17, 2002.

27. Thus, the remark of two Russian Orthodox laymen to me in Odessa, October 1984.

28. Terms used by the writer of the Pauline Epistle to the Ephesians, 2:17 (RSV).

29. In his "Address to the Electors of Bristol." I shall never forget the 1964 campaign speech by a North Carolina congressman in Raleigh, North Carolina, in which he reminded his rural audience that "in order to get my colleagues in Congress to vote for our agricultural interests, I have to support their urban interests."

30. *Devotions upon Emergent Occasions* (1634), "Meditation XVII," in *The Oxford Dictionary of Quotations* (Oxford: Oxford University Press, 1992), 253.

31. Ronald C. White Jr., *Lincoln's Greatest Speech: The Second Inaugural* (New York: Simon and Schuster, 2002), 189. Quoting from the negative editorial response to the address by the *New York Times* of March 6, 1865: "He makes no boasts of what he has done, or promises of what he will do. He does not reexpound the principles of the war; does not redeclare the worth of the Union; does not reproclaim that absolute submission of the Constitution is the only peace."

32. Forrest Church, *The American Creed: A Spiritual and Patiotic Primer* (New York: St. Martin's, 2002), 55.

33. David McCollough, *Truman* (New York: Simon and Schuster, 1992), 542–43.

34. Martin E. Marty, "The Real Luther," *The Christian Century*, November 1, 2003, p. 47.

35. Modern Americans can easily forget that the Revolution gained the support of only about a third of the colonial population in the 1770s, while a third opposed it and a third waited to see which side would win.

36. Howard Zinn notes that ten to fifteen million slaves had been transported alive from Africa to the west by 1800 and that deaths before and during transport brought the total to fifty million (Zinn, 29).

37. Congressman John Conyers of Detroit, in the wake of the Japanese American debate of the 1980s, proposed in his Judiciary Committee that Congress apologize for American slavery. His proposal (H.R. 40) has not yet come out of the committee. He has proposed it annually since 1988.

38. Paul A. Wee, head of the Luther Center in Wittenberg, Germany, in a paper, "Reflections on Terror and Justification," April 2002.

39. "World War II," *Encyclopedia Britannica*, 15th ed., vol. 19, p. 1011. This range of uncertainty about the total underscores the degree to which many twentieth-century wars have so buried, mutilated, and otherwise hidden human bodies that the deaths sink irretrievably into anonymity. Capital cities need to add an "Unknown Civilian" grave to that of their "Unknown Soldier."

40. Samantha Power, "War and Never Having to Say You're Sorry," *New York Times*, December 14, 2003, p. 33. "Whether regarding the Vietnam War, America's cold war assassinations, or our misguided former alliance with Saddam Hussein, American officials keep their eyes fixed on the future."

41. James Bennet, "Clinton Declares U.S., with World, Failed Rwandans," *New York Times*, March 26, 1998, pp. A6, A12. A few months after his Africa visit, Clinton delivered "an 'unplanned' semi-apology" for American slavery, "a half measure that satisfied many supporters and only moderately angered conservatives," says Elazar Barkan (*The Guilt of Nations*, 287). In a new definitive analysis of apology in international affairs, Girma Negash concludes that "Clinton's Kigali speech was a pseudo-apology because his carefully crafted words of regret, among other things, pleaded ignorance of the impending genocide in Rwanda, spread blames among other parties, and failed as a contrition" (*Apologia Politica* [Lanham, MD: Lexington Books, 2006].

42. Kofi Annan, Statement on Receiving the Report of the Independent Inquiry into the Actions of the United Nations During the 1994 Genocide in Rwanda, December 16, 1999, 1–2, and Report of the Secretary-General Pursuant to General Assembly Resolution 53/35, The Fall of Srebrenica, November 15, 1999, 6–7. At the beginning of the Rwanda report he calls attention to the 1948 UN enactment of the Convention against Genocide, "under which States accepted an obligation to 'prevent and punish' this most heinous of crimes."

43. National Public Radio News, November 23, 1999.

44. Nichoas Tavuchis, *Mea Culpa: A Sociology of Apology and Reconciliation* (Stanford, CA: Stanford University Press, 1991), 100. For further appropriation of Tavuchis's pioneering book and information on the relation of political apology to political forgiveness, see my *An Ethic for Enemies*, 220–24. In personal correspondence he notes wryly to me how, after the publication of this book in the 1990s, there emerged a flurry of public attention to collective apology and forgiveness. He was tempted, he said, to see himself as Aesop's rooster—by crowing one can cause the sun to rise. See Negash, referenced in note 41 above, for the most careful analysis to date of apology in international relations.

45. Albert Beveridge, *The Library of Oratory*, ed. Chauncey M. Depew (New York: 1902), 448–49; and William Graham Sumner, *War and Other Essays*, ed. A. G. Keller (New Haven, CT: n.p., 1911), 325–26, 334.

46. See Church, *The American Creed*, 73–77. Theological ground for Beveridge's imperialism had been prepared by Josiah Strong, leading liberal Congregational theologian of the nineteenth century. Strong did not always distinguish between the world mission of the Christian church and the mission of the United States. "Protestant Christianity and American democracy were exported in the same package" (Church, 74). Beveridge could have written Strong's proclamation: "We are the chosen people. We cannot afford to wait. The plans of God will not wait. Those plans seem to have brought us to one of the closing stages in the world's career, in which we can no longer *drift* with safety to our destiny." From Strong, *Our Country: Its Possible Future and Its Present Crisis* (Baker and Taylor, 1875), 218.

47. House Committee on International Relations hearing, as recorded by the East Asia Policy Education Project Web site, March 30, 2004, http://www.fcnl.org. Hyde went

on to say that North Korea should see U.S. determination in the Iraq War as a warning to its own aspiration to power.

48. U.S. Department of Defense, *Joint Vision 2020*, Fall 2002, http://www.dtic.mil/jointvision.

49. Power, *A Problem from Hell*, 509.

50. Charles Villa-Vicencio, personal correspondence, February 2004.

51. Edward LeRoy Long Jr., *Facing Terrorism: Responding as Christians* (Louisville: Westminster/John Knox, 2004), 111.

52. A distinction often made by the late H. Richard Niebuhr.

53. Joe Klein, "The Blinding Glare of His Certainty," *Time*, February 23, 2003, p. 19.

54. Reinhold Niebuhr, *The Irony of American History* (New York: Scribners and Sons, 1952), 148.

55. State of the Union Address, January 2003.

56. H. Richard Niebuhr, *The Responsible Self: An Essay in Christian Moral Philosophy* (New York: Harper and Row, 1963), 64.

57. Dietrich Stobbe, Governing Mayor of Berlin 1977–1981, Social Democratic member of the Bundestag 1983–1990, business executive in the 1990s, personal correspondence, December 2003.

58. Former *Bundespraesident* Richard von Weizsaecker, personal correspondence, December 2003.

59. Dr. Alex Boraine, personal correspondence, February 2004.

60. Rev. Peter J. Storey, now a professor at Duke University, personal correspondence, March 2004.

61. Drs. Helmut and Erika Reihlen of Berlin, December 2003.

Part II

Diverse Perspectives

Chapter 4

Where Is the Protestant Mainstream?

J. Philip Wogaman

Interpreting the "Protestant mainstream" is a formidable task. In the first place, how is one to define the term? Usually the denominations making up the National or World Councils of Churches are intended when commentators refer to the "mainstream," and yet it is more than questionable whether those churches are any longer at the center of contemporary American or world church life. Such churches certainly are not the fastest growing at least not in the United States. That honor now seems to belong to evangelical denominations and independent congregations. Moreover, the evangelicals seem to enjoy unprecedented (for them) political influence with mainstream churches relegated more and more to the sidelines.

Even if one accepts the traditional definition as I shall for purposes of this article, it is very difficult to locate the "mainstream's" fundamental position on any key issue such as the topic of patriotism. There are always huge exceptions to any generalizations one can offer. I do not propose to address the theme of this article through sociological analysis of the demographics of contemporary U.S. Protestantism; nor will I refer to data drawn from opinion polls. Such methods, valuable though they doubtless are in other contexts, can miss the point of how Protestant Christians draw conclusions when they are thinking as Protestant Christians. As I will note below, Protestant Christians and their churches can be influenced by social and cultural factors that have very little to do with the professed faith. So the deeper question is how to locate the essence of that professed faith as it relates to the subject of patriotism.

The "Protestant Principle" of Paul Tillich

A good starting point is Paul Tillich's proposed "Protestant principle" in which he sought to find the definitive contribution of Protestantism. As Tillich put it in his book *The Protestant Era*,

> The Protestant principle, in name derived from the protest of the "protestants" against decisions of the Catholic majority, contains the divine and human protest against any absolute claim made for a relative reality, even if this claim is made by a Protestant church. The Protestant principle is the judge of every religious and cultural reality, including the religion and culture which calls itself "Protestant."[1]

In more traditional language, this is the protest against idolatry: treating any relative reality as an absolute. Only God is absolute, and God transcends even our conceptions of God. In a novel interpretation of the classic and incontestably Protestant emphasis on justification by faith, Tillich remarks that this applies not only to humanity in its sinful condition but also in its doubts.[2] This means that we cannot reach God through external moral or cultural authorities.

Thus, the "Protestant principle" is negative—a rejection of the elevation of any relative reality to divine status. And yet this negative is based on a positive— faith in God, the one absolute. The fact that God is always something more than our intellectual conceptions and cultural expressions means that the critical task is never-ending. The application of the "Protestant principle" to the theme of patriotism seems obvious: Protestant Christians, when true to their faith, cannot make a god out of the nation. When veneration of one's country becomes absolute it is idolatry. It substitutes the nation, which is a relative reality, for God, who alone is absolute.

Centers of Value

In a somewhat different way of getting at the same point, H. Richard Niebuhr argues that every person has a "center of value" on the basis of which all other things are valued. In *Radical Monotheism and Western Culture*,[3] Niebuhr speaks of three characteristic forms that this can take. The first and arguably lowest is *polytheism*, which is the disintegrated valuing of different things. It often takes the form of materialism where now this and now that material object becomes the focus of one's valuing. In essence, one might suppose that this *polytheism* is really a self-centered form of valuing. But worship of the self is generally disintegrative, since there can be no value outside the self that is capable of commanding one's enduring loyalty.

The second kind of value center is more to the point: termed *henotheism* by Niebuhr (from the Greek *henos*, or tribe), this involves making one's primary group the center of one's valuing. The primary group can be a family, a tribe, a nation, a church, even humanity itself. Everything else is valued to the degree that it contributes to the well-being of this primary group; it is truly the center of one's affection and loyalty. *Henotheism* can lift a person above self-centeredness inspiring great generosity and noble self-sacrifice. That is often what patriotism truly is.

Niebuhr's third form is *radical monotheism*, which he defines as identifying the source of all being and goodness as the center of value. It challenges *henotheism*, for any group loyalty—even when the group is humanity itself—excludes everything beyond the group. In the case of national loyalty, other nations are excluded. Family loyalty excludes other families. When one's church becomes the center of value other churches and other religions are denigrated. Humanity as a whole, when made the center of value, treats every other aspect of creation as but a facility for human good. But the worship of the One who is the center and source of all being is the one form of worship that values the good as ulti-mate good and locates the self within a truly universal and eternal context. The object of this loyalty, unlike the other two, is not transitory.

Is Niebuhr's analysis faithful to the self-understanding of what we are calling the Protestant mainstream? The three-part typology of polytheism, henotheism, and radical monotheism, like all typologies, could be refined with endless elabo-rations.[4] Still, who could deny that the worship of God is central to the Protestant Christian mainstream and to other Christian streams as well? Does this not entail, explicitly or implicitly, a judgment against all idolatries? And is that not a theme to be encountered with some frequency from most Protestant pulpits?

Even so, there is a discernible Protestant ambivalence about all this when applied to the subject of patriotism. In the interest of honest appraisal, more needs to be said.

Protestant Ambivalence about Patriotism

While the basic theological perspective of mainstream Protestant Christianity is God-centered in Niebuhr's sense, there is a good deal of evidence of Niebuhr's *henotheism* when individual Protestants and their churches relate to the nation. Such data is not easily quantified so we must be content with an abundance of anecdotal evidence. I offer two illustrations.

First, consider the flags. In virtually all of the Protestant churches I have ever visited in all parts of the United States, the sanctuary will have an American flag positioned at one side of the chancel. Here it takes its place, virtually, as an object of worship symbolizing the national identity of the church and its people. True, in most of the churches I have visited there is also a Christian flag on the oppo-site side of the chancel thus balancing loyalty to country with loyalty to God. Any effort to remove the American flag, as sometimes happens, can be greeted with vigorous protest thus demonstrating the seriousness with which that loyalty is held. By the same token, removal of the Christian flag would also be protested for are we not also Christians? The one flag (with its set of loyalties) is balanced by the other (also with its loyalties). But isn't that revealing? Loyalty to country seems equal to loyalty to God. If that is not exactly out-and-out *henotheism*, it is surely far removed from Niebuhr's radical monotheism. Sometimes even this degree of balancing is lost. In the wake of the tragedy of September 11, 2001, I learned of a rural church served by a seminarian student pastor whose members sought to have the cloth on the communion table (or altar) replaced by an American flag.

Another slightly more refined expression of religious patriotism occurred in a number of Washington, DC church services for several decades up until the early 1970s. After the singing of the traditional *Doxology* ("Praise God from whom all blessings flow. . ."), the organist would modulate into *America*, the fourth verse of which would be belted out by the congregation ("Our fathers' God to thee, author of liberty, to thee we sing; long may our land be bright with freedom's holy light; protect us by thy might, great God, our King"). Happily, that practice seems to have disappeared although it is worthy of note that patriotic hymns, including *America*, continue to occupy space in the hymnals of several Protestant denominations thus facilitating their use in services of worship.

Not surprisingly, national patriotism tends to peak during wartime. Ray H. Abrams's study of sermons preached in Protestant pulpits during World War I explores the extent to which many preachers sought to rally national fervor in support of the war effort.[5] In fact, the egregious efforts by many in the churches to rally around the flag with total insensitivity to the deep human tragedy of the slaughter of millions in the trench warfare of France and Belgium led one thoughtful commentator to list this as a major cause of the disillusioned wave of secularism in American society during the 1920s.[6] Sharing in the disillusionment, if not the secularism, the mainstream Protestant churches were generally more restrained during World War II and thereafter, but appeals to national loyalty in time of war—including, of course, the cold war—have continued.

None of this should be surprising. "Mainstream" churches can be called that largely because their memberships have historically occupied the mainstream of American social and cultural life with attitudes deeply conditioned by that social location.[7] What is more surprising is that there has been so much criticism of patriotism within these churches. Some of that sprang out of disillusioned criticism of the Vietnam War during the 1960s and early 1970s and the partly related political disillusionments of that period. But it can also be argued that the extraordinary contributions of major twentieth-century theologians and the influence of Protestant seminaries upon new generations of clergy played an important role in sensitizing church leadership to the theological ramifications of all idolatries. Sometimes that has led to tense relationships between clergy and laity on issues of faith, but one can also observe changes in the attitudes of many lay Protestants as well.

Contrasting Versions of Patriotism

Are we then to conclude that mainstream Protestant Christians when true to their faith must reject patriotism? Certainly we are if patriotism is expressed as anything like Richard Niebuhr's *henotheistic* center of value. That cannot be the true center of value, the authentic focus of worship, by any Christian. It is properly understood to be idolatry. But is there not a distinction to be made between patriotism as *worship* of country and patriotism as *love* of country?

Worship of God must exclude all other forms of worship, but worship of God is not necessarily in conflict with other forms of love. Indeed, worship of God *leads* to other forms of love. The first great commandment, love of God, requires the second, love of neighbor. Who of us could say that because we worship God we cannot therefore love our families? Might that not also apply to other forms of human love, including our communities, our church groups, and our nation?

The point came clearer to me in the immediate aftermath of September 11, 2001, when, as pastor of a downtown Washington, DC church, I had to lead a spiritually wounded people in worship. In that situation, as we confronted the vulnerability of the nation of which most of us were citizens, the symbols of patriotism took on more of the character of love than of worship. Nationalistic arrogance was not the issue; rather, it was how we were to express our caring for one another in this broken nation. I even surprised myself by finding some value in that setting in one of the patriotic songs I have long disdained as the very essence of national pretension. It could even be considered at this time of national confusion and vulnerability as a kind of prayer: "God bless America, land that I love, stand beside her and guide her through the night with the light from above." There is nothing wrong with loving the land nor with asking for divine guidance in the midst of troubled confusion.

Of course, the scene changed quickly enough as a fearful nation turned to extreme measures in its insecurities. But, at least for me, the insight remained that there is a difference between love of country and idolatrous forms of patriotism.

One of the social gospel hymns expressed the problem in these words: "Forbid false love of country that blinds us to His call, Who lifts above the nations the unity of all."[8] That seems to suggest that there is a truer love of country, which is obedient to the call of Christ as the main point of loyalty. It also suggests that true worship for a Christian leads to a universal love that is not limited to one's nation. Another twentieth-century Protestant hymn is suggestive of that theme:

> This is my song, O God of all the nations,
> a song of peace for lands afar and mine.
> This is my home, the country where my heart is;
> here are my hopes, my dreams, my holy shrine;
> but other hearts in other lands are beating
> with hopes and dreams as true and high as mine.[9]

These words are expressive of deep love of country but hardly of idolatrous worship of the nation. Instead they express great sensitivity for the humanity of people everywhere. Such patriotism grounded in love is fundamentally positive. At the same time it embodies the critical principle to protect that love from idolatry.

Love of Nation Expressed in Practice

It is one thing to define a Christian conception of patriotism in broad terms as we have here sought to distinguish between a love of the national community and idolatrous worship of the nation. But, then, might such patriotism be expressed in practice? I wish to suggest five areas where the mainstream Protestant churches are especially put to the test.

1. International Relations (War and Peace)

Patriotic fervor seems most characteristically aroused in wartime when one's devotion to country is vividly contrasted with the other nations or forces against which one's own nation is in conflict. The virtues of "our people" are set up to oppose the evils of "the enemy." In that climate it is very difficult to venture criticism of "our side" without being accused of disloyalty or, in extreme cases, being prosecuted for sedition. Cold war-era anticommunism is a good illustration of this. Devout Anglicans during the Revolutionary War period were sometimes hounded as disloyal Tories, and even the Methodists of that period had to keep reassuring other American colonists that they were not compromised by their English Wesleyan roots. Loyalty to country can sweep all discerning criticism aside under such circumstances. One recalls the poignant story of Robert E. Lee's agonized decision on the eve of the Civil War: would he assume a command in the Union army or fight instead for his native Virginia? Virginia won out, slavery and all, and Lee's decision might practically have prolonged the conflict. After the United States' invasion of Iraq in 2003, the "support the troops" theme could mute criticism of the national policy itself.

Illustrations of conjunction between patriotism and military action abound throughout American history. Where have the mainline Protestant churches been throughout that history? Often, of course, they have lent uncritical support for the nation at war. But that is not the whole story.

Beginning early in the nineteenth century, the mainline churches have been deeply committed to global missionary activity. Sometimes that has been dismissed as merely an expression of American power and privilege, and doubtless there was some of that. But the mainstream of the missionary movement was an expression of concern for people (mostly in what we now call the Third World) not yet exposed to the gospel of God's love. And lest this be characterized as a purely individualistic version of the gospel, it must be remembered that there is a direct connection between much of this missionary activity and the emergence of twentieth-century ecumenism including the World Council of Churches. Insofar as the churches embraced the rest of the world as a part of God's global family, there was critical distance from idolatrous nationalism. The hymns cited above illustrate the point as embodied in the worship life of mainline churches.

A striking outcome of this attitude was expressed in the "Crusade for a New World Order" mounted by Methodist bishops during World War II and merged with the broader ecumenical movement for seven pillars of peace.[10]

This ecumenical venture sought to avoid the failure of the United States to support the League of Nations by encouraging the development of the proposed new United Nations organization. In the sixty years since the United Nations was founded, the mainline churches have generally continued to support the UN as an institutional expression of global solidarity.

What about war itself? No doubt the members of the mainline churches have continued to illustrate attitudes shared broadly within the society. But those churches have become much more critical of military actions especially since the trauma of the Vietnam War. Some of the mainline churches, such as Mennonites and Quakers, have opposed all war in principle. But a striking effect of the debates over Vietnam has been a mainline Protestant engagement with classical "just war" principles. While not pacifist, "just war" doctrines still define war as evil and place the burden of proof against any particular war. The practical effect of this is to encourage critical debate when America has contemplated military action—and even after war has begun—and thus to resist a fog of misplaced patriotism from muting that debate. At the heart of this is recognition that every "enemy" is also beloved of God and a part of God's intended community of humankind. Even if war or other military action is deemed to be necessary, it is a necessary evil undertaken to prevent an even greater evil. That is far removed from patriotism of "my country, right or wrong." Still, that seems fully consistent with a love of country and a protective attitude toward one's nation when its people and their basic rights are threatened.

A very large issue confronting the world community in the early twenty-first century is when, for the sake of those very values, it seems necessary to intervene militarily in other nations. An absolute conception of national sovereignty would be inconsistent with any intervention in the internal affairs of any nation, and yet such a conception encourages complacency in the face of gross evils like genocide. The "ethnic cleansing" begun in the Balkans and the Rwanda genocide illustrate the problem. The fact that, however belatedly, the North Atlantic Treaty Organization (NATO) powers intervened in the Balkans probably spared many lives and secured a better future for all of the people of Bosnia. The fact that the world community did not intervene in the conflict between the Tutsis and Hutus in Rwanda doubtless cost the lives of nearly a million people. A part of the moral risk of intervention is that it could become the vehicle for new forms of imperialism and narrow versions of national self-interest by intervening powers. The risk of total rejection of any intervention is that nationalistic forms of patriotism could be reinforced. Churches have yet to address this issue very effectively, except for the original vision of the United Nations as the vehicle for global collective security. Regional cooperative efforts or, when necessary and possible, the full employment of the United Nations might prove to be the best answer.

2. World Trade

Similar issues are raised now with the quickening pace of global economic activity. Emerging regional free trade zones, such as the European Economic Union

(EEU) and the North American Free Trade Agreement (NAFTA), are increasingly replacing protectionism with the World Trade Organization (WTO) encouraging this on a global scale. On the other hand, narrow forms of patriotism continue to be expressed with appeals to "buy American" or otherwise advance the perceived national economic self-interest. On the face of it, such appeals are counter to a Christian commitment to global community while not infrequently they are also economically counterproductive. Nevertheless, the issues are complex. For example, increased global trade can simply enrich economic elites and powerful transnational corporations while undercutting the welfare of workers in all countries. On the other hand, trade both within and among nations is a basic precondition for increased prosperity for all. The economic principle of "comparative advantage" helps us understand why very few, if any, countries can be entirely self-sufficient. All countries in a global trading market have things they can exchange for things they do not have. Bangladesh, one of the largest and poorest countries on earth and not well-endowed with natural resources and vulnerable to flooding and other natural disasters, has cheap labor—available to an increasingly global industrial and communications system—to offer in the global trading market. Absent its ability to provide labor in an integrated world economic system, Bangladesh has very little if anything to go on. But the question, illustrating the complexity, is how cheap can Bangladesh labor be without perpetuating deep poverty in that country and undercutting workers elsewhere who must compete with it?

The kind of patriotism that embodies love of one's country and its people while also expressing love for the rest of humankind might suggest the importance of the ground rules governing free trade agreements. The WTO and UN potentially can be vehicles for establishing global economic rules, but that will require concerted support from discerning people of good will including the members of the mainline churches.

3. Environmental Issues

The ecumenical movement began to address the environment in a major way during the 1970s. The World Council of Churches coined the slogan "Just, Participatory, and Sustainable Society" to speak of its ideals for human community and the "sustainable" aspect of this was directly in reference to environmental concerns coming to the fore. A "sustainable" society is one in which economic policies in one generation will not deplete resources and environmental health for future generations: what we do now must be consistent with the well-being of those who come after us. Will we so poison the atmosphere and water resources that future generations will be hurt? Will we use up resources—minerals, energy, agriculture—so future generations will be impoverished? Or will we consider those who come after us to have no less a moral claim upon us than our contemporaries?

H. Richard Niebuhr's radical monotheism remarkably anticipates this concern of contemporary mainline churches and their ecumenical movement. God is God of all being not just of those who live now and not just of people, either. All creation has its source in the Creator, and the worship of God entails responsibility before God for all that we touch.

As this relates to the theme of patriotism, we are challenged to see that the good of each is tied up in the good of all. Environmental pollution knows no national boundaries. Global warming potentially could devastate coastal cities worldwide. The effects of the rain forests of the Amazon are not felt only in Brazil but everywhere that the oxygen they generate flows. Again, we are challenged to see that true love of country necessarily reaches beyond the bounds of nation.

The churches continue to struggle with these issues generally employing high-minded rhetoric. There is much, however, that we do not know along with dilemmas we have yet to face squarely. If, for example, the economy of Brazil is enhanced by cutting into the rain forests too much—with attendant benefits to the poor of that country—then the rest of the world community must help Brazil find better ways. Moreover, forms of economic development consistent with environmental sustainability need to be encouraged. Not all economic development is bad; some can be very good. The recent invention of hybrid automobiles illustrates how human creativity can actually lead to greater conservation. Increased use of mass rapid transit and the development of alternative energy sources like solar heating and wind farms is even more promising.

4. Inclusiveness within the Nation

Patriotism, with its focus upon what binds a people together in nationhood, can often obscure injustices experienced by many within the nation. It can be a way of changing the subject when the subject of poverty, racism, or denial of civil liberties is raised. Patriotism, in that sense, has its analogy in the racism that undermined the possible political coalition of freed slaves and poor whites during the Reconstruction Era following the Civil War. The message to poor whites was something like, "you may be poor, but at least you're white"—and so a wedge was thrust between people of similar economic interest. Anticommunist extremism during the cold war-era might have employed narrow patriotism in a similar way thus inducing numbers of poor people to vote against their own interests. People like Martin Luther King Jr., whose views were far removed from Marxism, much less Soviet communism, found their concerns for social justice stigmatized and dismissed.

However, patriotism as love of country includes love of all its people. Mainline Protestant and Catholic churches, in common cause with Jewish groups and led mostly by African-American Protestants, worked hard at this agenda during the 1960s. There were, of course, huge exceptions for out-and-out racism was actively present in most of the mainline Protestant churches as well. Such churches were often bastions of racial segregation. Even the early social gospel movement was complacent about this. Having disposed of slavery, the mainline Protestants of the North were content to watch Reconstruction collapse and Jim Crow laws and customs to come into play. It is noteworthy that the first Social Creed of the churches, adopted initially by the Methodist Episcopal Church in 1908 and shortly after by the newly organized Federal Council of Churches, ignored the subject of race altogether. Still, there were active, prophetic spirits among the mainline churches from the 1930s on who pushed for greater racial justice.

The underlying issue here was whether African Americans were to be fully included in American society or only to be a tolerated and exploited subgroup. Ironically, from the standpoint of patriotism, racially excluded groups were sometimes in the forefront of military heroism during World War II. This was at least clear evidence that the African Americans and incarcerated Japanese Americans wanted to be included! As the nation moved into the 1950s with the school desegregation issue in the forefront and the 1960s with economic, housing, and voting rights at issue, mainline Protestantism came increasingly to see racial and ethnic inclusiveness as crucial to the health of the society as a whole. Black liberation was also necessary for white liberation—the former for physical and legal rights, the latter for social and spiritual wholeness. A true patriot could be seen as one who sought the full acceptance of all within the nation.

A remaining question, even yet not fully resolved, is whether racial and cultural pluralism is in conflict with racial and cultural integration. Does integration mean the absorption of people of color into the dominant "mainstream" of white American society with loss of previous cultural identity and with attendant continuation of white privilege? On the other hand, does racial and cultural pluralism mean a Balkanized coexistence of groups without an overall shared cultural and social identity? Mainline Protestant churches struggle inconclusively with such questions, but their theological commitments cannot, in the long run, allow new forms of social segregation to supplant the old. Perhaps the issue of integration must be reframed as what kind of integration is to be sought by Christians and what kind is to be rejected. An integration requiring previously oppressed groups to leave their cultural legacies behind as they enter increasingly into a dominant white culture is not true integration. Perhaps it is preferable to speak of a richer social mix in which the contributions of each is a benefit to all and where such diversity is taken as a gift and not an obstacle to genuine community. The principle applies to all forms of diversity, of course, and not only to those based upon ethnic identity or previous oppressions.

The goal of inclusiveness also affects the approach to poverty, a persistent reality in American society. A great strength in the Roman Catholic bishops' pastoral letter on the U.S. economy in 1986 was its identification of the relationship between economic poverty and social participation.[11] Human rights are not only social and legal, they are also economic. Every person should have the right to the economic conditions enabling their full participation in the life of the community.[12] As an expression of patriotism, this is an affirmation of all within the society.

Again, the policy issues are complex and there are dilemmas to be addressed. How far can a society go when including people who have no desire to be included or whose mental or physical handicapping conditions make full inclusion virtually impossible? It would take us too far afield to explore all of the complexities except to say that the commitment and the intent must be real and creative. Some economic provision for certain common needs can be handled collectively while other economic arrangements can rely upon free market mechanisms. American society currently provides free education to every child; in fact, all are required to be in school up to a certain age. Could similar provision be made for health care and higher education along with better systems for transportation and child care thus better enabling the employment of poor people?

In speaking of commitment to the inclusion of all, mainline Protestant churches have not done very well in relation to social offenders. The death penalty debate continues to rage, and the churches have not done very much to communicate their acceptance of the prison population. Those serving prison sentences have, in one sense, been removed from society. But are they not, in a large sense, still a part of the community? Most have family connections and friends of one kind or another; most also are stereotyped and stigmatized by others. Felony convicts generally have lost their voting rights, often permanently, thus symbolizing their formal rejection as participants in community decision-making. The rejection by society has two consequences: one is that the rate of recidivism is greatly increased and the other is that society itself is fragmented.

The capital punishment issue also has two facets worthy of notice. One is that this is the ultimate form of rejection by society of a fellow human being. Some of the mainstream churches, such as United Methodism, have gone against a larger American consensus to announce the church's rejection of the death penalty. The other facet is that the victims of capital offenses and of most other criminal offenses have been rejected by the injury or death they have suffered. When the surviving loved ones of a murder victim seek "closure" through the murderer's execution, as often they do, it seems to me that the closure being sought is a clear, emphatic, meaningful reaffirmation of their value and the value of their loved one by society. The death penalty can be seen as a way of doing that, but might there be other ways short of society having to take another life?[13] In all such issues, it may be that the true test of devotion to a nation is measured most by our attitude toward the least of its members.

5. Boundary Maintenance between Church and State

The mainstream Protestant attitudes toward patriotism come into sharper focus in the relationship between church and state. The First Amendment to the U.S. Constitution almost assures a perpetual tension between the two and so does the fact that the American religious scene is uniquely pluralistic. Contrary to a widespread perception, the First Amendment does not mandate a "separation" between church and state. Indeed, how could it if both institutions of religion and those of government exist side-by-side in the same society and with the same people populating both? The Constitutional provision establishes, rather, that Congress may not pass laws "respecting an establishment of religion, or prohibiting the free exercise thereof."[14] This language has given rise to endless debate and litigation.

In the contemporary debate, it is not just a question of what is or is not permitted legally. It is also about whether patriotism and Christian profession are inextricably combined and whether the state should symbolize the religious affirmations of its people. Maximum claims are readily disposed of in the courts, but there are culturally interesting issues at the margins. Should the flag be displayed in churches (not a legal issue, as we have seen, but a theological one)? Should the symbols of any religious faith be displayed on public property? An Alabama judge gained a fair amount of public attention and maybe some political support by displaying the Ten Commandments in the court house. A Denver mayor had to address a political and legal squabble over whether it was proper for a Christmas manger scene to be displayed in front of City Hall and whether it was proper for City Hall to continue to have a very large neon sign wishing everybody a merry Christmas.

At stake in such disputes is whether the state should cultivate identification between religious and patriotic loyalties. Seen from the standpoint of the state, the cultivation of such forms of patriotism is known as erastianism, which classically means state control of religious institutions for its own public ends. Seen from the standpoint of churches, this is theocracy with religion controlling the state for religious ends.

On the whole, mainline Protestant churches, together with their councils of churches, have strongly opposed both. This is partly for the theological reasons we have already surveyed. But it is also because these churches have, on the whole, been more sensitive to the rights of non-Christians than their Christian counterparts. When loyalty to church and state are mixed in a blending of patriotism and faith, the effect upon non-Christians is to have their patriotism questioned. At least they can be led to feel that they are not equal participants in the public life of their society.

A huge "gray area" develops, however, with the question of whether it is proper for people to act politically on the basis of religious motivation. In one sense, that is inevitable. If one's faith commitment is basic to one's values and purposes in life, one is likely to make the faith relevant to public life. That has certainly happened throughout American history with many people. There was strong religious opposition to slavery in the Northern states and strong religious support for its continuance in the Southern states. Mainstream churches weighed in forcefully, even if belatedly, in support of civil rights laws. Most of the mainstream Protestant denominations produce reams of resolutions instructing government to do this or that which those denominations consider essential in light of their faith. It can be a source of bemusement and sometimes anxiety among politicians to hear opposite views on a given issue from different Protestant and Catholic representatives, as in the abortion and same-gender marriage issues. At the same time, politicians are often not above using their faith commitments publicly in courting support among like-minded citizens. In the political arena, these attitudes and actions are permissible and maybe desirable.

But, consistent with the typical pronouncements of mainstream Protestant churches, two caveats must be entered. On the one hand, when churches witness on the basis of their faith in the public arena, there should also be an identifiable secular purpose. For instance, there are sound theological reasons for supporting an adequate city sanitary system, but there are also accompanying secular reasons as well. On the other hand, when politicians appeal to particular religious groups they need to bear in mind that they are potentially or actually public leaders for all of the people, including those who are of different faiths than their own. When a public leader so identifies with a particular group in articulating his or her reasons for policies, an implication is that those who do not share the faith are somehow lesser members of the community. But everybody, regardless of institutional religious commitments, can be encouraged to love their communities and their nations thus embodying a higher form of patriotism.

Notes

1. Paul Tillich, *The Protestant Era*, trans. James Luther Adams (Chicago: University of Chicago Press, 1951), xii.
2. Tillich, *The Protestant Era*, xiv.
3. H. Richard Niebuhr, *Radical Monotheism and Western Culture* (New York: Harper, 1960; Louisville: Westminster/John Knox, 1993).
4. I would prefer to define the first as hedonism, because it seems to me that the pleasure principle is what Niebuhr is really getting at when he speaks of polytheism. One could also insert aestheticism, beauty valued for its own sake, as yet another center of value for some people. Again, our mode of apprehending the One who is source of all being and value is worthy of much more discussion than Niebuhr could offer in this slim volume; his earlier work on the nature of Revelation is useful here.
5. Ray H. Abrams, *Preachers Present Arms* (New York: Round Table, 1933).
6. Paul A. Carter, *The Decline and Revival of the Social Gospel: Social and Political Liberalism in American Protestant Churches, 1920–1940* (Ithaca, NY: Cornell University Press, 1956), 44, 92–95.
7. It is noteworthy that the previously marginalized evangelicals who have come into greater political power and influence exhibit commensurate degrees of patriotism.
8. From S. Ralph Harlow's 1931 hymn, "O Young and Fearless Prophet." An alteration of words in the 1964 Methodist *Book of Hymns* marks a subtle diminishing of the point made by the original words, as it was revised to read "O grant that love of country may help us hear His call Who would unite the nations in brotherhood for all." This seems to suggest that love of country is the entry point into hearing the divine call, whereas in the original version it is the call of Christ that has priority and must not be obscured by love of country.
9. From Lloyd Stone's 1934 hymn, "This Is My Song," (Lorenz Publishing, 1964).
10. Walter G. Muelder, *Methodism and Society in the Twentieth Century* (New York: Abingdon, 1961), 186–94. Among other things, the Methodist "crusade" declared that "as Christians, we reject isolationism which subordinates the well-being of the world to national self-interest, and denies the Christian doctrine that all men are children of one Father and are members of one family. Jesus Christ is the Saviour of the World. The World is our Parish" (187).

11. *Economic Justice for All: Pastoral Letter on Catholic Social Teaching and the U.S. Economy* (Washington, DC: National Conference of Catholic Bishops, 1986).

12. I sought to express this theme in one of my first books, J. Philip Wogaman, *Guaranteed Annual Income: The Moral Issues* (Nashville, TN: Abingdon, 1968). I am less persuaded now of the possibilities of a clear-cut guaranteed income policy as it was being discussed nationally in the 1960s, but the concept of everybody's access to the economic resources enabling full participation in the life of society seems as compelling to me now as it did forty years ago.

13. I have explored this and similar issues in my *Christian Perspectives on Politics: Revised and Enlarged* (Louisville, KY: Westminster/John Knox, 2000), 336–39.

14. The origin of the "separation" language was a letter from Thomas Jefferson to a Baptist association.

Chapter 5

Can Christians Be Patriots?

William H. Willimon

In the middle of her wonderful, difficult book, *By the Renewing of Your Minds: The Pastoral Function of Christian Doctrine,*[1] Ellen Charry works through the Sermon on the Mount. After a blessed beginning with the Beatitudes, Jesus launches into a list of seemingly extravagant ethical demands on such matters as divorce, vengeance, and retaliation. Any sense of blessedness that we might feel at the beginning of his sermon dissipates as Jesus condemns lust of the heart, evil in the eye, anger, and other perfectly normal human emotions. I take some satisfaction in having steered clear of divorce, but the roving eye and the lustful heart is me all over. What does Charry make of such searing divine scrutiny? She concludes, "The rhetoric aims at making the hearers uncomfortable."

Uncomfortable? Is that all? Jesus preaches merely to make us uncomfortable? Perhaps dis-ease is a rather remarkable ethical achievement for Christians particularly in an age in which many seem all too willing patriotically to settle down, accommodate, and appease the claims of Caesar. Uncomfortability, a sense of dis-ease engendered in us when it comes to conflicting allegiances, is not a bad place to begin any Christian reflection about relations between God and government.

One evening, in a dormitory Bible study group with students, we were taking apart Matthew 22: Jesus and Caesar's coin. The Pharisees, seeking to entrap Jesus, ask him a difficult question about whether or not to pay taxes to Caesar. It is one of the rare moments in the gospels when the matter of politics comes up (note that the question is by the Pharisees, not Jesus).

"Jesus, should we pay taxes to Caesar?"

Jesus says, "Who's got some of that idolatrous coinage on him? My pockets are empty."

A nickel is produced.

"Whose picture is on it?"

"Er, uh, Thomas Jefferson," we say.

Jesus says, "Well, give it to him. But you be careful. Don't give to Caesar that which belongs to God. End of the lesson."

A student asks, "Did I miss something? He didn't answer the question! Should we pay taxes or not?"

"Yea," said another. "What's Caesar's and what's God's?"

Frustration with Jesus spreads within the group.

Finally, a student said something quite wise. "Perhaps," she said, "when it comes to what belongs to Caesar and what belongs to God, we never can be too sure. Maybe Jesus wants us to be permanently uneasy."

I was present when a seminarian asked my friend, Stanley Hauerwas, "Can Christians be involved in politics?" Hauerwas, crude Texan and orthodox theologian that he is, responded, "Christians ought to do politics the same way in which porcupines make love—very carefully."

Permanently uneasy. That's not a bad attempt at a response to the question, "Can Christians be patriots?" One faithful, biblical answer is, "It's possible for Christians to be patriots but never without great dis-ease." I'll admit that's not a whole theology of church and state, but it at least sets the context wherein we answer the question about our love of Christ and our love of America. Perhaps any attempt to devise a systematic, whole theology of church and state is not to be a Christian project in the first place. What's required is to be permanently uneasy.

Pity our founding father Thomas Jefferson for not having the moral courage to release his slaves even though he knew slavery was evil. Yet before he died, as he considered this peculiar institution, Jefferson said, "I tremble when I remember that God is just." At least Jefferson had the ethical insight to be able to tremble. Thank God that Abraham Lincoln learned enough backwoods Calvinism to admit in his Second Inaugural the ambiguity of even his righteous cause and the tragedy of violence, especially violence in the service of good. God save us from becoming too easy, too sure or too smug in our claims of righteousness.

My rabbi and I were talking about Jews and sports. "Basketball, baseball, just about everything except hunting," he noted.

"Why not hunting?" I asked.

"Jews don't hunt," he said authoritatively. "We are permitted to kill animals but never for joy, never out of pleasure. We can kill only with regret."

Regret? Isn't that a bit weak to serve as a basis for morality?

"Don't knock regret," said the rabbi. "It's tragedy's cousin. There are some things that are not so much right or wrong as deeply, unavoidably regrettable."

I've come, in the present context, to see the rabbi's wisdom. Don't knock regret. In a context in which Americans are able, without a twinge of regret, to march forth with banners flying and flags unfurled in righteous indignation to once again have the war to end all wars and urbanely cite theological doctrine as justification and then roll over and go back to sleep, God grant us someone who, in the words of that sophomore, has the grace to be "permanently uneasy" about the caughtness of human life and the injustice that infects our earnest efforts to work justice—in short, our sin.

Jesus warned us. A dozen chapters before this tensive exchange over taxes in Matthew 22, Jesus looks up and sees "great crowds around him" (Mt. 8:18). Jesus immediately tries to evade the crowds by going to the other side of the lake. A scribe comes up and asks to follow Jesus addressing him as "Teacher" and promising to follow Jesus "wherever" he goes (8:19). Jesus responds with a warning—the Son of Man (referring to himself with an eschatological designation rather than simply as "Teacher") has no real estate and is homeless and destitute (8:20). The man steps forward and offers to follow asking only one thing of Jesus—to be permitted to bury his late father (8:21). Jesus makes an insensitive comment: "let the dead bury their own dead" (8:22).

Isn't it good to have family values? Doesn't Scripture commend us to honor our parents? Do not our deceased loved ones deserve some show of respect? I love this episode principally because it shows that Jesus never makes discipleship appear easier than it really is. You can't accuse Jesus of false advertising. Move from consideration of him as a moral "teacher" to regard for him as a messianic "Son of Man" and the tensions escalate.

That I, as a preacher, would note this inherent tension between our ways and Jesus' way is significant because, like most preachers, I sometimes get confused into thinking that my job is to find some way to relax the tension between us and Jesus not accentuate it. Here is Jesus fostering dis-ease with some of our commitments, calling into question the true objects of our worship, refusing to give us clear answers to our legitimate questions, and I say, in effect, "Relax. I can explain what Jesus was trying to get at here if he had the benefit of a seminary education." The simple process of taking a tensive story, like the one about Caesar's coin in Matthew 22, and making two or three sermonic "points" that are extracted from the story is a sly preacher's attempt of relieving the Jesus-induced dis-ease of the story.

Marcus Borg does this one more time in his *The Heart of Christianity*. The motivation for such reductionism is always apologetics. Borg says that he writes because "there are no serious intellectual obstacles to being a Christian. There is a way of seeing Christianity that makes persuasive and compelling sense of life in the broadest sense."[2] There you have it. If you look at Christianity through the lens that is given to you by late, capitalistic, market driven, American, autonomous, individual liberalism and if you reduce the faith to some generality that makes "sense of life in the broadest sense," then there is no intellectual obstacle and no discomfort with Jesus. As a preacher I announce that I have been given the key to making Jesus less of a threat to present arrangements and then I preach those general principles from which you can select those that make the most sense to you in your present state and call that Good News. No dis-ease in that.

At a conference a few years ago at Messiah College on "Spirituality and Social Justice" in which a number of experts had articulated the doctrines of our churches on matters of justice, a young man rose out of his seat shaking with emotion and virtually shouting.

"I'm so frustrated! I've just returned from the Palestinian camps and the occupied territories and seen there the devastation. I'm not sure what I or my church ought to do, but I know we ought to do something more than sit here and have discussions!"

I felt ashamed that I had lost youthful frustration. I longed for some gospel induced sense of dis-ease. God forgive us of our middle-aged numbness, our calloused rationales, our informed complacency and our self-satisfied assurance that we are in the right or, if not in the right, at least doing the very best that we can.

When, after the horrid events of September 11, 2001, we were cast down into great national grief and needed help and hope, to whom did we turn? We reached, from what I observed, not for the cross but rather for the flag. After all, if right is to be done in our world and we are to be secure and have confidence in the future where will that be given to us if not from the hands of the all powerful state? One conviction unites politically conservative and politically liberal Christians in this country: It is up to the government to work peace, security, and justice, or peace, security, and justice won't be done.

After President Bush gave his famous speech to Congress shortly after September 11, 2001, a commentator said, "The American people desperately need to believe that the President has the character, the power, the intelligence, and the wisdom to bring us through this crisis safely." We tend to imbue our governmental leaders with divine attributes because we need a "god" to save us, even if we have to make up our "gods" for ourselves. It's all a matter of worship.

So that day, when asked about Caesar's tax, Jesus didn't tell us exactly what is the government's and what is God's. What he did was to place the question in the context of worship. He noted that, whereas the coin was stamped with the image of Caesar, we are created in the image of God. The coin belongs to Caesar; we belong to a different nationality. Thus we are called, as Christians, to bear two passports in our pockets. We are citizens of the United States of America, but we are also citizens of the Kingdom of God. We have our eyes fixed on "another city" and have here "no abiding city" (Heb. 13:14). It is no simple matter. When do we cross that line between valid affection and loyalty to the state and idolatry to the state? I don't always know. These matters are not that clear.

Perhaps the worst sin is not to give to Caesar that which ought only to be given to God—idolatry. The greatest sin is to not care—to act as if there is no problem, no cause for concern, no question of deep tension between our memberships in two very different principalities and no difficulty in the worship of the Trinity.

Reinhold Niebuhr taught us that, though there are historically deep tensions between Christians and government, though all governments are flawed and finite, and though we are never to put our ultimate loyalties in the hands of the government, if the government is a democratically elected government there is no real problem. Once we had trouble with kings and tyrants, but now the people are king. Because we live in a democracy where the government graciously gives religious people "freedom" to be religious (as long as our practice of religion disciplines itself never to question primacy of the government), when questions about patriotism and Christians arise we are able to say, "That doesn't apply to us. We're lucky enough to be Americans." Sadly, first liberal then conservative American Christians bought into Niebuhr's argument and American

Christians, when these issues are brought up, act as if the whole discussion has nothing to do with us.

Among the things that Niebuhr missed was the possibility that the people can be as tyrannical as the lone tyrant on the throne, that our alleged religious freedom has within it its own constraints, and that the liberal values of choice, individual autonomy, and personal authority that undergird democracy might be deeply at odds with the Christian faith. Niebuhr missed these tensions not because he was not a great political thinker, which he surely was, but because he was not a theological thinker. He thought without any prior acknowledgment of the peculiarity and the jealousy of the God of Israel and the Church. By making the Christian faith into an abstraction and detaching the practices of this faith from the particular, concrete stories of this faith, Niebuhr thought he had avoided the tensions and the incongruities. In modernity, a favorite tactic for accommodating the Christian faith to the limitations of the modern, Western, industrialized state is to make the Christian faith into an intellectual abstraction detached from the stories that make Christians such a problem for the state.

A Christian and an American patriot may have much in common. They may have similar values and seek comparable goals. They may join together to work on various projects of mutual concern. They may both vote and pay taxes and run for political office. They may both feel an equally strong affection for their native land and its real accomplishments.

Yet a Christian and an American patriot are different, even when they are the same person, because a Christian and an American have listened to a different set of stories. These stories teach us how to locate ourselves in the world; they are the lens through which we view the world, and they tell us who is in charge and who sits on the throne. And for that reason above all there are going to be tensions, and when Christians are patriots they can never be merely patriotic, simply loyal, or completely committed. Christians have their lives formed by a story that renders unto Jesus Christ and his Kingdom (a political claim if I ever heard one), and Americans answer to an Enlightenment engendered and often embroidered and even to untrue, sometimes inspiring but sometimes tragic stories of people who worship gods other than the one rendered by stories like the ones in Matthew 22. And one reason why, for Christians, a more important question than the patriotic, "What have I got to do to support the existence of the state?" is the ecclesiastical question, "What do I have to do to enable the church to be a living, breathing, visible example that the state is not God's answer to what's wrong with the world?" That divine answer is the church—that group of people who keep their eyes fixed on another kingdom and who keep telling one another a set of stories different from the governmentally subsidized, official account of what's going on in the world.

An egregious example of how not to think about these matters is provided by a *First Things* editorial by Richard John Neuhaus, "In Time of War."[3] Neuhaus was impressed by the President's "historic speech" (September 20, 2001) that he made before Congress calling for war. It was a speech, says Neuhaus, in which "boldness is touched by humility." In defending that claim, Neuhaus (who to my knowledge has never seen a war in recent years for which he could not find theological justification) said:

> Assured as we are and must be of the rightness of our cause, the President submits that cause in prayer to a higher authority. In a time of grave testing, America has once again given public expression to the belief that we are "one nation under God"—meaning that we are under both His protection and His judgment. . . . Most Americans are Christians who understand the mercy and justice of God as revealed in the gospel of Jesus Christ. Recognizing the danger that the motto "For God and country" can express an idolatrous identity of allegiances, most Americans act in the hope that it represents a convergence of duties.[4]

Note how quickly and effortlessly Neuhaus moves after a brief mention of "prayer" to some vague "higher authority" to the claim that this is evidence that we are, after all, "one nation under God." This has become the conventional American Christian move that assumes that, in loving our nation and in loving God, we are faced with a happy "convergence of duties." To make this sentimental move, it is important to keep as general and abstract as possible about the "mercy and justice of God as revealed in the gospel of Jesus Christ."

For Neuhaus and for many like him on the political left or the political right, there is little consideration that this alleged "convergence of duties" might obscure the deep tension between the worship of different gods. I can't tell much difference between the Web site of the National Council of Churches (NCC)[5] and their arch foe, the Institute for Religion and Democracy (IRD).[6] Both are preoccupied with issues of how we can be better citizens of the United States. They accept that project without much apparent reservation, though they squabble between themselves (rather vehemently at times) on how best to be patriots. While the NCC thinks that America can be made better by the politics of the left, the IRD advocates politics on the right. Both Web sites are devoid of any discernable theological content. I would defy anyone to surf their sites, read their pronouncements, and find out whether they are devotees of Islam, Christianity, Buddhism or New Age Spirituality. Probably both organizations realize that, in order to be helpful citizens, ideas of God need to be vague, abstract, large, general, and detached from a story about a specific Jew who lived briefly, died violently, and rose unexpectedly and happens to be God. The IRD has become the mirror image of the NCC.

In the modern world where the state is everything and all loyalties (including those of faith) must be subordinated to allegiance to the state, there isn't much room left for the worship of the God whose story is Scripture. Having been pushed out of the world and relegated to the realm of the private and the personal, Christianity has nothing essential left to do. In such a world, Christian apologetics attempts to argue for the faith on the basis of its utility. Following Jesus is good for you. Jesus is another technique for getting whatever it is that you think you must have. In a nation that has difficulty keeping itself together—mobilizing for the war effort, universal health care, national security, a living wage, or whatever it is that could make us the people we think we ought to be—it is understandable how the Christian faith gets used as a means of making America work. It's as if the world has never had the means to form a government without referencing god, even if we have to make that god up ourselves.

I find it odd that some Christians, of the right or the left, think that Jesus can so easily be enlisted in this project. To do so assumes that Jesus has an interest in our statecraft in the first place or that the patron gods of the state are left unchallenged by King Jesus. It wasn't that, in Matthew 22, Jesus gave some helpful hints about how to keep government in its place in regard to taxation laws, it was that it was Jesus who was doing the teaching: Jesus, the one who is not only often at odds with the authorities, but is also the Messiah, the Christ, the Son of God, the King of all Kings, and the Lamb who sits on the throne.

Isn't it revealing that George Bush did not say, when he ordered the invasion of Iraq, "Jesus Bless America," or that the billboard I see on my way to work would never say, "Jesus, Be with Our Troops"? Christians are tensive, uneasy patriots not primarily because we have misgivings about the American experiment in democracy but because we are trying to worship Jesus of Nazareth as God.

I was meeting with a group of students from a college in Mississippi a couple of years ago. During a discussion on the challenge of being a disciple, one of the students asked, "What do you do when people hate you because of Jesus?"

I told the young man that, as a Methodist, people usually hated me for reasons other than Jesus. What did he mean by his question?

"Well, in my fraternity one night, we got into a discussion of the war. Most of the guys were in favor of it. One had just enlisted to fight in it. I said that I didn't know that much about it, but I was against any big war like this for most any reason. Well, they started yelling at me! One of them told me if I didn't like living in America, I ought to move. Another told me that I was a disgrace to the fraternity for saying things like that. I thought they were going to try to hurt me!"

I told him that I thought this was an amazing story.

"Then one of them asked me," he continued, "'just what makes you think you know more than the president?' I responded that I didn't think I knew more than the President. All I knew was that I was a Baptist, and Baptists have always been suspicious of the government, any government. Baptists don't believe in much but Jesus and I just couldn't figure out how you could drag Jesus into something like this."

Such are the perils of trying to worship Jesus more than you worship anything else. I praise that young man's dis-ease.

I recall my own sense of discomfort, engendered in me through my attempt to listen to the biblical story more than other competing stories, one Christmas Eve. In preparing my sermon for Christmas Eve 2001, the Holy Spirit suddenly slapped me with the awareness that, in reading Luke chapters 1 and 2, I was reading an account of people (Mary, Joseph, the baby Jesus) caught under the heel of an occupying army (Rome and its Jewish collaborators). The Son of God was born in a manger, far from his hometown, and (according to Matthew) had to flee to

Egypt for safety because, even as a baby, he was a threat to the government. I had previously read the story from the standpoint of poor Mary, Joseph, and Jesus, but now I was reading it from the point of view of the Empire—the powerful Imperial army that had invaded and was now dominating God's people in the Near East. It was a sobering experience for me to read the scripture as a loyal American.

If we are so trustful of God, as the billboards claim, why do we have the largest military budget in the world? Why didn't we utilize Neuhaus's "prayer" rather than send in the troops? The answer lies partly in our inability to get from the God, who is the Trinity, what we think we need. Unlike other deities, this true, living God is free and sovereign, winning victories not through violence and power but through suffering, forgiving love, and by showing mercy to the kind and the ungrateful, dying for sinners no matter where they live, even in Iraq. That God requires a lifetime of training and sometimes painful transformation to worship. The god of the modern, officially atheistic nation requires only our money and sometimes the lives of our children while promising to deliver us security, safety, and control. The God whose name is Trinity requires a more totalitarian, imperialistic homage. He is the Way, the Truth, and the Life and is always causing difficulty for other possible ways, and truths, and lives. And that's why it's a challenge to be Christian and a patriot.

You're thinking that, as the invasion and occupation of Iraq drags on and the origins of this war and its results come to light, Neuhaus might put things differently on the "convergence of duties." I doubt it. The patriotic duty to support— or to at least work hard to improve—the state has trumped the duty to worship the God of Israel and the church with all our heart, soul, mind, and strength. We are complacently content in the assurance that our loyalty is vaguely sanctioned by some "higher authority."

"This is not a time for nay saying and carping criticism of the Administration's foreign policy," said a letter to a preacher friend of mine, complaining about his sermon. "This is a time for Americans to stand together, to stand with our leaders, and to show that we are loyal Americans."

Such sentiments may be fine for those who are not trying hard to follow Jesus. For Christians, we must take a moment to stand back, consider, critique, bring judgment to bear when we think our nation is wrong, and rectify those wrongs because our love for Christ is stronger than our affection for our country; we believe the best way we can love our country is by loving the God who is greater, wiser, and has a higher standard of righteousness than our country at its best. The greatest service patriotic Christians can render our country is to show the world that even in the most powerful, democratic country in the world, there are those who are free to bend their lives in worship toward the true and living God Who has turned toward us in Jesus Christ.

So, when the flag passes by, when you vote, when you are asked to support some government policy, and when you are considering the future of our nation, our town, our state and what you ought to do about it, be careful! And help me to be careful! Don't give to the state that which we ought to give to God! Don't be more concerned about the plight of the country than the fidelity of the church!

I can't always tell you exactly where that line lies, and I can't tell you in every case what belongs to Caesar and what belongs to God—but it's true that I probably know more about those lines and that ownership than I am yet able to live out. In the meantime, I can pray that God will grant us—unwillingly enlisted and not too faithful participants in the story of Jesus the Christ—the grace to be permanently uneasy.

Notes

1. Ellen Charry, *By the Renewing of Your Minds: The Pastoral Function of Christian Doctrine* (Oxford: Oxford University Press, 1997).
2. Marcus Borg, *The Heart of Christianity* (New York: HarperSanFrancisco, 2003), 5.
3. Richard John Neuhaus, "In Time of War," *First Things* 118 (December 2001): 11–17.
4. Neuhaus, "In Time of War," 12.
5. http://www.ncccusa.org
6. http://www.ird-renew.org

Chapter 6

Christian Patriotism?

Charles C. Colson

Whatever makes men good Christians makes them good citizens.

—Daniel Webster

In the kingdoms of man, young people learn the basics of good citizenship in high-school civics courses. Immigrants attend special classes to learn their new country's laws and their civic responsibilities; they must pass a test to prove they understand their new citizenship and then must swear their allegiance. Good citizenship requires such basic duties as paying taxes, voting, serving in the military and on juries, and obeying the laws of the land.

In the Kingdom of God one learns the obligations of citizenship from the Scriptures, the ultimate source of basic Christian truth. Unfortunately, most people, churched or unchurched, are woefully ignorant in this area. Though 500 million Bibles are published in America each year—that's two for every man, woman, and child—over 100 million Americans confess they never open one. In a recent survey only 42 percent could name who gave the Sermon on the Mount.[1] (Some thought it was delivered by a person on horseback.)

If the average churchgoer is uninformed, however, one does not have to look far to understand why. Church leaders have treated us to a smorgasbord of trendy theologies, pop philosophies, and religious variants of egocentric cultural values.

Recently, for example, a group of church scholars met to discuss which of Christ's words in the gospels could be accepted as authentic. Their modern critical analysis was carried out by ballot. Slips of colored paper were distributed to the group: a red slip meant the statement was authentic; pink meant probably authentic; gray meant probably not; and black meant not authentic. After intense discussion of each of Jesus' statements, participants cast their votes with the appropriate card. The Beatitudes and the Sermon on the Mount took a beating in the balloting. "Blessed are the peacemakers" was voted down; "blessed are the meek" garnered a paltry six red and pinks out of thirty votes. In the end only three of the twelve assorted woes and blessings from Matthew and Luke survived.

Such theological tomfoolery might be dismissed as too ludicrous to worry about except that this pink-slip mentality pervades the church. Orthodoxy—adherence to the historic tenets of Christianity—is under intense assault. This has been true since the Enlightenment, of course, but not until this century have so many in the church seriously argued that truth can be determined by majority vote or that the gospel should accommodate the whims of culture.

I have heard it said that reinterpreting the gospel in the context of modern culture is enlightened and progressive. Maybe some find that so, but Joseph Sobran better expresses my feelings: "It can be exalting to belong to a church that is five hundred years behind the times and sublimely indifferent to fashion; it is mortifying to belong to a church that is five minutes behind the times, huffing and puffing to catch up."[2]

Christianity rests on the belief that God is the source of truth and that He does not alter it according to the spirit of the times. When Christians sever their ties to absolute truth, relativism reigns, and the church becomes merely a religious adaptation of the culture.

Donald Bloesch maintains that modern "secularism is preparing the way for a new collectivism." He points to a historical precedent we have already looked at in some detail, the church in Germany. It was the confessing orthodox church in Germany that rose up in resistance to Hitler while "the church most infiltrated by the liberal ideology, the Enlightenment, was quickest to succumb to the beguilement of national societies."[3] Enticed by secular ideology, they saw the state as a vehicle for advancing the church.

Bloesch also points to a current illustration. In South Africa, 'it can be shown that of the three Reformed churches the most liberal theologically is the most illiberal in racial attitudes, whereas the most consciously Calvinist is the most courageous in speaking out against racial injustice."[4]

The effect of preaching a false theology can be disastrous. Most attribute the fall of Jim and Tammy Bakker to greed, sexual indiscretion, or the corruption of power. These were, of course, serious contributing factors. But the root cause of their downfall was that for years the Bakkers had preached a false gospel of material advancement: If people would only trust God, He would shower blessings upon them and indulge them with all the material desires of their hearts—a religious adaptation of the prevailing "what's in it for me" mentality. Tragically, the Bakkers deluded themselves into believing their own false message. Taking a two-million-dollar-a-year salary, living in splendor, and indulging their every whim didn't seem wrong; it was "God's blessing." And millions of followers continued to support them, even after their fall, because they too wanted such blessings.

The first responsibility for the citizens of the Kingdom, then, is to understand historic Christian truth: to know Scripture and the classic fundamentals of the faith. This is not to say that Christians are to mindlessly accept whatever they are told is an orthodox creed. Honest inquiry and thoughtful examination of the evidence, I believe, are healthy and should be encouraged, for these invariably lead to firmer belief in the truth of God's revelation interpreted by the great theologians through the ages. As Chesterton said, "Dogma does not mean the absence of thought but the end [result] of thought."[5]

When Christians either lack knowledge or are insecure about what they believe, as is the case with many today, they forfeit their place in contending for theological truth, and secularism advances. This is why James Schall implores Christians "to regain their confidence in their own dogmas. . .These are not idle speculations," he writes, "but the order of reality out of which a right order in human things alone can flow."[6] Such confidence is essential if Christians are to contend for values in culture and restore a sense of the transcendent to secular thought.

The problem is, as Harry Blamires states flatly, "there is no Christian mind."[7] By this he means that Christians have their own set of beliefs but, lacking confidence, keep them to themselves. As long as they are in a secular context, they act by secular values. When they return to the privacy of their enclaves where they can safely think and act in Christian terms, they do so. As a result their most fundamental beliefs never penetrate the culture. Jacques Ellul reminds us that the only way theological truth reaches the world is through the actions of laypeople in the marketplace.[8]

It is this first step of Christian citizenship in the Kingdom of God—knowledge and confidence in classical Christian truth—that enables the Christian to be a good citizen in the kingdoms of man. And it is in Scripture and classical doctrine that he or she finds the clearest expression of an individual's responsibility to both kingdoms.

On the one hand Scripture commands civil obedience—that individuals respect and live in subjection to governing authorities and pray for those in authority.[9] On the other it commands that Christians maintain their ultimate allegiance to the Kingdom of God. If there is a conflict, they are to obey God, not man.[10] That may mean holding the state to moral account through civil disobedience. This dual citizenship requires a delicate balance.

* * *

Christians who are faithful to Scripture should be patriots in the best sense of that word. They are "the salvation of the commonwealth," said Augustine, for they fulfill the highest role of citizenship.[11] Not because they are forced to or even choose to, not out of any chauvinistic motivations or allegiance to a political leader, but because they love and obey the King who is above all temporal leaders. Out of that love and obedience they live in subjection to governing authorities, love their neighbors, and promote justice. Since the state cannot legislate love, Christian citizens bring a humanizing element to civic life, helping to produce the spirit by which people do good out of compassion, not compulsion.

But Christians, at least in the United States, have all too often been confused about their biblical mandates and have therefore always had trouble with the concept of patriotism. They have vacillated between two extremes—the God-and-country, wrap-the-flag-around-the-cross mentality and the simply-passing-through mindset.

The former was illustrated a century ago by the president of Amherst College who said that the nation had achieved the "true American union, that sort of union which makes every patriot a Christian and every Christian a patriot."[12] This form of civil religion has endured as a peculiar American phenomenon supported by politicians who welcome it as a prop for the state and by Christians who see it enshrining the fulfillment of the vision of the early pilgrims.

The passing-through mindset is represented by those who believe they are simply sojourners with loyalties only in the Kingdom beyond. Patriotism has become a dirty word to them, particularly in the wake of Vietnam, and they believe it their real duty to oppose the United States in just about every endeavor on just about every front—from nuclear power to Nicaraguan policy to welfare for the homeless.

These two extremes miss the kind of patriotism Augustine had in mind. He believed that while as Christians we are commanded to love the whole world, practically speaking we cannot do so. Since we are placed as if by "divine lot" in a particular nation-state, it is God's calling that we "pay special regard" to those around us in that state. We love the world by loving the specific community in which we live.[13]

C. S. Lewis likened love of country to our love for the home and community in which we were raised. It is a natural love of the place where we grew up, he said, "love of old acquaintances, of familiar sights, sounds and smells." He also pointed out, however, that in love of country, as in love of family, we don't love our spouses only when they are good. Similarly, a patriot sees the flaws of his country, acknowledges them, weeps for them, but remains faithful in love.[14]

Dr. Martin Luther King Jr. spoke of love for his country even as he attempted to change its laws. "Whom you would change, you must first love," he said.[15]

That's the kind of tough love Christians must have for their country. To love the land faithfully, but not at the expense suspending moral judgment. Indeed, it is the addition of that moral judgment that makes Christian patriotism responsible. "Loyalty to the *civitas* can safely be nurtured only if the *civitas* is not the object of highest loyalty," is the way Richard Neuhaus expresses it.[16]

The basic principle from Scripture is straightforward: Civil authorities are to be obeyed unless they set themselves in opposition to divine law. As Augustine put it, "An unjust law is no law at all."[17] This is the other side of Caesar's coin and can lead to civil disobedience. Practical application of this principle, however, raises perplexing questions, as we have witnessed in recent decades.

Since the sixties, civil disobedience has become a preferred method of protest. As unlikely as it may seem to some, this is an area where the Christian church has a major contribution to make in public discussion. After all, we've wrestled with this matter for two thousand years.

If Scripture does give clear principles on the matter, as I believe it does, then when is civil disobedience justified? And how is it to be carried out?

Civil disobedience is clearly justified when government attempts to take over the role of the church or allegiance due only to God. Then the Christian has not just the right but the duty to resist. The Bible gives a dramatic example of this in its account of three young Jewish exiles who were drafted into the Babylonian civil service.[18]

All citizens of Babylon were required to worship the statue of Nebuchadnezzar, the king; those who disobeyed were incinerated. Like many political leaders, power and authority were not enough for King Nebuchadnezzar; he wanted spiritual submission as well. Shadrach, Meshach, and Abednego, the young Hebrews, refused. To worship an earthly king would be the ultimate offense against their holy God.

"Our God will deliver us," they told the king when they were condemned to death for their disobedience. "But if not, we will still not worship you."[19] (It is significant to note, a point we will address later, that they were willing to pay the price for their disobedience.) The three young men were thrown into a blazing furnace. God did miraculously deliver them—something we can't always count on—and as a result the king began to worship the one true God.

Civil disobedience is also mandated when the state restricts freedom of conscience, as in the case of Peter and John, two of Jesus' disciples.

Peter and John were arrested for disturbing the peace. They were taken before the Sanhedrin, a religious body holding authority from the government of Rome, and ordered to stop preaching about Jesus. Peter and John refused.

"Judge for yourselves whether it is right in God's sight to obey you rather than God," they said. "We cannot help speaking about what we have seen and heard."[20]

Their first allegiance was to the commandment they had been given by the resurrected Christ: the Great Commission to preach the gospel first to Jerusalem, then to the rest of Judea, and then to the ends of the earth. They could not permit the authority of the government-backed Sanhedrin to usurp the authority of God Himself.

This is a very real conflict for many Christians around the world. For example, Christians in India are imprisoned for proselytizing; in Saudi Arabia and Afghanistan they are imprisoned for even preaching the gospel. During a recent visit to the United States, a pastor from Nepal told of his imprisonment in his own country for just this offense. In conclusion he gave an excellent summary of Christian duty. "Of course I must obey my Lord and spread His Word," he said. "But even though we are persecuted, we who are Christians in Nepal pride ourselves on being the best citizens our king has. We try to be faithful to the fullest extent we can. We love our country—but we love our God more."[21]

The third justification for civil disobedience is probably the most difficult to call. It is applied when the state flagrantly ignores its divinely mandated responsibilities to preserve life and maintain order and justice. Those last words are key for Christians in deciding to disobey civil authority. Civil disobedience is never undertaken lightly or merely to create disorder. Replacing one bad situation with another is no solution, but when the state becomes an instrument of the very thing God has ordained it to restrain, the Christian must resist.

Inadequate though it was, the resistance of the German church to Hitler was a clear modern example of this necessity. In the sixties we saw it in the civil rights movement, as we do today in the right-to-life movement and nonviolent resistance to apartheid in South Africa.

When civil disobedience is justified, how is that disobedience to be carried out? When all recourse to civic obedience has been exhausted and the evil of the state is so entrenched as to be impenetrable, then the Christian may be justified. . .in organizing to overthrow the state. First recourse, however, is always minimum resistance. Good citizens always avoid breaking just laws to protest unjust laws.

Daniel in the Old Testament exemplifies the use of the least resistance necessary to accomplish the result.

Daniel was a contemporary of Shadrach, Meshach, and Abednego, another Jewish exile living in Babylon. King Nebuchadnezzar was impressed with Daniel and enlisted his service. As a member of the king's court, Daniel was required to eat from the king's table. While such delicacies were tempting, Daniel did not want to be "defiled"; that is, he did not want to break God's strict dietary laws for His people.[22] He quietly sought his superior's permission not to eat the food, and permission was granted. Daniel could have launched a hunger strike, but it was not necessary. He achieved his objections with minimum resistance.

Where peaceful means are available, force should be avoided. Clearly, at least in a democratic society, this should be the path civil disobedience takes. A person who, for example, feels the state's action in war is immoral has the right to pursue the matter of conscientious objection (although technically our government allows that preference only to those who practice pacifism at all times, not just for what they may perceive to be right or wrong wars).

Another important principle related to civil disobedience is illustrated by the apostles Peter and John as well as the three young Hebrews: though they disobeyed authority, they showed the appropriate respect for that authority by a willingness to accept their punishment. Those who practice civil disobedience must be prepared to pay the consequences of civil disobedience.

These general principles from Scripture are clear enough; but it is often another thing to apply them to specific circumstances, as the case of a zealous and deeply devout young woman illustrates.

Joan Andrews is a slight, soft-spoken Roman Catholic who on March 26, 1986, entered an abortion clinic for a pro-life sit-in and attempted to damage a suction machine used to perform abortions. She was charged and convicted of criminal mischief, burglary, and resisting arrest without violence. The prosecution asked for a one-year sentence. The judge gave her five.

Miss Andrews announced to the court, "The only way I can protest for unborn children now is by noncooperation in jail." She then dropped to the courtroom floor and refused to cooperate with prison officials at any stage of her processing. Labeled a troublemaker, she was transferred to Broward Correctional Institute, a tough maximum-security women's prison where she was placed in solitary confinement.

On one level, Joan Andrews's sentence was severe. For example, the same day she was sentenced, two men convicted as accessories to murder were sentenced by the same judge to four years. Five years for Joan Andrews's crime is disproportionately harsh.

On the other hand, in her protest against abortion Miss Andrews violated a trespassing law. Much like the civil rights movement, today's right-to-life activists engage in sit-ins and deliberately violate trespassing laws as a means of attracting public attention. In Joan Andrews's case, the fear of doing nothing, of standing by while innocent lives were being taken, was greater than the fear of prison. But even if the cause is just, as I believe both civil rights and right-to-life to be, are such means of opposition appropriate?

In a free or democratic society there are legal means available to express political opposition: we can picket, petition, vote, organize, advertise, or pressure political officials. Is it right to abandon our respect for the rule of law, the foundation for public order, simply to make statements that could be made legally in other forums? Can one break a just law in the name of protesting an unjust law? Few biblical precedents are set for us, and those that are clearly deal with laws that were themselves unjust. In our day, breaking laws to make a dramatic point is the ultimate logic of terrorism, not civil disobedience.

There may be situations, however, in which one has to respond to a higher law when life itself is at stake. Many Jews and Christians during World War II refused to obey Nazi laws requiring registration of aliens. On the surface those might have seemed just laws, no different than alien registration laws on the books of most Western countries today. But the citizens disobeyed because they knew those laws were being used to identify individuals for extermination.

Rightly exercised, civil disobedience is divine obedience. But when Christians engage in such activities, it must always be to demonstrate their submissiveness to God, not their defiance of government.

Unfortunately, no neat formulas for civil disobedience exist. The citizen must seek wisdom in striking the fine balance between disobedience and respect for the law. The state, though ordained by God and thus deserving of respect, is not God. The true patriot, therefore, is not one who always obeys the law. If that were so, the sheriff enforcing Jim Crow laws or the Auschwitz guard would be the best of citizens. On the other hand, disobedience can never be undertaken lightly.

Many on both the political right and left seem all too eager to defy civil authority and disrupt order to make a point on the six o'clock news. Their causes range from preventing CIA recruiters from entering college campuses to sheltering illegal immigrants to saving California condors to censoring bookstores. Some seem temperamentally disposed to such protest, as if they get high on the thrill of civil disobedience. But as Harvard law professor Alexander Bickel warns, "Civil disobedience, like law itself, is habit-forming, and the habit it forms is destructive of law."

Good citizenship requires both discernment and courage—discernment to soberly assess the issues and to know when duty calls one to obey or disobey, and courage, in the case of the latter, to take a stand.

The citizens of the Kingdom of God should be patriots in the highest sense, loving the world by loving those in the nation in which they live because that government is ordained by God to preserve order and promote justice. Perhaps this is why John Adams wrote that a patriot must be "a religious man."[23] Christians understand the phrase "a nation under God" not as a license for blind nationalism or racial superiority but as a humbling acknowledgement that all people live under the judgment of God.

Christian patriots spend more time washing feet than waving flags. Ideally, flags should not even be thought of as symbols of military and economic might, but of the common good of the specific people a sovereign God has called them to serve.

Notes

1. "Jesus Christ in the Lives of Americans Today," a poll conducted by the Gallup Organization, for the Robert H. Schuller Ministries, February 1983, p. 12.

2. Joseph Sobran, "Pensees: Notes for the Reactionary of Tomorrow," *National Review*, (December 31, 1985): 50.

3. Donald Bloesch, *Crumbling Foundations* (Grand Rapids, MI: Zondervan, 1984), 38.

4. Bloesch, *Crumbling Foundations*, 73.

5. G. K. Chesterton, *The Victorian Age in English Literature* (New York: Holt, 1913), 43.

6. James V. Schall, "The Altar as the Throne," in *Churches on the Wrong Road*, ed. Stanley Atkins and Theodore McConnell (Chicago: Regnery, 1986), 231-32.

7. Harry Blamires, *The Christian Mind* (Ann Arbor, MI: Servant Books, 1978), 3. Originally published, 1968.

8. Jacques Ellul, *Presence in the Kingdom* (New York: Seabury, 1967), 119. Originally published, 1948.

9. Romans 13:1; 1 Timothy 2:2.

10. Acts 5:29.

11. St. Augustine, *City of God* (Garden City, NY: Image/Doubleday, 1958).

12. Richard John Neuhaus, *The Naked Public Square* (Grand Rapids, MI: Eerdmans, 1984), 209.

13. St. Augustine, *City of God.*

14. C. S. Lewis, *The Four Loves* (New York: Harcourt, Brace, World, 1960), 41.

15. Neuhaus, *Naked Public Square*, 237.

16. Neuhaus, *Naked Public Square*, 75.

17. Lynn Buzzard and Paula Campbell, *Holy Disobedience: When Christians Must Resist the State* (Ann Arbor, MI: Servant Books, 1984), 123.

18. Daniel 1–3.

19. Paraphrase of Daniel 3:16–18.

20. Acts 4:19–20.

21. Charles Mendies in an interview with Ellen Santilli Vaughn, September 1986.

22. Daniel 1:8.

23. A. James Reichley, *Religion in American Public Life* (Washington, DC: Brookings Institute, 1986), 104.

Chapter 7

With Liberty and Justice for All?

Peter R. Gathje

Three mornings a week, as a member of the Emmanuel House Community, I join with others to welcome homeless persons to Manna House, a place of hospitality located in an inner-city neighborhood in Memphis, Tennessee. The men and women (and occasionally children) who come in for coffee, a sweet roll, a shower, and a change of clothes are among those people living in the United States to whom we need to pay attention if we are to evaluate patriotism as disciples of Jesus. For Jesus, the judgment of nations hinges upon how the most vulnerable members of a society are respected and honored in their human dignity as created in the image of God (Mt. 25:31–48). To follow Jesus means we must evaluate our lives as persons and as a nation by whether or not the hungry are fed, the thirsty are given something to drink, strangers are welcomed, the naked are clothed, the sick are cared for, and prisoners are visited.

The people I see at Manna House are among the hungry and thirsty in a country that spends $5 billion per month on an immoral war in Iraq, and where working forty hours a week at the federal minimum wage keeps a person nearly $8,000 below the poverty level. Many of them have been in prison, and many of them likely will be again as part of the two million prisoners in the United States—the highest rate of incarceration in the world. Prisons are now the second largest employer in the United States.[1] Many of those who come to Manna House are sick, suffering from physical ailments, mental illness, or addictions—none of which are adequately attended to by the limited health care available to homeless persons. Some of them are recent immigrants to the United States.

In conversations with the homeless who come through the front door of Manna House, I learned that many of them are military veterans. They are among the 200,000 veterans who, according to the Veterans Administration, are homeless on any given night.[2] Many of these veterans suffer from some form of mental illness. Yet treatment centers are few and far between. Jail often becomes the place where the mentally ill are housed.

My experience with the homeless at Manna House is a starting point for evaluating patriotism as a disciple of Jesus from the perspective of the poor. Like most Americans, I endured many years of the school ritual of reciting the Pledge of Allegiance with its rousing affirmation of "liberty and justice for all." This affirmation, of course, recalls the Preamble of the U.S. Constitution in which "we the people" pledge to "establish justice" and "secure the blessings of liberty."

The liberty and justice assumed to be inherent to life in America are often presented as reasons for patriotism and for a fervent love of and pride in this country. Such patriotism abides the criticism that liberty and justice do not extend to all. After all, the United States is a work in progress, moving sometimes slowly and at other times more rapidly toward that goal. But the experience of the poor in the United States and the following of Jesus who came to be good news to the poor (Lk. 4:18) suggest a deeper form of criticism that remembers both the realities of today and the history of this nation. This criticism finds patriotism, defined as love of country, incompatible with the practices of compassion and justice enacted by Jesus.

This criticism, informed by the history and experience of the poor in the United States, sees that the slogan "liberty and justice for all" is actually an ideological cover. From the standpoint of the poor, this nation has never been committed to liberty and justice for all. From the start, the U.S. Constitution was set up to protect the interests of a landowning, ruling class of white men.[3] Shays's Rebellion, it can legitimately be argued, scared the elite into the constitutional process. Further, the Constitution did not set forth requirements for the right to vote, and as a result at the outset of the Union only male property owners could vote. Women were not included as voters. Blacks counted as three-fifths of a person in determining political representation in the House but were also not included as voters. An appraisal of U.S. history from those on the margins—the poor and working class—must conclude that any expansion of liberty and justice in this country came through difficult and often bloody struggles with the elite yielding the minimum needed to prevent even more widespread revolt.[4]

The lack of liberty and justice for the poor continues today. Drawing from Jesus' judgment of the nations, we need to ask how those who are hungry, thirsty and lacking in basic necessities are faring in the United States. The official poverty rate in 2004 for the United States was 12.7 percent, up from 12.5 percent in 2003. In 2004, 37 million people in the United States were living in poverty, an increase of 1.1 million from 2003.[5] Of those in poverty, more than 36 million people lived in households experiencing "food insecurity," which is a fancy phrase for not knowing where your next meal is going to come from, and for the past three years the number of people experiencing "food insecurity" has risen.[6] Meanwhile, people whose income ranks in the top 10 percent continue to reap vast increases in wealth while the middle class continues to shrink. Income disparity in the United States is the worst of Western industrialized nations.[7]

Income disparity in the world has worsened as well, and at least some of this is attributable to policies and practices put into place and enforced by the United

States. In 1960 the poorest 20 percent of the world's population had 2.3 percent of the global income, and the top 20 percent of the world's population held 70.2 percent of the global income. By 1998 the poorest 20 percent of the world's population only had 1.2 percent of the global income while the top 20 percent of the world's population had 89 percent of the global income.[8] Every minute of every day, 20 children die in the world due to hunger and diseases related to poverty. Of these deaths, 90 percent occur in just 42 countries and 39 percent occur in sub-Saharan Africa.[9]

How does the United States welcome the stranger? Related to the economic disparity in the world is the rising tide of people migrating in search of better living conditions. There are more than 11 million undocumented immigrants in the United States today. In response to the rise of undocumented immigrants, legislation has been crafted that seeks to criminalize these strangers rather than welcome them. This criminalization response has been the consistent policy of the United States for several decades and represents a continuation of the nativist sentiment and policies enacted in the late nineteenth and early twentieth centuries. For example, the Chinese Exclusion Act of the late 1800s banned Chinese-born laborers from entering the country, and in what was called "Mexican Repatriation" more than 500,000 people of Mexican descent (including numerous U.S. citizens) were rounded up and deported during the Depression of the 1930s.[10]

How are the sick treated? Nearly 46 million U.S. residents have no health insurance, and the number continues to increase. Because employers increasingly move in the direction of shifting health care costs to employees, America's workers are being forced to pay higher premiums, deductibles, and co-payments or forego health insurance entirely. Additionally Medicare, the largest public health insurance program, which has more than 40 million beneficiaries in the United States, has been significantly altered by Bush administration legislation in ways that moves Medicare toward privatization. Increasingly, American health care tends to divide the population into insiders and outsiders. Insiders, who have good insurance, receive good health care. Outsiders, who have poor insurance or none at all, receive very little health care. Higher spending on insiders as medical costs rise leads the insurance industry to relegate more and more people to outsider status.[11] Of course people who are already poor suffer the most from the increasing inequities in medical care. Federal, state, and local government budget cuts over the past decade have severely hampered the capability of public hospitals to meet the medical needs of the poor and homeless.

Finally, how are prisoners treated in the United States? As indicated above, the United States leads the world with its rate of incarceration. Specifically, there are 2.1 million people behind bars in the United States and another 4.8 million on probation or parole.[12] The rise in the prison population has been caused by public policy changes that have increased the use of prison sentences as well as the length of time served. Mandatory minimum sentencing, three-strikes law, and reductions in the availability of parole or early release have resulted in higher levels of incarceration. New "super-max" prisons and the virtual elimination of rehabilitation programs contribute to the dehumanizing conditions pervasive in prisons in the United States.

The prison system reflects the economic injustice and racism endemic to American society. Prior to landing in prison, most prisoners were not employed full time or were unemployed, made less than $10,000 per year, and had a high school education or less.[13] These realities are nothing new. The United States has consistently imprisoned the poor, mentally ill, and mentally challenged.[14] The criminal justice system is also permeated by racism. According to the Justice Department, black men of all ages are incarcerated at more than seven times the rate of white men.[15] Additionally, one in six prisoners in the United States is mentally ill. These mentally ill prisoners are often the subject of mistreatment. They are victimized and exploited by other prisoners, punished by prison staff for symptoms of their illness, and are more likely to end up in isolation and enduring other forms of prison punishment.[16]

Massive military expenditures compound the failure of the United States to care for the poor, the stranger, the sick, and the imprisoned. These military expenditures represent not only preparation for and practice of the killing of other human beings but also resources that could be used for addressing the needs of the poor. For Fiscal Year 2006, the budget for military spending is $441.6 billion. This represents almost two-fifths of the total military spending in the world. Military spending by the United States is nearly seven times larger than the military budget of China, the second largest spender, and nearly twenty-nine times as large as the combined spending of the six "rogue" states of Cuba, Iran, Libya, North Korea, Sudan, and Syria, which spent $14.65 billion.[17]

Given this quick review of how the poor are faring in the United States today and given that as disciples of Jesus we must evaluate a nation, including our own, from the standpoint of the poor, the suffering, and the vulnerable, we can see that the promise of liberty and justice for all has not been kept and perhaps was never meant to be kept in the United States. As disciples of Jesus committed to being good news to the poor, we must see that any patriotism toward this nation constitutes bad news. How can we love a nation that treats the poor and the vulnerable with such disdain?

The problematic character of patriotism is further deepened if disciples of Jesus see that our liberty and justice as human beings can never be won through this or any other nation that organizes around the interests of the elite and regularly kills others in the name of liberty and justice. In contrast, faith in Jesus means that we see both liberty and justice as fruits of living in the way of Jesus, who provides a radical alternative to this and all nations—the Reign of God. Jesus provides us with a path to liberty and justice that goes through a life-giving way of love for all human beings, even our enemies. The story of Jesus' temptation in the desert is especially helpful here. In this political story, the devil showed Jesus "in an instant all the kingdoms of the world. And the devil said to him, 'To you I will give their glory and all this authority; for it has been given over to me, and I give it to anyone I please. If you, then, will worship me, it will all be yours'" (Lk. 4:6–7).

To say that the United States reflects a satanic control might not only seem an unnecessarily harsh judgment on this nation but also a kind of indelicate, simplistic view typical of backwoods preachers. And certainly this is not the only word about the state in the Bible. Romans 13:1–7 is often trotted out to provide balance so that we can feel more at ease with loyalty to our nation. After all, it is argued, Romans 13:1–7 indicates that God institutes the governing authorities and that they are God's servants.

But the differences between that passage, what precedes and what follows are telling. In Romans 12 and in Romans 13:8–14, the followers of Jesus are called to a way of life sharply in contrast to the state. Disciples of Jesus do not bear the sword for vengeance but overcome evil with good. For these disciples, "love is the fulfilling of the law." They are to "lay aside the works of darkness and put on the armor of light." They are to "put on the Lord Jesus Christ, and make no provision for the flesh to gratify its desires" (Rom. 13:10, 13:12, 13:14). Justice and freedom for the followers of Jesus come through being joined to his way of life. And if we remember both the history and current reality of the poor in relation to the United States, a harsh judgment is warranted.

But where does this leave those of us who share this judgment? What practices ought to characterize our relation to this nation other than patriotism? The temptation is either to retreat into sectarian withdrawal or to join some equally unrealistic sectarian political group. Drawing upon Paul's Letter to the Ephesians, I want to suggest some practices for following Jesus in the midst of a nation under judgment.

When Paul wrote this letter, he was in jail for engaging in activities considered disloyal or unpatriotic in relation to the empire. The people to whom Paul wrote stood in radical opposition to the Roman Empire. Their opposition was not political in the way we might typically think. But still their opposition was deeply political, because theirs was an alternative way of life that rejected imperial culture, politics, economics, and religion. In our lives today as followers of Jesus we should seek to do the same.

When Paul wrote to this small group of people, the Roman Empire was engaged in the usual business of empires—justifying massive military spending and perpetual wars in the name of national security and liberty, rewriting history to illustrate its political, economic, philosophical, and technological superiority, and using religion to assert that its way of life was divinely blessed. The parallels are easy enough to see with our situation in the United States today.

Like the small group of people to whom Paul wrote, we must be convinced that our liberty does not hinge upon military might, economic exploitation of subject peoples, or the imperial gods who bless both militarism and economic injustice. These convictions, then and now, are grounded in the life, death, and resurrection of Jesus. Jesus lived by the faith and he once said the truth would set you free. He was highly critical of a social order dependent upon the Roman Empire, its wars, and its disdain for the poor, and he showed his freedom by living in a way that welcomed the outcast, the poor, the sick, and the stranger. Jesus' way of liberty broke imperial politics by proclaiming a reign of God where the greatest would be those who served the least. His way of liberty broke imperial economics by sharing free food and by free healing, since he believed in God's economy of abundance through sharing, rather than in the imperial economy of scarcity through hoarding. And his way of liberty broke imperial religion by ignoring religious laws that divided people into pure and impure and those blessed by God and those not blessed by God.

The Romans, who had taken over Jesus' native land and then created a puppet government in the name of civilization and security (the Pax Romana), executed Jesus for his efforts. Jesus' crucifixion was supposed to help secure the Pax Romana by deterring others from entering into the way of liberty he had embodied and taught.

But like Paul and the people to whom he wrote, we need to see that this execution was not the end of Jesus and his way of liberty. Paul had had a powerful experience of Jesus being freed through the power of God from the execution the Romans had imposed. Paul had a powerful experience of liberty from the deadly power of the Roman Empire, and he had a powerful experience of liberty for the life-giving and liberating way of God.

Out of his powerful experience of liberty, Paul turned from persecuting followers of Jesus to living and teaching Jesus' way of liberty as God's way of liberty. In a letter to another of these small resistance communities, the Galatians, Paul wrote that "For freedom Christ has set us free. Stand firm, therefore, and do not submit again to a yoke of slavery" (Gal. 5:1).

Paul's experience of being free led him to embark on extensive travels and form resistance communities throughout the Roman Empire. He urged people to change their lives, to accept Jesus' way of liberty contrary to the imperial powers of the day and thus to live in resistance to those powers. Paul urged the formation of communities of prayer and mutual aid to stand in solidarity with each other and the poor. We need such communities today, and we can draw upon the example of the Catholic Worker Movement, Koinonia Farm, and others in forming and supporting these.

Moreover, Paul saw life in these faith communities as a difficult but deeply joyous and fulfilling way of liberty. And he continuously reminded such communities that, despite all appearances to the contrary, the Roman Empire would not last, but Jesus' way of liberty would endure forever. As he said in another of his letters, "When they say, 'There is peace and security,' then sudden destruction will come upon them" (1 Thess. 5:3).

For Paul and for us, liberty begins when we draw strength, vitality and life from a source greater than any nation, military might, or material wealth. Paul writes to the church in Ephesus, "Be strong in the Lord and in the strength of God's power" (Eph. 6:10). Paul saw that liberty is grounded in faith, not in fear or the desire for imperial security. Liberty, in other words, is grounded in divine liberation, not imperial domination.

Paul saw in the life of Jesus a clear demonstration of God's life-giving, loving, and liberating power. For Paul, God's power is the power of love and the power of justice, and these set us free. God's power does not reside with any one or with any nation that claims freedom comes through violent force. God's loving power, Paul wrote, empowers and frees us to love others as God has loved us. Moving far beyond the golden rule of "do unto others as you would have them do unto you," Paul gave this freedom rule: "Do unto others as God has done unto you." Just as God loves us, we are free to love others. Just as God forgives us, we are free to forgive others. Just as God welcomes us, we are free to welcome others—the hungry, the thirsty, the naked, the sick, the stranger, the imprisoned. In contrast to this liberating love graciously given to us by God, imperial security is grounded in fear, violence, and oppression.

Paul saw to the heart of a struggle in our lives—a struggle between trying to ground liberty in security and truly grounding our liberty in the giving of our lives in love. To take the risk of love, to take the risk of living for more than ourselves, and to take the risk of liberty, Paul saw that we need to be strong in the Lord and in the strength of God's power—a life-giving, loving, and liberating power—and that to enter into this risky way of freedom we need the whole armor of God (Eph. 6:13).

We need this whole armor of God, Paul states, because the world is warped by sin. We need the whole armor of God to stand against the wiles of the devil. Evil is tricky, confusing, underhanded, and seductive. It plays on our fears, our desire to secure ourselves from all harm, our pride and our desire to be invincible. Paul saw in his day an imperial spirit of evil that enslaves people even as it speaks of freedom. This imperial spirit urges a lie upon us that appeals to our fears—the lie that our liberty is won through the domination of others and enforced through violence done to others.

This imperial spirit and its lie link together fear and pride: We are the best and the brightest, so we have the right to impose our will on others—it is, after all, for their own good that our dominance is extended and protected. Paul knew that this imperial spirit and its lie are so powerful that anyone who stands up against them would be branded unrealistic, unpatriotic, and irreligious. In fact, followers of Jesus in Paul's day were often branded "atheists" because they rejected all religion that promised security through the empire and its gods. These "atheists" scoffed at the public displays of religion in government buildings, because they knew such religion was about slavery and not about serving the life-giving, loving, and liberating God.

Paul, in seeking liberty and justice, wrote of the need to resist this imperial spirit and its lie, the powers and principalities that employ fear, and the desire for security and domination; he believed that we need God's armor to protect and empower us in the struggle to live in Jesus' way of freedom. Fascinatingly, in his depiction of this armor of God, Paul subversively redescribed the imperial armor, the way Roman soldiers were outfitted for war, taking each piece of a Roman soldier's equipment and transforming it into God's alternative armor for a life of liberty. In doing this, Paul outlines for us six practices for liberty and justice that are alternatives to patriotism. Contrary to a narrow love of nation, these six practices reflect love and compassion for each and every human being as created in the image of God.

The first piece of God's alternative armor, Paul tells us, is the belt of truth (Eph. 6:14). We must fasten the belt of truth around our waists. To be truly free we cannot live by lies. Robert Penn Warren was reportedly asked once what ought to be done in response to the many problems facing American society. He responded, "Well, I think the first thing we ought to do is to stop lying to each other."

Lies and deception destroy both liberty and justice. Truth, on the other hand, is liberating. Remember that Jesus once said, "You will know the truth, and the truth will make you free" (Jn. 8:32). Paul knew that an empire is based upon lies, and he urged living by the truth. Truth means exposing deception and being honest in our relations with others. Truth requires love, mutual respect, and listening and learning from each other and from critics of other cultures and other lands.

Liberty requires vigilance for the truth that goes beyond imperial spin. Liberty requires listening to the truth that comes from the poor and the obscure corners of empires. In Paul's day truth came from a poor man living in Galilee, a Roman occupied territory in Palestine, and today truth remains with the poor. This is why I must go to places like Manna House: To find the truth in a land of lies by listening to the poor.

Truth requires the humility of accepting our humanity and so accepting our vulnerability and need for each other. Truth means dropping our self-righteousness and admitting that we and our nation are finite, fallible, and capable of evil. Truth requires repentance—that is, the work of recognizing and confessing our sins in order to change our lives and move toward just relations with each other. Being with people who are homeless, sick, imprisoned, and strangers, I begin to see my own complicity in the economic and political system that privileges a few at the expense of many. At places like Manna House I am led to repentance and to changing my life.

The next piece of God's alternative armor for a life of liberty is the breastplate of justice (Eph. 6:14). Freedom requires justice. We cannot be free by enslaving and dominating others. We cannot be free if our desire for security trumps justice. Paul knew that there was a reason all roads led to Rome. All roads led to Rome so that the world's goods could be brought cheaply to the center of the empire while impoverishing the rest of the world. Military force was required to maintain this unjust system. In Paul's day, Rome's reliance upon military force to secure its unjust accumulation of material goods had already subverted Rome's freedom. The rule of Caesar had replaced the Republic, so patriotism now meant uncritical support for Caesar, the military, and a way of life given to consumption and entertainment, bread and circuses.

In contrast, Paul urged putting on a breastplate of justice. Putting on the breastplate of justice means practicing the just sharing of the resources of God's abundant creation and resisting the seductions of wealth and over-consumption. Putting on the breastplate of justice means not being possessed by our possessions—that is, not desiring more and more possessions or fearing that our possessions are not secure. Putting on the breastplate of justice means living simply in solidarity with the poor, a life of sharing and service, and a life that seeks those changes that move our political and economic systems toward justice.

With the belt of truth and the breastplate of justice in place, the third piece of God's alternative armor of liberty are shoes—shoes that empower us to walk for peace and proclaim the gospel of peace (Eph. 6:15). When Paul wrote this letter, the Greek word that is translated "gospel" typically meant an announcement of military victory. But Paul's "gospel" is about peace rather than military victory—the peace that comes through the power of truth, love, and justice, not through military conquest and the oppression of others. Peace comes with truth and justice. Violence flourishes with lies and exploitation.

Paul was, after all, faithfully following Jesus who taught love of enemies and rejected the use of the sword even to defend himself. Paul and Jesus both knew that peace has never come through war and never will. It is one of the lies of the spirit of empires to say that this war or that war will end all wars; that this war or that war will finally rid the world of terrorism and make us secure. Paul speaks from the faith of Jesus when he says that truth and justice create peace. The way to peace is not through war; it is through the hard work of facing the truth about the vast economic inequities enforced by military and political domination. And from this truth there must come a commitment to building a just society and a just world. I must develop both an interior spirit of peace and practice nonviolent resistance to the war-making and injustices evident in the United States in both its domestic and international policies.

The fourth piece of God's alternative armor for a life of liberty is the shield of faith (Eph. 6:16). A soldier needed a shield to protect himself from flaming arrows. Under a shield, those arrows would bounce harmlessly away. Paul identifies faith as the shield that will keep away the flaming arrows that come from the imperial spirit and its way of lies and domination. If we attempt this way of freedom that requires living in the truth, living justly, and living the gospel of peace by nonviolently resisting evil, we can be sure there will be flaming arrows coming at us—arrows of ridicule accusing us of being unrealistic, arrows of patriotism accusing us of disloyalty to our nation, and arrows of an idolatrous religion accusing us of not being people of faith.

Paul's shield of faith affirms the truth that there is a loving power and purpose in our lives beyond self-interest and imperial domination. I believe Paul's shield of faith reflects the view of Dr. Martin Luther King Jr., who said that though the moral arc of the universe is long, it bends toward justice. Paul's shield of faith affirms that each human being is of infinite worth and should always be treated as a child of God and never as a thing to be used and abused. By such a faith I am empowered to see Christ in the poor, in those whose brokenness is not hidden under veneers of wealth and social respectability. By such a faith I am empowered to continue seeking transformation of injustices even as I am realistic about my own sinfulness and the ongoing power of sin in every human life and institution.

The fifth piece of God's alternative armor for a life of liberty is a helmet of salvation—of wholeness, integrity, and healing (Eph. 6:17). The Latin root of the word salvation is "salve," which means to heal, to make whole. If we are to be healed and live with integrity, our actions will have to match our words.

Our commitment to freedom will require that we work to liberate others, not dominate them. Our commitment to truth will require humility and even a sense of humor. Our commitment to justice will require rejecting self-righteousness. Our commitment to peace will require that we not demonize our enemies. We will need to be persons who recognize our own need for healing as we seek the healing of others. We will need to practice a compassion that suffers with those who suffer and in doing so allow ourselves to feel our own vulnerability and need for healing.

The final piece of God's alternative armor for a life of liberty is the sword of the Spirit, which is the word of God (Eph. 6:17). And this brings us full circle: Paul began with the strength of God's power, and he ends with God's word. God's word enters into history to redeem history. God's word enters into human life to restore us from our brokenness. God's word says that the way things are, are not the way things have to be. God's word proclaims that we are not bound to repeat over and over again the mistakes and wrongdoing so evident in human history and in our lives. God's word is thus the word of true liberty and justice. So I will need to pray and meditate daily on God's word in order to let God's loving and liberating presence inform and shape who I am and what I do.

In these six practices drawn from Paul, we enter into a way to liberty and justice that is not the imperial way of war, economic domination and exploitation, or religiously inspired hatred. This is a way to freedom that does not confuse freedom with security. This is a way of freedom that is risky and exciting and filled with a joy that is deeper than any suffering that might come in pursuing this way of freedom. This way of freedom emphasizes the need for a justice that stands in solidarity with the poor and seeks their liberation knowing that none of us can be truly free as long as others are in chains. The faith of Jesus, the way of freedom and justice, calls us to love the poor rather than a nation that proclaims liberty and justice but practices enslavement and oppression. With this faith, patriotism falls away.

Notes

1. For a Christian theological analysis of the prison system in the United States, see Mark Lewis Taylor, *The Executed God: The Way of the Cross in Lockdown America* (Minneapolis, MN: Fortress, 2001).

2. National Coalition for Homeless Veterans, http://www.nchv.org/background.cfm.

3. The classic analysis of the U.S. Constitution along these lines is by Charles Beard, *An Economic Interpretation of the Constitution*, (New York: Macmillan, 1937). For a more contemporary analysis, see Robert A. McGuire, "Economic Interests and the Adoption of the United States Constitution," Economic History Services, http://eh .net/encyclopedia/article/mcguire.constitution.us.economic.interests (accessed April 26, 2006).

4. Howard Zinn, *A People's History of the United States* (New York: Harper Perennial, 2003).

5. U.S. Census Bureau, http://www.census.gov/hhes/www/poverty/poverty.html.

6. "World Hunger Facts," http://www.elca.org/hunger/facts/facts.html#united-states.

7. Michael Forster and Mark Pearson, "Income Distribution and Poverty in the OECD Area: Trends and Driving Forces," *OECD Economic Studies* 34, 2002/I, http://www.oecd.org/dataoecd/16/33/2968109.pdf., accessed April 25, 2006.

8. "Growing Global Disparity (UNDP)—The Trickle Up Economy," http://poorcity.richcity.org/entundp.htm.

9. Global Health Council, "Child Health," http://www.globalhealth.org/view_top.php3?id=226.

10. "Understanding Anti-Immigrant Movements," http://www.afsc.org/immigrants-rights/learn/anti-immigrant.htm.

11. Paul Krugman and Robin Wells, "The Health Care Crisis and What to Do About It," *New York Review of Books* 51, no. 5 (March 23, 2006), http://www.nybooks.com/articles/18802.

12. "U.S. prison, parole population sets record: One in 32 Americans in jail or on parole in 2003," July 26, 2004, *MSNBC.com*, http://www.msnbc.msn.com/id/5517618/.

13. Matthew B. Robinson, *Justice Blind? Ideals and Realities of American Criminal Justice* (Upper Saddle River, NJ: Prentice Hall, 2002), 306.

14. David Rothman, *The Discovery of the Asylum*, (Boston: Little Brown, 1971).

15. Marc Mauer, *Race to Incarcerate*, (New York: New Press, 1999).

16. "Ill-Equipped: U.S. Prisons and Offenders with Mental Illness," Human Rights Watch, http://www.hrw.org/reports/2003/usa1003/.

17. http://www.globalissues.org/Geopolitics/ArmsTrade/Spending.asp.

Chapter 8

A Distinctively Catholic Patriotism?

Christine Firer Hinze

The United States, a traditionally Christian nation, is today confronted with a troubling reality: the growing presence and influence of believers adhering to a foreign religious sect whose worldview and creed put them at odds with the fundamental tenets of freedom, religious toleration, and human rights on which this country is founded. Followers of this sect, many of them recent immigrants, give their fealty to a faith and form of religious leadership that arrogates to itself the trappings of a competing theocratic government. Despite members' claims to civic loyalty, their faith's official tenets unabashedly contend that their religious law supersedes and in fact ought to dictate the law of states and governments. The influx into the United States of members of this foreign sect thus is creating a growing pool of antipatriots in our midst. Should these antipatriots gain majority political power or influence, they would not hesitate to install the theocratic rule that their religion teaches is the norm and ideal.

To twenty-first-century U.S. ears, the above statement may sound like the ill-informed rhetoric frequently employed against Muslims in the days following September 11, 2001. In fact, it captures a viewpoint historically prevalent in official and popular attitudes toward American Catholics whose aftereffects linger to this day.[1] From the earliest days of the republic, Catholics have been suspected of harboring fealty to a foreign, authoritarian power whose rule precluded them from genuinely loyal U.S. citizenship. Like its contemporary anti-Muslim counterparts, anti-Catholic polemic in the nineteenth and twentieth centuries sprang from and fed on the fears of a majority citizenry confronted with the presence of a community growing in size and influence and regarded as different, inscrutable, unassimilable, and threatening. In both Catholic and recent Muslim cases, the truth about the religious beliefs that have prompted the polemic is complex and generally misunderstood, even by many adherents. And within both the Muslim and Catholic communities one finds a variety of responses to the question of how to be loyal U.S. citizens while remaining true to deeply held religious convictions that ultimately supersede civic commitments.

Is there a distinctively Roman Catholic approach to patriotism? What, in particular, characterizes U.S. Catholic patriotism for the twenty-first century? To address these questions, we must first take a brief look at Catholic Christianity's historical approach to loyalty to one's country. Second, we need to explore how particular Catholic experiences in America have affected U.S. Catholic understandings and expressions of patriotism. These forays into Catholic, then American Catholic, tradition and experience will help us consider the contours of a contemporary U.S. Catholic approach to patriotism. Of course, given the vast historical sweep and enormous diversity that mark two millennia of Catholic Christianity and four and a half centuries of American Catholic history, we undertake this exploration with great modesty. The best this short essay can hope to accomplish is a bird's-eye view of terrain encompassed by the subjects of patriotism and Catholicism with particular attention to the United States.

Our investigation will show that Catholics in the United States have enacted the relationship between their religious and national identities and loyalties in complex ways. A strong sense of national identity has motivated U.S. Catholics to emphasize the compatibility between being Catholic and being American. Yet their Catholic identity has precluded any simple, uncritical embrace of all that being American may comprise. These two identities, Catholic and American, substantially overlap but remain in real tension. The patriotism required of Catholics is thus both affirmative and critical and prohibits either blind obedience to the state or withdrawal from civic participation. U.S. Catholics have addressed the matter of civic loyalty in diverse ways, but these varying expressions have been marked by a devotion to advancing a communitarian and personalist vision of justice and the common good, grounded in ecclesiastically-mediated religious commitments to God and service of neighbor. Catholic citizens should speak up, contribute, and act wherever human dignity and the common good are in jeopardy and wherever they are being protected and advanced—all the while doing so from a capacious perspective that places national interest and well-being within the larger arc of a universal justice and multi-textured common good in which every human being is meant to share.[2] This, I will contend, describes the heart of a distinctly Catholic understanding of *amor pro patria*, love of one's country, in the American setting.

Christianity and Civic Loyalty

Christianity's scriptures, creeds, prayers, and moral practices center on the worship of God as revealed in the person, life, death, and destiny of a first-century Palestinian Jew, Jesus of Nazareth. Jesus bequeathed to his followers the radically theocentric orientation of his Jewish faith. The first commandment, "I am the Lord your God. . .you shall have no other gods before me" (Ex. 20:2–3), enshrined a bedrock truth for Jews that was reinforced in worship, law, and daily life. Jews, and Christians after them, embraced a covenantal relation with a God who commanded their ultimate and unswerving loyalty and forbade them from making an object of ultimate loyalty anything other than God. Jesus' teaching affirmed that the greatest commandment is that of utter loyalty to God: "Love the Lord your God with all your heart, with all your soul, and with all your mind" (Mt. 22:37). By anchoring their loyalty in One who transcends any earthly kingdom, power, or concern, the Jewish and Christian traditions, as the later Muslim tradition does, reject any form of patriotism that supplants God by requiring unconditional fealty. By definition this places Christians in a double-edged relationship with the civic polity and state. On the one hand, Christian scriptures and tradition include affirmations of loyalty and obedience to the state (e.g. Rom. 13:1–4, 13:7), as well as statements that suggest a distinction but no necessary conflict between "rendering to Caesar and rendering to God" (Mt. 22:21). On the other hand, when conflicts have occurred, Christians' unquestioned priority of religious over political loyalty has compelled them to affirm that "we must obey God rather than human beings" (Acts 5:29), and in the extreme, to relegate secular governments to the "powers and principalities" under God's condemnatory judgment (Rev. 13)

The history of Christianity in various epochs and cultures has been punctuated by this inherent and varyingly explicit tension between civic and religious loyalties. When their dual loyalties have clashed, Christians who have chosen "God rather than human beings" have become the objects of governmental scrutiny, suspicion, oppression, or even martyrdom. At other times, these loyalties have been framed as compatible, and Christians have found themselves assimilated into, or comprising, the powerful majority.[3] The history of Christianity also reveals an array of strategies for holding allegiance to God together with beneficent forms of civic participation and commitment. In the third century, the *Letter to Diognetus* speaks of the obedient and beneficent presence of Christians in all countries and cities yet also of their transcendence of narrow national loyalties.[4] In the middle ages, the doctrine of the "two swords" articulated by Pope Gelasius I (492–496 CE) laid the groundwork for the freedom of the church from secular dominion and underscored the dual loyalties expected of Christians.[5] In the post-Reformation period, the tension between civic and religious loyalties was frequently resolved in a different direction with the separation of church and state becoming a hallmark of Western liberalism.

Within this grand Christian narrative, Western Catholic approaches to patriotism have had their own distinctive grammar and syntax. Roman Catholicism's highly visible, hierarchical and institutionalized church organization, the close relationship obtained between the powers of church and state from the Constantinian to the Reformation eras, the progressive dissolution of the temporal power of the Roman church in the modern period, and Catholics' encounters with the Enlightenment and Protestant religious sensibilities that shaped the United States both in its origins and subsequent history—all of these have contributed to the particular ways that Catholics, including U.S. Catholics, have apprehended what love and loyalty to country might mean.

Roman Catholicism, *Pietas*, and *Patria*

"Patriotism" understood as identification with a secular nation-state and its people is a modern Western phenomenon. But love of and devotion to one's country—understood as encompassing a homeland, a heritage passed on by one's ancestors, and a people—has a lineage traceable to ancient times. Classical Greeks and Romans, and later Western thinkers indebted to them, counted devotion to country as a primary form of the virtue of *pietas*, or dutifulness. *Pietas pro patria*, rooted in respectful gratitude and expressed in obedience and service to one's country, was one mark of the just person and good citizen.

In the pre-Constantinian era, Christianity's status as a minority religious movement within the Roman Empire, whose members refused to engage in acts of political fealty they deemed idolatrous, put believers at odds with the ruling powers, often at the cost of their lives.[6] Writings recounting the deaths of Christian martyrs frequently highlighted their subjects' refusal to offer sacrifices to state gods, to serve in the military, or to pay obeisance to a divinized emperor and reject the lordship of Christ, even in the face of the most grisly torture and execution. Besides directing its members' loyalties elsewhere, Christianity also inculcated a sense of community of all humankind. Thus Tertullian's *Apology* (197 CE) could insist that "Nothing is more foreign to us [Christians] than the state (*res publica*), for there is only one state that we recognize and that consists of the entire world."[7] Writings such as the *Letter to Diognetus*, (ca. 200 CE) and Augustine's *City of God* (413–426 CE), exemplify efforts of learned Christians to convince ruling powers that the presence of this God-fearing sect in their midst was not a threat but indeed a blessing to the civic community.

From the Edict of Milan and the installation of Christianity as the official religion of the Empire by Constantine in 313 CE forward, *pietas* toward one's country and its rulers was promoted by the Catholic Church. In a classic scholastic presentation, St. Thomas Aquinas (1221–1274), drawing on Aristotle, described *pietas* as a virtue connected to justice. Aquinas identified three primary forms of *pietas*, each of which reflect and accord with human nature: *pietas* toward God, one's parents, and one's country. These different sorts of dutifulness obligated one in descending order of priority. *Pietas* toward one's country encompassed respectful obedience toward its rulers who, following Romans 13, were regarded to have derived their authority from God. Rulers and subjects alike were subject to God and to the revelation of God's will discoverable by reason in the natural law. Rulers who failed to legislate according to divine and natural law were still owed *pietas* by virtue of their office but would be under divine judgment. With its strong emphasis on social order and an organically unified and hierarchical society in which all had their pre-ordained place, medieval political thought underscored the fact that *pietas* was owed even a bad ruler and left little room for revolution by subjects. Yet by affirming the shared accountability of citizens and governors to God and to the dictates of the natural law, Catholic understandings of love of country provided grounds for condemning tyranny and for taking to task rulers who failed to serve the common good and their subjects. Devotion to country and rulers was therefore relativized in relation to the larger orders of natural, moral, and divine law.[8]

Approbation for patriotism in this sense of *pietas* remained the steady teaching of the church during the post-Reformation period that stretched from the Council of Trent (1545–1563) to Vatican II (1962–1965) and thereafter. Writing about patriotism in the late 1930s, for instance, the American Jesuit Stephen Brown described it as *amor patriae*, love of country. Love of one's country, he explained, encompasses homeland, people, and ancestors, as well as love for the "spiritual elements" that are the "natural heritage" of a nation. These latter include the nation's culture, its languages and literature, its artistic, technical and civic achievements, its shared historical memories, and its religion. Natural affection for and sense of identification with one's country grounds a Catholic understanding of patriotism as respect for rightful authorities, commitment to civic duty, and willingness to sacrifice for the common good.[9]

But the countervailing resistance to unquestioned fealty to the state or conformity to the times also remained and was in some ways accentuated. The Catholic Church was by no means the beneficiary of the waves of religious, political, and cultural revolution that swept Europe from the seventeenth century forward. Indeed, as modernity's anti-authoritarian, secularist, and anticlerical champions, Roman Catholicism became the symbolic embodiment of all things antimodern. For its part, the institutional church's reaction to Enlightenment and modern developments did little to assuage its critics. The rise of nationalism, liberal democracies, and the modern secular nation state were regarded with deep suspicion by the post-Reformation church. Religion's exclusion from status or influence in the secular state represented a sharp departure from Catholicism's traditionally powerful position in church-state relations and it was a change that Catholic officialdom resisted. Until the Second Vatican Council, official Catholic teaching continued to insist that in the ideal state the "one true Roman Catholic Church" would be the privileged state religion. As for patriotism, Catholic teaching during this period maintained its emphasis on civic loyalty and support for existing governments but accentuated its requirement that believers hold church and religious law in first place. Catholic citizens were also enjoined to promote political arrangements that, at minimum, allowed the church to freely and fully carry out its mission or that, optimally, publicly acknowledged religion—more specifically, Catholicism—and its spiritual superiority distinct from all temporal powers.[10]

Popes in the nineteenth and early twentieth centuries explicitly condemned "modernism" and its support for a fully secularized state as well as the secularized versions of freedom of conscience and freedom of religion they perceived as dominating the European, and to some extent the American, scene. Influenced by this official vantage point, Catholic forms of civic engagement between the two Vatican councils (1870–1963), especially in Europe, had in common "their sense of critical distance from the dominant culture; their specifically Catholic inspiration;. . .and their understanding of Catholicism as an alternative culture with its own vision of society and politics. Catholics, unlike many others, did not take separation [from dominant culture] and pluralism as final: they intended neither to withdraw into a counter culture nor to live in peaceful coexistence with others, but ultimately to restore a more integrated society, a new Christendom."[11]

Pope Leo XIII's 1885 *Immortale Dei* repeated Pius IX's condemnations of modern secular states but also supported pluralism in purely political matters, extolled a properly-oriented patriotism, and urged Catholics to participate in all facets of the political order, seeking to turn the methods of government, "so far as is possible, to the genuine and true public good, and to use their best endeavors at the same time to infuse, as it were, into all the veins of the State the healthy sap and blood of Christian wisdom and virtue."[12] Leo XIII also inaugurated the era of modern Catholic social teaching with his 1891 encyclical *Rerum Novarum*. Pius X in 1909 praised *amor patriae*.[13] The rise of Nazi socialism in the 1930s prompted Pius XI in *Mit Brennender Sorge* to sound the contrasting Catholic theme of a higher loyalty, reminding his German audience that no state, nation, or leader could legitimately aggrandize citizens' ultimate or absolute loyalty. Similarly, in the cold war era Pius XII castigated communist governments for demanding total loyalty to a godless state under the guise of patriotism.[14]

The short papacy of John XXIII (1958–1963) and the ecumenical council he called, Vatican II (1962–1965), marked a watershed shift in the posture of the Catholic church toward modernity and modern political systems. In treating political community and related topics both John XXIII and Vatican II's *Gaudium et Spes* brought forward the two-pronged Catholic understanding of patriotism as loyalty to country and government for the sake of a genuine common good, grounded and limited by prior fundamental loyalty to natural moral law and divine revelation. But it did so with a new receptivity to many of the hallmarks of modern democracy that popes during the preceding century had regarded with deep suspicion or outright condemnation.[15]

In the post-conciliar era, particularly during the papacy of John Paul II (1979–2005), these teachings on Catholics and patriotism continued to be echoed with two notable recent emphases. First and most significantly is the development of the notion of "solidarity" as a framework for contemporary understandings of Christian social participation. A theme in *Gaudium et Spes* that was self-consciously advanced by Pope John Paul II, solidarity denotes both the fact of human interdependence and the normative response this interdependence requires.[16] When such interdependence becomes recognized, the proper "correlative response as a moral and social attitude, as a 'virtue,' is solidarity. This is not a feeling of vague compassion or shallow distress at the misfortunes of so many people, both near and far. . .but rather a firm and persevering determination to commit oneself to the common good. . .to the good of all and of each individual."[17] Pope John Paul's social writings from the late 1980s underscore the fact that solidarity comprises a special preference for the poor and vulnerable. In particular, Christians and the church are called to take their stand beside the poor—"to become a church of and for the poor…while keeping in mind the common good." Ultimately, solidarity is a religious virtue and the "social face of Christian charity."[18] Solidarity, the late pontiff argued forcefully, is the primary antidote to and weapon for confronting and dismantling sinful social structures and patterns that undermine the well-being and survival of so many today. Patriotism understood from within the framework of solidarity funds a love of country that is infused with a commitment to the common good, which transcends national boundaries.

Second, some recent teaching concerning political engagement has been marked by a cautionary emphasis on the need for Catholics to detect and combat elements of moral and religious relativism and irreligious secularism in their particular political and social circumstances. In 2003, a papally-sanctioned document issued by Cardinal Joseph Ratzinger's Congregation for the Doctrine of the Faith, "Doctrinal Note on Some Questions Regarding the Participation of Catholics in Political Life," reflected the support for democratic forms of polity found in *Gaudium et Spes* but also echoed Leo XIII's *Immortale Dei* in stressing that "If Christians must recognize the legitimacy of differing points of view about the organization of worldly affairs, they are also called to reject, as injurious to democratic life, a conception of pluralism that reflects moral relativism. Democracy must be based on the true and solid foundation of non-negotiable ethical principles, which are the underpinning of life in society."[19]

American Catholics and Patriotism

The peculiarly American mix of Protestant culture and Enlightenment-influenced political sensibilities that arose in the English colonies of the New World during the colonial and revolutionary eras—retaining its influence since—decisively shaped U.S. Catholics' experience and expression of their political allegiances. From the eighteenth century to the present, questions about the compatibility of Catholic and American loyalties have been raised on both cultural and political grounds. Catholics' adherence to a hierarchical institution with an international structure and foreign "headquarters" whose pre-Vatican II teachings explicitly opposed liberal conceptions of freedom, conscience, religion, rights and politics and made their growing presence a persistent thorn in the sides of many non-Catholic observers. Nineteenth- and early twentieth-century arrivals of huge numbers of immigrant Catholics heightened fears that the growing political and economic influence of Catholics endangered American culture and values, and a general, frequently explicit, climate of anti-Catholicism prevailed. In the face of this, Church leaders and ordinary believers felt, on the one hand, pressed to demonstrate their patriotism as "one-hundred percent Americans," and on the other hand, a protective pride in their distinct religious-institutional and ethnic-cultural identities. One visible symbol of this dual pull common to this day was the prominent placement in local Catholic church sanctuaries of two flags, side by side—the gold and white papal flag and the American flag. The second half of the twentieth century saw an increasing acceptance of Catholics into mainstream middle-class culture and politics—particularly white, economically-mobile. The election of John F. Kennedy to the presidency in 1960 symbolized this progress; but the fact that Kennedy encountered pressure to waylay public fears concerning potential conflicts between his Catholic faith and his ability to fulfill governmental duties, as did Supreme Court Chief Justice nominee John Roberts in 2005, confirms that the dual pull between Catholic and American identities continues to be felt.[20]

The complicated historical relationship between their religious and political identities has educed two primary responses from U.S. Catholics. On the one hand, a dominant, compatibilist tradition has emphasized the harmony between being American and being Catholic. A contrasting, nonaccommodationist tradition has accentuated the differences and conflicts between American and Catholic identities. This nonaccommodationist viewpoint has led Catholics at various historical points down more radical paths.

Catholic Compatibilism

The compatibilist claim has been a recurring *leitmotif* in the history of Catholicism in America. From the late eighteenth century into the twentieth, David O'Brien notes, American Catholics "never ceased telling Rome and native Protestants that Catholic religious teachings and American political and social beliefs complemented each other perfectly. 'To understand the Catholic Church in America,' wrote the church's leading historian in 1926, 'one must see how naturally and integrally the spiritual allegiance of its members knits into the national allegiance so as to round each other out.'"[21]

American Catholics' burgeoning numbers and institutional visibility—by the civil war, Catholicism had become the single largest U.S. denomination, and by the late nineteenth century Catholicism was "by far the largest. . .denomination. . .and well-institutionalized from coast to coast"—coupled with their different religious and ethnic-cultural ways made them liable to be viewed as threatening to the non-Catholic majority. But in the United States, unlike in some parts of Catholic Europe, "the idea of an integral Catholic society and culture as a future possibility lay beyond the imagination of almost all Catholics."[22] The American Catholic church accepted, in practice, certain tenets of liberalism: the separation of church and state; pluralism in which a claim to be "the church" was considered a religious affirmation, not tethered to any conspiracy to establish Catholicism as the state religion; and, most of the time, the civic obligation to present Catholic claims in terms intelligible to a non-Catholic public.[23] During this period, church leaders like Archbishop John Ireland of St. Paul, Minnesota and Cardinal James Gibbons of Baltimore were vocal official representatives of this Catholic American view. [24] In different ways before and after the 1960s and the second Vatican Council, this position has been associated with interpretations of Thomism that highlight Catholicism's active embrace and participation in what is true and valuable in its cultural and political context.[25]

U.S. bishops and other Catholic church officials, "anxious not to arouse anti-Catholic passions," have historically tended to restrict their political activism to matters of explicit church interests,[26] and on other issues to favor what Bryan Hehir calls an "educational cultural" approach to civic engagement.[27] This strategy is geared toward forming Catholic consciences and making persuasive, reasoned arguments in the public arena. It is a form of engagement modeled consistently by official Catholic social teaching from both the Vatican and the U.S. bishops. Modern Catholic social teaching, spanning from Leo XIII to the present, sounds a set of themes pivoting around the God-given, socially-realized, personal dignity of every human being, themes that frame an understanding of patriotism as civic participation on behalf of a substantively envisioned common good.[28] The practice of the U.S. bishops since 1976 of publishing a guide for Catholic voters entitled "Faithful Citizenship" as well as their public process of drafting and issuing major pastoral letters on peace and on the economy in 1983 and 1986 are illustrative of the efforts of U.S. church leadership since Vatican II to educate and form the Catholic populace in principles, sensibilities, and political implications of their church's social teaching.[29] Yet, as O'Brien points out, its inevitably broad and general messages, acceptance of a wide variety of interpretations and responses (or lack thereof), and failure to enact coordinated pastoral and societal strategies have allowed this U.S. Catholic civic style to gain wide public exposure at the expense of a united front of Catholic voters or activism on particular political issues.[30]

On the grassroots level, a more effective form of compatibilism was enacted by Catholics who threw themselves into American political life via interest group type organizing that frequently revolved around immigrant and ethnic communities.[31] Distinct from and complementing the more idealist, teaching-oriented approach to civic engagement modeled by U.S. bishops and scholars, this second posture evinced a realist, populist activism.[32] Gaining its momentum from appeals to a strong and defined group identity whose makeup combined ethnic, cultural, spiritual and institutional elements, this style of being Catholic and American has traded on Catholics' sense of existing as an outsider group fighting for its voice and rights within the U.S. political and social scene. Later nineteenth- and twentieth-century working-class Catholics' strong identification with the Democratic party, their participation in machine politics in cities like New York, Chicago, and Boston, their prominent role in labor union organizing and in support of social programs associated with the New Deal,[33] Hispanic Catholic involvement in Cesar Chavez's United Farm Worker movement, and Catholic grassroots activism and political lobbying on behalf of legislation concerning "life issues" such as abortion, euthanasia, and capital punishment—all these are examples of politically engaged Catholic American citizens. Strong on participation but more prone to thinking and acting with interest groups rather than for the common good, this style of civic engagement has been the most characteristic form of Catholic activism up through the latter part of the twentieth century.[34]

Catholic Nonaccommodationism

A more countercultural form of civic participation by Catholics emerged most distinctly in the 1930s. In contrast to compatibilist efforts to communicate in public, nonsectarian terms, this radical evangelical style of Catholic engagement has attempted more directly to translate church teaching into personal commitment and political activism. In the 1930s, Dorothy Day and the Catholic Worker Movement refused tax-exempt status and embraced a radically pacifist stance. Virgil Michel and John Hanley Furfey called for Catholics to work toward a liturgically-grounded Eucharistic society that would be explicitly permeated with Catholic piety.[35] In the 1960s and thereafter, the nonaccommodationist stance was expressed in the antiwar civil disobedience of the Berrigans, in the pacifism of Pax Christi, and in resistance to liberal notions of rights and privacy by some Catholic pro-life activists.[36]

Dorothy Day and the pacifist, anarchist Catholic Worker Movement have epitomized this sort of Catholic radicalism. Significantly, Catholic Worker actions of public resistance against government war-making efforts or other forms of state-sponsored violence are presented in terms of love of country. As Day once put it, "We love our country and are only saddened to see its great virtues matched by equally great faults. We are part of it, we are responsible too." While resorting to civil disobedience of laws they judge unjust, Catholic Workers are explicit in their support for just laws and those who enforce them: "We bend over backward to show our respect for and desire for the common good, which most laws are for."[37]

Still, radical Catholic nonaccommodationists are crystal clear about their opposition to what they regard as the anti-Christian aspects of American society, politics, and economy. This opposition has led some, like Catholic Worker and theologian Michael Baxter, to hold suspect the very identification of "American." Writing soon after the terrorist attacks of September 11, 2001, he explained: "My resistance to the usage 'we Americans' comes from my conviction that in times like these it is important for Christians to identify themselves first and foremost as Christians, coupled with the fact that all too often in times such as these Christians fail to do so." Baxter contends that "This rejection of Christian identity on the part of Christians rarely occurs overtly or explicitly. Rather, Christian identity is simply merged into American identity, as if they are perfectly harmonious, as if there is absolutely no conflict between them. And thus Christianity gets subordinated to the aims and purposes of the state."[38]

The contrast between this view and that of Catholic compatibilists is plain. Catholic nonaccommodationists often draw but do not fear charges of civic disloyalty. But most, like Dorothy Day, continue to see their actions as reflecting loyalty to ideals and values that their country, at its best, ought to embody.

Hybrid Stances

There have also been hybrids of these two responses across the history of U.S. Catholicism. In the cold war era, Catholics who joined in obviously patriotic anticommunist activities found themselves in a more culture-resistant position of combating trends toward secularism in schools and society. In the post-Vatican II era, U.S. Catholics working for nuclear disarmament, racial justice, or the repeal of abortion laws have frequently contended that they do so for patriotic as well as religious and moral reasons. America, they argue, will not be living up to its own authentic identity, promises, and ideals until the changes they are advocating occur. And official teachings that affirm the legitimacy of both nonaccommodationist and compatibilist forms of engagement have encouraged the coexistence of both styles in places where Catholics gather. On many Catholic college campuses, for instance, both ROTC students in military uniform and Catholic Workers protesting the presence of ROTC programs are common sights.

Amid their differences, characteristic Catholic understandings of civic life are discernable in all the stripes of social engagement. John Coleman describes a certain drift or "tilt" to Catholic approaches to civic engagement, a leaning that expresses a fruitful affirmation and tension between Catholicism and overarching framework of U.S. civic thought and practice. Optimally, Catholics' social teaching and tradition marks their civic involvement with this particular slant expressed in what Coleman calls several distinctive "biases": a rejection of untrammeled capitalism and liberalism (though also of communistic socialism); a bias toward social rather than political revolution; a bias toward a pluralist, multi-associational view of society coupled with a more recent embrace of the merits of democratic polity; and a bias toward social and economic as well as individual rights.[39]

U.S. Catholic Patriotism in the Twenty-First Century

In Catholic discussions of what it means to be a patriot in post-9/11, twenty-first-century America and how faith shapes understandings of civic devotion or loyalty, one can detect contemporary versions of the compatibilist and nonaccommodationist strands that have woven their way throughout the U.S. Catholic story.[40] In her 2006 study, moral theologian Kristin Heyer uses the terms "public" and "prophetic" to identify the two major positions on Catholicism and U.S. citizenship that we have called compatibilitist and nonaccommodationist.[41] Advocates of public Catholicism focus on Catholics' capacity and obligation to be critically engaged in civic life, participating in mainstream avenues for involvement that include voting, participation in voluntary civic associations, support for political parties and lobbying efforts, military service, and so forth. All of these are considered legitimate avenues for promoting and protecting the common good of U.S. society, something that Catholics have an obligation to do. Public Catholic patriots may be of liberal or conservative political or economic stripes. Public Catholics are neither jingoistic nor gullible; they are enjoined by their leaders and scholars to a critical engagement that reflects the moral and divine law's prior claim. But those in this camp embrace U.S. political institutions and many of its cultural and social values as basically sound and salutary.

"Prophetic" Catholics are contemporary heirs to the nonaccommodationist aspect of Catholic teachings on state and civic loyalty. These citizens share the conviction that attachment to gospel values entails a suspicious, at times separatist, stance toward U.S. cultural values and political institutions and practices. For prophetic Catholics, patriotism is a problematic concept to the degree that it implies unmitigated acceptance of national identity, values, and policies. Rather than feeling at home, such Catholics experience themselves as "resident aliens" in any political order.[42] Catholics like Baxter and Day have been convinced that Christian discipleship places one on the margins of mainstream U.S. culture. From this vantage point, prophetic Catholics can see societal flaws more clearly and nurture communities that witness to an alternative, Gospel-inspired way of living.

Is it possible to be a "prophetic Catholic patriot"? Or is the prophetic stance antithetical to the sort of civic *pietas* that the Catholic tradition has historically upheld? Theologian Tracey Rowland attempts to address this question by way of the Augustinian tradition of the "two cities." True Christians whose allegiance is to the City of God do not remove themselves from the worldly political order nor do they seek to destroy it. Instead, Augustine argues, these authentic Christians are a salutary force within the *polis*. When the political order is corrupt or led astray by vice or evil, however, Christians are bound to withdraw or resist. In the contemporary United States, prophetic Catholics regard American culture and institutions with an eye sensitized to corruption and misdirection. *Pietas* or loyalty toward one's country is likely to be understood as a duty to protest corruption and error and to witness to a better way.

As with public Catholicism, prophetic Catholicism takes different forms. One divergence is between social transformationists and social separatists. Over the past forty years, varieties of liberationist theology and practice (feminist and womanist, black and Hispanic, and others) have proffered radical criticism of social ills infused with a culturally and institutionally transformative hope and intent.[43] While clear-eyed about the depth of the disease in culture, *polis*, and economy, these "radical transformationists" hold forth hope for and the obligation to struggle toward structural changes that will lead to a better approximation of the just world they envision. Other prominent representatives of the radicalist prophetic tradition hold up less hope for social transformation and focus instead on faithful witness in a fallen world. Prophetic Catholics in this group do not fit in; they are not skilled or savvy political strategists, and they refuse to conform to "this world." While locally engaged in works of mercy and witness, they neither expect nor aspire to a structurally transformed social order.

How ought Catholics adhering to these varying positions enact their religious convictions *vis-à-vis* the public square? Bryan Hehir argues that cultural education, policy reform, and radical styles each make particular contributions and that each one should remain in dialectical relation with the other two. Alternatively, Kristin Heyer argues that what is needed is a critical correlation of the prophetic and public strands in Catholic approaches to civic obligation. I concur with Heyer and further suggest that a fruitful avenue for twenty-first-century

U.S. Catholic patriotism is a strategy that catches up the transformationist impulses of Bryan Hehir's first two models but weds them to a radical social critique and vision of a renovated social order compatible with the gospel-based norms of justice and love that animate modern Catholic social teaching. Unless sufficiently radical, Catholic civic loyalty is too vulnerable to acquiescence in the status quo. Absent a practical transformationist thrust, Catholic civic critique is in danger of succumbing to an ultimately anti-Catholic despair or rejection of the public realm. A radical transformationist approach would seek to bring prophetic witness into dialectical solidarity with reformist policy initiatives; to hone a nuanced public discourse overtly anchored in and accountable to the gospel; and to insert Christians into secular society to serve their neighbors in response to and as witnesses of the love of Jesus Christ.[44]

The current challenge for Catholic citizens in the United States—a context complicated by war, terrorism, globalization, and glaring disparities between rich and poor—is the problem of crafting a patriotism that is accountable to the compatibilities and tensions between their religious and national allegiances. Catholics who swerve to unquestioning national loyalty will err in one direction; those who fail to see that their tradition compels them into active civic participation and service will err in the other. An authentic Catholic patriotism will be represented in a range of energized forms of engagement in the great debates, concerns and needs that surround the emerging common good of local, national, and global communities.

Is there a distinctively Catholic patriotism? One would more accurately speak of Catholic forms of patriotism. *Amor pro patria* for contemporary Catholics will be expressed in varied ways, all sharing an embodied appreciation for country in its land, peoples, cultures, history, and heritage; a moral commitment to advance the common good of local community, nation, and world; and an encompassing religious and ecclesial loyalty that provides the perspective from which to sift the wheat from the chaff in the laws and practices of the land, and to discern the appropriate forms of their obligations and duties to serve their neighbor and the common good.

At its best, Catholic Americans' civic participation will exhibit a passionate commitment to upholding the dignity of each human person realized in community. Their patriotism will be grounded in and counterweighted by faith commitments that are prior to and relativize commitments to nation or state. Love of country as a particular form of neighbor love will preclude any patriotism that divides the world into "us" against "them." Finally, patriotism as an expression of the virtue of justice will be framed by the post-Vatican II Catholic vision of solidarity: a factual interdependence among fellow citizens—local, national, and global—that calls for generous, serving responses that can never be limited to the pursuit of local or national self-interest.[45] Displaying these characteristics in new circumstances, patriotic U.S. Catholics will continue to find themselves in the dynamic, now supportive, now critical relationship to American values and practices that has been their heritage from the start.

Notes

1. Mark Massa, *Catholics and American Culture: Fulton Sheen, Dorothy Day, and the Notre Dame Football Team* (New York: Crossroad, 1999), describes Robert Blanshard's *American Freedom and Catholic Power* (Boston: Beacon, 1949) as "arguably the classic twentieth-century American statement of 'progressive' fears of Catholic authoritarianism." Blanshard wrote: "Unfortunately the Catholic people of the United States are not citizens but *subjects* in their own religious commonwealth. The secular as well as the religious policies of their Church are made in Rome by an organization that is alien in spirit and control. . . . They are compelled by the very nature of their Church's authoritarian structure to accept nonreligious as well as religious policies that have been imposed on them from abroad." For a glimpse at popular and organized legislative forms of anti-Catholicism as illustrated in the public school battles in Oregon in 1922, see "Catholic Patriotism on Trial: The Oregon School Case," http://libraries.cua .edu/achrcua/OSC/welcome.htm. Sharp claims about anti-Catholicism on the U.S. left are leveled by Philip Jenkins, *The New Anti-Catholicism: The Last Acceptable Prejudice* (New York: Oxford University Press, 2003).
2. The term "common good," which appears repeatedly in this essay, is a central concept in Catholic social thought, denoting "the sum total of those conditions of social living whereby persons are enabled more fully and more readily to achieve their own perfection." Pope John XXIII, *Mater et Magistra*, no. 65; David O'Brien and Thomas A. Shannon, eds., *Catholic Social Thought: The Documentary Heritage* (Maryknoll, NY: Orbis, 1996). Essential to personal well-being but not reducible to the sum of individual interests, the political common good is a substantive set of conditions and resources in which all members share and to which all are to contribute. This political notion of the good is grounded theologically in humanity's shared participation in and bonds with God—the ultimate "common good" on whom all depend, and in whom all are connected.
3. Early Christian martyrs, for example, often met their fates for refusal to serve in the military or to pay obeisance to emperors or state gods. Fealty to the Christian gospel motivated the withdrawal from civic participation by the Schleitheim Brethren and other radical reformers and has continued to ground the pacifism and eschewal of political office of the modern "peace churches." Conversely, one finds strong identification between Christian and civic loyalties espoused, in very different forms, in the fifth-century writings of Eusebius, in sixteenth-century Geneva under the leadership of John Calvin, and in the writings of Catholic Americanists of the nineteenth and twentieth centuries.
4. Chapter 6 of *The Letter to Diognetus* includes this point: "They dwell in their own countries, but simply as sojourners. As citizens, they share in all things with others, and yet endure all things as if foreigners. Every foreign land is to them as their native country, and every land of their birth as a land of strangers. They marry, as do all [others]; they beget children; but they do not destroy their offspring. They have a common table, but not a common bed. They are in the flesh, but they do not live after the flesh. They pass their days on earth, but they are citizens of heaven. They obey the prescribed laws, and at the same time surpass the laws by their lives." This famous letter is quoted in both *Gaudium et Spes* and the *Catechism of the Catholic Church*.
5. Lester L. Field Jr., *Liberty, Dominion, and the Two Swords: The Origins of Western Political Theology* (Notre Dame, IN: University of Notre Dame Press, 1997), 180–398.

6. John Hegeland, Robert J. Daly, and J. Patout Burns, eds., *Christians and the Military: The Early Experience* (Philadelphia: Fortress, 1985); Lisa Sowle Cahill, *Love Your Enemies: Discipleship, Pacifism, and Just War Theory* (Minneapolis, MN: Fortress, 1994).

7. Tertullian quoted in John A. Coleman, "Catholics and International Life," 234. Bringing Tertullian's sentiment into the present U.S. scene, Coleman argues that "American Catholicism's major contribution to international life [has] consisted in providing some vivid symbols of belonging to and having bonds with an international community." Cahill, *Love Your Enemies*, notes that Tertullian is typical of early Western Fathers in that he is a "pacifist but not a separatist," who "supports the legitimate and necessary function of the state and its rulers" and "does not discourage Christian participation [though he all but rules out military service and perhaps, public office] to the extent that idolatry, killing, and other immorality can be avoided" (48).

8. Thomas Aquinas, *Summa Theologiae*, 2a 2ae Q. 101.

9. Stephen Brown, "What Is Patriotism?" *Catholic World* 10, no. 10 (November 1939): 169.

10. Pope Leo XIII, *Immortale Dei*, nos. 11–13, 33.

11. David J. O'Brien, "A History of Christian Political Action: A Catholic Experience," *The Catholic Church, Morality, and Politics: Readings in Moral Theology*, 12th ed., ed. Charles E. Curran and Leslie Griffin (New York: Paulist, 2001), 83.

12. Pope Leo XIII, *Immortale Dei*, no 45; see also nos. 4, 44, and 88 on political pluralism; and nos. 23–27, 30–31 on the errors of the modern secular state.

13. Pius X, in an address to French pilgrims on April 19, 1909, stated that "if Catholicism were the enemy of the country, it would no longer be a divine religion. . . . Yes, it is worthy not only of love but of predilection, that country (*patrie*) whose sacred name awakens in your mind the most cherished memories and makes quiver every fiber of your soul, that common country which has cradled you, to which you are bound by bonds of blood and by still nobler bonds of affection and tradition" (cited and translated in Brown, "What Is Patriotism?" 168).

14. Pius XI, *Mit Brennender Sorge*: "Whoever exalts race, or the people, or the State, or a particular form of State, or the depositories of power, or any other fundamental value of the human community—however necessary and honorable be their function in worldly things—whoever raises these notions above their standard value and divinizes them to an idolatrous level, distorts and perverts an order of the world planned and created by God; he is far from the true faith in God and from the concept of life which that faith upholds" (no. 8). No. 11 is also helpful here: "None but superficial minds could stumble into concepts of a national God, of a national religion; or attempt to lock within the frontiers of a single people, within the narrow limits of a single race, God, the Creator of the universe, King and Legislator of all nations before whose immensity they are 'as a drop of a bucket'" (Isa. 11:15). See also Pope Pius XI, *Ad Apostolorum Principis*: "The Church exhorts and encourages Catholics to love their country with sincere and strong love, to give due obedience in accord with natural and positive divine law to those who hold public office, to give them active and ready assistance for the promotion of those undertakings by which their native land can in peace and order daily achieve greater prosperity and further true development" (no. 21). However, "those who control the state, cannot exact obedience when they would be usurping God's rights or forcing Christians either to act at variance with their religious duties or to sever themselves from the unity of the Church and its lawful hierarchy" (no. 23). "Under such circumstances, every Christian should cast aside all doubt and calmly and firmly repeat. . . .' We must obey God rather than men.'" (no. 24).

15. *Gaudium et Spes*, nos. 74 and 75, in O'Brien and Shannon, *Catholic Social Thought*. Pope Pius XI's Christmas addresses in the 1940s show growing support for Western democratic governance. See John Langan, "Commentary on the Christmas Messages of Pius XII (1939–1945)," in *Modern Catholic Social Teaching: Commentaries and Interpretations*, ed. Kenneth R. Himes, 181–85 (Washington, DC: Georgetown University Press, 2005). See also J. Bryan Hehir, "Catholicism and Democracy," in *Change in Official Catholic Moral Teachings: Readings in Moral Theology, No. 13*, ed. Charles E. Curran, 20–37 (New York: Paulist, 2003).

16. Pope John Paul II, *Sollicitudo Rei Socialis*, nos. 37–38, in O'Brien and Shannon, *Catholic Social Thought*. The theme of solidarity in *Gaudium et Spes* and thereafter is analyzed in Christine Firer Hinze, "Straining Toward Solidarity in a Suffering World: *Gaudium et Spes* 'Forty Years After,'" in *Vatican II: Forty Years Later*, ed. William Madges (Maryknoll, NY: Orbis, 2006).

17. *Sollicitudo Rei Socialis*, no. 39. Consistent with Catholic social thought's appreciation for subsidiarity within a multi-associational communal life, solidarity's expansive sweep is understood to be grounded in concrete bonds with neighbors in local and civil society. David Hollenbach, *The Common Good and Christian Ethics* (Cambridge: Cambridge University Press, 2002), thus contends that "Civil society, not the state, is the primary locus in which human solidarity is realized. . . . [C]ivil society is the soil in which the seeds of human sociality grow. When communities are small or of intermediate size, they enable persons to come together in ways that can be vividly experienced. The bonds of communal solidarity formed in them enable persons to act together, empowering them to shape some of the contours of public life and its social institutions such as the state and the economy" (102).

18. *Sollicitudo Rei Socialis*, no. 40.

19. See footnote 15 in Cardinal Joseph Ratzinger, Congregation for the Doctrine of the Faith, "Doctrinal Note on Some Questions Regarding the Participation of Catholics in Political Life," http://www.catholicnewsagency.com/document.php?n=3.

20. Both Kennedy and Roberts assuaged concerns about their capacity for office by emphasizing that their Catholicism would have no direct impact on their political or legal judgments or actions. As we will see, this places them in one, but by no means the only, stream of Catholic interpretations of the relation between faith and national allegiance.

21. David J. O'Brien, *American Catholics and Social Reform: The New Deal Years* (New York: Oxford University Press, 1968), 214–15, cites Peter Guilday, "The Catholic Church in the United States," *Thought* 1 (June 1926): 7.

22. O'Brien, "A History," 83. U.S. Catholics were not restorationists but neither did they fully imbibe "that deep commitment to the common good of one's own people which was the foundation of the more constructive activism of European Christian Democratic parties."

23. O'Brien, "A History," 83–84.

24. See, for example, J. T. Ellis, "Gibbons, James." *New Catholic Encyclopedia* 6, 2nd ed. (Detroit: Gale, 2003), 204–7; and J. P. Shannon, "Ireland, John," *New Catholic Encyclopedia* 7, pp. 549–52.

25. The works of David Hollenbach, Bryan Hehir, and the U.S. Bishops Conference are examples of this approach. See Kristin E. Heyer, *Prophetic and Public: The Social Witness of U.S. Catholicism* (Washington, DC: Georgetown University Press, 2006); and Tracey Rowland, *Culture and the Thomist Tradition after Vatican II* (New York: Routledge, 2003).

26. O'Brien, "A History," 84.

27. Hehir describes "educational-cultural," "legislative-reform," and "prophetic-witness" models of U.S. Catholic civic engagement in "The Right and Competence of the Church in the American Case," in *One Hundred Years of Catholic Social Thought*, ed. John A. Coleman, 66–69 (Maryknoll, NY: Orbis, 1991).

28. Fleshing out its centerpiece affirmation of the personal dignity of each human being, substantive themes of modern Catholic social thought include a communitarian anthropology that affirms human realization as both personal and social; solidarity as both a fact and a norm; a preferential option for the poor and vulnerable; vocal support for the dignity of work and rights of workers; a focus on family as the basic cell of society and seedbed of faith; a thick notion of justice as commutative, distributive, and social; a multi-associational view of society that leads to a critical stance toward both untrammeled liberal capitalism and consumerism, and communistic socialism; and concerns with environmental responsibility.

29. See U.S. Catholic Bishops, "The Challenge of Peace," and "Economic Justice for All," in O'Brien and Shannon, *Catholic Social Thought*, 492–680; U.S. Conference of Catholic Bishops, "Faithful Citizenship: A Catholic Call to Political Responsibility," issued September 2003, http://www.usccb.org/faithfulcitizenship/bishopStatement.html.

30. David J. O'Brien, *Public Catholicism*, 2nd ed. (Maryknoll, NY: Orbis, 1996), xi. Coleman, *One Hundred Years*, writes of "the failure of this tradition to propose workable alternative institutions and ideals," and warns that "[i]n actual fact, in the absence of alternative models of institutional implementation, social Catholicism will embrace the status quo" (39). The failure of most U.S. Catholics in 2003 to heed the public objections to the United States engaging in preemptive war on Iraq raised by both Pope John Paul II and the U.S. bishops provides a recent example of the limits of this educational-cultural style.

31. O'Brien, *Public Catholicism*, xi. Marvin Mich's *Catholic Social Teaching and Movements* (Mystic, CT: Twenty-Third Publications, 1998) focuses on the interaction between official Catholic social teaching and particular social movements with special attention to the United States in the twentieth century.

32. O'Brien, "A History," 85.

33. Another legislative reform model of Catholic civic engagement can be found in some activities of the U.S. Bishops Conference, especially between 1919–1945 in the work of the Social Action Department under the direction of Msgr. John A. Ryan of the Catholic University of America; and in the ongoing lobbying efforts of the present day U.S. Conference of Catholic Bishops. See O'Brien, *Public Catholicism*, 137–51; and Charles E. Curran, *American Catholic Social Ethics: Twentieth-Century Approaches* (Notre Dame, IN: University of Notre Dame, 1982).

34. O'Brien, "A History," 85.

35. Dorothy Day, Virgil Michel and John Hanley Furfey are discussed in Curran, *American Catholic Social Ethics*.

36. See Patrick W. Carey, ed., *American Catholic Religious Thought: The Shaping of a Theological and Social Tradition* (New York: Paulist, 1987), 124–26. Carey also summarizes Catholic activism and struggles around concerns of African-Americans, Hispanic-Americans and women between 1965–1990 (128–34).

37. Dorothy Day quoted in Massa, *Catholics and American Culture*, 104.

38. Michael Baxter, "After September 11, 2001, What Should We, As Catholics, Do? Patriotism and Pacifism," *Houston Catholic Worker* 21, no. 6 (November 2001).

39. John Coleman, "Neither Socialist Nor Liberal," in Coleman, ed., *One Hundred Years*, 32–35.

40. Compare, for example, Baxter's "After September 11" with Jospeph A. Varacalli, "Catholicism and Democracy," *Homiletic and Pastoral Review* (May 2002): 26–30.

41. See Kristin Heyer, "Bridging the Divide in Contemporary U.S. Catholic Social Ethics," *Theological Studies* 66, no. 2 (June 2005): 401–40; and *Prophetic and Public*. Heyer analyzes the writings of J. Bryan Hehir and Michael Baxter as contemporary representatives, respectively, of public and prophetic U.S. Catholic political postures.

42. This term is used by United Methodist theologian Stanley Hauerwas who is a prominent representative of an "evangelical" or "prophetic-witness" vision of Christians' relation to the *polis*. Hauerwas and his work have influenced Baxter and other like-minded Catholics. See, for example, Stanley Hauerwas and William Willimon, *Resident Aliens: Life in the Christian Colony* (Nashville: Abingdon, 1989).

43. Over the past four decades, liberationist theologies have emerged within communities of oppressed and marginalized believers (the poor, women, racial-ethnic minorities), first in Latin America and subsequently around the globe. Liberationists approach theology as reflection on Christian *praxis* oriented by the perspective of the poor and oppressed, and regard social critique and transformative action as intrinsic elements of Christian faith and practice. See, for example, Gustavo Gutierrez, *A Theology of Liberation* (Maryknoll, NY: Orbis, 1971). On North American liberationist theologies, see M. Shawn Copeland, "Black, Hispanic/Latino, and Native American Theologies," and Rebecca S. Chopp, "Feminist and Womanist Theologies," in *The Modern Theologians: An Introduction to Christian Theology in the Twentieth Century*, rev. ed., ed. David F. Ford, chaps. 19 and 20 (Cambridge, MA: Blackwell, 1997).

44. Heyer, "Bridging the Divide," 439–40; and Christine Firer Hinze, "Response to Michael J. Baxter," *Proceedings of the Catholic Theological Society of America* 59 (2004): 42–49.

Chapter 9

Is Patriotism a Virtue?

Robert W. Jenson

A lisdair McIntyre famously insisted that we must always ask about a presumed virtue, whose virtue is this? Virtues are specific to human communities and associations, so to understand a virtue you have to ask what group honors it.[1] To be sure, a community fully in tune with its own construal of reality would not think to pose such a question about its own typifying virtues. But in the case of America,[2] which is not now well in tune with itself, and in the case of the presumed virtue of patriotism we have to ask. When we do, the answer is not far to seek: when we invoke patriotism in any plausible sense of the notion, we pull from our grab bag of virtues one that belonged to the old Romans.[3] It is the Roman sense of *patria* and *virtus* that must provide such force as the notion of a virtue, "patriotism," may still have for us.

Republican Roman patriotism was in its own terms a splendid thing. Even St. Augustine, who saw such utter difference between God's city, with its virtues, and all polities of this world, with their virtues, harbored a nostalgic admiration for it. But can patriotism be a Christian virtue? That is the question that the title of this volume suggests I should first undertake. Following consideration of that question, we must—in apparently backward fashion—ask whether patriotism can truly be a virtue for anyone.

I

So much can be firmly established: the Roman virtue cannot be a specifically Christian virtue; it could at most be a virtue Christians should cultivate under circumstances not directly given with their faith. According to the most splendid and succinct evocation of the Roman virtue, patriots are those who find it "sweet and fitting, to die for the *patria*."[4] *Patria* is usually translated "fatherland," but this may be misleading; it was not so much a piece of Italian territory for which old Romans found it sweet to die as the fathering political entity enabled by possession of that territory, the *res publica,* "our shared public thing."[5] And this happy willingness to die for something like a city or nation must indeed be an essential mark of any characteristic that might reasonably have the same name as the old Roman quality.

We must be clear: willing acceptance of death for a *res publica* is not an option for the patriot; it defines the virtue he or she claims. Approval of or liking for one's polity or culture is not necessarily patriotism no matter how vehement. My own decided preference for living in the United States and within its polity and society rather than in other countries I have inhabited and indeed for living in the very city where I write this is not patriotism. My utter contempt for Europeans who trade in anti-Americanism is not patriotism. Those who "support our troops" may or may not be patriots. Nationalists may or may not be patriots and vice versa. Indeed, those under no immediate deadly threat on account of a *res publica* should be very cautious in speaking of patriotism at all—as I will try to be here. The patriot is one who stands in the gate of the beleaguered city or at the border of the threatened empire, finding it sweet to die rather than be the one to admit the enemy. "I regret that I have but one life to give for my country" was indeed the archetypical utterance of American patriotism, just as the public schools used to teach.[6]

For Christians, however, the only violent death that can be sweet and regretted, like Nathan Hale's, is martyrdom. This is death solely for testimony to Christ, not for Rome or the United States. One can die sweetly and in a way fitting to one's own integrity[7] only, in Paul Tillich's phrase, for one's "ultimate concern." For the old Romans, Rome was their ultimate concern along with their gods, and all images of Rome and its life. But no polity of this world can be the ultimate concern of Christians. It is exactly this relativizing of all earthly *patria, in fact,* that has throughout history brought many Christians to martyrdom, their appropriate sweet death.

To be sure, there is one polity for which Christians can and do die sweetly: the church. This claim is not in conflict with what has just been said. According to the New Testament, the church is the body of Christ himself, and since dying is a matter of bodies, the distinction between Christ as the head and the church as the body is not relevant at this point. Thus any who die for Christ die for the church die for Christ. One must, of course, note that this equivalence must be carefully defined. It is the one catholic church of the creeds, and not, for example, the Presbyterian or Lutheran church, or American church or for which martyrdom may be right. At the end of this essay we will come back to martyrdom and the church.

So far, this is straightforward, as it was for the church's first centuries. But in the fourth century a complication appeared. The locally dominant worldly polity reversed its policy and called—indeed entreated—the church to emerge from hiding and join in combating a crisis of morale. Then the church had to face questions posed by this unexpected new relation to the world. When the emperor professed Christ and the empire supplied incense for the churches rather than demand incense for itself, Rome or New Rome could no longer be seen in simple antithesis to the church. What responsibility did the church have to such polities?

The question arose in many contexts. To our present point, the majority church came to think that under some circumstances Christians could rightly serve in arms for a relatively beneficent polity and so accept dying—and killing—for it. Facing death in the armed service of a Rome that no longer persecuted Christ could not be sweet for Christians,[8] but it might sometimes be necessary within God's providence for this world, insofar as mandated by God, and insofar as it is praiseworthy also among Christians.

Was this decision of the ancient majority church correct? Theologians whom I honor and whose thought otherwise runs close to mine[9] are emphatic that it was not correct. And of course a consistent pacifism will no more countenance dying for the *patria* than it will countenance killing for it. When I am with these friends or read most of their writings I wish I could agree. But I am unable to evade the banal logic of the majority church's position. Christians are indeed no longer "of" the world, but they are still "in" it; and that means they are in a world pervaded by violence, in which God's work to restrain that violence is itself—by the massive testimony of Scripture[10]—sometimes violent. A Christian must indeed be pacifist in his own cause, but can hardly be so in the cause of his neighbors in the world. Suppose the robbers had been still beating their victim when the "good Samaritan" came along? I know this question is a clichéd cheap shot, but it nevertheless demands answer.

I know also that "two kingdoms" and "just war" doctrines and the like generate antinomies but so do attempts to work out pacifist principles in this world.[11] If the neighbors under threat constitute a polity other than the church, a polity to which I too belong, it seems I may be called to face others' and my own death in its cause. It may be asked why it should not be the "enemy" polity for which I should be willing to face death, since this too is a collection of my neighbors. The consistent answer is that this may sometimes be the case; "just war theory" is in part an attempt to sort out the cases. Sometimes I may be called to defend my neighbor by risking death for his and my worldly polity, by withdrawing from its summons, or by passive resistance to my worldly polity's unjust violence or by actively fighting against it, as did some European resistance movements of World War II.

So I have to agree with the ancient church's decision. But what then? Can such derived—even rather grudging—willingness to die for a worldly polity reasonably be called "patriotism"? Or indeed be regarded as a virtue at all? Perhaps Christians must say to those who are our fellow citizens in some other polity than the church, "This is the most we can offer, and you must judge what to call it."

II

We now need to consider the notion of virtue itself. We will say you have the virtue of, for example, courage if we know that in the past you have responded to danger with the kind of action we call courageous and if we think we have reason to suppose you will continue to do so in future—that is, if we think we can rely on you to perform courageous acts. Thus a virtue is a quality displayed by a life taken as a diachronic whole. Two specifications must be noted.

The first specification: If we think we can rely on—to stay in the same general range of behaviors—your cowardly action and that you have diachronically the quality of cowardice, we will not call that a virtue. This refusal cannot be accounted for by a calculus of benefits, since in some situations the rest of us might very well benefit from relying on your cowardly behavior, as indeed you yourself might. Thus it seems that a virtue must be constituted in cultivation of what in premodern theory was called "a good," a substantial goal of action that obtains somehow beyond calculations of benefit.

Let me propose a definition of virtue: virtues are qualities of character that establish dramatic continuity in lives moving to a good, which subsists independently of anyone's actual possession of or desire for the relevant virtue.[12] This notion of virtue, I suggest, rests on a metaphysical assumption: to live a human life is to be subject to a teleology that obtains independently of the actions that do or do not approach to it. If there is no God or substitute for Him, the notion of virtue is a delusion.

The adjective "dramatic" is, I think, needed. How is a life morally diachronic, or how does it hang together morally? Surely not by sameness; the idea that someone's actions are easily predictable because they are repetitive is commonly regarded as diminishing to their moral character. Indeed, how do we judge that two successive actions of one person are both "courageous"? If they have been done in very different contexts, neutral description may very well report, for example, that in one case Horatius stepped toward the threat and in another case retreated from it, and moral judgment may then say that both showed his virtue of courage. A personal life hangs together the same way a dramatic narrative hangs together.

The second specification: A life does not make a diachronic whole until it is over. Thus the attribution of a virtue is a very special sort of proposition. The judgment that someone is courageous is always provisional and thus different from the way in which empirical judgments are generally open to correction. We may rightly judge we should rely on Horatius's courageous action, but until he has finally gone down bravely this reliance involves accepting a risk. Indeed, if there is no risk involved in relying on someone's persisting in a certain kind of action, that pattern of persistence is not a virtue but simply a trait. Thus to vary the instance, the judgment that someone is intelligent is a different kind of judgment than that he is reasonable. If someone is intelligent, she will be that way come what may and willingly or not,[13] whereas someone we judge reasonable may yet let us down without necessarily ceasing to be herself.[14] This is why reasonableness is a virtue and intelligence is not.

III

So what would a Christian virtue be? It would be a quality of character that establishes continuity in a life being moved toward the Kingdom of God.

Millennia of reflection have been devoted to this matter, circling around a standard biblical list of specifically Christian—in scholastic language "theological"—virtues: faith, hope and love. If the Spirit is drawing us toward the Kingdom, faith, hope and love will establish continuity in our lives, at least as God sees us. If, again at least in God's view, these characteristics do not so structure our lives, we are not moving to the Kingdom. We do not find patriotism on this list nor anything related to it.

Traditional teaching recognized also basic virtues that while not specific to Christianity are nevertheless bound to be cultivated by Christians as by others: prudence, temperance, fortitude, and justice. We do not find patriotism on this second list either. But we should note that—presuming pacifism is not an option—these virtues between them will under certain circumstances produce the same actions as patriotism.

Here, a further consideration may be relevant. Faith, hope and love would be virtues even if we and our world were not fallen. According to Martin Luther's exegesis of Genesis 1–3, it was in order to give humankind opportunity to practice these very virtues that God picked one tree in the garden and prohibited its use. They were thus given the possibility of trusting this word from God, hoping in its promise of life, and loving the one who gave them such opportunity. Humankind was not and is not begun in the perfection for which it is intended; God placed the tree and spoke his word in order to give humankind opportunity to practice virtue and eventually be brought *to* perfection. Thus, trust in God and hope in his promise were needed also before the fall and would have been needed in a continuing unfallen world while love is the very perfection intended. But although justice—or at least what Scripture means by justice— would seem to be such a supralapsarian virtue, temperance, fortitude and prudence are needed only if there is the sort of temptation posed in a fallen world. Therefore, patriotism too could be a virtue only in a fallen, violent world.

From another angle, we have again arrived at the judgment: happy willingness to die for a *patria* of this world is not a virtue appropriate for Christians directly because they are Christians. If anyone wishes to regard as a virtue the "patriotism," which certain circumstances of life in this fallen world sometimes compel Christians to practice, they may do so.

IV

So what is the good for which, in a fallen world, patriots find it sweet to die and for which Christians may sometimes find it mandated to die? The Romans called it the *patria*. What is that? And indeed, does such a good really obtain at all? Which is to say, is there really a possible virtue of patriotism? Were the Romans on to anything real?

In *The City of God*, Augustine turned the tables on the Romans and their patriotism by citing two of their own great authorities in matters political. He quotes Cicero citing Scipio. There can be, said Cicero-Scipio, a true *res publica* only where there is mutual commitment to the rule of agreed upon law; there can be such a community of law only where there is an antecedent community in virtue, and there can be such community in virtue only where there is shared desire for some good. Very fine, said Augustine. But what, he then asked, are the goods available to fund community in this way? Biblical faith says there are only two sorts of goods—the Creator and the created goods.

No community of this fallen world can be united by desire for the Creator, since rejection of the Creator is precisely what constitutes this world as fallen. Thus Rome, Athens and the United States can only hang together by desire for some created good or set of created goods. But whereas the Creator is good for all, created goods are particular; none are in themselves *common* goods. Therefore, argued Augustine, the good around which a community of this world unites fills this role only precariously for its particularity makes it simultaneously a temptation to individual rather than shared appropriation. Only the Creator is intrinsically a common good; *per contra*, every good around which a polity of this world may unite is by its particularity inevitably a temptation also to disunity or the political form of self-love: the *libido dominandi*, desire for dominance. Thus the chief good in pursuit of which Romans were bound together was the "glory" of Rome. But what about when getting glory for Rome became a way of getting glory for oneself, as in Augustine's diagnosis it was likely sooner or later to do and in fact had done? What about when the returning victor's triumph was considered "his," even perhaps over other Romans? What about when Caesar's pursuit of glory for Rome carried him across the Rubicon?

It follows from Scipio-Cicero's analysis that a *patria* does not subsist as itself a good—for which one might find it fitting or mandated to die—except as it is a commonality bound and enabled by some good that it desires. If there is no vision then there is no *patria*. And it follows from Augustine's deployment of the difference between Creator and creatures that all goods around which a polity of this world may unite are treacherous in that role. Thus it seems that a *patria* subsists only as an inwardly endangered—indeed evanescent—entity. Is our nation now a *patria*? We cannot assume it; it often appears that there is no longer anything of the sort in place.

Is then sweet willingness to die for so unreliable an entity a virtue? Earlier I said that we would have to leave it to others to say whether Christians' conditional willingness to die for some polity of this world deserved the label. Now it appears that patriotism is in any case an intrinsically uncertain virtue. Some characteristics are clearly virtues in a quite straightforward sense. It is perhaps a matter merely of honorific usage whether or not we put patriotism under one label with them.

And therewith a remarkable reversal appears. For it follows from Augustine's further analysis that while the *patriae* of this world are unreliable goods and the patriotism of this world are often a self-defeating virtue, there is a *patria* that is reliably a good and therefore a "patriotism" that is reliably a virtue. For the good around which the church is gathered is the Creator himself, the one good who is ineluctably common to all and whose desirability cannot occasion the *libido dominandi*.[15] The polity that is the church is the one polity within which patriotism is reliably a virtue, because only in the church is dying for the community's uniting good always sweet and fitting.

Notes

1. Even if there should turn out to be virtues universally acknowledged and practiced, this would only prove that humankind somehow makes one community. On the practicalities of this, the drafting and acceptance of the United Nations' "Universal Declaration of Human Rights" is instructive. As a chief drafter, Jacques Maritain recounted afterward that it was relatively easy to draw up a list of human rights so long as one did not ask why the things on the list were, in fact, rights; as soon as one did ask, sessions became acrimonious. But it would be precisely in asking that question that virtue discourse would appear.
2. Or any polity of the late modern West.
3. That a grab bag of variously inherited virtues is all the late modern West has is the contention that made McIntyre famous the second time.
4. Horace, *Satires*, bk. III, ii: *Dulce et decorum est pro patria mori*.
5. We should note that recent German enthusiasm for the *Vaterland* was a qualitatively different matter.
6. And whether Nathan Hale actually said it.
7. Perhaps the best translation of *decorum*.
8. Though it must be supposed that the last Christian emperor in the East, Constantine XI Paleologus, and those who fell with him on the walls of dying Constantinople in foredoomed defense of Christendom's capital from the *jihad* that was devouring the Eastern church thought they died as martyrs.
9. Most notably, Stanley Hauerwas.
10. Some theologians' confident assertion that you cannot fight violence with violence is remarkably lacking in evidence and oblivious to the actual biblical account of God's work.
11. For a blatant instance, see Stanley Hauerwas and Frank Lentricchia, eds., *Dissent from the Homeland: Essays after September 11* (Durham, NC: Duke University Press, 2003).
12. The standard framework of this definition I have adapted from one whose original form and source I have simply forgotten.
13. Barring, obviously, neurological injury. Even an intelligent schizophrenic or depressive remains intelligent, sometimes fiendishly so.
14. Supposing that other elements of continuity seem sufficient to warrant the judgment of identity.
15. This assertion may seem to be contradicted by church history. But on closer inspection of each apparent instance of *libido dominandi* in the name of God, it will be seen, that some manifest idol has been making mischief.

Chapter 10

Can Pacifists Be Patriots?

Keith Graber Miller

Just eight days after September 11, 2001, our local newspaper, *The Goshen News*, carried a critical letter by a Goshenite responding to an earlier letter written by my friend Albert J. Meyer, former head of the Mennonite Board of Education. "Al," the critic wrote, "if you think serving tea and crumpets in your den to Moammar Gadhafi, Yasser Arafat, and Osama bin Laden would bring lasting peace from terrorism, you go for it. I think it's been proven that diplomacy with these people has not been real effective!" In his closing paragraph, the critic stated that "if some people. . .want to hold discussions on world peace or sew quilts or what not for the cause," they should realize that they can do so only because the United States, unlike Iraq and Afghanistan, treasures freedom of speech. "But understand," he concluded, "that you're in the great minority of Americans."[1]

A week later the *News* carried a banner headline that proclaimed, "Dissenting Voices Not Welcome in a Flag-Waving Chorus across America."[2] Two days after that, the newspaper ran a letter penned by Don Rhude, a military captain disenchanted with pacifists. "If this group," Rhude wrote, "truly believes that their message of 'love and neighborly compassion' is the correct answer, then they need to go as a group to Afghanistan and place their bodies in harm's way to deliver that message to the people who caused the spiral [of violence] in the first place."[3] And then, in early October, Indiana state representative John Ulmer published his own tome in the *News*. "Let's look at this situation seriously, folks," he pleaded. "The pacifists and the media experts are in way over their heads. . . . I am sorry to have to break it to the pacifists: War is not pretty. In order to maintain the pretty parts of life, we sometimes need to get ugly. It is just a fact. All the liberal rhetoric in the world will not save us from 25,000 strategically positioned human time bombs, all aimed straight at the United States, all under the finger of Osama bin Laden."[4]

In the opening months of the War on Terror, these four local critiques of Mennonites and other pacifists were echoed in numerous national publications. One of the most vehement critiques was from Michael Kelly, editor of the *Atlantic Monthly*. Kelly, never one to shy away from using volatile language, labeled pacifist American war critics as "evil" and "objectively pro-terrorist," adding that opponents of the war "are on the side of future mass murderers of Americans."[5]

In all of these cases, and hundreds more like them, the message was transparent: In the world in which we live, pacifism is not only irrelevant, it's also antithetical to good citizenship. Go ahead and sew your quilts, march for peace, hold your teas, but the rest of us are going to take the action required to end terror and protect our nation. We're going to drive those evildoers into the ground.

Mennonites, of course, were not alone in calling for a reasoned, multilateral, peaceful response in the aftermath of September 11, 2001. Nor were we surprised by the marginalization and delegitimation that most peacemakers experienced shortly after September 11, 2001. If we were surprised, that is likely because we had become too comfortable in Middle America and too forgetful of our peace heritage. At the outset of every war fought in U.S. history we have found ourselves on the margins of society, pushed there because we have been "traitors" to the national cause. In this post-9/11 age, we are on the margins once again.

Mennonites and "the Sword"

Contemporary Mennonites and related groups trace their faith origins to the sixteenth-century Anabaptists (rebaptizers) who were part of what became known as the "left wing" of the Protestant Reformation. The Anabaptists largely agreed with the Reformers but believed they were not going far enough on some issues. Of central importance to the early Anabaptists (to whom contemporary Mennonites, Hutterites, and Amish trace their ancestry) was the autonomy of the church from the state in matters of worship and religious practice and voluntary baptism based on an adult commitment to follow in the way of Christ. Most importantly, the Anabaptists were concerned about separating Christians from the "worldly" realm of secular government and distancing themselves from the use of "the sword."[6]

The earliest Anabaptist confession of faith, usually known as *The Schleitheim Confession* (1527), addresses the question of the sword—"whether a Christian may or should use the sword against the wicked for the protection and defense of the good, or for the sake of love"—in the sixth of its seven articles on which the Swiss Anabaptists were united. The answer, according to the confession, is "unanimously revealed: Christ teaches and commands us to learn from Him. . . . For He Himself says: 'Whoever would come after me, let him deny himself and take up his cross and follow me.'" The confession further described the sword as "an ordering of God outside the perfection of Christ" and forbade the use of the sword in churchly affairs. It also discouraged Christians from passing sentences in disputes about worldly matters and argued that "it does not befit a Christian to be a magistrate: the rule of the government is according to the flesh, that of Christians according to the spirit."[7]

Just over a decade later, Menno Simons, after whom Mennonites are named, drew a similar conclusion about the use of the sword noting in an allusion to Romans 13 that "the civil sword we leave to those to whom it is committed."[8] In another treatise later that same year (1539), Simons wrote:

> [W]e seek, desire, teach, and preach that all magistrates, emperors, kings, dukes, counts, barons, mayors, knights, junkers, and burgomasters may be so taught and trained by the Spirit and Word of God that they may sincerely seek, honor, fear, and serve Christ Jesus, the true head of all lords and potentates; so that they may rightly administer and prosecute their office and use the sword given them of God in His fear and in brotherly love to the praise of God, to the protection of the good, and to the punishment of the evil according to the Word of God (Rom. 13:3; I Pet. 2:13) as did the dear men of God, such as Moses, Joshua, David, Ezekiel, Josiah, and others.[9]

Most sixteenth-century Anabaptists recognized the theological legitimacy of and necessity for the state's use of occasional coercive force in the exercise of its duties; that was partly why most Anabaptist leaders discouraged their followers from becoming magistrates. In the words of the confession, the sword is "an ordering of God. . .and the secular rulers are established to wield the same."[10] Anabaptists also believed that, given the lordship of Christ and the divine requirement that magistrates "rightly administer and prosecute their office. . .in brotherly love to the praise of God," they should speak to and challenge governing authorities, calling them to live up to their own highest ideals.[11]

While few sixteenth-century Anabaptists served in the civil government, they publicly communicated their opposition or praise to princes and rulers. Menno Simons, for instance, frequently referred to governing authorities in his voluminous writings and in 1552 wrote "A Pathetic Supplication to All Magistrates" requesting kinder treatment of Anabaptists and urging the "noble sirs" to repent and serve God by doing justice and following the way of Christ.[12] Other Anabaptists also spoke radically about both the government and the economic system, and magistrates came to believe that, because of their "seditious" ramblings about the poor and their refusal to cooperate with those wielding governmental power, the Anabaptists posed a significant threat to the economic and political order.[13]

In that volatile and fragile world, pacifistic Anabaptists experienced intense persecution and martyrdom at the hands of civil and ecclesial authorities. With persecution of the Anabaptists continuing through the sixteenth and into the early seventeenth century in parts of Europe, most Anabaptists became increasingly withdrawn from public life. By the late seventeenth century, some Mennonites made the voyage across the Atlantic, lured by land, the promise of a fresh start, and the hope for greater religious freedom.

U.S. Mennonite Responses to Previous Wars

Historian Richard K. MacMaster has documented that Mennonites were far from withdrawn from public life in colonial America: they voted, helped select candidates, and held certain local offices. Prior to the American Revolution, MacMaster contends, "pacifism" was considered compatible with "good citizenship."[14] By the early stages of the revolution, however, the test of membership in the newly forming American state was willingness to participate in local "associations" and to pledge to bear arms to protect American liberties. Nonresistant Mennonites "failed the test." Although patriots sought to include Mennonites in the new democracy, Mennonites felt increasingly alienated. Eventually, observes MacMaster, "the revolution induced in Mennonites a mood and strategy of inwardness and withdrawal."[15] In subsequent years this pacifistic withdrawal was solidified with the public "outsider" status given to Mennonites in a nation frequently at war. Before long, nonresistant Mennonites were among the most politically marginalized religious groups in the country.

During World War I, when U.S. Mennonites were still a relatively withdrawn people and when they had not negotiated any leeway for conscientious objection to warfare, many young Mennonite men were drafted into military service. Often this was in noncombatant roles, but in military camps these pacifists were treated abusively.[16] Back home, a number of their churches were painted yellow, and church leaders—my great-grandfather Niles among them[17]—were persecuted for their unwillingness to buy war bonds.

By the time of World War II, Mennonites and other peace churches were ready to move forward with Civilian Public Service, an arrangement that allowed conscientious objectors to perform "work of national importance" in place of military service.[18] In spite of the alternative service option, the strong, patriotic pull of that "war against evil" drew more than half (53 percent) of U.S. Mennonite men into noncombatant or active duty in military service (39.5 percent went into active service).[19] That suggests that pacifists were a functional minority among mid-century Mennonites, a troubling point for those of us who see faith-based peacemaking as central to Christ's gospel.

Following the Civilian Public Service years of World War II, Mennonites were involved with similar nonmilitary programs such as 1-W service during the Korean War and Voluntary Service during the Vietnam era. Vietnam, a far less popular engagement than World Wars I and II, gave Mennonites many allies in resistance. Vietnam also gave Mennonites an aggressive Selective Service System against which some young Mennonites defined themselves. The Persian Gulf War of the early 1990s, because of its brevity and its distance from the United States, did not marginalize pacifists as dramatically as some earlier wars had nor as much as the more recent U.S. military invasions have.

During and since the Vietnam War, North American and European Mennonites frequently have issued public statements opposing various warmaking initiatives; taught their young men and women the "way of peace"; supported their young people who have refused Selective Service registration in the

United States and conscription elsewhere; engaged in ecumenical dialogues with those from nonpacifist religious traditions; peacefully participated in demonstrations opposing war and other forms of violence; argued for significant reductions in or elimination of military budgets; and increased their service efforts in suffering nations around the globe. Mennonites also have become aware that with "volunteer" armies, technological developments, and the corresponding need for fewer conscripted soldiers to fight modern wars, the impact of individual conscientious objection has lessened. Instead, peacemaking Christians' financial and social entanglement in their nations' war-making has become a more pressing issue. Some Mennonites have refused to voluntarily pay the percentage of their income taxes that goes to support present and past wars, and Mennonites have been at the forefront of the Peace Tax Fund efforts in the United States.[20]

The War in Afghanistan and Iraq

The recent U.S. military invasions of Afghanistan and Iraq have strained the peace position of U.S. Mennonites, many of whom are largely acculturated in the early twenty-first century and some of whom have imbibed and embraced American patriotism. Some Mennonites have too uncritically accepted the rhetoric of the Christian Right, while others have done the same with the rhetoric of the left. Divisions have been evident within congregations and across the denomination regarding appropriate responses: should Mennonites be supportive of the war or at least the troops, silent in the face of our unwillingness to fight, or vocal in our resistance to the U.S. military interventions in Afghanistan and Iraq?

In many ways this war is similar to other wars. But it also is radically different than a war against the Axis powers or a definable nation. The contours and limits of a "war on terror" are yet to be defined. The rhetoric used in the recent war has been more closely aligned with the Christian crusade tradition than with "just war" or the more recent "just peace" theories. In the crusade tradition, crusaders set absolute goals that they relentlessly pursue against opponents considered to be entirely evil. The tradition was most clearly articulated and most often explicitly practiced during the Middle Ages when the nations of Western Christendom sought to take back the Holy Lands from Islam. It is unfortunate and ironic, if not surprising, that the military actions in Afghanistan and Iraq have had radical Muslims as their target.

This war also is different from some previous ones because the initiating event, at least from the perspective of most Americans, was an attack on our soil. In reality, of course, the earlier bombing attempt on the World Trade Center towers, the attacks on U.S. embassies in Africa, the ramming of the U.S.S. Cole, and the bombing of the U.S. marine barracks in Beirut all were prior events in this same "war." And those events were not caused by but related to U.S. expansionism around the globe. What we are seeing is an ongoing struggle between the United States and a significant portion of the world that opposes U.S. interests.

The Japanese attack on Pearl Harbor at the outset of our involvement in World War II happened in the homeland also, but most of the targets then were clearly military ones. In New York and Washington, the several thousand killed on September 11, 2001, were noncombatants. It could have been us, and for many people around the country it was indeed "us"—our sons and daughters, our parents, our cousins, our friends from college, our beloveds. It was a horrific event, too close to home, too brutal, evil. I watched the tragedy unfold with my ethics and morality class that Tuesday morning, and I remember speaking with the class in the days that followed about being a conflicted pacifist though a pacifist nonetheless.

The present military engagement also is different because it is unclear to us who "the enemy" is. Everyone is suspect, and that potentially divides us along ethnic and religious lines, engaging us informally as well as institutionally in racial profiling. It is also unclear when "the enemy" may strike again. That raises the stakes considerably and places us into a military state or warfare state for the foreseeable future.

In an interview with *USA Today* in October 2001, U.S. Defense Secretary Donald Rumsfeld acknowledged that "even if Osama bin Laden were gone tomorrow, the same problem would exist." He explained that bin Laden had trained many lieutenants, and the Al Qaeda network had bank accounts in fifty or sixty countries. "If we do a terrific job arresting people all over the globe," said Rumsfeld, "interrogating them, jailing them, finding out what they know, and if we do a wonderful job of blocking bank accounts and drying up their funds, and if we systematically go around the world and find terrorists and see that they stop terrorizing, and if we make it very unpleasant for the countries who are actively harboring and facilitating and financing and maybe even just tolerating terrorists, terrorism will be reduced. Will it go away completely? No."[21] Events more than four years after the World Trade Center towers came down evidenced even further the partial truth of Rumsfeld's early observations. The grim reality Rumsfeld describes makes opposition to the wars in Afghanistan and Iraq, even more so than for earlier wars, incomprehensible for many Americans.[22]

This war also is different from some past wars because in the previous century conscientious objectors generally had a draft to resist. That Selective Service reality has elicited Mennonites' denominational passion, driving us to disciple our young toward a pacifist response. Previous wars also have compelled us to serve in ways other than militarily. Historian James Juhnke has written that wartime persecution has sent Mennonites to seek "a moral equivalent to war's sacrifices."[23] Or, as many other Mennonite leaders have quipped with humiliating irony, "It takes a good war to bring out the best in Mennonites."

Historically Mennonites have recognized that there is a certain kind of expectation in American society—usually implicit but now sometimes spoken by presidents or used against candidates in election campaigns—which insists that service to the country is something everyone must do. If people are unwilling, for reasons of faith or conscience, to serve in the military forces, they must contribute to the country in some other way.[24] Drawing partly on our centuries-old traditions of discipleship and service, we have offered ourselves for nonmilitary social needs. As early as the French and Indian War, our forebears gave relief to war sufferers. In the revolutionary colonies, some Mennonites pleaded for exemption from militias on the grounds that they had done some prior meritorious public service.[25] In the Civil War, Mennonites responded with humanitarian assistance and, in some cases, "compromised" by providing wagons and other military-related supplies,[26] paying commutation fees, or hiring soldier substitutes, a provision made possible by the national draft law.[27]

By 1920 Mennonites institutionalized our tradition of service in the Mennonite Central Committee (MCC). James C. Juhnke, in one of the first analytical accounts of the development of MCC, suggests that World War I forced us to accommodate to the nature of twentieth-century nationalism—a nationalism perceived to be even stronger now. "[Our] felt need for some corresponding positive act through which [we], like [our] fellow Americans, could stand up among people without shame was at the core of [our] postwar behavior."[28] P. C. Hiebert, the first chair of the Mennonite Central Committee, and MCC leader Orie O. Miller wrote that there was "little satisfaction in just maintaining a negative position toward war." Hiebert and Miller said what was needed was "an opportunity to disprove the charges of cowardice and selfishness made against the conscientious objectors, and to express in a positive, concrete way the principles of peace and goodwill."[29]

Juhnke contends that the Mennonite tragedy was not that we became Americans so slowly, but that "[we] so desperately wanted to be good American citizens and could not fulfill the requirements without violating [our] consciences or abandoning the traditions of [our] forebears." Juhnke attributes to this tension "whatever was creative in the Mennonite experience"—relief programs, development of positive alternatives to military service, and scattered criticism of American nationalism from a pacifist perspective.[30]

Traditionally, the peace position of Mennonites has been rooted in the biblical portrayal of Jesus' way of love and his willingness to suffer on the cross.[31] Such a principled pacifism, in its roots and origins, is different from some forms of pacifism that have emerged in more recent centuries. Early twentieth-century liberal pacifists, for example, had a more optimistic view of human nature believing that sustained peace may be possible if people became sufficiently educated and enlightened. In this view, pacifism was not only possible but also practical and effective. Mennonites have been less optimistic about human nature but have instead believed that Jesus calls his followers to be nonviolent.[32] Sometimes this pacifism "works" and sometimes it does not. But in the Anabaptist-Mennonite tradition, as in many other religious traditions, faithfulness has long taken priority over effectiveness. Faithfulness is near the heart of Mennonite theological and ethical thinking with the deep, confident, eschatological hope and belief that God has structured the world in a way that faithfulness will ultimately be effective.

The pacifism of Mennonites is rooted, then, in the belief that Jesus' demonstration of love in all relationships should be normative for his followers.

Although we have not applied such teachings slavishly, Mennonites have believed that what Jesus says about turning the other cheek, giving a cloak to someone who asks for your shirt, going the second mile, loving enemies, and praying for persecutors has something to do with Christian discipleship. Menno Simons wrote in 1537, "[The regenerated] are children of peace who have beaten their swords into plowshares and their spears into pruning hooks, and know war no more."[33]

Often in Mennonite history the faithful response to violence has been characterized as "nonresistance," a term derived from Jesus' injunction to "resist not evil" but to turn the other cheek (Mt. 5:39). For Mennonites, nonresistance has been a way of being a faithful disciple of Jesus Christ—not a strategy for achieving peace. Such a posture, espoused most articulately by Guy F. Hershberger in his mid-twentieth-century book *War, Peace, and Nonresistance*, was broader than simple conscientious objection or refusal to participate in warfare; nonresistance had implications for all dimensions of Christian life. While some Mennonites still use the language of "nonresistance," over the last fifty years Mennonites have debated the appropriateness of nonviolent resistance, sociopolitical activism, and justice-making. Such debates, influenced by the activism of Mahatma Gandhi and Martin Luther King, Jr., have pushed at Mennonites' traditional theological and ethical boundaries.[34] More than a decade ago two Mennonite leaders published a small book detailing the plethora of contemporary Mennonite peace theologies, including "historic nonresistance," "culturally engaged pacifism," "social responsibility," and "radical pacifism," as well as a half dozen other types.[35]

At least since Mennonite theologian John Howard Yoder's 1972 publication of *The Politics of Jesus*,[36] many Mennonites have perceived Jesus as a markedly political person, constantly having run-ins with religious and political authorities and perpetually confronting those seeking to thwart the reign of God. Jesus was unafraid of verbal confrontations and conflicts, and he was crucified on political charges. Even though Jesus had some disciples who were prone to violence, he chose to confront authorities directly—and nonviolently—while also willingly submitting to the cross, a cross that can be identified "as the punishment of a [person] who threatens society by creating a new kind of community leading a radically new kind of life."[37]

In the face of this socially and politically engaged Jesus, one organizational response of activist Mennonites and other Christian pacifists has been the formation of Christian Peacemaker Teams (CPT).[38] CPT does something similar to what Captain Rhude proposed in his *Goshen News* letter recommending that peace activists go overseas and place their bodies "in harm's way"—in hot spots such as Haiti, Hebron, Afghanistan, and Iraq, CPT sends small teams of workers to stand between hostile groups, document and report atrocities and human-rights violations, and actively but nonviolently intervene in violent situations. The banner on the organization's Web site (http://www.cpt.org) asks, "What would happen if Christians devoted the same discipline and self-sacrifice to nonviolent peacemaking that armies devote to war?" Impetus for the group's formation came from a speech delivered by Ronald Sider at the 1984 Mennonite World Conference gathering in Strasbourg, France:

> Over the past 450 years of martyrdom, immigration and missionary proclamation, the God of shalom has been preparing us Anabaptists for a late twentieth-century rendezvous with history. The next twenty years will be the most dangerous—and perhaps the most vicious and violent—in human history. If we are ready to embrace the cross, God's reconciling people will profoundly impact the course of world history. . . . Now is the time to risk everything for our belief that Jesus is the way to peace. If we still believe it, now is the time to live what we have spoken. . . . Unless we. . .are ready to start to die by the thousands in dramatic, vigorous, new exploits for peace and justice, we should sadly confess that we never really meant what we said, and we dare never whisper another word about pacifism to our sisters and brothers in those desperate lands filled with injustice. Unless we are ready to die developing new nonviolent attempts to reduce conflict, we should confess that we never really meant that the cross was an alternative to the sword.[39]

About forty people from various Christian communities are full-time members of Christian Peacemaker Teams, and about 125 people are in the organization's Reserve Corps.[40]

Patriotism, Citizenship, and Civil Religion

Partly because of their tensions with ruling authorities in most of the countries in which they have lived and partly because of the necessity of frequent emigration because of persecution or a lack of religious freedom Mennonites have not developed a particularly nationalistic or patriotic spirit, in the way those terms are generally understood in the United States. Mennonites have supported this lack of devotion to one's nation by tempering Romans 13:1 ("let every person be subject to the governing authorities") with Acts 5:29 ("obey God rather than human authorities"). When governmental push has come to shove, Mennonites generally have gone with Peter's counsel in Acts.[41]

Mennonite ethicist John Richard Burkholder once responded to a critic by noting that what the critic had called "anti-Americanism" could better be described as "more-than-Americanism." "Pacifists identify with the entire human community and the long sweep of history," wrote Burkholder. "For the pacifist, citizenship in a particular nation-state is just not that important. He [or she] cares less about national interests than about the well-being of the people of all nations. Since most pacifist leaders are not parochial in their worldview, they do not see the U.S. national interest as paramount."[42] Burkholder added that pacifists "consciously adopt a more global worldview than most Americans. They wear tribal identifications lightly and see themselves as global citizens."[43] In the midst of the wars against Afghanistan and Iraq, among the pro- and antiwar bumper stickers in our region is one stating, "God Bless the Whole World: No Exceptions."

The question of citizenship is essentially one of competing loyalties, all of which may demand our wholehearted—and therefore perhaps contradictory—allegiance. For those of us who are Christians living in the United States, we are citizens of a particular nation, we are global citizens, and we are Christians. Pacifistic Mennonites have traditionally viewed themselves as first and foremost disciples of Christ and citizens of God's reign, then citizens of the world, and finally citizens of a given country. In contrast to that ordering, during times of warfare many people in the United States, including some Mennonites in recent years, have believed American citizenship should trump nearly all other loyalties, or at least that Christian allegiance can be aligned with American patriotism. For principled pacifists, such a conflation is more difficult, especially in a powerful nation frequently at war.

The rise of patriotism during periods of warfare is evidence of what sociologists refer to as civil religion—a religion that has remained relatively dormant in nonbellicose times. Civil religion is part of what holds together a nation composed of highly differentiated, heterogeneous subgroups. It seeks to pull together disparate religious and ethnic groups into a cohesive whole by pulling down divisive barriers and finding a common rallying point and often marginalizing those who do not fully board the patriotic train.

Christian Century noted that sociologist Robert Putnam identified a new civil mood in the nation after September 11, 2001. Putnam, who coined the term "bowling alone" and has written provocatively about the collapse of community life, wrote in the *American Prospect* that "people's trust in national and local governments has increased significantly." Polling data from the fall of 2001, said Putnam, indicated that "Americans are more confident that their neighbors will cooperate in a time of crisis. And they express more interest in politics." The terrorist attacks, the sociologist concluded, have made Americans "more united, readier for collective sacrifice and more attuned to public purpose" than they have been for decades.[44]

Civil religion in the United States exists alongside churches with its own theology, ethics, symbols, and rituals. A sense of a special mission, destiny, and calling is an integral part of the "legitimating myth" of American civil religion. The symbols and rituals of American civil religion include a variety of sacred objects and sacred spaces. We have national saints such as George Washington who is sometimes depicted in nineteenth-century engravings as ascending to heaven on a throne surrounded by angels. Thomas Jefferson, Abraham Lincoln and a host of other presidents and military leaders also function as saints in American civil religion. Other cultic rituals and objects include the citing of the pledge of allegiance in schools and at public gatherings and the singing of the "Star Spangled Banner" at high school sporting events.

The flag is the primary symbol of American civil religion. Strict rules are in place for how a flag can be flown: it must be lighted at night, it must be cared for in severe weather, and it cannot be publicly displayed in tattered form. In the aftermath of September 11, 2001, flags emerged in places where they had never flown before.[45] Among those novel locations was the bodice and train of the bridal gown of one local bride whose wedding photo appeared in *The Goshen News* as I was writing this chapter. The front-page article, headlined "Patriotic Couple Holds All-American Wedding," began by saying, "Sheri and Bill Dunlap celebrated the love they have for each other and their love of America at Grace Community Church July 2."

Those who walked through the parking lots of many U.S. Mennonite churches on Sunday mornings in September and October 2001 also found freshly purchased flags flying from the antenna or plastered to the bumpers of a number of cars.[46] In the weeks after the attacks on the World Trade Center towers and the Pentagon, Goshen General Hospital hoisted a dozen flags across the front of its property, a stone's throw across State Road 15 to Goshen College where I teach. Later in the fall the hospital erected a mammoth pole and flag that, from where I sit in my third-floor office, seems aimed at our Mennonite campus.

Sociologist Robert Bellah wrote a seminal article on American civil religion in 1967, during the heart of the Vietnam War and the revolutionary 1960s.[47] Given the threat of national disintegration at the time, Bellah affirmed the civil religion phenomenon even though he concluded by suggesting that Americans should move toward an international and ecumenical faith that transcends national boundaries. In the post-Reagan world, Bellah has recognized the dangers of civil religion run amok, but even back in 1967, he proposed that civil religion should function not in only one but in two ways for the nation. First, it should justify and provide meaning for the way we arrange our social life, and should draw us together as a people. This is the priestly version of American civil religion with the American president as the chief priest. It is the belief that the United States is great because it is a good nation and the conviction that God has promised to care for and build up America. Second, civil religion should prophetically criticize the nation, recognizing that God is the ultimate, sovereign authority. This prophetic dimension relativizes our existence, recognizes our failures, and calls us to live up to our highest ideals. As President Theodore Roosevelt said, "To announce that there must be no criticism of the President, or that we are to stand by the President right or wrong, is not only unpatriotic and servile, but is morally treasonable to the American public."[48] These two differing dimensions, both equally part of American civil religion, were exemplified during the Vietnam War with a set of bumper stickers. The priestly version proclaimed, "America—Love it or leave it!" And the prophetic version countered, "America—Change it or lose it!"

Eight Modest Proposals: On Being Pacifist Christians and U.S. Citizens

Many Mennonites and other peacemaking Christians continue to feel deeply ambivalent about the language of citizenship, as well as the rise of wartime patriotism. Without question, principled pacifists need to acknowledge both the ways in which we benefit by living in the United States and the responsibility we share for our nation's actions through our uncritical enjoyment of some of these benefits, our payment of taxes, and our silence. As part of good American citizenship, I would like to reclaim—with Bellah and in the spirit of my Anabaptist forebears—a prophetic critique of the government as an essential counterpoint to unmitigated support for our nation's aggression.

I also want to continue to look for ways to be creatively Christian and creatively American, drawing on the best from both traditions. With both traditions in mind, I recommend the following eight postures and practices,[49] hoping that they will enable Mennonites and other conscientious Christians to work at God's calling on us at this point in history.

1. Teach our congregations about the historic, faith-rooted tradition of peacemaking.

We must remember that we are disciples of a nonviolent Christ, one whose upside-down way of encountering the world often seems nonsensical and leaves others uncomfortable. We need to revisit the Christian origins of our peacemaking, examine more closely the various permutations our peace theologies have undergone, and tell stories from our faith traditions about those who lived, and died, for their commitments to peace. We need to train our young people to understand that nonviolent peacemaking is faithful to the Jesus way, even if it is sometimes perceived as ineffective or irrelevant.[50] And when the winds of war subside, we need to sustain the teachings of peace.

2. Reinterpret the meaning of the flag.

We ought to commit ourselves to not jumping on board the red, white, and blue bandwagon. If we fly the flag in an effort to be good citizens, we should fly it alongside a United Nations flag, attach purple and green ribbons to it, or otherwise recognize symbolically that God loves all people from all nations. With our neighbors we should affirm the values our flag can stand for, including freedom of conscience, separation of church and state, the rule of law and the efficiency of representational government. If we choose to fly the flag, we should recognize our responsibility, through the taxes we pay, for the military repression our flag symbolizes to many people around the world. We should be "alternative patriots,"[51] combining our appreciation for our country with our love for all of God's children, and following the example of the Hebrew prophets who witnessed to their nation and its leaders while expressing loving care and concern for the well-being of its people.

3. Maintain our humility as we share with our
neighbors and speak to national leaders.

As people who follow the Prince of Peace, we must admit that we do not have quick or easy answers for responding to complex, twenty-first-century world conflicts. When we disagree with decisions our political leaders make, we must respond in a more gracious manner than our natural inclinations might normally take us. As good citizens of the United States who hope for God's reign, we should respect and pray for our country's decision-makers, even while we challenge and critique their decisions when necessary.

4. Listen to those who believe differently than we do.

We need to seek out ways to share with those who do not agree with us and genuinely listen to their stories. We need to listen to Muslims, Jews, and other Christians, to peacemakers and patriots, to people in our own communities and country, and to those in other parts of the world.[52] We need to be open to learning from others. Part of our "listening" should include learning to know our differently-minded neighbors as well as engaging ourselves in the public welfare of our local communities, participating fully in community organizations devoted to the common good, seeking justice for those who experience oppression and exploitation, and sharing ourselves and our resources with others.

5. Challenge our nation to end its reliance on violence to solve problems, and call our nation to live up to its highest ideals.

Our nation responded to the violent September 11, 2001, attacks with violence in kind, which resulted in yet more violence and continues to perpetuate perceptions of injustice and oppression. It is likely that our violence-for-violence response in the recent war has created more rather than less danger and more rather than fewer terrorists.[53] We hope the United States and other countries responding to terrorism can work at the roots of terrorism—poverty and gross economic disparity, the arrogance of nations, imperialism, exploitation, injustice—rather than reacting only militarily. As a nation, we must pay attention to the causes of terrorism as much as to the manifestations of terrorism.

6. Hold our military, political, and media leaders responsible for reporting the truth, and seek out that truth.

Americans often are in the dark about the extent of the casualties of our military actions. By 2005 the number of Afghanis and Iraqis killed in the ongoing war were more than fifty-fold the number of Americans killed in the September 11, 2001, tragedy. We need to seek out alternative sources for news reports some of which are available on the Internet.[54] Being knowledgeable about our country's actions is part of the practice of good citizenship.

7. Live responsibly by reducing our consumption of the world's resources.

We need to model for our children and our communities a lifestyle that needs less defending by our military. A standard of living that demands a disproportionate share of the world's resources increases our perceived need for a military to protect us. As conscientious Christians, we ought to reduce our consumption of oil and other goods so that our calls for justice in other parts of the world have integrity.

8. Serve our brothers and sisters at home and around the world.

For those unwilling to participate in warfare for conscientious reasons, we need to work to find contemporary moral equivalents to the sacrifices of war. Many of us have lowered our expectations for our young people to consider volunteer work; instead, as parents and church leaders we have urged them to be more responsible by moving into careers more quickly. We need to repent of that embrace of American individualism and economic success, and instead model lives of service to our young people. We should encourage all of those who believe in peace to participate in a one-year or multi-year service assignment, at home or overseas, through one of many faithful church agencies or through other worthwhile humanitarian organizations around the world.

In short, pacifist Christians can be good U.S. citizens in a conflict-ridden time by being faithful disciples of Jesus Christ, impassioned peacemakers, and hospitable neighbors and friends to those we perceive as "the other" whether they are our nation's leaders, our Muslim sisters and brothers, or our flag-hoisting neighbors. In a complex twenty-first-century world, conscientious Christians can be good citizens by giving our first allegiance to Jesus Christ, the Prince of Peace. We can live our lives in ways that are faithful to the gospel. And we can share Christ's message of peace in a world often drawn to violence. Such a way of life is faithful to Jesus' teaching, and that may be sufficient. But it also is a way of being that (we can humbly hope) is as relevant in a violence-prone world as are alternative responses. I am all for holding teas, and marching for peace, and for writing letters, and for sewing comforters, and for praying in the spirit of a nonviolent Christ, and for thinking and acting creatively in ways other than violence to make for peace.

Notes

1. Mike Keim, "Treaty Actions Not Cause of Attacks," *Goshen News*, September 19, 2001, p. 4.

2. *Goshen News*, September 26, 2001, p. 4.

3. Capt. Don Rhude, "Group Should Go to Afghanistan," *Goshen News*, September 28, 2001, p. 4.

4. John D. Ulmer, "Terrorist Attacks Are More than Crimes," *Goshen News*, October 2, 2001, p. 4.

5. Michael Kelly, ". . .Pacifist Claptrap," *Washington Post*, September 26, 2001, p. A25.

6. Not all of the early Anabaptists, or people considered Anabaptists, were convinced pacifists, as history has clearly shown (e.g., the Münsterites of 1534–35), but the surviving groups of Mennonites' ancestors were. See James M. Stayer, *Anabaptists and the Sword* (Lawrence, KS: Coronado Press, 1972). Because the Anabaptist movement's origins coincided with the Peasants' Revolt of 1524–25 and because of unclear delineations between the various people and groups seeking social and religious change in sixteenth-century Europe, "Anabaptist" became a derisive term covering a wide range of people responding to Europe's unrest.

7. John H. Yoder, trans. and ed., *The Schleitheim Confession*, in *The Legacy of Michael Sattler* (Scottdale, PA: Herald Press, 1973), 39–40. The confession also states that the sword "punishes and kills the wicked, and guards and protects the good. In the law

the sword is established over the wicked for punishment and for death, and the secular rulers are established to wield the same."

8. Menno Simons, "Foundation of Christian Doctrine," in *The Complete Writings of Menno Simons*, ed. J. C. Wenger (Scottdale, PA: Herald Press, 1956), 200.

9. Menno Simons, "Why I Do Not Cease Teaching and Writing," in *The Complete Writings*, 304.

10. *The Schleitheim Confession*, in *The Legacy of Michael Sattler*, 39.

11. Contemporary Mennonites are conscious of and self-reflective about the differences between living under foreign occupation, in a kingship, in a communist state, in a democracy, or under another governing system.

12. Menno Simons, "A Pathetic Supplication to All Magistrates," in *The Complete Writings*, 523–31. Some twentieth- and twenty-first-century Mennonites were ready to speak to government officials when their actions conflicted with Mennonites' self-interests but reticent to speak on other issues. Many other Mennonites have noted and challenged this inconsistency. On this, see, Keith Graber Miller, *Wise as Serpents, Innocent as Doves: American Mennonites Engage Washington* (Knoxville: University of Tennessee Press, 1996), especially 113–14 and 201–2. It is clear that Simons and other Anabaptist leaders spoke out to the magistrates on behalf of their own interests and the interests of others outside their fold.

13. Walter Klaassen, *Anabaptism: Neither Catholic Nor Protestant* (Waterloo, ON: Conrad, 1973), 60–63.

14. Richard K. MacMaster, *Land, Piety, Peoplehood: The Establishment of Mennonite Communities in America, 1683–1790* (Scottdale, PA: Herald Press, 1985), 250–51.

15. MacMaster, *Land, Piety, Peoplehood*, 250–51.

16. On this, see Paul Toews, "The Impact of Alternative Service on the American Mennonite World: A Critical Evaluation," *Mennonite Quarterly Review* 66:4 (October 1992): 615–27; and Rodney J. Sawatsky, "History and Ideology: American Mennonite Identity Definition through History" (PhD diss., Princeton University, 1977). While American Mennonites prospered economically during World War I, they also suffered various forms of harassment and persecution during the war. About 138 of the 2,000 Mennonites drafted were court-martialed and sentenced to federal prisons (where some died) for refusing to obey military orders, and others were ridiculed for being pacifists during their time of service at stateside military camps. About 1,000 Mennonites and Hutterites (the communal Anabaptists) fled to Canada.

17. For the story of Niles Slabaugh's persecution by a dozen "loyal citizens" of Miami County, Indiana, see Gerlof Homan, "A Pastor Pays a Price for Peace," *Gospel Herald*, May 1, 1990, p. 308–9. The vigilantes took Slabaugh, partly dressed, from his home in the middle of the night, then shaved his head and face and applied a coat of yellow paint to his body, leaving him on a road about twelve miles from his home. According to *The Peru Republican's* account of the August 14, 1918 event, Slabaugh's offense was that he had insisted "he would do nothing towards helping his Uncle Samuel in winning the war from the Huns."

18. Civilian Public Service was a collaborative effort of the Mennonite Church, Church of the Brethren, and Friends, and was provided under the U.S. Selective Service and Training Act of 1940. See Albert N. Keim, *The CPS Story: An Illustrated History of Civilian Public Service* (Intercourse, PA: Good Books, 1990). For a broader look at U.S. wars in the first half of the twentieth century, see Albert N. Keim and Grant M. Stoltzfus, *The Politics of Conscience: The Historic Peace Churches and America at War, 1917–1955* (Scottdale, PA: Herald Press, 1988).

19. Paul Toews, *Mennonites in American Society, 1930–1970* (Scottdale, PA: Herald Press, 1996), 173. These figures are little known among Mennonites even though they were first gathered at the war's end by former CPSer Howard Charles and updated in 1949 by Mennonite leader Guy F. Hershberger. Toews writes that the story of those Mennonites who served in the military during World War II "remains marginal to Mennonite memory. No doubt due to a Mennonite ideological bias, there is little research published on them. Indeed the marginality of the story reflects a larger marginalization of persons who defied the official denominational stance" (173).

20. For information about the National Campaign for a Peace Tax Fund, see the organization's Web site, http://www.peacetaxfund.org.

21. "Rumsfeld: As the World Changes, So Must USA," *USA Today*, October 25, 2001, p. A19. Interview conducted by *USA Today* Editorial Board.

22. The leadership group of my local congregation, Assembly Mennonite Church, wrote in its 2002 "State of the Assembly" newsletter to the congregation: "In the midst of our professed efforts as a congregation to welcome visitors and engage our local community, we have been challenged to discover appropriate ways of expressing our counter-cultural convictions without alienating our neighbors."

23. James C. Juhnke, *A People of Two Kingdoms: The Political Acculturation of the Kansas Mennonites* (Newton, KS: Faith and Life Press, 1975), 115–16.

24. Since the early twentieth century, from World War I to both Persian Gulf Wars, major U.S. conflicts have served to remind American Mennonites of their identity; compelled them to reiterate for themselves and the public their reasons for not participating in warfare; and prompted them to contribute something, short of taking up arms, to the societies in which they live. Many Mennonite leaders also have called on Mennonite churches to promote local, national, and international peacemaking whether their nation is involved in warfare or not and to work at peace in their congregations and communities at all times.

25. MacMaster, *Land, Piety*, 257. MacMaster rightly observes that this plea evidences the first stirrings of "alternative" service.

26. On the Mennonite response to the Civil War, see especially Theron F. Schlabach, *Peace, Faith, Nation: Mennonites and Amish in Nineteenth-Century America* (Scottdale, PA: Herald Press, 1988), particularly chapter 7. Schlabach notes that some of the contributions were "not purely voluntary" (179).

27. Schlabach, *Peace, Faith, Nation*, 185–89. Some Mennonites and Amish, of course, also simply served in the military. Some were unable to afford the commutation fees or pay the required $300 to $1,000 to hire a substitute, others refused to support the war in any fashion, and still others could not imagine paying another person to serve in their stead.

28. Juhnke, *A People of Two Kingdoms*, 115–16. On this subject, see also Juhnke's *Vision, Doctrine, War: Mennonite Identity and Organization in America, 1890–1930* (Scottdale, PA: Herald Press, 1989), especially chaps. 8 and 9.

29. P. C. Hiebert and Orie O. Miller, *Feeding the Hungry: Russia Famine, 1919–1925* (Scottdale, PA: Mennonite Central Committee, 1929), 29. Parts of this also were cited in Juhnke's *A People*, 115–16.

30. Juhnke, *A People*, 156–57. On 192, Juhnke says a corollary to his argument is that the Mennonite relief program would not have arisen had there been no contact with American culture and no desire to be good Americans. He suggests that a comparison with the Amish, who remained isolated and uninterested in relief programs, would be instructive. Acculturation among the more progressive Amish has led to

relief and mission work in recent years. Juhnke also notes that the link between American nationalism and Mennonite discipleship again could be seen in the early 1970s, when the number of Mennonites volunteering for church-related service declined, partly in response to the end of the military draft.

31. Various recent Mennonite biblical scholars and theologians have deepened the scriptural basis of peace theology by addressing the themes of *shalom*, holy war, the question of God's violence, Jesus' politics, and salvation and atonement theology. For an overview of some of these developments, see John Richard Burkholder, "Peace," in *The Mennonite Encyclopedia*, vol. 5, eds. Cornelius J. Dyck and Dennis D. Martin (Scottdale, PA: Herald Press, 1990), 681–85.

32. Many younger Mennonites, including many of the students in my ethics and theology courses, are initially unaware that their contemporary form of pacifism is quite different from that of their faith ancestors in this regard.

33. Menno Simons, "The New Birth," in *The Complete Writings*, 94. In the same 1537 essay, Simons wrote: "Evil [the regenerated] do not repay with evil, but with good. They do not seek merely their own good but that which is good for their neighbors both as to body and soul. They feed the hungry, give drink to the thirsty. They entertain the needy, release prisoners, visit the sick, comfort the fainthearted, admonish the erring, are ready after their Master's example to give their lives for their brethren" (93).

34. I am keenly aware here of the critiques of theologian and political realist Reinhold Niebuhr and others who offered tempered affirmation for Mennonite-style nonresistance. Niebuhr considered the Mennonite nonresistant ethic of his day as consistent with the nonresistant love taught by Jesus. But Niebuhr also contended that such an ethic is impossible to achieve in a world peopled by fallen human beings. He suggested that if Mennonites were sufficiently humble, they could serve as a prod to the nation's conscience reminding pragmatically oriented people that love is the ideal toward which Christians strive. However, Niebuhr expected Mennonites to remain disengaged from the real world of politics where compromise is essential to effecting change and violence is an inherent part of governing. Reinhold Niebuhr, "Why the Christian Church Is Not Pacifist," in *The Essential Reinhold Niebuhr: Selected Essays and Addressed*, ed. Robert McAfee Brown (New Haven, CT: Yale University Press, 1986), 106–7. Many mid-twentieth-century Mennonites welcomed Niebuhr's backhanded compliment. On Mennonite responses to Niebuhr, see especially John H. Yoder, *Christian Attitudes to War, Peace, and Revolution: A Companion to Bainton* (Elkhart, IN: Co-op Bookstore, 1983), 343–418.

35. John Richard Burkholder and Barbara Nelson Gingerich, eds., *Mennonite Peace Theology: A Panorama of Types* (Akron, PA: Mennonite Central Committee Peace Office, 1991). Earlier John H. Yoder had published *Nevertheless: The Varieties of Religious Pacifism* (Scottdale, PA: Herald Press, 1971). Yoder's book was revised in 1992 and retitled, interestingly enough, *Nevertheless: The Varieties and Shortcomings of Religious Pacifism* (Scottdale, PA: Herald Press, 1992).

36. John H. Yoder, *The Politics of Jesus: Vicit Agnus Noster*, 2nd ed. (Grand Rapids, MI: Eerdmans, 1994).

37. Yoder, *The Politics of Jesus*, 53.

38. See http://www.cpt.org. For first-person narratives about CPT's work, see Tricia Gates Brown, ed., *Getting in the Way: Stories from Christian Peacemaker Teams* (Scottdale, PA: Herald Press, 2005).

39. From Christian Peacemaker Teams' Web site at http://www.cpt.org. The full text of Sider's speech is available on the site. Sider, long-time president of Evangelicals for

Social Action, is professor of theology, holistic ministry, and public policy and director of the Sider Center on Ministry and Public Policy at Eastern Baptist Theological Seminary.

40. Christian Peacemaker Teams came into the international spotlight in November 2005 when four of its team members in Iraq—Tom Fox, James Loney, Hameet Singh Sooden, and Norman Kember—were kidnapped. In March 2006 Fox was found dead with gunshot wounds, but the other three CPTers survived four months in captivity.

41. Mennonite scholars also have significantly tempered the Romans 13 directives by looking at the larger context of the passage. See John H. Yoder, *The Politics of Jesus*, 193–211.

42. J. R. Burkholder, "Pacifist Ethics and Pacifist Politics," in *Peace Betrayed? Essays on Pacifism and Politics*, ed. Michael Cromartie, 198 (New York: University Press of America, 1990).

43. Burkholder, "Pacifist Ethics and Pacifist Politics," 205. See also Wilbert Shenk, "Missions, Service and the Globalization of North American Mennonites," *Mennonite Quarterly Review* 70, no. 1 (January 1996): 7–22.

44. Robert Putnam, "Flag-Waving," *Christian Century* (January 30, 2002): 5. Much of that spirited cooperation, community support, collective purpose, and sacrifice is good, especially when it contributes to increased conversations at the community, state, and national levels.

45. See Monica Joseph, "Patriotic Couple Holds All-American Wedding," *Goshen News*, July 10, 2005, p. A1.

46. Most Mennonite meetinghouses in the United States still do not have flags of any kind in their sanctuaries, though American flags are slowly creeping into these sacred spaces. For an additional perspective on U.S. Mennonites and the flag, see the short piece by Susan Mark Landis, minister of peace and justice for Mennonite Church USA, at http://www.peace.mennolink.org/articles/flag_reflections.html.

47. Bellah's essay appears in multiple texts, including Robert N. Bellah, *Beyond Belief Essays on Religion in a Post-Traditional World* (New York: Harper and Row, 1970). The piece originally was written for a *Daedalus* conference on American religion in 1966. Many scholars, including Bellah himself, have critiqued the "civil religion" thesis over the past 40 years. One of the more recent challenges to Bellah and others in his stream was from Ira Chernus in a review of Richard T. Hughes's book *Myths America Lives By* (Chicago: University of Illinois Press, 2003). Chernus wrote: "The 'we' of the civil religion literature, offered as a representation of all Americans, too often represented the views of an elite group, consisting mainly of wealthy white men. Writers on 'our' civil religion seemed unable to break out of the prejudicial premise that this elite represented the views of the entire nation. No matter how much the literature called 'our' civil religion into question, somehow 'we' always ended up having a core of ideals and values that gave 'us' a privileged place in the forefront of humanity. Once these biases were widely recognized, everything written on U.S. civil religion became deservedly suspect." See Ira Chernus, "Review of *Myths America Lives By*," *Journal of the American Academy of Religion* 73, no. 2 (June 2005): 539–41.

48. This oft-cited statement by Roosevelt was made by the president during World War I in an editorial published in the *Kansas City Star*, May 7, 1918.

49. I am grateful to a number of people for responding to this section of the essay or to the full chapter. Among those who provided thorough, insightful critiques of earlier drafts of the entire chapter are J. R. Burkholder, Carolyn Schrock-Shenk, David Schrock-Shenk, Susan Mark Landis, and Doug Kaufman. Those who helpfully reviewed and

commented on these final points include Ron Byler, J. Daryl Byler, John Rempel, Kathryn Rodgers, Mary Schertz, and André Gingerich Stoner. In spite of such erudite counsel, some errors of fact or interpretation likely remain; those remaining misstatements are my responsibility alone.

50. Recently at a gathering of Mennonite youth and sponsors, I was one of several speakers responding to the possibility of a draft. After we finished our presentations, one youth teacher stood and, shaking with anger, said, "You're just filling these kids' heads with these silly stories. And they're going to get out in the world, and those ways of responding just won't work." Most of what I and other speakers had been describing was Jesus' teachings related to peace.

51. The language of "alternative patriots" was used by my Goshen College Bible and Religion colleague Paul Keim in his article "My Struggle with the Flag," in *Where Was God on Sept. 11? Seeds of Faith and Hope*, eds. Donald B. Kraybill and Linda Gehman Peachey, 163–65 (Scottdale, PA: Herald Press, 2002).

52. In the months following September 11, 2001, one rural Mennonite congregation in Ohio invited a local Muslim physician in to speak to the congregation about Islamic faith. My Peace, Justice, and Conflict Studies colleague Carolyn Schrock-Shenk requires students in her Conflict Transformation course to approach someone who they perceive to be "the Other" for them, an experience that is always transformative for students.

53. Mennonite peacemaker John Paul Lederach said in a Fall 2001 lecture, "Warfare was and remains the choice of greatest risk in terms of perpetuating the perceptions of injustice and oppression in the social milieu that gives rise to the regeneration of recruitment into Terror." See John Paul Lederach, "Quo Vadis?" Colonel Richard Dunn, former chief of the Army's internal think tank, commented that "you can go and kill every one of their terrorists and hang bin Laden in front of the White House and you will not have solved the problem—and you probably have created hundreds of new terrorists. So you could win tactically, and lose strategically." Quoted in *Washington Post*, October 21, 2001, p. A19, and cited in Lederach's speech.

54. Among the multiple alternative news sources available are *Sojourners* magazine and its online news source available at http://www.sojo.net; *Truthout*, available at http://www.truthout.org; *Common Dreams Newscenter* at http://www.commondreams.org; and *The Christian Century*. These and many other online sources provide links to articles from other mainstream and alternative publications and sites. All of the alternative news sources noted here have a peace and justice bias.

Chapter 11

Called to Christian Anarchy?

Lee Griffith

The Journey Out of Babylon

Whether Samuel Johnson was correct or not in observing "patriotism is the last refuge of a scoundrel," in times of crisis it is the first refuge of many, including those who are not scoundrels. In the days following September 11, 2001, "God bless America" was the slogan displayed on the billboards of burger joints and on the bumpers of vehicles across the nation. While those displaying the slogan clearly wanted us to know of their patriotism, were they also trying to say something about "God," or does that particular name appear "in vain," as the Decalogue calls it? Alongside Jesus' teachings on the plain (Lk. 6:17–38), any possible theological content to the slogan is incomprehensible. It is the peacemakers and those who refrain from violent retaliation who are blessed, not we who spend more on the military than the next top twenty nations combined. It is the poor, the hungry, and the persecuted that are blessed. To pray that we might be those people who receive God's blessing is either a masochistic prayer or an indication that we are praying to another god entirely—perhaps the god of nation, power and wealth.

But maybe those who use the slogan, "God bless America," intend "blessing" to mean something other than what Jesus meant—something less eschatological, less enmeshed with suffering. Perhaps they mean that the mission of America is of such import that God ought to be concerned for the United States in a manner more urgent than the divine concerns for, say, Sri Lanka or Burundi. Perhaps God has even chosen America for this mission, thus giving credence to the characterization of the United States as "New Israel." Yet, the biblical witness again raises doubts about whether being "chosen" can be counted as a happy turn of events in any conventional sense. Chosen as it was, the biblical Israel was never blessed with invulnerability. Even at the short-lived apex of its historical trajectory, Israel was always a backwater country subject to the whims of the imperial powers that marched across it. A nearer historical analogy for contemporary America would be to the slave master of Egypt (Ex. 14:5–9), or the golden cup of Babylon (Jer. 51:7–9), or the beast of Rome (Rev. 13:1–8).

Of course, the characterization of the United States as "New Israel" did not originate in the recent days of American imperial might but in the less secure milieu of the European colonization of the "New World." Even as the Puritan colonizers were establishing their "city on a hill," they somehow had to address the inconvenient presence of natives and the fact that the hill on which they proposed to do their establishing did not belong to them. It was the same inconvenient fact that greeted nineteenth-century Boer settlers in South Africa and the whites in North America and South Africa hit upon similar exculpatory solutions—namely, the settlers were people who had been chosen by God to go out into the wilderness and to seize the land that had been promised to them.[1] From the beginning of European settlement in America and South Africa, the sense of being chosen was inextricably linked with the need for conquest, occupation and possession.[2] It was also linked to the nurturing of some talents that are very odd indeed—the ability to not see or hear certain people, the ability to ignore certain events, and the ability intentionally to forget that which happened yesterday. To forget intentionally—to remember something in such a way that we do not remember it—is possible only in a world of delusion or a world of bad faith.

America can be presented as the city on the hill only by ignoring the city of Watts and the hills of Wounded Knee. America can be presented as the land of liberty only by deploying a carefully nurtured amnesia regarding the Trail of Tears, the slave ships that frequented our shores, the prison camps for Americans of Japanese ancestry, and more recently, by turning a blind eye to the "free speech zones" that confine and isolate the expression of dissent, and to the prison gulags that cage nearly one percent of our population. America can be presented as the embodiment of justice only by refusing to acknowledge the growing gap between rich and poor, the homeless people near Capitol Hill, the gay-bashing rhetoric of our political leaders, and the incremental authoritarianism that goes by the name of the "Patriot Act." America can be presented as an advocate of democracy abroad only by ignoring the U.S. support for Saddam Hussein in the 1980s when he was using chemical weapons against our Iranian enemies, the U.S. support for the anti-Soviet Afghan Mujahedeen in the 1980s when they were bombing hospitals and schools and civilian airliners, and more recently, the U.S. support for brutal regimes in Uzbekistan and Tajikistan when they were providing bases for the U.S. invasions of Afghanistan and Iraq to overthrow our former friends. America can be presented as exemplary of compassion only by refusing to speak the names of Dresden, Hiroshima, Nagasaki, My Lai, and Abu Ghraib or by viewing these as mere bumps in the road of our otherwise profound respect for human life—mere aberrations in an otherwise pristine record of warfare in which our cause is always just and our bombs are always smart.[3]

However, to refrain from christening the United States as the "city on the hill" or the "land of liberty" is not to engage in demonization. The American people are no more sinful (or more righteous) than people of other nations. Our elected officials and bureaucrats are no less gifted (or more wise) than leaders of other nations. Indeed, if there is one salient feature that distinguishes the United States from other nations, it is the American surfeit of power.

There is a widespread misperception of power as a neutral entity. In this view, power is "wielded" in pursuit of various objectives, and therefore the goodness or badness that attaches to the use of power is highly dependent on who is doing the wielding toward what goals. Power might be used for good by Americans who ostensibly espouse the spread of freedom, but it might be used for evil by our adversaries who are persistently portrayed as reincarnations of Hitler.

A markedly contrasting perception of power pervades the texts of the Hebrew Bible and the New Testament. In biblical perspective, contrary to the modern myth of power as a possession that we wield, power possesses us as if it were a creature or a demonic spirit. Indeed, it is; however, the creaturely and spiritual dimensions of power are not singular in their manifestations.[4] In the New Testament alone, we are confronted by a bewildering array of names for power and for the creatures who are the principalities and powers.[5] In the Pauline and deutero-Pauline writings, we meet a veritable menagerie of creatures: the angels (Rom. 8:38), the governing authorities (Rom. 13:1), the rulers of this age (1 Cor. 2:8), the authorities and powers that are allied with death itself (1 Cor. 15:24–26), the elemental spirits that enslave us in this world (Gal. 4:3), the rule and dominion below (Eph. 1:20–21), the ruler of the power of the air above (Eph. 2:1–2), the cosmic powers of this present darkness (Eph. 6:12), the thrones and dominions (Col. 1:16), and all of the principalities that need to be disarmed (Col. 2:15). In the Revelation of John, some of these creatures are representatives of ornery but ostensibly benign institutions and communities (such as the angels of the seven churches in Rev. 1–3) while others are depicted with a grotesquerie which is pervasively malignant (such as the dragon who gives the beast his power in Rev. 13:2). In Luke 22:53, the "power of darkness" is associated with incumbent political and religious authorities.

Many biblical scholars agree that this language of the powers had its origins in the idea of a heavenly council created to serve *YHWH*. On occasion, the council assembled as a court for testing individuals (Job 1:6–12) while at other times the council gathered to strategize the ways in which the angelic powers could serve God's will among the nations (1 Kings 22:19–23). It was this latter function that issued in the belief that each nation was represented in the council by its own heavenly power, its angel (Dan. 10).

But all was not well in the heavenly council. Already in the Hebrew Bible, there is a depiction of heavenly powers in rebellion against the will of God. Indeed, the J redactor of Genesis depicts not one Fall but two. Human beings are fallen (Gen. 3), but so too are "the sons of God" (Gen. 6:1–4), specifically, the heavenly powers along with the nations and the earthly powers that they represent.[6] Struggles on earth were mirrored in the struggles among the stars (Judg.

5:20), and a nation's disaster signaled the fall of its star, its heavenly power. Whatever the pretenses of earthly rulers, the nations are substantially controlled by the plotting of heavenly powers (for example, in 1 Enoch 56:5–7, angels "shake" and "stir" the kings to war). Phrases like "principalities and powers" became a way of referring to neither socio-political structures nor their heavenly counterparts alone but naming both at once in their inextricable combination.[7] Increasingly, biblical witnesses discern that the powers that were created by God have fallen under the dominion of Satan (Mt. 4:8–9; Lk. 4:5–7; 1 Jn. 5:19). The powers that were created to be servants of God are now arrayed against God's will (Ps. 82; Acts 4:26). The powers that were created to aid in the restraint of chaos have become the perpetrators of chaos, disorder and violence (Eph. 6:12).

But why should we allow our view of nations and governments to be shaped by mythologies that are dated by two millennia and more? Should we not judge the achievements of the state by standards of empirical evidence rather than by esoteric ruminations about fallen creatures? Or is it possible that the biblical perspective challenges our modern myths and our patriotic prejudices so as to enable us to see the empirical evidence in a new light?

Do governments provide for the poor and needy? In fact, government intervention in the economy usually serves to channel wealth toward the already wealthy.[8] Historically, welfare programs for the poor have been motivated less by compassion than by the need for social control; with no regard for actual poverty rates, these programs expand during times of social unrest and contract when "order" has been restored.[9] The bulk of U.S. foreign aid is in the form of military "assistance," but even with humanitarian aid or disaster relief, government programs are often designed to serve ideological purposes or to benefit American corporations.[10]

Do governments serve to defend the rights of threatened minorities? For Americans, the court rulings and civil rights legislation of the 1950s and 1960s are the most frequently cited examples of effective government intervention on behalf of equality. Yet, only a few decades later, we see resegregation and grotesque disparities between white and black rates of unemployment, imprisonment and early mortality.[11] Rather than defending threatened minorities, governments often seek to consolidate their power by manipulating public sentiments against minorities in ways which are discriminatory (for example, against "undocumented" Hispanic immigrants in the United States, or against gays and lesbians) or even genocidal (for example, against the Armenians in the Ottoman Empire, the Tutsis in Rwanda, the Jews in Germany and elsewhere). Indeed, some scholars have noted that the rejection and suppression of vulnerable minorities has been a decisive factor in the history of the creation of nation states.[12]

In democracies, at least, do governments represent the will of the people? This is a fair question to which others must be added. To what degree is our will shaped and manipulated by leaders who tell blatant lies or by more subtle governmental, corporate and media propaganda? In view of the fact that a plurality of Americans polled once favored the use of nuclear weapons in Korea and

Vietnam, in what sense might public opinion be equated with wisdom or insight? How extensive is the *de facto* disenfranchisement of the poor, of felons, and of people with odd ideas—such as the pacifists and anarchists who want no commander-in-chief and are unlikely to go to the polls to select one? Is the candidate for whom you vote (for example, Lyndon Johnson, the 1964 peace candidate) the leader you get (for example, Johnson, the war president)? How often do democratic elections have decidedly undemocratic outcomes? Recall that the Nazi Party won by a clear plurality of votes in the 1932 Reichstag election thus setting the stage for dictatorship. Recall that Bush lost by a clear plurality in the 2000 U.S. election. All of these vagaries of public opinion and elections notwithstanding, sociological studies by Vilfredo Pareto, Robert Michels and others indicate that governments function on the basis of elite rule rather than popular will, regardless of the constitutional forms of the governments.[13]

Do governments restrain violence? On the contrary, governments organize violence. While Thomas Hobbes maintained that governments arose out of the social contract, which enabled humanity to leave behind the brutish state of nature, it would take an extraordinary amount of brutishness to match the body count of the organized violence of the nation state. This violence is exacerbated by the tendencies of adversarial states to engage in mimesis. The Nazi targeting of civilian population was matched by the Allies at Dresden, Hiroshima and elsewhere. After the 2003 ouster of Iraqi dictator Saddam Hussein, the interim American authority in Iraq shut down newspapers and established state-run media, launched military attacks against Iraqi dissidents, ignored civilian casualties or claimed that they were "light," structured the economy in favor of military spending and oil production rather than humanitarian needs, engaged in mass arrests and torture of prisoners—all actions that mirrored the behavior of no one so much as Hussein himself.

Power does not restrain chaos. Power is chaos. But for many Christian anarchists, this biblical insight does not lead to any illusions that the elimination of governments will foster the birth of paradise. As the powers are fallen, people are also fallen—individually and collectively. A vision of Christian anarchy need not be based on any pretenses to human righteousness or perfectibility.[14] Indeed, it is an awareness of our own fallibility that might warn us against participation in coercive institutions.

The refusal to give allegiance to the fatherland and to the powers does not mean that Christian anarchists are people without allegiance. Giving allegiance means keeping faith and the refusal to give allegiance to nation or state enhances the possibilities for keeping faith with others. Above all, believers are called to keep faith with God rather than with any human authority (Acts 5:29), and all other acts of faith issue from this singular allegiance. Believers are called to keep faith with the creation (Gen. 1:11), and not only with a portion that is artificially bounded and labeled as "our country."[15] Believers are called to keep faith with the aliens (Lev. 19:33–34), and not only with "our own kind."[16] Believers are called to keep faith with the enemy (Mt. 5:43–48; Lk. 6:27–36), a form of keeping faith that is rarely acceptable to those of patriotic bent.[17]

Believers are called to keep faith with the prisoners, the rejected and the despised (Mt. 25:31–46).[18]

In contrast to some forms of anarchism, Christian anarchy is marked by spirituality. Voltaire wrote, "If God did not exist, it would be necessary to invent him." Michael Bakunin wrote, "If God really existed, it would be necessary to abolish him."[19] Among anarchists, Bakunin is certainly not alone in his atheism. If there is blame to be assigned for this atheism, it lies squarely with those churches that have pronounced blessings over every principality, power, and war to come down the pike. Small wonder that many anarchists have viewed deity as a mere sanctifying accoutrement to a system of domination. Yet for Christian anarchists, a transcendent God offers the surest hope that all of the penultimate powers will meet judgment and resistance.

In contrast to some forms of anarchism, Christian anarchy is committed to nonviolence. Indeed, it is not unfair to wonder about the degree to which a "violent anarchist" is an oxymoron. Violence and the threat of it are the very essence of coercive power. The words of Ephesians 6:12 are pertinent: "For our struggle is not against enemies of blood and flesh, but against the rulers, against the authorities, against the cosmic powers of this present darkness, against the spiritual forces of evil in the heavenly places."

In contrast to some forms of anarchism, Christian anarchy is communitarian. From Max Stirner to contemporary libertarians, individualistic anarchists have focused on freedom as the removal of constraints on personal behavior (freedom from). The communitarian orientation insists on freedom to love and freedom for others. Some of the most interesting Christian anarchists are those who have lived in intentional communities and who have devoted far more energy to advocating for the freedom of others rather than to their own freedom. As Simone Weil observed, patriotism is a false substitute for genuine community.[20] Patriotism co-opts the language of kinship, neighborliness and sacrifice, but in its abstraction, the fatherland is no more a point of genuine human encounter than is the "Internet community" or the World Wide Web.

In contrast to some anarchists who have hatched all kinds of schemes for the final eradication of domination, Christian anarchy is best conceived as a journey rather than a destination. Thomas More (1478–1535) coined "utopia" as a word that could carry two divergent meanings; from the Greek, *eutopos* would mean "good place," but *outopos* would mean "no place." Visions of utopia serve us well if we retain the tension inherent to the word itself. Visions of a good place protect humanity against resigned acceptance of the powers that be, but the admission that humanity can create no place of perfect peace and freedom guards against the Orwellian pursuit of paradise.

Like any people who hold onto visions of a new heaven and earth, anarchists must forever confess, "We have not arrived." Those who hope for a new earth live in perpetual exile, yet they can sense the new life that is already in their midst (Lk. 17:20–21). Even with fallibility, they can seek to live a new life within the shell of old power arrangements. If anarchy is a place, a destination of freedom from all oppression, then it can only appear as the eschatological gift from God. But if anarchy is a journey of resistance to the powers and compassion for the power-less, then it is a continuing journey. It is a journey of hope because of the stories that have been making the rounds. Word has it that the powers have already been unmasked. Word has it that death has already lost its sting. Word has it that Babylon has already fallen. Depart, then, on the journey out of Babylon.

A Great Cloud of Witnesses

The word "anarchy" itself is suggestive of negation with a negative prefix (*an*) attached to a Greek word for "power" (*arche*), but rarely have anarchists been proponents of mere nihilism. The first prominent figure to identify himself pub-licly as an "anarchist" might have been the nineteenth-century French theorist and activist, Pierre-Joseph Proudhon. The writings of Proudhon and those of the many "classical anarchists" who came after him (for example, Michael Bakunin, Peter Kropotkin, and Emma Goldman) are awash with proposals for decentralized social organization without the power of domination. Rather than promoting nihilism, these writings offer debatable but creative visions of labor federations and mutual aid, of public safety without police and decision making without hierarchy, and of education that resists conformity and voluntary com-munities that resist the allure of wealth and greed.

Historians of the anarchist movement have focused rather exclusively on this period of "classical anarchism" in the West—a period that extends from the French Revolution to 1939, the year that the fascist troops of Francisco Franco rounded up the anarchists of Barcelona.[21] The historians' choice of these chronological parameters has been influenced to no small degree by linguistics. Prior to the French Revolution, there were no identifiable movements of people who embraced the title "anarchist," insofar as "anarchy" was regarded as a syn-onym for "chaos."[22] Therefore, relying solely on the linguistic criterion, it would be anachronistic to find "anarchists" prior to the late eighteenth century.

The focus of historians on "classical anarchism" suffers from both geograph-ical and chronological limitations. In its Eurocentrism, this focus ignores the impact of indigenous communitarian traditions on the anarchism of Latin America and Africa, as well as the significant convergence of pacifism, anar-chism and Christianity among activists in twentieth-century Korea and Japan.[23] In the name of avoiding anachronism, historians risk ignoring anarchist themes, which date back to the philosophies of Zeno (circa 342–267 BCE), Chuang Tzu (fourth century BCE), Heraclitus (circa 540–475 BCE) and beyond. If one asks whether the word "anarchist" was used as a self-designation by the Doukhobors in the nineteenth century, the Diggers in the seventeenth century, the Donatists in the fourth century, Jesus in the first century, the proto-Israelites in the twelfth century BCE—in each case, the answer is clearly "no." But clearly in each of these cases there was a fundamental challenge to power and repudiation of it—the power of empire and king, the power of violence and coercion, the power of wealth and exploitation—and dogmatic cronyism ought not prevent us from seeing the anarchist nature of that.[24]

In the history of the church, there are witnesses aplenty to a faith in God that is subversive toward allegiance to temporal authorities. In the pre-Constantinian era especially, the power of government was less celebrated as a great constraint on evil than it was remembered as integral to the juridical murder of Jesus. What of patriotic loyalty to homeland? Listen to the anonymous author of the letter to Diognetus, one of the earliest of the extra-canonical writings from the Jesus sect of Judaism. Of believers, he or she says,

> They dwell in their own countries, but simply as sojourners. As citizens, they share in all things with others, and yet endure all things as if foreigners. Every foreign land is to them as their native country, and every land of their birth as a land of strangers. . . . They pass their days on earth, but they are citizens of heaven.[25]

In the three centuries following the crucifixion and resurrection of Jesus, the question of the extent to which believers should fulfill the responsibilities of provisional citizenship in various localities hinged on two defining issues: whether Christians could honor the divinity of the emperor and whether Christians could wield weapons of war. "No" was the resounding answer on both counts with very few exceptions to prove the rule. The *Apostolic Tradition* of Hippolytus (circa 218) counseled that "military constables" and "magistrates" could be admitted to the assembly of believers only if they agreed to refrain from all killing, and if any believers who were already baptized should decide to become soldiers, they "shall be sent away."

Dramatic changes loomed with the so-called conversion of the Emperor Constantine in 312, but it was the church that changed, not Rome or its Emperor. The Empire lumbered along as before with its palace intrigues, murders, slavery, colonial thievery, wars and juridical bloodletting. Constantine persisted in his reverence for Apollo, the sun god, but after 312 Jesus was incorporated into the solar pantheon as a sort of son of the sun god.[26] It was the church that sustained the only significant changes in the sudden transformation from being persecuted minority to being persecutors in the name of the official religion of the Empire.

Eusebius, Ambrose of Milan, and Augustine of Hippo were complicit in shaping an imperial theology to bolster the new status of the church. As they did so, there emerged the earliest hints of Christian "patriotism" in the suggestions that certain lands and leaders (the Romans) were godlier than others (the barbarians). Nonetheless, the vision of the early church persisted not on the broad thoroughfare of official, post-Constantinian Christendom but in the alleyways of dissent and among those who were formally branded as "heretics."[27] North Africa, a seedbed of political and ecclesiastical dissent, provided a home for Montanism and Donatism both of which were renounced as deviant by the emerging ecclesiastical powerbrokers who insisted on an orthopraxis in religion to match the imperial hegemony of Rome. Montanists were unacceptable in their attentiveness to biblical eschatology and in their willingness to be led by the anarchistic movement of the Spirit rather than by officially sanctioned doctrine; equally suspect was the respect that they accorded to female prophets.[28] The Donatists were unacceptable for having sought to build a faith community that was free of any taint of allegiance to the Roman Empire, even if the allegiance had been pledged under the pressures of persecution.[29]

Among anchorites and cenobites, the rejection of what passed for civilization was implicit in their lifestyles and often explicit in their writings. The strategy of the church hierarchy to deal with these movements of separation was to co-opt them or, failing that, to suppress them. In late antiquity and throughout the middle ages, the social order faced multiple challenges from communitarian visionaries. The very foundation of the economic order was challenged by the voluntary poverty embraced and preached by Peter John Olivi and the Spiritual Franciscans.[30] The security of patriarchal power was undermined by new perceptions of the feminine in God.[31] The technological power to plunder the creation met resistance in the visions of Francis that the animals, the trees, and the earth itself are our sisters and our brothers.

Clearly, dissent in medieval Europe antedated the Protestant Reformation by centuries. Authorities both political and ecclesiastical (insofar as that distinction applied) met resistance from Cathars, Lollards, Waldensians, Hussites and others, and the historian Norman Cohn is not amiss in labeling some of these dissidents as "anarchists."[32] At times, the resistance was violent, such as that mounted by the fifteenth-century Taborites. A movement of early Bohemian nationalism, the Taborites did not seek to renounce power so much as to usurp it. More far-reaching was the vision of a contemporary of the Taborites, Peter Chelcický.[33] Basing his faith on the authority of the New Testament, Chelcický was an advocate of absolute pacifism and the elimination of all class distinctions. He believed that Christians should not rely on civil courts. While John Huss believed that the emperor should intervene to reform a corrupt papacy, Chelcický maintained that the community of believers should remain totally separate from political authority. Indeed, Chelcický traced the fall of the church to that sad day when Constantine embraced it.

With the dawn of the Protestant Reformation, Lutherans and Calvinists were critical of papal power, but they were more enamored of the princely powers and emerging nationalism in northern Europe. Anabaptism represented a third way of free communities of believers who were beholden to neither ecclesiastical nor political power, a stance that left them vulnerable to persecution by both bishops and princes. Anarchist themes that found expression among groups like the Hutterites included a total refusal to rely on violence, a literal communism, and a practice of mutual aid that Peter Kropotkin could only match in theory. It must be emphasized, however, that most Anabaptists did not overtly resist political authority. For some Anabaptists, the governing authorities were viewed as gifts from God for the restraint of evil, but for others the powers were perceived to be part of the way of the world that was being overcome by Christ. Through noncooperation with all violence and coercion, the faithful could participate in the love of Christ that was already overcoming power.[34]

A vision of anarchy was planted in the hills of seventeenth-century England—planted literally, as Gerard Winstanley and friends gathered on April 1, 1649, to sow beans, carrots and parsnips on the commons at St. George's Hill in Surrey. Traditionally, common land had served as a refuge for the poor, a locale in which the landless could gather firewood and plant subsistence gardens without fear of arrest by claimants to "private property." By the seventeenth century, however, enclosure acts were dramatically decreasing the acreage set aside as commons. In a bold act of reclamation, Winstanley and the Diggers sought to establish communities for the poor at St. George's Hill and Cobham.

Winstanley was a pacifist, and he believed that the beheading of Charles I on January 30, 1649, was a poor substitute for genuine revolution. "Do these men throw down kingly power?" No, wrote Winstanley, because the hankering for domination still persists among the lawyers, clerics, armies and wealthy lords of manor. But do not presume to kill them all as well, because faith in power has become embedded within the souls of people everywhere. Kingly power is overcome by exposing it to "the Sun of Righteousness" (Mal. 4:1–2) and the alchemy of God's love.[35] Later in his life, Winstanley joined the Quakers, another group to emerge from the nonconformist and antinomian milieu of the English Revolution. The fundamental Quaker respect for "the Light" abiding within each person issued in a critique of all hierarchal governance including majority rule. Since all are equal in the Light, heads should not be bowed to potentates and thieves in prison should be accorded as much respect as bishops in cathedrals. The power of the king is not overcome by violence. The power of the king is overcome by calling him (like everyone else) "friend."

There were plentiful "no government" Christians among the antebellum abolitionists of America including Frederick Douglass, William Lloyd Garrison and Adin Ballou. In the "Standard of Practical Christianity," the founding document of the nineteenth-century Hopedale Community, Ballou wrote:

> Placing unlimited confidence in our Heavenly Father, we distrust all other guidance. We cannot be governed by the will of man, however solemnly and formally declared, nor put our trust in an arm of flesh. Hence we voluntarily withdraw from all interference with the governments of this world. We can take no part in the politics, the administration, or the defense of these governments, either by voting at their polls, holding their offices, aiding in the execution of their legal vengeance, fighting under their banners, claiming their protection against violence, seeking redress in their courts, petitioning their legislatures to enact laws, or obeying their unrighteous requirements.[36]

The Hopedale Community became a model for egalitarianism, a forum for women's rights advocates, and a refuge for escaped slaves. Even as other nonresistants compromised to endorse the Union during the Civil War, Ballou continued to espouse both pacifism and abolitionism.

As Northerners were pleading the cause of abolition, some escaped slaves participated in establishing communities that were free of the domination of both slave owners and government authorities. In various regions of the South, escaped slaves were able to make their way to the relative safety of territory inhabited by Native Americans. The free "maroon" communities shaped by Native Americans and former slaves are a vital part of the story of antebellum anarchism in America.[37]

While Russians have been stereotyped as people constrained by a history of authoritarian rule, Russia might have given the world more theorists and practitioners of anarchism than any other land. The Christian anarchists of Russia included the Doukhobors ("Spirit Wrestlers," that is, those who struggle by means of the spirit rather than arms or coercion). When the Doukhobor refusal of conscription led to persecution by the state in the late nineteenth century, it was another Russian anarchist, Leo Tolstoy, who came to their aid and helped to organize their eventual emigration to Canada. Christian anarchism persisted in twentieth-century Russia in the peasant communities inspired by Tolstoy and in Nicolas Berdyaev's writings on freedom in communion with God.[38] The impact of Tolstoy's vision of Christian anarchism was not confined by boundaries of culture or religion. In the twentieth century, Tolstoy's work had an influence on Jewish thought (through the writings of Gustav Landauer and Martin Buber) and on Hindu activism (through Mohandas Gandhi and Vinoba Bhave). In turn, the impact of these Jewish and Hindu witnesses rebounded to influence Christian spirituality (Thomas Merton and Dorothy Day) and Christian resistance (Dan and Phil Berrigan and Elizabeth McAlister).

In *The Holy Way: A Word to the Jews and the Nations*, Martin Buber presents Jesus as an anarchist. Jesus saw that the power of Rome would collapse, not due to armed rebellion, but due to a renewal in the very soul of Judaism. In Buber's view, God was present for humanity in "the between" of loving and compassionate relationships. Thus, a compassionate community (*Gemeinschaft*) of mutual aid is "the realization of the Divine" in human history, and Buber maintained that Jesus was offering this community as a response to Roman oppression.

> 'Do not resist evil,' means: resist evil by doing good; do not attack the reign of evil, but unhesitatingly bond together for the reign of good—and that will come when evil can no longer resist you, not because you have conquered it, but because you have redeemed it. Jesus wished to build the temple of true community out of Judaism, a community whose mere sight would cause the despotic state's walls to crumble.[39]

The Holy Way bore the dedication, "In memory of my friend Gustav Landauer." Landauer was a pacifist (owing in part to the writings of Tolstoy) who was murdered by German troops in 1919. There is substantial agreement in the perspectives of Landauer and Buber regarding community as an antidote to the state. For Landauer, the state represents relationships based on force (*Gewalt*), but in true community, relationships are grounded in spirit (*Geist*). Through the creation of independent countercommunities (*Gegen-Gemeinschaft*), people have the potential to free themselves of "the superstition of the state." The spread of

Gegen-Gemeinschaft will mark the fall of the state not because it will be over-thrown but because it will be ignored.[40]

Tolstoy's reading of the Gospels also left its mark on the nonviolent revolutionaries of India. In the 1950s, a frail ascetic clad only in homespun *khadi* walked the length and breadth of India stopping along the way at the homes of wealthy landowners and introducing himself by saying, "I have come to rob you with love." The man was Vinoba Bhave, whose movement of *Bhu Dan* ("gift of land") led some to call him the successor to Gandhi. His vision was for nothing less than the voluntary redistribution of all of the land of India, and before his death he had secured the transfer of hundreds of thousands of acres to the poor. *Bhu Dan* was not well-loved by capitalists or socialists. The capitalists believed that large landholdings were essential for productive economic activity, and the socialists believed that only state intervention could achieve an equitable redistribution; but *Bhu Dan* was less an economic plan than a spiritual movement of anarchy—the anarchy of giving.

Vinoba's vision of *Bhu Dan* was inspired by Gandhi's proposal for *Swadeshi*, or "economic independence." The struggle for independence was to be waged on multiple levels; India should be free of British imports and British rule, and Indian villages should be economically and politically free of central governance, and individuals should be free of economics itself—free of the buying and the selling and the striving after wealth. Gandhi loved to tell of the criticism with which one opponent had confronted him: "Political economy is concerned with the distribution of wealth, but you and your spinning wheel are concerned with the distribution of poverty." After expressing delight that his critic had understood him so well, Gandhi quoted Luke 6:20: "Blessed are you who are poor, for yours is the kingdom of God."[41] Although Gandhi was Hindu, his familiarity with the Gospels surpassed that of most of the British rulers of India.

The most cogent expressions of Christian anarchism in America today are to be found among intentional communities of resistance, service and voluntary poverty. Ranging from Jonah House to the Pacific Life Community to the Community for Creative Nonviolence, many of these communities have found an inspirational model in the Catholic Worker movement. In the early days of the movement, Peter Maurin told Dorothy Day that he believed that one of the greatest curses of modern humanity was the endless reflection about "what the other guy ought to do." In democracies where voting is presented as the highest form of civic engagement, this reflection usually focuses on what the government ought to do. The government ought to feed the hungry, house the homeless, and work for peace. Day and Maurin believed that, whenever responsibility for these "works of mercy" is relegated to the government, there is a spiritual impoverishment of human community and a perverse presumption that we have managed to bureaucratize love. Whenever responsibility for peace is relegated to the state, governments make the inevitable Orwellian claim that militarism is peace. *I* must be engaged in works of mercy and peace, and *we* must be engaged in them together, not because it is an effective form of social engagement, but because it is the Gospel.

But in our technological era, we want effectiveness, do we not? How effective can they be—these anarchistic communities with their free kitchens and their hospitality houses for the homeless, these protesters standing on the rainy sidewalks with their signs and sitting in the jail cells for their civil disobedience? If they really want to be effective, why not get involved with electoral politics and with making real changes in the structure of power instead of dismissing it all as (in the words of Dorothy Day) "that filthy, rotten system?" Day knew of the faint praise that damned the Catholic Workers as "good humanitarians" but ineffective in the "real" world:

> You people are impractical, they tell us, nice idealists, but not headed anywhere big and important. They are right. We *are* impractical. . .as impractical as Calvary. . . . If an outsider who comes to visit doesn't pay attention to our praying and what that means, then he'll miss the whole point of things. We are here to bear witness to our Lord.[42]

The Antistatist Tradition in the Bible

Everything—absolutely everything—depended on two women with little power. Everything depended on the fragility of the moment in which these women decided whether to obey or disobey the direct order of the most powerful ruler on earth. The ruler had at his disposal an unprecedented military force, while the only power available to the women was the power of refusal, and everything depended on it. Shiphrah and Puah disobeyed the Pharaoh (Ex. 1:15–20). Had they decided to obey him instead, there would have been no people of God, no biblical story, no hope for the future.

Questions of historical factuality aside, the story of Shiphrah and Puah is remarkable for the light it sheds on the nature of power. Pharaoh ordered the midwives, Shiphrah and Puah, to kill all of the male children born to Hebrew slaves. Contrary to popular illusions that power is wielded in the pursuit of rational objectives, there was something irrational and self-defeating at the very core of Pharaoh's command. Like the monuments it left behind, Egypt itself was a pyramid with the well-being of the few at the apex fully dependent on the many slaves at the base. But when Pharaoh, who wanted many slaves, felt threatened because his slaves had become so many he ordered the diminution of the pool of slaves on which his own well-being depended. The irrationality of it all indicates that Pharaoh was less a power-wielder than a man possessed by power. It is not insignificant that the command was for birth to be followed straightaway by death. (As with Pharaoh, so with Herod in Mt. 2:16–18.) Contrary to popular illusions that power is wielded in the service of life, death is unveiled as the very foundation and content of power. In his anthropological study of power, Eli Sagan put it succinctly: "A king was a king because he could kill at will."[43]

If its perspective on power is bleak, the story of Shiphrah and Puah offers hopeful insight on the potential for resistance. But the hope-filled resistance commended by Exodus 1:15–20 is not the sort of resistance that customarily fills the annals of political science and history. Forget about amassing your cache of weapons in preparation for the revolution; Pharaoh always wins that game, and even if he is overthrown the "revolutionary Pharaoh" who takes his place will resemble no one so much as his predecessor. Forget about wheedling your way into the halls of power or winning the next election so that you can pursue your resistance from within; by the time you get within, power itself will own your heart, head and "keester," and the urgency of resistance will be replaced by the need for compromise and accommodation in pursuit of "meaningful change." Forget about devoting years to gathering together the mass of people who can take to the streets and cajole the Pharaoh from his throne; the masses are too busy with "making a living," and they are unlikely to be mobilized by concern over the killings of a few Hebrew slave babies. No, the resistance commended by the book of Exodus is hope-filled precisely because it is not dependent on force of arms or politics or numbers. It is dependent only on the noncooperation of two women and the noncooperation of one God.

How did Shiphrah and Puah know that this was a God of resistance who willed noncooperation with the only earthly authority known to them? The text does not tell us. There are no burning bushes, no voices from on high. We are only told of allegiance and disobedience as if these were two sides of one faith: allegiance to God and disobedience to the powers. It is this God alone who is cited as the motivator for the actions of the midwives. Interpretations that posit nationalism or ethnocentrism as providing the impetus for this resistance to the Pharaoh are owing less to the words of Exodus than to the extra-biblical elevation of patriotism to the status of a core ethical value. Readers of the text might be prepared to risk all in defense of homeland or of "our own kind," but such a view is foreign to the story of Shiphrah and Puah. Indeed, the text asks us to imagine a time when there was no homeland for the Hebrew people or, more precisely, the homeland was Egypt—the very source of the oppression that merited resistance. Moreover, there is no certainty that Shiphrah and Puah were even Hebrews. While the names of these two women have Semitic etymologies, the text itself (1:15) is beguiling on the question of whether these were "Hebrew midwives" or "midwives to the Hebrews."[44] Their disobedience was not motivated by loyalty to clan or race or nation but by loyalty to God.

Who were these "Hebrew" people who had no nation and no homeland save the land of their oppressors? Insofar as there was any unity among the Hebrews, it was not based in ethnicity and certainly not in race. Prior to the first millennium BCE, the word *hapiru* (Hebrew) might have functioned simply as a designation for outcastes, rabble, and people of no account. In the Amarna letters and other extra-biblical sources, *hapiru* referred to people of low social standing but with the added connotation that these people were outlaws, fugitives and rebels.[45] When a degree of unity was eventually forged among these outcastes and fugitives, its source was God alone. The covenant at Sinai provided a vision of a free people of *YHWH*, a "kingdom of God," a community with no rulers except for God. The Empire, Pharaoh, pyramid and all of the accoutrements of power were to be left behind in the flight to freedom.

Questions about the identity of the *hapiru* have contributed to an ongoing debate among biblical scholars regarding the origins of Israel. There have been three positions.

1. Some traditional scholars insist that the books of Exodus, Deuteronomy, Joshua and Judges provide straightforward historical accounts of events as they transpired. Thus the Hebrews, an ethno-religious group, escaped slavery in Egypt, led a nomadic life for forty years, and then invaded and conquered Canaan. This is the "conquest model" for the origins of Israel.

2. Other scholars have asserted that it is a misrepresentation of both the Bible and historiography to claim that biblical writers were merely attempting to provide a factual account of events. There is no extra-biblical evidence to corroborate such momentous events as the escape of tens of thousands of slaves from Egypt and their subsequent military conquest of Canaan. The biblical narrative might be a telescoped version of events that transpired over centuries. The Hebrews (still an ethno-religious group in this model) were nomadic people who gradually migrated into the land of Canaan. When their numbers reached sufficient mass, the Hebrews took possession of the land from the Canaanites. This is the "migration model" for the origins of Israel.

3. Thanks in large part to the work of George Mendenhall and Norman Gottwald, there is a third possibility: the "revolt model." This model takes seriously the biblical and extrabiblical identification of the *hapiru* not as an ethnic group but as dispossessed fugitives and rebels. The *hapiru* were those who opposed the monarchies of the Canaanite city-states, and the majority of the *hapiru* might have lived in Canaan for all of their lives. But the revolt model does not discount the Exodus narrative. The small bands of fugitive slaves who escaped from Egypt brought to Canaan a faith in *YHWH* and a vision of a kingdom of God which was free of tyranny. In this model, the origin of Israel is less a tale of bloody conquest and genocide than a story of alliance and cooperation among escaped slaves, oppressed Canaanites and fugitive outlaws united by *YHWH*'s promise for a new land of milk and honey. As the kings of Canaan were deposed, the proto-Israelites shaped a nonhierarchical society—a confederation of tribes including those of escaped slaves and liberated Canaanites, all of whom became known as the Hebrews.

While the debate on the origins of Israel continues, there is little debate that the proto-Israelites managed to shape a confederated society that was broadly egalitarian and devoid of central governance. Like the "primitive," stateless societies of Africa and Latin America, Israel produced its charismatic leaders (judges) during times of crisis, but there was no institution of kingship or other enduring locus of rule. As the early Israelites rejected political power, they were also profoundly suspect of military power. As Gideon set out to face the Midianites (Judg. 7:1–23), the anxiety was to decrease the size of available military force lest the people fall under the illusion that they were winning a victory of armies. *YHWH* was the only king, and *YHWH* would be Israel's defense.

A land without hierarchal governance is not a land without social organization. The social structures of premonarchal Israel included families and extended families, mutual aid associations of families, tribes, and eventually, a confederation of tribes.[46] These extended families and mutual aid associations were the basic structures to which Israel and Judah returned in times of crisis, including the crisis of Babylonian exile when the monarchy had been swept away and segments of the population were carried away to captivity. There in exile, the people discovered anew that the glue that held them together was neither king nor homeland but faith in God. While in exile, Jews were separated from the families of their birth, and they formed new "families"—the *beth 'abhoth*, voluntary communities of mutual aid and encouragement in which the "family" connectedness was a useful social fiction.[47] When Babylon fell and these communities of Jews returned from exile, the prophet Zechariah urged them not to return to the ways of monarchy: "Not by might, nor by power, but by my spirit, says the LORD of hosts" (Zech. 4:6).

Given that much of the biblical history of Israel passed through redaction by the palace scribes and court historians of Israel's monarchal period, it is remarkable that even the "greatest" kings are still presented as radically flawed—David with his lies and his murders and Solomon with his greed and his idolatry.[48] It is even more remarkable that the texts of the Hebrew Bible retained and perpetuated the antistatist perspectives from the period of Israel's origins. In Jotham's fable (Judg. 9), the useful trees and vines produce olives, figs and grapes, but the king is identified with the bramble, which produces nothing but fire and destruction. The portrayal of kingship in 1 Samuel 8 gives pause for its negativity. Through Samuel, *YHWH* warns the people of Israel that a king will take away their sons to be soldiers and take away their daughters to be servants. A king will demand of the people one-tenth of the product of their labor, thus usurping the tithe that properly belongs to God. A king will cause the people to cry out for liberation as if they were still enslaved in Egypt, but this hankering for freedom will come too late. The people of Israel ignored all of the warnings because they wanted to "be like other nations."

Jacques Ellul notes a peculiar pattern in the biblical accounts of the kings of Israel and Judah.[49] Drawing specifically on the text of 2 Kings, Ellul discovered that the idolatrous and faithless kings were highly skilled in the political arts and victorious in their wars while the kings who were concerned with faithfulness to God and integrity in their dealings with people were disastrous in both politics and war. The pattern is so pronounced that it constitutes a veritable judgment on the world of power politics and on the world's criteria of success.

The skepticism toward power that pervades the "historical writings" becomes a torrent of opposition to power in prophetic literature. If a prophet took a favorable attitude toward the king—encouraging him, consoling him, obeying him—it was a sign that he was a false prophet. The genuine prophets of Israel were unrelenting in their condemnation of power, in their judgment that the official policy was the wrong policy, in their repudiation of wealth, in their contempt for the religious displays that passed for righteousness, and in their revulsion at the bloodlust that passed for peace. However, the prophets must not be depicted as proponents of proto-democracy as if they were espousing the will of the majority of the people in the face of tyrannical rule. On the contrary, it was the prophetic contention that the most urgent truths were represented by only one—the widow whose neglect and suffering was sufficient cause to cast doubt on the future of the entire nation (Isa. 1:23), the one prophet whose proclamations were subjected to universal scorn and ridicule (Jer. 20:7), and the one God who was abandoned by all of the covenanted partners who had once most earnestly declared their loyalty (Hos. 4:1).

With the prophets, the very foundation of Israel's hope, the Messiah, is envisioned anew with the image of the "shoot" or "branch" (Isa. 11:1; Zech. 3:8). It is an image that acknowledges that the glory and power of Israel's monarchy has been cut off like a great tree that has been felled; out of the fallen tree's stump, a tender shoot grows as a sign of the perseverance of God's promise. Gone are the images of the promised one as an iron rod who will shatter the nations (Ps. 2:7–9), and as a lion who will maul the ungodly (2 Esdras 12:31–33).

Isaiah totally subverts any association of messianic hope with a coercive, militarized monarchy (Isa. 11:1–9). In Isaiah's vision, the only rod that shatters is the rod of the mouth (11:4)—that is, the word of God. The only lion is the lion that eats straw and is led about by a little child (11:6–7). The military paraphernalia belted around the waist are replaced by righteousness and faithfulness (11:5). While the powerbrokers have assiduously ignored the plight of the lowly with the shoot there will be justice for the meek and the poor (11:4). All of this will be accomplished not by power but by the spirit of God (Isa. 11:2; Zech. 4:6).

This critique of power is continued and expanded in the apocalyptic literature of the Hebrew Bible and the New Testament. The apocalyptic vision itself constitutes a judgment on all nations and all temporal authority, for in the end, the visionary perceives that all power will be overthrown "and not by human hands" (Dan. 8:25).[50] By its very nature, apocalyptic is about revealing and unveiling. Apocalyptic is a mode of seeing from the vantage points that are rarely granted to us—seeing underneath the robes of power, seeing through the pomposity of the Empire, seeing with the eyes of all the martyrs, and seeing at the very behest of God—and what is seen is chilling. When we see the nations and the kings, we see no shining city on a hill; we see the whore of Babylon seated on the seven hills of Rome (Rev. 17).[51] Where some would hope to see that God is on the side of free nations with high moral principles, we see instead that every nation (*nota bene*) follows beast and dragon (Rev. 13:7). Where some would hope to see the loyal patriots, we see instead those who worship the beast (13:4, 13:8). Apocalyptic seeing penetrates patina and veneer. Prosperity and victory in war are not signs of God's blessing but veritable marks of the beast. The saints are not victorious; they are defeated (13:7).

But apocalyptic vision is certainly not without hope; it merely says that hope is neither to be found in loyalty to nation or to state nor in coercion or in violence. If you believe that hope lies in "killing all the terrorists" (a refrain from both sides in the 2004 election campaign), then read again Revelation 13:3. Like Hydra, both the dragon and the beast thrive on all violent assault. Hope, for John of Patmos, resides with the most improbable of figures, the slaughtered

Lamb. The only weapons in the arsenal of the Lamb are the word of God (the "sword of the mouth" and the "sword of truth" of Rev. 1:16, 2:16, 19:15) and the blood of the martyrs (14:13–20).[52] The torrents of blood become a means of purification (7:14) for those who proclaim that "power and might" belong to God alone (7:12), but for the acolytes of the Empire, the blood of the martyrs produces the final intoxication that marks the fall of Babylon (17:2, 17:6, 18:3). The copious bloodshed by which the nations sought to be victorious becomes the very medium of their fall, but the end of Revelation is not the fall of Babylon and certainly not the destruction of the earth. The victory of the slaughtered Lamb is only completed with the new heaven and new earth (21:1–4). The "slaughtered Lamb" is John's favored image for the risen Christ, the crucified Jesus.

The Gospel depictions of Jesus constitute a parody of conventional kingship, with his birth in a cow barn, his aides comprised of fishermen and carpenters, his triumphal entry into Jerusalem riding on a donkey rather than a warhorse. The Gospels also present Jesus as inaugurating a radically "upside-down kingdom."[53] Jesus renounces political power in the temptations accounts as he refuses Satan's offer of governance over all the kingdoms of the world. Jesus renounces economic power in his calls for giving to extremity and his pronouncements of God's blessing on the poor. Jesus renounces juridical power and the power of the prison in his proclamation of liberty for the captives. Jesus renounces technological powers in the lessons that he draws from the birds of the air and the flowers of the field. Jesus renounces military power as he tells Peter to put away his sword. Jesus invites his disciples to live in a new community of love that is present even now as "the kingdom of God." With Jesus, there is the establishment once again of the nonhierarchical "kingdom of *YHWH*" that was first received as a gift by the *hapiru* who had been freed from domination.

Given Jesus' radical turn away from power, what are we to make of the "Render unto Caesar" periscope well-loved by the proponents of temporal power? With only the slightest variation, these words appear in all three of the synoptic Gospels (Mt. 22:21; Mk. 12:17; Lk. 20:25): "Give therefore to the emperor the things that are the emperor's, and to God the things that are God's." Even the hard-boiled skeptics of the "Jesus Seminar" assert without reservation that this is a genuine saying attributable to the historical Jesus. Does this saying, then, provide a viable foundation for a theology of two kingdoms in which God should be heeded in the spiritual realm and Caesar should be obeyed in all temporal matters?

In all three synoptics, the saying is actually Jesus' response to a trap that had been laid for him and (the Jesus Seminar notwithstanding) the meaning of the saying is totally skewed if it is separated from this context.[54] In Matthew and Mark, the trap is laid by Pharisees and Herodians while in Luke, it is laid by "spies" of the chief priests who wished "to hand him over to the jurisdiction and authority of the governor." In all three versions, they sought to trap Jesus with the question of whether it was "lawful" to pay taxes to Caesar. The question was not whether the payment of taxes was good or righteous. Clearly, the laws of Rome not only allowed for tax payments but required them. In the codes of Judaism, it was clearly "lawful" to pay taxes for the temple (e.g., Mt. 17:24–27). Was it also lawful to pay taxes to this occupying emperor who claimed to be a god? A response of "yes" would have constituted an endorsement of the occupying power and a refutation of the faith of Israel. A response of "no" would have constituted sedition and would have provided cause for immediate arrest. That was the trap, but Jesus said neither. Instead, he asked to see a denarius, a coin that bore the graven image of Caesar. By producing it, those who sought to entrap Jesus showed that they were violating Jewish law themselves by carrying around this miniature idol, this symbol of apostasy.[55] Therefore, give to Caesar everything that belongs to him, namely all of the graven images, apostasy, idolatry, and faithlessness. All else belongs to God. Whenever the "Render unto Caesar" saying is divorced from its context, it is made to do what the Herodians and spies wanted Jesus to do—that is, endorse submission to Caesar. In fact, Jesus rebukes Caesar and his followers.

But what of Paul? It certainly does not seem to be a repudiation of Caesar when Paul writes in Romans 13:1–7, "Let every person be subject to the governing authorities." Was Paul practicing what he preached? If he was enamored of authority, why did Paul admonish believers not to rely on the "unrighteous" civil courts (1 Cor. 6:1)? If Paul was urging obedience to rulers, what accounts for his repeated arrests and his reputation as a troublemaker?

Romans 13:1–7 is a text well-loved by Nazis in Germany (after they came to power), by white racists in South Africa (before they lost their apartheid grip on power), and by patriotic Americans (after they were able to extricate themselves from subjection to the governing authority of George III).[56] If the criteria for what constitutes a "governing authority" is not static neither are categories like "nations" and "countries." Patriotic as we may be, nations are mortal creatures. There are no Reichs to last a thousand years and no empires on which the sun will never set. Like the Soviet Union, Rome, and Babylon, the United States will surely pass away.

Both Paul and the pseudo-Pauline writers were keenly aware that empires, rulers and powers are historically ephemeral and grounded in contingency rather than wisdom (1 Cor. 2:6–8). They are doomed (1 Cor. 15:24–26), and they will be disarmed by Christ (Col. 2:15) and made subject to him (Eph. 1:20–21). An awareness of the eschatological nature of the Pauline writings led William Stringfellow to urge an exchange in the traditional readings of Romans 13 and Revelation 13—two texts that appear to be in opposition. In the traditional readings, subjection (Rom. 13) is moral guidance for the present while "the beast" (Rev. 13) is only an apocalyptic vision relevant to some future era. In fact, John of Patmos may be admonishing believers about "the beast" that is being worshiped now, and Paul may be counseling "subjection" only when and insofar as it witnesses to Christ's ultimate victory over the powers.[57]

If the verses of Romans 13:1–7 are well-remembered, Dale W. Brown is certainly correct in observing that Romans 13:8 is often overlooked.[58] What is owed to others is not taxes or obedience but love. Love is the fulfillment of God's law, and that is the one law that believers are called to obey. While Caesar is the head of the body politic, Christ is the head of the body of believers (Col. 1:15–18).

These references to God's law and Christ's lordship raise a final question for Christian anarchists. Is it not an intolerable contradiction to renounce temporal power while simultaneously proclaiming faith in a Celestial Autocrat? In several of the Psalms of Israel an association is posited between the glory of God and the enthronement of earthly kings. It is an association that has persisted as a dominant theme in no small number of historical and contemporary theologies. Enthronement is suggestive of stasis and immovability, as are the divine attributes of omnipotence and omniscience. These are attributes that are envied by the mightiest of earthly rulers. Omnipotence means never having to suffer defeat.

In 1 Samuel 4, *YHWH* suffers defeat. What is described in this text is not only a military defeat of Israel by the Philistines; it is also a defeat of God as the Ark is carried into captivity.[59] It is a narrative that does not fit well with theologies of triumphalism and omnipotence, but it is by no means the only text to challenge the association of God with victorious power. In Revelation, John of Patmos offers a subversive rereading of the hymns that herald the enthronement of the divine warrior (e.g., Ps. 96, 97, 98) as he reconfigures them into hymns for the slaughtered Lamb. As Sallie McFague observes, the struggle for a viable "model of God" does not originate in the speculations of post-biblical theologians; it is a pursuit that is integral to the biblical text itself.[60] God is the Majestic Sovereign (Ps. 8) and God is the Seamstress (Gen. 3:21). God is the King who subdues (Ps. 47) and God is the Midwife who serves (Ps. 22:9–10). God is the Lion who drags away and devours the young (Jer. 50:44–46), God is the Shepherd (Ps. 23), God is the Warrior (Ex. 15:3), and God is the Compassionate Mother (Isa. 49:14–15).

So yes, it is a paradox for anarchists to renounce the earthly powers while also proclaiming faith in the Lord of lords. But that is the least interesting of the paradoxes. More interesting is the Almighty who suffers, blesses the persecuted, and stands with the defeated. More interesting is the power of God made manifest through cross and empty tomb.

Notes

1. Besides the historical accident of happening to show up at a certain place and time, how did the settlers know that they had been chosen? Jonathan Edwards argued the case based on the "analogy" (his word) between the Puritan settlers and the Hebrew people passing through the wilderness. Prior to the arrival of the godly, the wilderness had been inhabited by demons. Thus, Cotton Mather was not surprised to learn that the devil that possessed the seventeen-year-old Mercy Short appeared to be a man "of an Indian color." Marion L. Starkey, *The Devil in Massachusetts: A Modern Enquiry into the Salem Witch Trials* (Garden City, NY: Doubleday, 1969), 240.

2. Mark Noll notes the similarities between the "national messianism" that developed in the United States and in apartheid South Africa. Noll, *One Nation Under God? Christian Faith and Political Action in America* (New York: Harper and Row, 1988), 189–92.

3. In 1995, as the Smithsonian Institution prepared an exhibit to mark the fiftieth anniversary of the end of World War II, there were howls of protest over plans for

the exhibit to include photographs of the victims of the atomic bombings of Hiroshima and Nagasaki. The Smithsonian altered the exhibit to quiet the controversy. The effort to control historical narration so as to present America's wars as heroic, bloodless affairs was also evident in the 2003 war in Iraq: the Pentagon prohibited coverage of returning U.S. caskets, declined to count enemy and civilian casualties, and directed news coverage by "embedded" journalists.

4. It is a limitation of English that the single word "power" is used to describe both "the ability to act" (an ability shared by all animate creatures) and "the ability to coerce." Anarchists do not protest the power of the muscles that built the pyramids but the coercive power that enslaved people and forced them to do the building. Nonetheless, it must be acknowledged that there is coercive potential even in "the power of nonviolence." Therefore, those who are engaged in nonviolent struggle must avoid the temptation to choose tactics based on calculations about how best to coerce the adversary. Mark Juergensmeyer explains Gandhi's view that nonviolent revolution entails not the seizure of power but "the transformation of relationships." Victory does not belong to the one who wins but to all who enter into this transformation. "In a Gandhian fight, you can claim to have won only if your opponent can say the same." Juergensmeyer, *Gandhi's Way: A Handbook of Conflict Resolution* (Berkeley: University of California Press, 2002), 64.

5. On the meanings of *arche, dynamis, exousia, thronos,* and other names for the powers, see Walter Wink, *Naming the Powers: The Language of Power in the New Testament,* vol. 1, *The Powers* (Philadelphia: Fortress, 1984). Wink's trilogy offers the most exhaustive treatment of biblical perspectives on the powers, but he is not alone in discerning that the biblical view is at odds with the modern myth of power. The theme has also been explored by Markus Barth, Dale Brown, Jacques Ellul, William Stringfellow, John Howard Yoder and others. Most of the writings by Ellul and Stringfellow are pervaded by awareness that the principalities are fallen and that the human pretense to control power is disastrous.

6. The second Fall has been called "the watchers myth," and although it is cited elsewhere in canonical writing, 1 Enoch offers the most extensive commentary. In 1 Enoch, the fallen angels are the source of human governments, and they introduce humanity to the instruments of war (8:1) and the ways of oppression (9:6).

7. Throughout his trilogy, Wink explains this combination as the interior and exterior lives of institutions. While the nations and their governing structures constituted a premier manifestation of the powers in the Bible, Wink, Ellul and Stringfellow are in agreement that the powers are legion. The powers include institutions and social forces ranging from Wall Street to the media, from social movements to technology, from ideology to religion. The ideologies that are manifest as powers include not only nationalism, socialism and capitalism but also anarchism whenever it (like the other ideologies) functions in such a way as to control people and to offer predetermined solutions for all human predicaments. Religion (*including Christian religion*) functions as a power whenever it seeks to supplant the living word of God or the vibrancy of faith with reliance on sacerdotal hierarchies or "traditional values." Religion is manifest as a fallen power whenever it engages in triumphalism by seeking to assert its own primacy over "other religions" or by allying with the powers of the nations in their assorted crusades. When Franklin Graham and Pat Robertson characterized Islam as a bloodthirsty religion, it was an example of religion as a fallen power (in this case, not the religion of Islam, but the religion of Graham and Robertson). On October 24, 2004, in an interview on CNN, Jerry Falwell gave voice to religion as a

fallen power allied with nation: "But you've got to kill the terrorists before the killing stops. . . . If it takes 10 years, blow them all away in the name of the Lord."

8. For recent documentation on this phenomenon, see Mark Zepezauer, *Take the Rich Off Welfare* (Cambridge, MA: South End, 2004).

9. The social control function of welfare programs is documented in the classic work by Frances Fox Piven and Richard A. Cloward, *Regulating the Poor: The Functions of Public Welfare* (New York: Vintage, 1971).

10. Graham Hancock, *Lords of Poverty: The Power, Prestige, and Corruption of the International Aid Business* (New York: Atlantic Monthly Press, 1989), 160–68. Real humanitarian assistance is more effectively provided by independent aid organizations that manage to avoid entanglements with governments; examples include Oxfam and Médecins Sans Frontières (Doctors Without Borders). Some church-related agencies manage to provide valuable services while avoiding high overhead expenses and also avoiding any temptations to use needy people's vulnerabilities as an opportunity for coercive proselytism; many worthy groups could be mentioned here, but I am most familiar with Mennonite Central Committee.

11. On resegregation, see "Beyond Black, White and *Brown*: A Forum," *The Nation* (May 3 2004): 17–24. More than any legislative achievements, the most enduring legacy of the civil rights movement may be the witness of the nonviolent struggle itself. Clearly, Martin Luther King Jr. was no anarchist; he pursued legislative changes and embraced a dream of equality and freedom, which he posed as a specifically American dream. Yet, in the last months of his life, King was focused less on legislative agendas than on advocacy for exploited workers and on his stance against the war in Vietnam. Without surrendering his hope for a "beloved community," King had a growing sense of what Malcolm X called "the American nightmare" rather than "the American dream." On the continuing need to heed the voices of both King and Malcolm X, see James H. Cone, *Martin & Malcolm & America: A Dream or a Nightmare* (Maryknoll, NY: Orbis, 1992).

12. See the recent work by Anthony W. Marx, *Faith in Nation: Exclusionary Origins of Nationalism* (New York: Oxford University Press, 2003).

13. For a summary of these studies and of the critical theorists of elite rule, see J. S. McClelland, *A History of Western Political Thought* (New York: Routledge, 1996), 637–58.

14. It is understandable that, given the brevity of his account, J. Philip Wogaman lacks nuance in his treatment of the Christian anarchism of Leo Tolstoy. It is true that Tolstoy "delegitimized existing state structures," but it is less clear that he believed that the eradication of the state "would set the stage for a flowering of the essential goodness of humanity." Wogaman, *Christian Perspectives on Politics*, rev. ed. (Louisville: Westminster/John Knox, 2000), 57. In both his essays and his works of fiction, Tolstoy expressed the view that structures of violence and coercion are grounded in human proclivities for self-love, and therefore, the struggle against structural violence is also necessarily a struggle with oneself. See Richard F. Gustafson, *Leo Tolstoy, Resident and Stranger: A Study in Fiction and Theology* (Princeton, NJ: Princeton University Press, 1989), 161–213.

15. This is not to ignore the vital insight by Wendell Berry that all claims to love people and places half-a-world away are doomed to abstraction unless we have first practiced love of people and land in a local place. As Berry also observes, we live in watersheds that are stubbornly oblivious to political boundaries and "private property" lines. Berry, *Citizenship Papers* (Washington, DC: Shoemaker & Hoard, 2004), 135–41.

16. The impact of U.S. border patrol policies in the Southwest has been to increase dramatically the number of deaths among those who are crossing from Mexico without "documentation." The Rev. Robin Hoover and the Humane Borders project have saved lives by merely giving water to those who are crossing the desert.

17. Examples of keeping faith with the enemy include the shipments of food and medical supplies to Vietnam by the American Friends Service Committee in the 1960s and 1970s and to Iraq by Jubilee Partners in the 1990s and 2000s. Examples include the nonviolent presence and intervention of Witnesses for Peace in Nicaragua in the 1980s and the Christian Peacemaker Teams in Iraq in 2002 and 2006. Examples include the Peaceful Tomorrows organization of surviving family members of the World Trade Center attacks and the nonviolent resistance of communities like Jonah House.

18. Recent prison abolitionists who have been active in advocating for both offenders and victims of crime include Angela Davis, Fay Honey Knopp, and Ruth Morris. See Morris, *Crumbling Walls: Why Prisons Fail* (Oakville, ON: Mosaic, 1989).

19. Bakunin, *God and the State* (New York: Dover, 1970), 3.

20. In one of her final letters, Weil renounced attachment to any "earthly country." Weil, *Waiting for God*, Emma Craufurd, trans. (New York: Harper Torchbooks, 1973), 96–97.

21. The prominent historians who confine their focus to this period in the West include Paul Avrich, *Anarchist Portraits* (Princeton, NJ: Princeton University Press, 1988); Daniel Guérin, ed., *No Gods, No Masters: An Anthology of Anarchism*, 2 vols., Paul Sharkey, trans. (San Francisco: A K Press, 1998); James Joll, *The Anarchists* (New York: Grosset & Dunlap, 1966); George Woodcock, *Anarchism: A History of Libertarian Ideas and Movements*, 2nd ed. (New York: Penguin, 1986).

22. The treatment of "anarchy" and "chaos" as synonymous persists today. Following the 2003 invasion of Iraq, embedded reporters commented on the "anarchy" that prevailed in the clashes among remnants of Hussein loyalists, U.S. and British troops, Shi'ites, Sunnis, Kurds, Turkmen, and "foreign terrorists" who found a new home in the chaos. This was not an absence of power (*an-arche*). It was an overabundance of that lethal power by which all of the petty and self-exalted factions asserted their claims to rule. Advocates of anarchy do not propose that greater thugs should be overthrown so that lesser thugs may rule in their stead. The debate on what constitutes "anarchy" figured prominently in the struggle over slavery in antebellum America. Abolitionists like William Lloyd Garrison and other members of the New England Non-Resistance Society renounced all institutional rule and openly identified themselves as "no government people" while simultaneously renouncing "chaotic anarchy." John C. Calhoun, a strong proponent of slavery, charged that the abolitionists were in fact fostering anarchy through their subversion of authority. The abolitionists responded that there was no greater "anarchy"—that is, chaos—than the wars of governments and the brutality of slavery. A helpful summary of the debate is provided by Lewis Perry, *Radical Abolitionism: Anarchy and the Government of God in Antislavery Thought* (Knoxville: University of Tennessee Press, 1995).

23. On the plentiful native groups of Latin America whose communities were devoid of chieftainship or other hierarchal structures of governance, see Pierre Clastres, *Society Against the State: Essays in Political Anthropology* (New York: Zone Books, 1989). The communitarian legacy of "stateless societies" in Africa is traced by Sam Mbah and I. E. Igariwey, *African Anarchism: The History of a Movement* (Tucson, AZ: See Sharp Press, 1997). Some early twentieth-century Japanese Christians faced persecution over one of the same issues that had plagued the church of the second

and third centuries, namely, the precise nature of the respect that was to be shown to the emperor. As he witnessed the persecution of Japanese Christians, the anarchist and pacifist, *Osugi Sakae*, was attracted to this faith "that transcended national boundaries and. . .recognized no temporal authority." *Osugi* was baptized, but he left the church during the Russo-Japanese war as Christians on both sides of that conflict prayed for victory and preached sermons on the virtues of patriotism. *Osugi Sakae, The Autobiography of Osugi Sakae*, trans. Byron K. Marshall (Berkeley: University of California Press, 1992), 124–25. After numerous beatings and arrests, *Osugi* was murdered by the police in 1923.

24. Despite the dangers of anachronism, a rigid chronism can warp the perspectives of historians even more, a point effectively argued by James Holston, *Ehud's Dagger: Class Struggle in the English Revolution* (New York: Verso, 2002), 9–45. With historical study and biblical exegesis alike, there is a diachronic responsibility to represent fairly the setting in life (*Sitz im Leben*) of the subject of inquiry while rendering it comprehensible to the setting in life of the inquirer; such a responsibility is rarely fulfilled through the simple avoidance or embrace of either anachronism or chronism. Jesus as Warrior (in the crusading theology of the eleventh and twelfth centuries), as Pantocrator (in Eastern Orthodoxy), as Mother (in the thirteenth and fourteenth-century writings by Margaret of Oingt and Julian of Norwich), as Chief (in Bantu theology), as Revolutionary (in Latin American liberation theology), as Businessman (in Bruce Barton's 1925 bestseller, *The Man Nobody Knows*)—all of these titles are anachronistic, but some might do less violence than others to the evidence provided by research on "the historical Jesus," which is another anachronism. On the other hand, the title "Savior" (*soter*) is not anachronistic to the milieu of the Jesus movement of the first century, but the twenty-first-century meanings attached to the title are at considerable variance from earlier usage. Declaring that an emperor or a king had been a "Savior" was a proclamation that he had provided for the welfare and defense of the people and that he merited the obedience and worship that ensued. Thus, as indicated by Acts 5:27–33, there is a subversive element to the acclamation of Jesus as "Savior." Proclaiming that Jesus is "King" would be a direct threat to the kingship of Caesar (Jn. 19:15), and so too, proclaiming that Jesus is "Savior" would deny obedience and worship to other would-be saviors. On the title "savior" in the ruler cults and emperor worship of the Greco-Roman world, see Werner Foerster, "*soter*," in *Theological Dictionary of the New Testament*, vol. 7, ed. Gerhard Friedrich, trans. Geoffrey W. Bromiley, 1003–12 (Grand Rapids, MI: Eerdmans, 1971).

25. "The Epistle to Diognetus," in *Ante-Nicene Fathers*, vol. 1, trans. and ed. Alexander Roberts and James Donaldson, 26–27 (Peabody, MA: Hendrickson, 1994). Regarding citizenship in heaven, see Philippians 3:20.

26. Even after he had the cross sewn onto his military standards, Constantine ordered that coins be minted in honor of Apollo. As late as March 321, the Emperor issued a decree that all work should cease on "the venerable day of the Sun," i.e., Sunday. A. H. M. Jones, *Constantine and the Conversion of Europe*, rev. ed. (New York: Collier, 1962), 88.

27. I acknowledge kinship between the position presented here and the "sectarian" readings of church history dating back to Gottfried Arnold (1666–1714). While I agree with the sectarians that God's reign has never been without its witnesses and that these witnesses are most often found among despised minorities, I fail to perceive the need to trace an unbroken historical transmission of a theoretically pristine faith from the primitive church to its modern expressions. The epistolary

admonitions of Paul alone provide evidence that even the faith of the primitive era was shot through with ambiguity. On the sectarian readings of church history, see Donald F. Durnbaugh, *The Believers' Church: The History and Character of Radical Protestantism* (New York: Macmillan, 1968), 9–16.

28. The anarchistic nature of Montanist appeals to the Spirit were noted by Adolf Harnack, *History of Dogma*, vol. 2, trans. Neil Buchanan (London: Williams & Norgate, 1910), 103. Harnack observed that Montanists tried to raise warning cries as the church "marched through the open door into the Roman state." A recent work that recognizes the prominent role of women in the movement is Christine Trevett, *Montanism: Gender, Authority and the New Prophecy* (New York: Cambridge University Press, 2002).

29. Even before the reign of Constantine, attacks on Donatists at Carthage in 304 marked the first collaboration of church leaders with political authorities in the suppression of other Christians. See Introduction to *Donatist Martyr Stories: The Church in Conflict in Roman North Africa*, trans. and ed. Maureen A. Tilley (Liverpool: Liverpool University Press, 1996), xi–xviii. Later, by reliance on a strained exegesis of Luke 14:23 ("compel people to come in"), Augustine defended the use of coercion against Donatists. Since I have been an admiring student of the writings of Stanley Hauerwas, allow me to express misgivings at his defense of Augustine's reliance on coercion. "Christian Peace: A Conversation between Stanley Hauerwas and John Milbank," *Must Christianity Be Violent? Reflections on History, Practice and Theology*, ed. Kenneth R. Chase and Alan Jacobs (Grand Rapids, MI: Brazos, 2003), 216. Hauerwas asserts that "heresy is a worse sin than violence." Yet, as a Christian peacemaker, Hauerwas surely knows that violence is heresy—or more precisely, the fruit of a specific manifestation of heresy that has done more to undermine the church than all of the dissident movements of history put together.

30. It is more than coincidence that the vast majority of those who were persecuted as heretics in medieval Europe were advocates and practitioners of voluntary poverty. The hierarchal church was allied with powerful financial interests, and a relaxation in the ecclesiastical understanding of the sin of usury proved to be important groundwork for the eventual emergence of capitalism. On this latter point, see Jacques Le Goff, *Your Money or Your Life: Economy and Religion in the Middle Ages* (New York: Zone, 1990).

31. Best known is Hildegard of Bingen and her presentation of God as Sophia, Sapientia and Caritas, all female images drawn from the wisdom literature of the Hebrew Bible. Barbara Newman, *Sister of Wisdom: St. Hildegard's Theology of the Feminine* (Berkeley: University of California Press, 1989), 42–88.

32. Cohn's characterization appears in his classic work, *The Pursuit of the Millennium: Revolutionary Millenarians and Mystical Anarchists of the Middle Ages* (New York: Oxford University Press, 1970).

33. One of the few studies available in English is by Murray L. Wagner, *Petr Chelcický: A Radical Separatist in Hussite Bohemia* (Scottdale, PA: Herald Press, 1983).

34. Considerable tension is inherent to the stance of seeking to live in subjection to the powers who are being overcome by Christ. The implications are still being worked out today among Mennonites, Amish and Brethren. There is common agreement that refusal is the proper response if the state orders believers to take up arms, but what about the taxes to pay for those arms? Might believers accept benefits from state programs like Social Security? What are the faithful responses to all of the state's intrusions ranging from compulsory schooling to mandated flashing lights on

horse-drawn buggies? For insights on Amish responses to some of these dilemmas, see the collection edited by Donald B. Kraybill, *The Amish and the State* (Baltimore: Johns Hopkins University Press, 1993).

35. T. Wilson Hayes, *Winstanley the Digger: A Literary Analysis of Radical Ideas in the English Revolution* (Cambridge, MA: Harvard University Press, 1979), 117–19.

36. Adin Ballou, *Practical Christianity*, ed. Lynn Gordon Hughes (Providence: Blackstone Editions, 2002), 243–44.

37. John Tidwell, "The Maroons," *American Legacy: The Magazine of African-American History and Culture* (Winter 2003): 41–50.

38. On the struggle for survival of the Christian anarchist communities during the Soviet era, see William Edgerton, trans. and ed., *Memoirs of Peasant Tolstoyans in Soviet Russia* (Bloomington: Indiana University Press, 1993). Of the many books by Berdyaev, a helpful introduction to his unique version of anarchism is *Slavery and Freedom*, trans. R. M. French (New York: Charles Scribner's Sons, 1944).

39. Martin Buber, *The Holy Way*, trans. Walter Kaufmann (New York: Charles Scribner's Sons, 1970), 124–25.

40. While Landauer renounced patriotism and ethnocentrism, he believed that belonging to a "nation" was integral to each person's identity and that unique nationalities are of service to all humanity. Landauer identified himself as having three "nationalities"—Bavarian, German and Jewish. Charles B. Maurer, *Call to Revolution: The Mystical Anarchism of Gustav Landauer* (Detroit: Wayne State University Press, 1971), 78–81.

41. Lanza del Vasto, *Gandhi to Vinoba: The New Pilgrimage*, trans. Philip Leon (New York: Schocken Books, 1974), 33.

42. Robert Coles, *Dorothy Day: A Radical Devotion* (Reading, MA: Perseus Books, 1987), 97.

43. Eli Sagan, *At the Dawn of Tyranny: The Origins of Individualism, Political Oppression, and the State* (New York: Alfred A. Knopf, 1985), 321.

44. Brevard S. Childs, *The Book of Exodus: A Critical, Theological Commentary*, The Old Testament Library (Philadelphia: Westminster, 1974), 16.

45. George E. Mendenhall, *The Tenth Generation: The Origins of the Biblical Tradition* (Baltimore: Johns Hopkins University Press, 1973), 135–38. See also Norman K. Gottwald, *The Tribes of Yahweh: A Sociology of the Religion of Liberated Israel, 1250–1050 BCE* (Maryknoll, MD: Orbis, 1979), 213.

46. These are among the social structures cited by Gottwald, *Tribes of Yahweh*, 245–92.

47. On the "fictional families" of the exilic and post-exilic periods, see Daniel L. Smith, *The Religion of the Landless: The Social Context of the Babylonian Exile* (Bloomington, IN: Meyer-Stone Books, 1989), 93–126.

48. For more on how the ambiguous portrayals of David survived the censorship of royal propagandists, see Baruch Halpern, *David's Secret Demons: Messiah, Murderer, Traitor, King* (Grand Rapids, MI: Eerdmans, 2001).

49. Jacques Ellul, *The Politics of God and the Politics of Man*, trans. Geoffrey W. Bromiley (Grand Rapids, MI: Eerdmans, 1972).

50. Flannery O'Connor once wrote, "You shall know the truth and the truth shall make you odd." To Westerners accustomed to linear modes of thought and transparency in symbols, apocalyptic literature seems very odd indeed. From where does it come? Proposals have been put forth that it was imported from the dualistic world of Persian Zoroastrianism, or it was a desperate pipe dream and a grab for extra-temporal hope by oppressed people who had no earthly reason to hope, or it was simply

prophetic utterance taken up a notch and carried to an illogical extreme by voices too shrill. One cogent alternative theory for the origins of Jewish apocalyptic traces it to the context of revolution betrayed. When Maccabean revolutionaries fought to overthrow the despotic rule of Antiochus IV Epiphanes (175–164 BCE), they compromised their faith by forging foreign alliances, fighting on the Sabbath, and engaging in atrocities. A party of "the Just" arose to renounce the rule not only of Antiochus but of the Maccabees as well. The book of Daniel might be a surviving writing from the party of the Just. The case is presented by Otto Plöger, *Theocracy and Eschatology*, trans. S. Rudman (Richmond, VA: John Knox, 1968).

51. John of Patmos did not manage to escape the sexism prevalent in his culture and in ours. The female imagery that he deployed fits too neatly into the caricatures of women as virgins (21:2), mothers (Rev. 12) or whores (Rev. 17). See Susan R. Garrett, "Revelation," in *The Women's Bible Commentary*, ed. Carol A. Newsom and Sharon H. Ringe, 377 (Louisville: Westminster/John Knox, 1992).

52. As it is used in the patriotic anthem, "The Battle Hymn of the Republic," the winepress of God's wrath functions as an incitement to violence, which is the exact opposite of the way the image functions in Rev. 14. In John's vision, it is clear that neither God nor the faithful are killing people and shoving them into the winepress. John's term for "harvest" (the noun *therismos* and the verb *therizo*) is used consistently in the Septuagint and the New Testament to refer to an ingathering of the faithful (e.g., Mt. 9:36–38). G. B. Caird, *The Revelation of Saint John*, Black's New Testament Commentaries (Peabody, UK: Hendrickson, 1966), 190. The winepress is "trodden outside the city" (Rev. 14:20), which is the locale of Jesus' crucifixion and the martyrdom of his disciples (Heb. 13:12–13). It is the blood of the Empire's victims that flows from the winepress. Babylon does not fall because God finally decides to start shedding blood. The Empire falls because of its own incessant bloodshed.

53. The phrase is from the excellent book by Donald B. Kraybill, *The Upside-Down Kingdom* (Scottdale, PA: Herald Press, 1978).

54. The Jesus Seminar folks like the Gospel of Thomas, and the "Caesar" saying also appears there (100), but totally devoid of context. Thus, Thomas's Jesus simply approves of tax payments. Such temporal affairs matter little to true Gnostics.

55. This position is presented in greater detail in Donald D. Kaufman, *What Belongs to Caesar? A Discussion on the Christian's Response to the Payment of War Taxes* (Scottdale, PA: Herald Press, 1969).

56. This question of who is the "governing authority" was more than theoretical for some Christians in America in the 1770s. Those Christians who refused to take up arms were suspected of treason by both the Tories and the rebels. Richard K. MacMaster, *Christian Obedience in Revolutionary Times: The Peace Churches and the American Revolution* (Akron, PA: Mennonite Central Committee Peace Section, 1976).

57. Stringfellow, *Conscience and Obedience: The Politics of Romans 13 and Revelation 13 in the Light of the Second Coming* (Waco, TX: Word Books, 1973). Mark D. Nanos argues that Paul was not even referring to political rulers in Romans 13:1–7. Nanos contends that Paul was calling upon the members of the Jesus sect in Rome to be subject to the governing authorities of the Roman synagogue. Nanos, *The Mystery of Romans: The Jewish Context of Paul's Letter* (Minneapolis, MN: Fortress, 1996), 289–336. For an overview of possibilities in the exegesis of Romans 13 from someone who survived the apartheid era in South Africa, see Jan Botha, *Subject to Whose Authority? Multiple Readings of Romans 13*, Emory University Studies in Early Christianity (Atlanta: Scholars Press, 1994).

58. Brown, *Biblical Pacifism*, 2nd ed. (Nappanee, IN.: Evangel, 2003), 123–25.

59. For insightful and poignant commentary on this text, see Walter Brueggemann, *Ichabod Toward Home: The Journey of God's Glory* (Grand Rapids, MI: Eerdmans, 2002).

60. Sallie McFague, *Models of God: Theology for an Ecological, Nuclear Age* (Philadelphia: Fortress, 1987).

Part III

Issues in an Age of Terror

Chapter 12

Patriotism Transformed by Terror?

Thomas Massaro, S.J.

This essay addresses the ways in which the understanding and practice of patriotism on the part of Christians in the United States is transformed now that we have entered an era of serious terrorist threats. Because I approach the topic from the perspective of Catholic social thought, I will simultaneously treat the question: What does American Catholicism have to offer by way of reflection on the topic of patriotism in the contemporary world? Comprising approximately one-quarter of the U.S. population, the Catholic community draws on a distinctive set of experiences and sensibilities that illuminate certain aspects of what all Americans are facing as we discern vital questions about the contemporary meaning of patriotism.

Before tackling these questions directly, it is necessary to examine a few preliminary considerations regarding the meaning of patriotism and the related concept of "civil religion." Two items will then comprise the bulk of this essay: 1) an examination of what American Catholicism "brings to the table" regarding patriotism; and 2) an exploration of how these findings apply to the contemporary situation of the United States. My thesis is that the age of terrorism along with the heretofore ill-conceived policy response to it by the U.S. government present a set of new and serious challenges to Christians who take seriously the obligation to limit the resort to violence in our world. Resisting the temptation to paint the world in stark black and white terms, we must take into account many complex global realities if we hope to speak meaningfully of fulfilling our patriotic duty. True patriotism may even call us to a stance of resistance against national policies that amount to little more than "hitting back" at those whom our national leaders target, whether actual, imagined or surrogate enemies. While many bedrock principles and familiar sentiments regarding our nation remain relevant, we who care about both our nation and the Gospel of Jesus Christ certainly need to reconsider and revise many of our judgments and courses of action in order authentically to support the perennial values we hold dear.

Preliminary Observations about Patriotism and Civil Religion

Patriotism is an abstract noun, one that defies easy definition. Like so many terms ending with "ism," it tends to conceal at least as much as it reveals. People using the word often mean rather different things by it. We all have certain intuitions regarding the look of "patriotic behavior" and the feel of "patriotic attitudes," but the content of these phrases is not at all self-evident. Precisely which forms of thinking and acting are justified and allowable against the horizon of patriotic regard remains a perennially open question. Further, like all abstractions, patriotism is subject to the vicissitudes of various historical eras, so what seems to be a sturdy truth at one time may cease to be an appropriate or reliable guide to thought and action even a short time later.

The phrase "civil religion" captures an important bundle of concepts relating to the role of patriotism in U.S. public life and perhaps in other societies as well.[1] With roots in the practices of Greek and Roman civilizations as well as in the writings of Rousseau, Hegel and others, civil religion identifies the ways that patriotism elicits a quasi-religious response from citizens of a given polity. In at least the case of the United States, our love of and allegiance to our country has throughout our history been at once distinguished from and yet closely aligned to our faith in ultimate things. Robert Bellah's seminal 1967 essay that fixed the term in the lexicon of American discourse called attention to the ways that the symbols and trappings of civil religion at once mirror "church religion" and yet are distinguished from it.[2] In parallel ways, church religion and civil religion both serve the function of binding together American society, supplying the social glue that provides a sense of legitimacy to our polity.

Because civil religion aspires to universal acceptance in a denominationally pluralistic society, it represents something of a least common denominator. Hence the "God" of civil religion invoked in political speeches remains a rather austere and abstract deity (indeed a Unitarian one, deliberately fashioned in that mode so as not to give offense). Likewise, the set of propositions contained in the core message of civil religion ("America is specially blessed; America has a duty to justice," etc.) is generally kept to a minimal bundle. Bellah wisely hastened to add that civil religion also includes a "prophetic role," a power capable of calling us back to collective values that may have fallen by the wayside when the "priestly role" of legitimating and animating national projects has grown overly strong and potentially even perverted by hubris and national ambition. Civil religion, then, not only ties us together and makes us feel good about our collective identity and action but also functions as an ever-present word of implicit judgment and a potential check on the unrestrained exercise of national power.[3]

Long before Bellah thematized these aspects of American public life, great statesmen and political leaders lived them out in word and deed and none with greater eloquence than Abraham Lincoln. His struggles to make sense of the excruciating experience of a bloody civil war led him to the most profound reflection on the notion of patriotism as witnessed in the public addresses and writings of his final years. Even while Lincoln rallied the Union around the embattled national flag, he tempered his enthusiasm for the cause with a poignant sense of the culpability of all Americans for the injustices of our national history. Behind his soaring rhetoric, often redolent as it was with scriptural themes and explicit biblical references, lay an awareness of both the priestly and prophetic functions of American civil religion at its best. His example of constructive invocation of patriotism supplies a necessary counterpoint to Samuel Johnson's famous quip that appeals to patriotism as "the last refuge of a scoundrel."

Patriotism emerges, then, as a rather plastic concept. It can be used to elicit entirely appropriate and necessary sacrifices for the collective good, but it can just as easily be enlisted to support courses of action that are morally objectionable, blatantly self-serving or otherwise misguided. The prophetic aspect of civil religion suggests that patriotism may contain the inner resources to exercise a beneficial self-limitation, but history demonstrates that this promise is not always kept. Surely, a healthy dose of skepticism should greet those who appeal to patriotism as a motivator of others' actions. Americans with religious sensibilities and affiliations should be especially eager to situate patriotism within the larger constellations of our most profound loyalties. In the following section, I sketch out how this task may unfold against the background of the religious tradition in which I walk, and the only one I know well—Roman Catholicism.

The Distinctive Contribution of American Catholicism

Like members of all religious denominations, Catholics wrestle with the dynamics of our dual membership. We are aware of simultaneously belonging to earthly associations, such as nations, kinship groups and local communities, and to the transcendent realm of God's Kingdom. While assenting to St. Paul's claim in Philippians 3:20 that "Our citizenship is in heaven,. . ." we nevertheless feel very much at home in this world. While it would be impossible, at least in the absence of an ambitious scientific survey of opinions, to draw reliable generalizations about the inner attitudes of American Catholics regarding subtle issues of church and state, it seems safe to articulate at least two observations. The first is that Catholics by and large experience the same set of tensions as other Americans regarding the task of balancing devotion to God and to country in appropriate ways. There is no reason to believe, for example, that Catholics in America are any less susceptible to the perennial temptation to conflate the purposes of God and those of the nation than adherents of any other religion. Nothing about Catholic belief renders us immune from the arduous and necessary work of establishing and sustaining a proper set of equilibriums regarding our loyalties.

The second observation stands somewhat in tension with the first. It is that Catholics are less likely than many other religious Americans to experience the feeling of living out earthly existence as "strangers and aliens." Our acknowledgement that the world as we know it is a passing reality somehow does not prevent us from displaying an ethos characteristic of those who are very much at home in the temporal realm. The general ambience of Catholic life is markedly world-affirming, to borrow a category from the sociology of Max Weber. By and large we do not expect our religious and temporal projects or loyalties to conflict very often nor do we slide readily into the idiom of blunt-edged prophetic denunciation of worldly "principalities and powers." At the risk of over-generalizing, I think it is fair to say that an ordinary American Catholic would be quite startled to hear the opinion that the state is to be categorically distrusted as a potential source of idolatry, as somehow a rival to or even an enemy of God. Admittedly, there are Catholics who look for inspiration to radically countercultural voices such as Dorothy Day and the Berrigan brothers. But this small group is the exception that proves the general rule—namely, that the rhetoric of anarchism and prophetic condemnation of government find little resonance among Roman Catholics on these shores. There is simply more in us and our community of the message of Romans 13 (wherein Paul urges harmonious cooperation with civil authorities) than of Revelation 13 (where John portrays earthly powers as demonic). Our awareness of being on pilgrimage (an image invoked in several of the influential documents of Vatican II) in no way deters us from investing quite lavishly in our semi-permanent earthly dwellings.

One manifestation of this attitude is that Catholic Americans appear to have fewer scruples than perhaps any other Americans regarding the cooperation of the agencies of church and state for potentially constructive purposes. We were quiet pioneers in faith-based social service initiatives, for example, taking for granted the benefits of public-private partnerships as Catholic charitable organizations began contracting with federal and local governments decades ago. For generations, Catholics lobbied in vain for state assistance to parochial schools long before recent court victories for the school voucher movement. In the typology of First Amendment stances, the opinions of most mainstream Catholics would surely be closer to the "moderate accommodation" than the "strict separation" end of the spectrum regarding church-and-state issues.

There is a range of potential reasons why this is the case. Catholics may be more at ease with church-state interaction because of the history of the worldwide Catholic Church, which, until surprisingly recently, worked hand-in-glove with governments in many parts of the world, particularly in Europe but also in regions such as Latin America and Oceania with long colonial histories. Indeed, for centuries official church leadership openly preferred maximal throne-and-altar arrangements to liberal separationist regimes. The memory of painful setbacks for the Catholic Church in Europe during the French Revolution and the Italian Risorgimento (particularly the loss of the Papal States in the nineteenth century) cast a long shadow on church teaching and activity over many subsequent decades. It led the Catholic hierarchy to express great suspicion of nationalism and to strike an unflattering reactionary pose toward many features of modernity.

Not incidentally, the lingering memory of these wounds was among the historical reasons that the project of updating church teaching on the vital topic of religious liberty was regrettably so long delayed. In fact, until the Second Vatican Council approved its Declaration on Religious Freedom (*Dignitatis*

Humanae) in 1965, the Catholic Church's official position did not explicitly support the granting of the basic right to religious liberty we take for granted today. There may indeed be a bit of a "Constantinian hangover" lingering in the minds even of American Catholics, some of whom seem to harbor nostalgia for a supposed golden age of Caesaropapism—that is, the unified administration of spiritual authority and temporal power. The memory of those days when the state and the church (and in pre-Reformation Europe, this meant the Catholic Church) were in effect arms of each other may still exert considerable influence on the thinking of certain American Catholics, particularly those of a conservative or even "restorationist" bent.

As intriguing as these speculations may be, it turns out to be far more productive to explore predominant Catholic attitudes toward the state on the level of cultural and spiritual sensibilities than on the level of historical memory narrowly understood. If American Catholics do not expect to have to make sharp choices between their allegiance to their church and their nation, it is at least partially because they share an inherited culture that leads them to perceive the world in a certain way. A common shorthand way of characterizing this style refers to this dominant Catholic sensibility as a "both/and" rather than an "either/or" approach to most issues. One manifestation of this tendency is the preference within Catholic theology for patterns of thought that embrace reason and revelation, grace and nature, material and spiritual concerns. Adherents to this approach are eager to arrive at a synthesis that unites and integrates rather than a dichotomy that divides the world into discrete and incompatible categories. In our desire to overcome sharp oppositions, we show a marked preference for being "lumpers" rather than "splitters." Often to the surprise of outside observers, there is room in the Catholic tent for great diversity of thought, a variety of sources of wisdom and many centers of value.

How does this cultural predilection apply to the specific topic of patriotism? By what mechanism is this general pattern transmitted to succeeding generations of particular Catholics? One promising line of inquiry considers the type of personal and moral formation many American Catholics receive from an early age. I suspect my own experience is somewhat typical. Like most Catholic parish churches to this day, the church of my boyhood years on the East coast displayed two flags within its sanctuary: the red, white and blue of the U.S. flag was matched by the gold and white of the papal banner directly across from it. The symmetry is not lost on churchgoers; the unambiguous message it sends is that the reality standing behind each of these symbols merits our allegiance. While church and nation may not occupy precisely commensurable space within our interior landscape, loyalty to both is certainly accorded great importance in the arena of American Catholic culture. Relying again on personal experience that I believe to be typical, I recall that the Catholic secondary school I attended in New York City boasted the official motto *Deo et Patriae*—for God and country. In fact, the precise syntactical form of that motto served as an excellent lesson illustrating the proper use of the dative case in an early session of my freshman Latin course.

That my high school had adopted this particular motto in the year of its founding, 1914, stands as no idle coincidence. Despite isolationist rhetoric to the contrary, the United States was beginning to mobilize toward its eventual entry into the Great War in Europe and was conducting something of a "gut check" at the time. A new Catholic school, particularly one founded by the wily Jesuits, was eager to allay nativist suspicions. After all, buildings housing Catholic institutions had been burned to the ground by members of such groups as the Know-Nothing Party not so far away and not so many years earlier. Though such violent and destructive flare-ups of anti-Catholicism were only occasional, members of the Catholic community had grown accustomed to a barrage of more mundane indignities, such as verbal slurs (the epithet "Papists" was common) and discrimination in hiring and educational admissions policies. Announcing a patriotic intent and wearing it on one's sleeve was a shrewd way to signal the desire for definitive acceptance in a pluralistic culture. To this day, such quintessentially Catholic institutions as the University of Notre Dame and the Knights of Columbus feature patriotic slogans, symbols, and motifs in their official literature and even on letterheads.

One of the most delicious ironies regarding the history of Catholicism in the United States involves precisely this challenge regarding identity and patriotism as it was faced in the era just mentioned. In order to prove that they had assimilated successfully and were now genuinely and fully Americans, Catholics went to extremes to display their patriotism. Participation in the horrific sequence of bloody wars of the twentieth century became the paradigmatic act to demonstrate loyalty to the United States. Ethnic Catholics in particular felt pressure not only to answer the ordinary call of national duty but indeed to become super-patriots, a dynamic confirmed by depictions of Catholic GIs in film, literature, and other vehicles of popular culture. Stereotypes as they are, the gung ho Italian-American private from Brooklyn, the "Boston Irish" doughboy volunteering for hazardous duty, and the German Catholic farm boy from the Midwest vowing with all his might to defeat Hitler—all are enduring icons of a faith community eager to prove its patriotism.

But it is hard to escape the conclusion that this was also a tragic irony. In order to prove that they were in no way harboring a rival allegiance to a foreign leader who went by the title of Pope, immigrant Catholics or those who were offspring of immigrant Italians, Irish, Germans and Poles among others took up arms in great numbers to support the foreign adventures of their newly adopted nation. In some cases they found themselves shooting at enemy soldiers who shared their faith and ethnic background. All of them, regardless of their familiarity with the nuances of the just war theory, found themselves putting on the shelf many of the teachings of the man they acknowledged as their Lord and Savior. Still, they returned home from war in Europe or the Pacific Theater, or from Korea or Vietnam, whether healthy, wounded or dead, as heroes whose deeds had proven that their ethnic and religious communities were as genuinely American as any.

If American Catholics display a marked propensity for loyalty to country, then, we came by it honestly. We have inherited patterns of thought and culture (traceable back to the common good theories of Aristotle and Thomas Aquinas, seminal figures who still exert a dominant influence in Catholic intellectual circles) that place a premium on group belonging and the willingness to make sacrifices for the collective good. Our communitarian leanings stand out as rather distinctive within an American culture that is quite probably the most individualistic culture the world has known. Of course, it is overly simple to characterize U.S. Catholics as merely a bunch of "good company men and women." Much available evidence suggests that the lines separating Catholic culture from the American mainstream have been blurring considerably over time, particularly as Catholics gain in material affluence and continue to enjoy upward mobility. But it may still be instructive for anyone seeking to analyze the roots of patriotism to consider the experience of Catholics in the United States. Because it has been shaped by the historical and cultural factors sketched above, the American Catholic community demonstrates a disposition toward stalwart patriotism and a tendency to revere and trust national leaders, perhaps excessively. Anecdotal evidence suggests that the Central Intelligence Agency (CIA) and the Federal Bureau of Investigation (FBI) recruiters are particularly eager to receive applications from Catholics because of this perceived disposition toward obedience and unrelenting patriotism. In this, Catholics reflect a more general cultural tendency to accord the benefit of the doubt to those projects identified by our political leaders as urgently in the national interest and that, on this basis, supposedly deserve our unquestioned support.

The stage is thus set for the analysis of contemporary challenges to patriotism, to be taken up in the final section of this essay. But first, in order to round out our treatment of what the Catholic perspective has to offer, a brief word regarding official Catholic teachings on the subject of patriotism will be helpful. This is not the place for an exhaustive survey of papal encyclicals or statements of conferences of bishops on the theme of loyalty to one's country. Suffice it to say that the tradition of Catholic social thought demonstrates a high regard for the functioning of national communities as the political arena where many issues of proper social order are appropriately addressed and where many social injustices should ideally be remedied. In keeping with its principle of subsidiarity (first articulated in the 1931 encyclical of Pope Pius XI, *Quadragesimo Anno*), Catholic social teaching cautions that not all social problems are to be addressed on the national level as this might foster excessive centralization and even totalitarianism. However, many items of social concern do legitimately fall to the nation-state—the level of social organization at which, for example, taxes are most reliably collected, industry is most efficiently regulated, and military security most readily guaranteed. National governments emerge as privileged agents of the common good, and the importance of loyalty to them is in no way slighted in modern Catholic social teaching. Honoring one's country by abiding by its laws, paying its fairly assessed taxes, and participating in its public life are all part of the personal duties each person faces as a citizen of some particular national community.

While no comprehensive document devoted primarily to the theme of patriotism is to be found in official Vatican teaching, the topic of the rights and responsibilities of individuals to the various levels of civil association surfaces in many places, including in papal addresses to audiences of diplomats and social organizations in recent decades. General principles governing these relationships are treated particularly prominently in the two social encyclicals issued by Pope John XXIII (*Mater et Magistra* in 1961 and *Pacem in Terris* in 1963) as well as in *Gaudium et Spes*, the major social teaching document promulgated by the Second Vatican Council in 1965. In line with the Thomism that still dominates Catholic social theory, voices of the official church urge a careful balancing of claims and values within the increasingly intricate web of human relationships. The nation-state as we know it today (something Aquinas could not have foreseen) has emerged as a legitimate level at which we as individuals and as members of distinctive social groups organize our social and political life. A well-ordered set of loyalties surely includes a healthy measure of patriotism, as long as rampant nationalism does not shade over into chauvinism or jingoistic militarism, abuses that church leadership would presumably be eager to denounce.[4]

In keeping with the theological predilections we have already seen, the Catholic approach to patriotism includes the quest to find a way to honor both God and country appropriately. These duties need not conflict. If they should be found to be incompatible for some reason (e.g., when the public authorities of a given state demand an excessive loyalty that amounts to absolutism, abridges religious freedom, or leads to xenophobia or aggression), a genuinely Catholic position would insist upon reform. It would advocate for a reestablishment of proper balance, a renewed ranking of loyalties that places devotion to God (and, by extension, devotion to the absolute demands of universal well-being) above the relative value of loyalty to one's particular nation. The language and general analytic framework employed in the 1963 encyclical *Pacem in Terris* support this conclusion especially clearly. Here, Pope John XXIII, horrified at superpower rivalries and aggression that had repeatedly led the world to the brink of nuclear warfare, introduces the term "universal common good." Enshrined in subsequent Catholic social thought, it has continued to play a significant role as a regulative principle of international relations in an increasingly interdependent world. Among the functions exercised by this term is the provision of a summary rationale for limiting the otherwise absolute rights of sovereign states. For example, in the face of emergencies such as genocide or famine, the ordinary right of a state to control its borders and resources gives way to the universal common good of protecting human life, promoting stability, and enhancing security.

In a roundabout way, employing this distinctive bundle of concepts finds the Catholic community joining all other Christians in a set of common priorities. We join ranks with all followers of Jesus Christ in insisting that fidelity to the Gospel and adherence to religiously grounded principles of social concern ultimately trump allegiance to any national flag. This is a sentiment St. Paul expressed most succinctly with his assertion that "Our allegiance is to Christ" (2 Cor. 5:20). This imperative to order our affections properly is also captured in the multivalent spiritual motto *Deus semper major*—God is always greater. The deity is not only larger than our imaginings (the usual sense in which this Latin phrase is taken) but, further, the place of God in our lives outweighs the role of all other created things and entities (such as nations) to which we find ourselves related. In this regard, especially when the stakes are so high, the usual Catholic "both/and" approach may find itself giving way to the occasional "either/or" solution.

Patriotism in a New Era: Terrorism and our National Response

I have already stated my conclusion that, at least for Christians, the meaning of American patriotism is indeed transformed in the light of contemporary challenges to our nation. There are numerous distinctive and unprecedented global realities that substantially alter the equation of how Christians feel and act regarding our allegiance to the United States. By no means is our adjustment to contemporary circumstances a simple matter of experiencing either the tug of greater patriotism or the strains of diminished loyalty to our nation. Rather, our new world situation calls forth from us a set of more deliberate and problematic judgments than ever before. With the advent of terrorism on a massive scale, something has qualitatively changed in our world and how we perceive it, and these discontinuities must be addressed if we are to speak meaningfully of fulfilling our patriotic duty. Drawing from the foregoing analysis, the following four propositions and explanatory paragraphs, while far from complete, lay out the major challenges:

1. More than ever before in U.S. history, it is crucial to distinguish between the tentative and qualified support we might offer to current political leaders and their agendas on one hand, and the much deeper and abiding loyalty or reverence we hold for our nation itself and its transcendent ideals on the other hand.

To disagree with the policy and actions of a sitting president (or even with the courses of action pursued by all branches of government simultaneously) does not mean that one has withdrawn support from the overall project of the nation *per se*. This has always been a relevant distinction but bears repeating with renewed emphasis today. Whatever else they altered, the terrorist attacks of September 11, 2001, certainly ushered in an era of more sharply divergent interpretations of the proper role of the United States in the world. While President Bush was able to paper over differences of opinion in the early months of this new era as he presided over a seemingly broad consensus supporting the forcible removal of the Taliban government in Afghanistan, the fragile sense of agreement had definitively evaporated by the time the United States invaded Iraq in March 2003. The war in Iraq, rather than uniting the nation in a common cause has proven to be an enormous wedge issue for the American public. While every American military involvement produces some level of disagreement between hawks and doves—between interventionists and isolationists—questions regarding how to respond appropriately to terrorism today have split us especially profoundly with no prospect of resolution in sight. This is so because the stakes are so high with the numbers of casualties piling up in Iraq and Afghanistan, billions of dollars consumed in war-related expenses and the deterioration throughout the world of trust and good will toward the United States.

Are those who oppose Bush and who fault our government for its handling of these matters any less patriotic than other Americans? Do their protests and expressions of dismay constitute a type of treason? Do they deserve the often heard accusation that they are letting down the country by withholding support sorely needed by our nation in its desperate hour? Anyone who answers affirmatively has overlooked a key distinction between dissent and disloyalty and has so reduced the meaning of patriotism that it is no longer recognizable. It seems not only unfair but also intellectually dishonest to characterize as disloyal those who perceive serious national mistakes in the "war against terrorism" as it has been executed. It is greatly distressing to witness the conflation of a genuine love of country with positive support for the policies of the officeholders of the moment. In less divisive times, this mistake might be considered a mere bit of foolish dogmatism, a harmless foible. In this dangerous age of terrorism, to deny the very possibility of a loyal opposition betrays a serious blind spot, one that potentially imperils civil liberties and human rights here and abroad.

Patriotic duty has traditionally included the obligation to speak out with the hope of correcting flawed policies that, if continued, could cause grave harm to the nation. People of good will and of commendable patriotic devotion are surely to be found on both sides of these complex issues. It is demonstrably foolish to use the brush of treason to paint anyone whose interpretation of facts and policy directions differs from those in the ascendancy. This misguided reasoning threatens to unleash a ceaseless witch hunt against any and all who speak a contrary word or cast a dissenting vote. The absurdity of such a position is exposed when we consider what conclusions would logically follow from a reversal of national policy. Would changing direction in America's official response to terrorist threats suddenly render all the "white hats" suspect and conversely turn the "black hats" into instant super-patriots? Patriotism is more than mere compliance with directives and obedience to authorities. If anything, the search for those with a deficit of patriotism should begin with the people on the sidelines, those who have not invested sufficiently in thinking through these important matters of state to form a solid opinion or who do not muster the energy to speak out publicly about the conclusions that they do reach.

If we are unable to maintain this key distinction between deep abiding loyalty to a nation and support for current leaders and their momentary agendas, then we forfeit whatever we have learned about the prophetic aspect of civil religion. We saw above that the hard work of calling the nation back to values and principles that might have become obscured or forgotten makes an indispensable contribution to our common life. In the absence of this type of witness to justice and equity, our nation faces the danger of finding itself trapped in an endless cycle of power and domination, acting like a bully without a trace of conscience. These observations support the argument proposed by many ethicists (particularly those of a Kantian stripe) that universal moral principles themselves deserve a share of our loyalty, precisely because these summaries of received moral wisdom help us to remember who we are as a people and what abiding values we stand for.

Consistently affirming core principles helps us distinguish which of our loyalties are unconditional and which are conditional—that is, dependent upon changing circumstances and exigencies. In the arena of international affairs, principles regarding right order and self-restraint supply badly needed leverage against the positivistic approach that can justify any course of action in the name of expanded power or, in the rallying cry of today, enhanced security. The old slogan "might makes right" has morphed into "whatever protects us from terrorists is justified," but this assertion still needs to be exposed and rejected.

The theme of conflicting loyalties (and specifically, pitting obedience to current political authorities against obedience to the dictates of one's conscience) dates back at least as far as the fifth century BCE. In the world of Greek drama, Sophocles's character, Antigone, is forced to choose between the conventional civic duty to follow the directives of Creon, monarch of her polis of Thebes, and her sense of family piety. Her conscience and devotion to family ultimately impel her to defy the king and to accord a dignified burial to the corpse of her fallen insurrectionist brother Polyneices. Much great literature of the subsequent millennia has revisited the various ways humans handle and suffer from stark conflicts in loyalties, many of which involve the sense of patriotic duty. Even when they do not produce a pile of corpses in the course of the drama, forced choices such as Antigone endured display dimensions of profound tragedy. The parameters of the conflict she faced exhibit perennial relevance; the political community (whether polis or nation-state or empire) stakes a claim upon each of us as a legitimate object of loyalty, but it is never the only center of our concern and affection. The questions raised by this example lead us to a second proposition.

2. In this age of terrorism, citizens of the United States face a heightened urgency to sort out rival moral claims upon us, and no such claim is more problematic than patriotic duty.

Feeling and displaying loyalty to a nation is more complex and fraught with difficulty than feeling and displaying loyalty to a kinship group or an alma mater or any other type of affinity group. It is hard to imagine such small-scale groupings growing too strong or aggressive for the welfare of the environment they inhabit. But nations, by their very definition, are ways of organizing and maintaining power. The risk of a great nation using its power to dominate others is so endemic that we cannot ignore the consequences of our individual acts and practices regarding patriotic duty. To lend open-ended support to a nation that abuses its power for self-aggrandizement entails complicity in the injustices committed. Indeed, while knee-jerk patriotism may be tolerable in a nation with inconsequential power on the world scene, it is incumbent on the citizens of great powers not to fall into a dogmatic slumber of mindless obedience to their regime, a stance summarized by the vintage bumper-sticker slogan: "My country, right or wrong." There is simply too much at stake to drift into such an irresponsible position. The lives and well-being of people all around the world depend on citizens of great superpowers exercising their influence to restrain the excesses of their nation's projection of political, military and even economic power. Have we not all heard the appeals of people of weaker nations pleading for Americans to lobby our government to change its foreign policies? Luckily, our democratic tradition gives us substantial cause for hope that reversals of policy are possible at least in comparison to previous world empires in which entrenched cabals and dynasties enjoyed unchallenged power for long stretches of time.

The use of the term "empire" signals an important debate currently underway about the semantics of American power on the global stage. Is it accurate to refer to the United States as an empire? To what extent does the American place in the world today resemble that of ancient empires such as Rome or the great European colonial empires of the early modern world? Obviously, the term empire is not a univocal one, and points of similarity as well as dissimilarity need to be considered. The United States has never, of course, established a full-blown empire of colonies and territorial acquisitions in the classic sense, but it has assumed certain salient features of empires. Most ominous among these are America's remarkably far-flung string of military bases around the world, its construction of undeniable spheres of military and economic influence in many regions, and a disturbing preference in recent years for unilateralism over cooperative arrangements for security and related matters.[5]

A close study of these trends in U.S. foreign policy must precede any set of ethical judgments regarding the proper actions of citizens in this new context. Opinions will surely run a rather wide gamut regarding precisely to what extent and in what ways America deserves the title "empire" and how we should consequently relate to our nation. Questions abound: Should empire continue to be employed exclusively as a term of opprobrium, so that our loyalty to an alleged "American Empire" comes sharply into question? Or is a new possibility dawning, whereby the growth of U.S. power might have more positive connotations, representing actual gains for the cause of universal well-being rather than oppressive domination? Might the unrivaled power of the United States be put to good use, ushering in an era of enhanced mutual security for all against terrorist threats? Those with the most optimistic interpretation of these possibilities hasten to remind us that power in itself is not necessarily evil, and that history does contain at least a few instances when hegemonic power was employed for broad mutual benefit (the eras of the *Pax Romana* and *Pax Britannica* are most often cited).[6] Nevertheless, pivotal questions remain regarding how we might expect imperial power to be managed in the future and to what ends it will most likely be employed.

Since America began to mobilize against terrorism in 2001, numerous interpretations of this new exertion of power have appeared. In foreign policy journals, scholarly volumes, Web logs, talk radio programs and editorial columns in the popular media, a wide-ranging debate has raged. Commentators have coined several new terms to describe America's unique new role in the world, as the sole superpower to emerge from the cold war and now to array its forces against international terrorism. The United States has been called a "reluctant empire," a "benevolent empire," an "inadvertent empire,"[7] an "empire by improvisation,"[8] and even (by human rights scholar Michael Ignatieff) "empire lite."[9] Some commentators treat the "American Empire" as an incontestably constructive development while others, often speaking from a religious perspective, hasten to articulate scruples about the wisdom of assuming this role and embracing the attendant consequences.[10]

As citizens with a profound stake in such matters, our judgments on these disputed questions ultimately hinge upon how the putative empire conducts itself. If a great power is able to continue to respect the self-determination of its neighbors and resist the urge toward expansionism to the detriment of others, then its power might well be wielded in a constructive way, one that merits the continued loyalty of its citizens. But if economic and political power devolves into opportunism and exploitation, characterized by arbitrary and unilateral efforts at control that are quick to resort to military force to press its advantage, then citizens of that nation ought to do all they can to resist such injustices and to right the ship of state. Withholding support from tyrannical uses of power is not disloyalty, but the highest form of patriotism, one that recalls principles like fairness and self-restraint. Whether the United States has strayed onto this side of the ledger sheet is, of course, a topic of vehement current debate. But what is beyond all doubt is the proposition that, as citizens, we all have the solemn obligation to pursue these questions as far as our abilities to discern take us and then to act steadfastly and in good faith according to our conscience, whatever our ultimate judgment.

3. Terrorism and the threat of "Weapons of Mass Destruction" introduce a new set of perils that make it more difficult to continue the practice of an open and free society as the United States has historically known it.

America today feels threatened and rightfully so. While it is easy to chide our leaders for attempting to make political hay out of our anxieties, it nevertheless remains true that a worldwide network of violent and vengeful terrorists does exist, and thwarting their harmful intentions against U.S. citizens and American interests will continue to require great effort on the part of the military and intelligence communities. We are all called upon to make at least modest sacrifices to provide security officers with the tools, information, and resources they need to conduct their work as successfully as possible. While some politicians from time to time might be guilty of exploiting the message of counterterrorist priorities ("Be afraid, be very afraid. . .and support my agenda"), it would be foolhardy to forego reasonable and well considered measures to enhance the physical security of our nation.

Among the pivotal questions that arise is this: How many of our civil rights and accustomed practices in a free and open society need we sacrifice in this struggle against terrorism? While no tidy summary answer is possible, it is not hard to perceive the broad outlines of what is at stake and what attendant perils confront us. If we do too little, we leave ourselves unnecessarily vulnerable to further terrorist attacks, missing opportunities to defend our nation from threats that might well be anticipated and prevented. Conversely, if we act too aggressively, our counterterrorism measures themselves become oppressive and undercut the freedoms we as a society prize. Even if no bombs are ever detonated, the terrorists win when we yield to the temptation to abridge civil liberties too sharply or engage in such excessive surveillance that key constitutional rights are trampled underfoot.

No one holds the definitive answer on precisely where to draw the line. For this reason, the provisions of the USA PATRIOT Act of 2001 and proposals for its renewal and reauthorization in subsequent years are hotly debated and rightly so. The rough and tumble of the political process is healthy, and repeated deliberations and compromises have a remarkable way of finding the "sensible center," especially when all parties to the debate receive accurate information regarding what is at stake. Repeated public review adds to the legitimacy and enforceability of such legislation, whether it involves airport screening or FBI surveillance. Over time we sharpen our understanding of the trade-offs between rights and liberties on one hand, and the good of security on the other hand. It is especially important that our national debate on antiterrorist measures proceeds in a rational way without exaggerated fears of perceived threats that have no basis in reality. Nothing is gained by encouraging hysteria or by truncating genuine dialogue through trite sloganeering ("The constitution was not intended as a suicide pact" and "Principles mean little when we are the only side playing by the rules"). Regardless of external threats, we should continue to treat our fellow Americans and friendly foreign nationals with the greatest of respect and see that our government provides all members of society with as much freedom as is compatible with reasonable security. This is what patriots do in times of national trial.

It is equally important not to give in to the temptation to treat suspected terrorists in brutal and inhumane ways. Adherence to the Geneva Conventions and to other international instruments insuring fair treatment of enemy combatants and detainees of all types are minimal requirements of any defensible antiterrorist policy. Our government's reluctance to renounce categorically any form of torture or coercive interrogation of detainees has demonstrably damaged the reputation of the United States and has probably produced no reliable and valuable intelligence. Our good name as a defender of human rights around the world suffered immeasurable damage when U.S. personnel abused and humiliated prisoners at Abu Ghraib. The ongoing extralegal detention of hundreds of detainees at Guantanamo Bay similarly sullies our reputation. U.S. officials at the highest levels have only dug a deeper hole through repeated efforts to obfuscate the issue, first by "defining torture down" and then by creating spurious new categories to describe the legal status of captured foreign nationals who are suspected of links to terrorist organizations. Government policies that produce such shameless dissembling and that seek to mislead citizens about what is being done in their name fail a fundamental test of legitimacy. An administration that continues such abuses forfeits the good will and support of those it seeks to protect. This entire series of episodes in the war against terrorism provides a disturbing case study illustrating the many ways in which cutting ethical and procedural corners is not only immoral but ultimately self-defeating.

Students of history will identify certain of these perils as familiar while others are quite novel. Abuses of executive power in wartime date back to the early years of the republic, including most egregiously the Alien and Sedition Acts of 1797 and Executive Order 9066 that interred thousands of innocent Japanese-Americans during World War II. Revered presidents and other officials of all party affiliations have repeatedly crossed the line separating prudence and excess. The ante has been raised now that we have reason to fear that our enemies may be able to acquire atomic, bacteriological, chemical, and other weapons of mass destruction. We have entered an era when it is increasingly likely that our leaders will appeal to the danger of grave and imminent threats in order to win support for restrictions of our civil rights and the human rights of others. This constitutes yet another reason to revisit the concepts of loyalty and patriotism and to renew our practice of the special virtues of citizens, such as the quality of vigilance considered below.

> *4. Citizens seeking to practice an informed loyalty today bear a burden to be more vigilant than ever before.*

If there is a new meaning of patriotism, then surely the quality of vigilance is its particular virtue. The often repeated advice of Thomas Jefferson that "eternal vigilance is the price of liberty" well expresses the insight that it would be dangerous to let down our guard amidst contemporary challenges. Besides the reasons for vigilance we have already seen, there is at least one additional item for which all citizens, but perhaps especially American Christians must be on constant watch.

This is not so much a definable political problem but rather the pernicious influence of an overarching ideology, a pattern of thought and symbol-making that threatens to warp the way we see the world. One name for this is "zealous nationalism," a term employed in an intriguing recent volume about U.S. culture and foreign policy coauthored by scripture scholar Robert Jewett and social philosopher John Shelton Lawrence.[11] To view America as we sometimes do, as categorically beyond reproach, and making its way in a fallen and dangerous world where it frequently needs to resort to "redemptive violence,"[12] is a recipe for justifying heavy-handed meddling in the affairs of other states and regions. An America in this mold, which is unfortunately supported by many images in our popular culture, is likely to exploit the threat of terrorism as an excuse for self-serving interventions abroad. Indeed, those who perceive the Second Gulf War as a thinly veiled grab for power and for access to oil supplies point to United States action in Iraq as a shining example of this type of zealous nationalism. If American foreign policy is out of control, it is at least partially due to the images in our heads—mythic subtexts that distort reality by demonizing our opponents and too readily equating our selfish agendas with God's purposes in history. This is a lethal mistake that leads to sanctioning otherwise indefensible courses of national action.

From a Christian perspective, one of the worst aspects of such a nationalistic ideology is its tendency to exhibit the ancient heresy of Manichaeism, a philosophical approach that sharply and glibly divides the world into good and evil. Painting our nation as a force for unlimited and untainted good and setting it up against supposedly irredeemably corrupt enemies supports a never-ending and unlimited crusade that respects no bounds in its use of military force. There was ample evidence of Manichaeism at work in the overly grandiose rhetoric surrounding U.S. antiterrorism policy in the days after September 11, 2001, particularly in President Bush's repeated avowals to "eliminate evil from the face of the earth," a phrase that betrays a disturbingly dualistic perspective. Christians should be especially on guard against the ways that such a mythic ideology distorts scriptural portrayals of cosmology and eschatology and threatens to run roughshod over both constitutional constraints and international conventions that aim to limit coercive force.

The project of limiting violence is a special concern of Christians both in America and elsewhere. We should be eager to join efforts with people of other faiths to advocate the path of reconciliation and peacemaking, urging political leaders to renounce warfare as a tool of international policy. There was a brief moment shortly before the invasion of Iraq in March 2003 when it appeared that the leadership of a majority of the largest religious denominations in the United States might be able to launch an effective appeal to prevent war. Detecting a profound disconnect between the exigencies of the world situation and the moral demands of their respective traditions, all of which ultimately seek to limit violence except as a last resort, they spoke out boldly to halt the lurch toward this "war of choice." Many such appeals went out of their way to emphasize that patriotism is not synonymous with displaying a quick trigger. Although these diverse religious leaders did not carry the day, they rendered the considerable service of displaying the rich fruits of their peace-loving traditions for all to see. They also demonstrated precisely the type of constructive vigilance I propose.

****

The leadership of the Catholic Church played a prominent role in this last-minute appeal to prevent the invasion of Iraq. Both U.S. bishops (led by Archbishop Wilton Gregory, then president of the United States Conference of Catholic Bishops) and Vatican prelates (such as Cardinals Angelo Sodano and Pio Laghi)[13] made repeated appeals and formal visits to the White House to forestall hostilities to no avail. These sincere and extraordinary efforts at peacemaking introduce a final element of irony pertaining to U.S. Catholics and the subject of patriotism. In a word, the "other shoe" had finally fallen, and issues of peace and war once again came to play a key role in advancing Catholic understanding of the meaning of patriotism.

What unfolded in 2003 was the next act in a drama that had begun twenty years earlier. When American Catholics think about the ethics of war today, they look back to a ground-breaking document of the U.S. bishops published in 1983, *The Challenge of Peace: God's Promise and Our Response*. In a forthright and discerning way, the bishops took this opportunity during the twilight of the cold war to issue a word of concern and even condemnation regarding America's nuclear targeting policies, particularly its reliance on the strategy of "mutually assured destruction" *vis-à-vis* the Soviet Union. Grappling profoundly with the dual traditions of nonviolence and the just-war theory as they inherited them from centuries of Christian reflection, the bishops announced a prophetic judgment against a core tenet of U.S. defense policy. A more consistent application of age-old Christian principles regarding the presumption against war and the solemn duty to prevent harm to civilian noncombatants demanded this reasoned demurral from conventional wisdom in policy circles.

Was the Catholic community still to be considered a loyal group of patriots? While some expressed consternation, perceptive observers rejoiced that American Catholics had at last come into their maturity as full participants in national policy debates. With this breakthrough, the Catholic Church had found its voice as a "public church." It no longer felt a compulsion to prove its patriotism by rubber-stamping policies of the U.S. government or swallowing legitimate objections to foreign policy. This community of faith was wriggling free of the earlier insecurities that had prevented it from drawing from its heritage of theological riches in a fully authentic way. With this pastoral letter, the church was declaring its intention to discern the signs of the times fearlessly and to reach and teach ethical judgments without the constraints of undue social pressures that muted the voice of conscience. With the assistance of strong leadership, Catholic Americans were suddenly free to encounter Jesus anew under the title of "Prince of Peace" and to appropriate the full range of peacemaking priorities of their tradition. The *Challenge of Peace* opened the door to the further development of American Catholicism toward responsible participation in policy analysis in many areas, including the writing of the bishops' monumental pastoral letter *Economic Justice for All* in 1986.[14] Above all, it signaled that the Catholic Church was at long last ready to claim the mantle of "peace church"— something it should always logically have been, but an identity it has assumed only recently as its appeals for peace in March 2003 demonstrate.

This case study of growth toward a more genuine version of patriotism within the American Catholic community illustrates the virtue of vigilance that all Americans need to practice in a heightened way in this age of terrorism. To continue the sleepwalking of conventional notions of patriotism simply will not do. Unless we reflect more profoundly and inform our conscience more deliberately, Americans risk falling under the influence of ideologies that sanction practically any U.S. policy as justified, even as God-given. Courage and inner freedom are required in order to penetrate the fog of rhetoric and to question and oppose policies that we judge in conscience to be immoral and counterproductive in a dangerous world. True patriotism insists on the clarity of vision that is afforded by a critical distance from familiar patterns of thought and behavior.

The excessive reliance on the unilateral use of force to solve problems, the adoption of a dangerous policy of preemptive wars, a preference for secrecy over transparency, and coercive treatment of other nations and their citizens—all are objectionable and cry out to be opposed by people of principle. Even when our nation adopts laudable goals (the democratization of the Middle East, the disruption of terrorist networks), people of conscience serve their country well when they speak out against employing immoral means to achieving these ends. Very few purposes, no matter how commendable, are best carried out at gunpoint.

Because of these recent policy responses to our new era of terrorist threats, the United States has squandered the good will of people around the world as evidenced in their expressions of sympathy in the aftermath of September 11, 2001. We have, by and large, drawn the wrong lessons from the terrorist attacks. We have missed the opportunity to explore and address the deep roots of terrorism in the humiliation and despair experienced by members of societies that feel themselves to be exploited and marginalized in the global community. Until we change the fundamental style of how we relate to international tensions, our interventions can only fan the flames of hatred and resentment. In these challenging times, the American Christian who wishes to be a true patriot will walk a path illuminated not just by a narrow conception of national interest but also by the light of ethical principles and virtues grounded in the Gospel.

Notes

1. Scholars speculate as to whether the term "civil religion" applies univocally in different societies. This question is addressed through a series of intriguing national case studies in Robert Bellah and Phillip Hammond, *Varieties of Civil Religion* (San Francisco: Harper and Row, 1980).

2. Robert Bellah, "Civil Religion in America." This 1967 essay appears most conveniently in reprinted form as chapter 9 in his *Beyond Belief: Essays on Religion in a Post-Traditionalist World* (Berkeley: University of California Press, 1970), 168–89.

3. Bellah strikes this cautionary note in several later essays. See Robert Bellah, "Religion and the Legitimation of the American Republic," the afterword to his book *The Broken Covenant: American Civil Religion in Time of Trial*, 2nd ed. (Chicago: University of Chicago Press, 1992), 164–98. Of closely related interest is Robert Bellah, "Is There a Common American Culture?" *Journal of the American Academy of Religion* 66, no. 3 (1998): 613–25.

4. In fact, the failure of Pope Pius XII to denounce the excessive nationalism and subsequent atrocities of Nazi Germany in more unequivocal terms is still hotly debated in academic circles. Some scholars of the era judge the Pope's silence regarding racial hatred and the Holocaust to be a grave scandal while others defend Pius as having acted with prudent caution against a foe who unfortunately held all the cards.

5. An especially insightful account of the ways in which the United States has come to resemble an empire is Chalmers Johnson, *The Sorrows of Empire: Militarism, Secrecy and the End of the Republic* (New York: Metropolitan Books of Henry Holt, 2004).

6. Perhaps the most sanguine interpreter of the possibilities of U.S. imperial power is historian Niall Ferguson. See his *Colossus: The Rise and Fall of the American Empire* (New York: Penguin, 2004).

7. William E. Odom and Robert Dujarric, *America's Inadvertent Empire* (New Haven, CT: Yale University Press, 2005).

8. Ferguson, *Colossus*, 73.

9. Michael Ignatieff, *Empire Lite: Nation Building in Bosnia, Kosovo and Afghanistan* (London: Vintage, 2003).

10. Perhaps the best single resource to emerge from theological circles is Wes Avram, ed., *Anxious About Empire: Theological Essays on the New Global Realities* (Grand Rapids, MI: Brazos, 2004). The most prominent secular voice to denounce an imperial approach has surely been that of Noam Chomsky.

11. Robert Jewett and John Shelton Lawrence, *Captain America and the Crusade against Evil: The Dilemma of Zealous Nationalism* (Grand Rapids, MI: Eerdmans, 2003).

12. Jewett and Lawrence, *Captain America*, 245–72.

13. Sodano acted in his capacity as Secretary of State of the Holy See. Laghi was chosen by Pope John Paul II as a special envoy on an ad hoc basis, largely because of his longstanding cordial relationship with the Bush family and his previous service as Apostolic Nuncio to the United States.

14. For a fuller analysis of these developments, see David J. O'Brien, *Public Catholicism* (Maryknoll, NY: Orbis, 1996).

Chapter 13

Patriotic Legislating in the Context of Grace?

Theodore R. Weber

The principal legislative response to the tragedy of September 11, 2001, was the U.S. PATRIOT Act of 2001. Despite its titular designation, the Patriot Act is not about patriotism in some explicit and defined sense. It is about expanding and extending the powers of the U.S. government in order to deter and destroy terrorism deriving mainly from radical Islamist sources and to protect against further terrorist acts.[1] The introductory statement makes this purpose clear: it is "An act to deter and punish terrorist acts in the United States and around the world, to enhance law enforcement investigatory tools, and for other purposes." One suspects that the bill was called the "Patriot Act" as a defensive gimmick—that is, as a means to preempt challenges to the further intrusion of governmental power into the rights and privacies of the people entailed by its antiterrorism proposals and to suggest that anyone who is unwilling to sacrifice additional rights and liberties for this purpose is unpatriotic. In any event the bill is not about patriotism but about the uses and limits of governmental power in an extreme situation that threatens the American nation from several directions.[2]

So what? What difference does it make whether the bill lives up to its "patriot" label so long as it serves the purposes for which it is intended? The difference it makes depends on our understanding of patriotism and whether our definition of patriotism pertains to the legislative process itself and not only to the responses of citizens. A comprehensive definition with a legislative reference could have provided Congress with a richer and more inclusive understanding of governmental responsibilities—one that embraces the defensive purposes of government but is not limited to them. In that event it might well have avoided some of the negative and even fearful reactions provoked by this particular legislation and provided more effective service to the government's and the public's concerns with terrorism. It would have yielded an example of the U.S. Congress acting patriotically.

This question of patriotism and its definition is not just about what might have been but also about what needs to be. Legislative reconsideration of the Patriot Act continues because terrorism persists unrelentingly. The Bush Administration wants all provisions of the act renewed, even though many have drawn sharp criticism and some have been ruled unconstitutional. The Department of Justice wants additional and more intrusive investigative permissions. Critics in Congress and elsewhere want some of its provisions repealed, especially those having to do with library investigations and searches without judicial permission. Will the review process finally make the bill a patriotic act and not merely one carrying the "patriot" title to make it more palatable? And if it becomes patriotic, what will be the substance of its patriotism?

I mean to address the issue of legislative patriotism and its substance from the standpoint of Christian theology. In a collection of essays on Christianity and patriotism, that should come as no surprise. This approach is neither an extraneous nor an artificial matter because theology deals with reality in its fullest and is capable of exposing dimensions of political reality not readily discernible from other perspectives. In the case of a legislative act of this kind theological inquiry is especially important. When a nation is subject to such grievous threats the appeals to patriotism tend to reduce all diverse points of identity to a single one manufactured in the national image and to condense all loyalties into a single focus on national survival. These patriotic reductions are idolatrous. They create inevitable tensions with Christian faith, which accords primacy of identity to life in Christ and primacy of loyalty to the one God who transcends and judges all nations. The question here is not whether but how concepts drawn from Christian theology are relevant to the issue at hand and how they can guide and inform the patriotism of the legislative process in response to the threats of terrorism.

Patriotism and the Patriot Act of 2001

What is a "comprehensive" definition of patriotism that governmental officials should will to make operative in their deliberations and enactments? Let us try this one: patriotism in the legislative process is about using the power of government to protect, strengthen, and develop the *patria*. The *patria*, literally, is the "fatherland," but more fully it is the nation, its people, institutions, ethos, and traditions.[3] Any item of legislation and any executive action should be framed with the intent to secure the *patria* in the totality of its present life and future prospects.[4] Doubtless that is what the legislators had in mind in enacting the Patriot Act of 2001. After all, "Uniting and Strengthening America" is part of the title they assigned to it. Why then should the bill not qualify as "patriotic" under this definition?

The answer is that the bill focuses narrowly on acquiring and justifying instruments for the defense of the *patria* but does not do so in a context of concern for the totality of the *patria*. To the words about "uniting and strengthening" it adds, "by providing appropriate tools required to intercept and obstruct terrorism." The legislative focus is on threats, instruments, and terrorism but not on the totality of the national society. It is necessary, but it is not enough. Probably that is why the act did not in fact unite America but instead evoked widespread and hostile response. Did it even strengthen America? That may depend on whether the relative gains in antiterrorist protection were achieved without significant loss of individual rights and of defenses against the intrusive powers of government, as well as some loss of confidence in the government's willingness to observe limits—both informal and institutional—to its exercise of intrusive power on the public's behalf. If the bill divided America and did not unite it, and if it weakened America by damaging the rights structures and the essential tissues of confidence, then it should be judged unpatriotic in those respects even if it served its defensive purposes.

My purpose here is not to evaluate the particular legislation in force nor to produce a model bill. Rather, it is to come to an understanding of how the legislative process can be patriotic in terms of service to the *patria* in a situation where unusual exertions of governmental power are required to cope with extreme threats to public and private welfare. As I indicated previously, I shall pursue this inquiry with perspectives on governmental power drawn from the Christian faith.

Theology in the Legislative Process

There is nothing novel about connecting Christian theology with political problems. Jesus of Nazareth was crucified as a political subversive, and the Apostle Paul admonished the Christians in Rome to "be subject to the governing authorities, because they are ordained of God."[5] Theologians throughout the centuries have discussed and debated questions of law, power, political authority, the relations of church and government, and other related issues that emerged in their times and required reflection and action in the light of the Christian message. The same themes with which they worked are pertinent to our own times and to the awesome responsibilities that confront governments as they attempt to cope with the incalculable and unpredictable menaces of the terrorists.

Contexts of Grace and National Community

Basic to theological orientation is the recognition that all of God's dealings with the world and its peoples take place in a context of grace. Grace is the lens through which we read the meanings of creation, judgment, preservation and salvation. Because grace is prevenient—that is, it is the action of God that goes before all our actions—it is the power of the future over the present. Because grace is justifying, it forgives our sins and opens the possibilities for new directions in life. Because grace is sanctifying, it develops the spirit of love and justice in relationships and encourages the maturation of the connecting tissues and substance of community. Each of these dimensions of grace is significant in political application, because each in its own way points to the explosive power of hope for dead-end situations, the canceling of the pride and insecurity that prevent the admission of wrongdoing, and the healing and renewing of the common life. Grace centers every action in a matrix that discloses its relation to every other action, person and value.

Just as grace is the context for every action, so also the *patria* in the fullness of its relationships is the context for every legislative operation and product. In the case of terrorism, Congress is prompted to act in response to anticipated terroristic actions. However, it must do so in the context of the *patria* and the multiplicity of its values and relationships and not as though responses to threats were engineering projects with their own self-contained rationality. That is, Congress should not pass laws designed just to thwart and nail the terrorists without considering the implications of such laws for all other related aspects and elements of the society. In particular, the legislative efforts must respect the existing fabric of rights and liberties as a limit to the extension of governmental power and must wrestle to produce an unusual degree of justification for any infringements. The legislators must recognize that their own subjective authority is at stake in any and every violation of individual and corporate rights and liberties, and any questioning of authority provoked by such violations reflects reduced public confidence in government.

The dimensions of grace have their counterparts in the interpretive work of counterterrorist legislation. What factors of resistance to terrorism are operative already in American society, and how can legislative actions cooperate with them and not frustrate them? Can the leaders of government own up to the occasions when policies of the administration or Congress have contributed to the climate that has spawned and nurtured terrorism, and if they do so, do they have the political will to turn around and do what is right? Do the leaders recognize that the sensitivity with which they deal with these complicated issues will contribute either to the unity or to the disunity of the country?

Of course, the context of grace is the Kingdom of God. The *patria* is not the Kingdom of God, although the inflated rhetoric of religious nationalism tends to equate the two. It is essential to maintain this critical distinction and to hold the former over the latter as both judgment and limited possibility. Nevertheless, it is possible to learn important lessons from the analogy of one to the other—especially with regard to the awareness of the total context within which the legislative efforts proceed and of the dimensions of grace that illuminate and empower the processes of action, reaction, and recovery.

Order and Defense

"The primary purpose of this government is to protect the American people against terrorism." The words are those of Attorney General Alberto Gonzales addressed to television host Charlie Rose in an interview aired in July 2005. Gonzales's comment reflects accurately the sentiments of President George W.

Bush who often has said words to the same effect and indeed has used the tragedy of September 11, 2001, as the defining moment and theme of his presidency. Important elements in their plan of protection were codified into law in the Patriot Act of 2001.

Both Gonzales and Bush are on sound theological grounds in acting to protect the country. Theologians always have held that the primary purpose of government is to provide for domestic order and for defense against all enemies both foreign and domestic. One finds it in one form or another in Augustine, Aquinas, Luther, Calvin, John Wesley, Reinhold Niebuhr, and others. The basic argument is that the creation has been plunged into chaos because of original sin, and this chaos has been countered by the divine work of preservation, which turns the forces of sin against themselves. The instrument of preservation is government, and because preservation of the fallen creation is part of the divine plan, the institution of government receives divine ordination for its work. Even *The Schleitheim Confession*, a sixteenth-century pacifist document that serves as a political ethics foundation for Mennonites, acknowledges the coercive and ordering work of government while nevertheless excluding Christians from participation.

Clearly the administration and the Congress are right in organizing the powers of government to defend against terrorism and, in doing so, to pass legislation to help implement that defense. Terrorism is a continuing and largely unpredictable eruption of chaos into the order that societies achieve in their histories for the protection and nurturing of public and private life. Defense against destructive and chaos-producing terrorism is a theologically grounded work of government. It is patriotic in providing necessary service to the *patria*. The necessity of this defense and its theological grounding should be recognized even by those Christians who dissent from policies of the Bush Administration and from particular provisions of the Patriot Act.

However, the government is committed also to protect the social and legal fabric of the rights and liberties of the American people. This fabric and its particulars are established in constitutions, laws, and customs, and are monitored by the courts. In reading the Patriot Act of 2001, one notes with appreciation that its authors have recognized the vulnerability of Muslims and Arabs in the tense and emotionally overheated conditions of the present and have specified protections for their rights and persons. The same sensitivity is not so apparent for threats to rights and liberties of all Americans resulting from the newly-defined, intrusive powers of the government.

If Attorney-General Gonzales had spoken with Charlie Rose with the *patria* as the context of his political responsibility, he would have had to say that defense against terrorism is an immediate and fundamental commitment of this government but not "the central purpose." Certainly the defensive responsibilities evoked by terrorism are clear, constitutionally and theologically, but so are the responsibilities of the government to protect American rights and liberties against its own expanding interventions when it is "at war" to protect them. If the U.S. Congress had used the *patria* as the framework of its legislative efforts, would it have enacted this highly controversial bill in such utter haste? We have been told that the bill was delivered to the members of Congress at night and was voted on the next morning with very few of the members having the opportunity to read much of its lengthy text. Does that process suggest serious attention to the impact of this aggressive expansion of governmental power on the rights and liberties of the American people? Does it invite and encourage the consent of the American people to the bill's intrusive provisions and especially to those provisions that allow investigative agencies to invade the sanctity of individual liberties and privacy without judicial permission and with insufficient judicial oversight? It should be evident that placing the threats of terrorism in the context of the *patria* with its totality of values and relationships produces a different legislative and executive outlook and result from when the terroristic threats themselves are used to define the context of governmental action and are allowed to subordinate all other considerations.

Let us remember that government as order of preservation resides in the context of grace leading to salvation. Preservation is not an end in itself nor can its justification be limited to the emergencies of the moment. The government that protects also must affirm and reinforce the law. It must support and strengthen the sinews and substance of community and elicit a maturation of the common consciousness that enhances increasingly its own authority. It must respect and defend the freedom of groups and persons within the society that subject its policies and practices to criticism, especially the severe criticism that exposes fraud, duplicity and arrogance and the subordination of public interest to partisan political advantage. None of these practices of government sets aside the compelling duty to arrange and execute the defenses against terrorism or other challenges to the security of the republic, its people, and its territory. However, they place that duty in the context of the comprehensive and interacting duties generated by the total reality of the *patria*. When that happens, the placement reflects the embodiment of the order of preservation in the context of divine redeeming grace.

Suspicion of Power

A theology of government deriving from biblical sources carries with it a deep suspicion of power despite or perhaps because of the divine ordination of governing authority. One tradition in the Hebrew Bible resisted the establishment of the kingship because of the fear that the king would exalt his own majesty to the point of putting himself in the place of God. Another tradition accepted the kingship reluctantly but warned that the king would oppress the people (2 Sam. 8). The story of David and Bathsheba and of David's encounter with the prophet Nathan records the temptation to arrogance and abuse of power inherent in unlimited royal authority. The prophets warned of the alliance of political power with economic power and the resultant exploitation of the poor and powerless. Jesus also raised the theme of the arrogance of power when he said to the disciples, "the rulers of the Gentiles lord it over them. . .[but] It will not be so among you" (Mt. 20:25–26).

From the beginning, the theologians who developed the teaching concerning the role of government as order of preservation in the total economy of God have incorporated this biblical suspicion of governing power into their political doctrine. They made clear that governments exercise their power under God. They are not themselves divine, and any pretensions to divinity will lead them to catastrophe. Governments are accountable to God, and they are under the judgment of God. All theologians have held governments to be limited by law—divine and natural law, in any case, and in many cases by human law as well. For the past four centuries or more, most theologians have held that governments are limited in important respects by their accountability to the people. Increasingly they found theological justification for embodying this accountability in constitutions and political structures that translated suspicion of power into means of control of power by members of the *patria.*

Suspicion of power is built into the political structure of the United States with its separation into executive, legislative, and judicial branches; the division of the legislature into Senate and House of Representatives; and the reservation to the states of most powers not awarded expressly by the Constitution to the federal government. It is a conservative system designed to prevent direct democratic policy-making, the domination of the government by any single faction or power center in the society, and the hasty passage of ill-considered—or inadequately considered—legislation. It is designed also to allow for the weight of majority sentiment while preventing majorities, determined minorities, or the government itself, from ignoring or abridging the rights of persons or groups not enjoying majority favor or governmental support at any given time. Although conservative in those respects, it is not intended simply to stifle governmental actions in the public interest.

For the most part, this system works more or less as intended. However, its conservative restraints are threatened by at least two types of conditions. One is when a single political party controls both the executive and legislative branches and uses that control to appoint federal judges who will confirm its ideology and its interests. A second is when the public welfare is threatened to such a degree that impetuous political action sweeps over the restraints. Both of these conditions have been present to support the passage and reconsideration of the Patriot Act of 2001. The intensity of the terrorist threat explains why some highly questionable provisions survived in the bill and why it moved through the Congress at such a rapid and unreflective pace. Fear of terrorism suppressed the usual warnings deriving from the suspicion of power, and major party control rode the wave of that fear.

Nevertheless, some provisions reflecting suspicion of governmental power are incorporated into the bill itself. "Section 1001 of the USA PATRIOT Act. . .directs the Office of the Inspector General (OIG) in the U.S. Department of Justice (DOJ or Department) to undertake a series of actions related to claims of civil rights or civil liberties violations allegedly committed by DOJ employees. It also requires the OIG to provide semiannual reports to Congress on the implementation of the OIG's responsibilities under Section 1001."[6] These semiannual reports go to the Committee on the Judiciary of the House of Representatives and the Committee on the Judiciary of the Senate. Also, "On a semiannual basis, the Attorney General shall fully inform the Permanent Select Committee on Intelligence of the House of Representatives and the Select Committee on Intelligence of the Senate concerning all requests for the production of tangible things under section 402."[7] Similar reports are to go semiannually to the aforementioned Judiciary Committees. The requests refer presumably to such matters as demands for library records, seizure of computers, etc.

The fact that this reporting is only on a semiannual basis suggests something less than constant and rigorous congressional oversight. Moreover, the focus of attention seems to be mainly on possible or alleged violation of the rights of Muslims and Arabs. There is no specific provision for possible violations of the rights of the general public by employees of the Department of Justice.

Suspicion of governmental power becomes concrete when libraries, universities, and other institutions and professions anticipate having to respond to antiterrorist investigators armed with new provisions of the Patriot Act that challenge some of their basic commitments. Section 215 of the act allows representatives of the Justice Department to seize library records, books, computers, and other "tangibles" armed only with warrants—which allow immediate action— rather than subpoenas—which may allow the targeted persons or institutions some time to prepare a response. Patrons are not to be informed of intrusions that affect themselves. Employees of the institutions are not allowed to inform anyone else—attorneys are a possible exception—of these investigative actions. It is oppressive power acting in a good cause and with weakened limits to its exercise.

Librarians, their libraries and professional associations, want to cooperate with justifiable investigations and they do not want to disobey the law. However, they also want to protect their patrons and their freedom of reading, research, and privacy. The result is that they have become highly self-conscious about their own situations and practices, about revising their procedures to accommodate the new demands without sacrificing the other values they are bound to protect, about instructing employees on how to respond to official requests (or demands), about what to erase or destroy, and about how to inform their patrons about the new conditions. Instructions are formulated about how to protect patron privacy without breaking the law and "What to do before, during, and after a 'knock at the door.'" Universities and other institutions face similar problems.

The attempt on the part of Congress and the administration to do what is right with regard to protecting the country against terrorist issues in more than a curtailing of rights and liberties, which the people have come to take for granted. It produces a climate of intimidation, which restricts action and invites uneasiness even when no governmental action is forthcoming. Thus, the suspicion of power, which is latent in the relationships of governors and those governed, takes on invisible but menacing form as an effective curtailment of freedom through the means developed to protect freedom.

More than seventy years ago, the theologian Reinhold Niebuhr argued that groups are more powerfully self-righteous than individuals, because they combine the egoism of individual members into the power of group self-interest and unite that amalgam with the moral certainty that their leaders are acting righteously and perhaps self-sacrificially on behalf of the group.[8] What can be said of groups in their struggle with each other can be recognized also in the moral certitude of leaders who encounter resistance from within the group itself: the leaders tend to lose the self-transcendence that would allow them to acknowledge that complaints against their policies and actions from within the society spring from anxiety over threats to constitutional rights arising from the government's own use of power to defend the society and cannot be dismissed as subversive or naïve. The same moral certitude tends to suppress the biblically-derived suspicion of power when the righteous actions of the leaders arouse suspicion. This tendency surely must be exacerbated when the president of the United States announces that the aim of his "war on terrorism" is to "eradicate evil from the earth" or when he understands himself to be on "a mission for God."

Suspicion of power is not intended to paralyze the government in its proper pursuit of legitimate tasks. It is intended, in one dimension, to keep the exercise of power fully subordinate to the rich and ranging demands of the *patria*, and in another dimension, to keep it publicly under the judgment of God. For that to happen, it is necessary for the constitutional restraints to work as they are designed to do and not to be set aside by one-party dominance or overriding emotions of the moment. Constitutional restraints will work only when the minority party is included fully in debates over public policy and when all parties strive to maintain a judiciary that is independent and not ideologically biased. It is necessary also for the public conscience to incorporate the notion of the context of grace that keeps the *patria*, its institutions, and its leaders under a critical judgment not directed by partisan loyalties, and that leads to a richer, more just, and more participatory common life.

Power and the Wholeness of the Patria

All of the actions of God in the context of grace are directed toward healing the brokenness of the fallen creation and encouraging the development of its latent possibilities. Preservation has its purpose in that context and is never alone and in isolation from it. We must think of the work of government in similar terms. When the government defends against terrorism, as it is required to do by the U.S. Constitution and by divine mandate, it must incorporate that defense into a comprehensive strategy of healing American society and encouraging the realization of public and private goods. That is to say, its thinking, planning, and legislating must be contextual in the richest sense and not focused exclusively on particular threats and objectives—even though these particularities provide the occasion for governmental response. Only that contextual orientation can make the defense against terrorism "patriotic" in the true meaning of the term. Does the defense serve the *patria* by strengthening and deepening the common life in all its substance and relationships?

Let us put the matter in the form of imperative principles: in defending against terrorism—or any other threat—the government should act in such manner as to confirm and strengthen the institutions that monitor the actions of government, and to increase the confidence of the people that it is acting in a truly patriotic manner. These principles require that the government act always to reaffirm and solidify constitutional and statutory restraints on government intrusion, even and especially when it is intruding on individual and group rights in the name of erecting defenses against terrorists. The law should elicit public acceptance, even when it authorizes governmental intrusions. That can happen only when the legislative process is fully transparent to the media and to the public and when the minority party is drawn into the process respectfully and meaningfully.

Every national administration is reluctant to admit mistakes and to reverse course on failed and destructive policies. Certainly the administration of President George W. Bush exhibits that reluctance—to a very high degree, some would insist. Yet any administration will feel more secure in admitting mistakes and changing policies if it enjoys public confidence. Public confidence that an administration is doing the right thing for the right reasons confers on it a large measure of freedom to open itself to self-criticism and the criticism of others and to change course. In that respect it corresponds roughly to the divine grace of justification that confers forgiveness of sins and allows for a new birth in righteousness. The two are not simply the same, of course. Justification—the forgiveness of sins—is totally free grace and cannot be earned. Public confidence must be earned by a reputation for integrity and truthfulness as well as effectiveness in the administration of public power. It is not enhanced by public relations and spin doctoring. However, both justification and public confidence point in the same direction: The freedom to change and to act is not freedom in any absolute sense but an allowance and encouragement to create more confidence and trust to support future policies and actions that may make additional stringent demands in their service to the public good. Theologically, that is known as growth in grace and in love. Politically, it is the transformation of partisan advantage into patriotic authority and with it the maturation of authentic cohesion of the *patria*. The active principle is a commitment to making the *patria* whole incorporated into every exercise of executive and legislative power.

The Churches and the Power of the *Patria*

When we move beyond theological analysis of power relations to Christian practice, we encounter the age-old problem that Christians are citizens of the earthly *patria* and sons and daughters in the Kingdom of God. It is a problem that every generation in every land must deal with until the Lord comes again. Neither of these contexts rightly can be denied; both of them generate occasions for loyalty and obedience. These calls for loyalty and obedience cannot simply and rightfully be reduced to each other. Inevitably there is tension between the two, and in a moment of critical decision one of them will prevail. There should be no doubt in the mind of a well-instructed Christian—one who believes that God is present in Christ reconciling the world to the divine self and that the risen Christ has defeated the demonic powers that control the world—that the priority in Christian loyalty is to God in Christ above all earthly loyalties and that true identity is not the national image but the image of God recovered through the sacrificial and sanctifying love of Christ. Nevertheless, the tension between the two contexts and foci of loyalty remains, and if they cannot rightly be merged neither can they rightly be disconnected.

In the managing of this tension, the temptations and risks are several. One that is increasingly prominent and compelling is to unite the cause of Christ with the national cause, erasing any distinction between the two and staging the conflict as between the goodness of Christian America and the unmitigated evil of the terrorist menace. In this scenario, the religion of nationalism becomes the healing and inspiring force, the president of the United States emerges as national spiritual leader, and "God Bless America" (our national hymn) replaces "Take Me Out to the Ballgame" in the seventh-inning stretch (But what is more American than "Take Me Out to the Ballgame"?). The major objection to this tendency is that it corrupts the cause of Christ, which knows no national boundaries, into an ideology of national power and righteousness. Not incidentally, it is a very large gift to radical Muslim terrorists who take it as evidence that the Christian West indeed is conducting a crusade against Islam.

Another option—a temptation and risk—is the secularist one of declaring religious faith to be a private matter irrelevant to political matters and related to political matters only unjustifiably and dangerously. Yet another is the pious stance that declares "values" to be basic to political responsibility and then limits the scope of "values" by excluding such matters as poverty, environment, rights of women and minorities, and restraints on the use of military force.

None of these options with their temptations and risks is acceptable as a way of dealing with the tension between Christian life in the *patria* and membership in the Kingdom of God. All of them are fraught with danger for both faith and politics. It is essential that persons of faith recognize these temptations for the siren songs that they are and in their Christian communities learn to identify and discard them and to find biblically defensible ways of honoring God while fulfilling their patriotic responsibilities. Some suggestions follow.

Worship and Preaching

From Moses before Pharaoh to Jesus before Pontius Pilate, the Bible has recognized the critical transcendence of divine worship over the impressive claims of political power. "You shall have no other gods before me" (Ex. 20:3) is a call to faithfulness with respect not only to other tribal gods but also to the looming power that controls the temporal realm and claims divinity for itself. Temporal values or authorities that exalt themselves and that we allow to take the place of God are false idols. We must learn to discern them as such and then dethrone them. "'You would have no power over me unless it had been given you from above'" (Jn. 19:11a) is the answer Jesus gives to the Roman governor who reminds him that he has the power to release or to crucify him. The cultic practices of worship may seem remote from such dramatic encounters, but they shape the Christian character and form the Christian memory to meet the challenges of faith and understanding when loyalty to the *patria* threatens to override loyalty to God. In the planning and practice of divine worship we never should forget how often the two forms of loyalty intersect with other and how fateful the results of their meeting can be.

Preaching of the Gospel always should hold the prospect, the possibilities, and the risks of this intersection in mind. The engagement of preaching with political existence is not in the first instance a matter of taking stands publicly on political issues, although it may come to that. Rather, it is a matter of opening up a political experience that the people share and that may threaten or at least puzzle them and showing how it is to be understood in the light of Christian faith. What do we discover when we explore the issues in the context of divine reconciliation? What evidences are there of prevenient grace—of justifying and sanctifying grace? What is the relevance of "war on terror" in Iraq to our belief that all human beings are created in the image of God? Do we understand ourselves and our nation to be under the judgment of God for our individual and collective sins and not merely victims or righteous warriors? What is the difference between the peace that Christ gives and the peace that the world gives, and what relationship—if any—is there between them in the situation before us? For what can we hope and on what basis?

The possibilities for preaching politically with theological insight—and theologically with political insight—are almost endless, and they are the stuff of faithful pulpit proclamation. Such preaching is essential to keeping and guiding the patriotism of the faithful in the context of grace.

Prophetic Criticism

If we are not there already, here is where we "Quit preachin' and go to meddlin'!" Prophetic criticism in this case has to do with whether the government is fulfilling its divine commission to provide order and defense (and other benefits) in the context of divine grace. It is not out of bounds for church people to ask prophetically whether the government is providing adequate defense against terrorism and other threats or whether it has become negligent or has spent its counterterrorist resources on "pork barrel" awards to powerful members of Congress. But more in the ancient prophetic line, it is entirely within bounds to ask whether the government is protecting American citizens and their rights, liberties, and privacies against its own vast and expanding power. Inquiry into the particulars of these issues may be more properly the province of investigative journalists, scholars, whistle-blowers, and others who have the knowledge and the vocation to conduct such investigations and be alert to failures and violations. Yet surely it is within the range of the church's prophetic responsibility to register warnings concerning abuses of power and the failure of the government to protect the weak and vulnerable in the society—especially against the government's own well-motivated efforts to provide protection. There is no doubt that at times the government requires unusual measures to cope with threats to the nation, its people and its institutions. However, the tendency toward violation with a sense of justification is so great that these measures also must be under unusual and constant scrutiny and especially the prophetic watchfulness of those who know how easy it is for the human heart to turn the power of protection into the power of oppression.

Education

It is a scandal of the churches that persons looked upon as faithful members can rise to the highest offices in the land without a clue as to what their denominations teach concerning issues with which they deal politically. When that happens they are not clueless altogether, of course. The gaps in their religious instruction are filled quickly and influentially by the interests and ideology of corporations, gun clubs, unions, and a variety of political action committees, nongovernmental organizations, and political commentators. "Faith" then becomes a matter of affirming certain "values" of part of their political constituency, attending prayer breakfasts, saying grace before meals, and associating with prominent religious figures. Faith as articulated in their own Christian traditions has no discernible bearing on their most significant political decisions.

Should we settle for this result—a testimony to the irrelevance of Christian faith to fundamental issues of the common life, that is, of the *patria*? Is that true patriotism? Why should we fail to school laity and clergy in the theological-political concepts examined above: the context of grace and national community, the theological groundings and limits of order and defense, the biblical suspicion of power, and the bearing of judgment and movement toward healing and wholeness on every action of the political institutions of the *patria*? Can the churches and their leaders and members be patriotic in the proper sense without providing this fundamental education in Christian political thinking?

Sacramental Perspectives

In the sacrament of the Lord's Supper, we are reminded that Christ died for the sins of the whole world. A sacramental perspective on the government's efforts to defend against terrorists requires it to bring the whole world into the picture and not only the United States, its people, territory, and property. It contextualizes the *patria* in the society of nations with its web of relationships and away from the tendency to work in isolation or to move unilaterally. Of course, that revisioning imposes limitations—often unwanted—on a country inclined to look internally and to resist external restraints. Nevertheless, it makes political sense, because terrorism is a problem for the international society and not just for one country, and effective measures to cope with it require international cooperation.

Political leaders who think sacramentally will recognize the reality and significance of this international context for national action.

The sacrament reflects the fact that the body of the world is broken, as does the conflict with radical Islamic terrorism. The two perspectives interpret this brokenness differently, however. Sacramentally, we speak of it as the result of sin. That identifies it as a human problem and therefore our problem as well as everyone else's. We must engage in restraint of sin where that is called for, but we also must examine our own practices and policies under the judgment of God and with due respect to the criticisms of others. In the reciprocity of conflict with terrorism, the problem of brokenness is cast as a good against evil dichotomy. There is no acknowledgment of complicity and none of the possibility of merit in the opponent's cause or critique. Where one stands with regard to these alternative interpretations is ultimately a matter of faith and not of political wisdom or calculation. Whoever poses the conflict as one simply between good and evil is not thinking sacramentally and therefore is not using Christian theology to interpret issues and decide responses.

The sacrament is the presence of the holy in the mundane. Thus the Holy Spirit is met in the water of baptism, and the crucified and risen Lord is present in the breaking of bread and the pouring out of the wine. There are lessons from the sacrament for patriotism in the process of legislating defense against terrorism. In addition to what has been said, a further lesson is that we never are justified in treating the *patria* itself as holy and according it a degree of loyalty that belongs only to the divine. Sacramentally understood, the *patria*—in this case, the United States—is merely temporal, limited, relative and nothing more. It is true that we meet the holy in the experience of the body politic, but our first encounter with it is as a word of judgment that denies any basis for national exaltation or political self-righteousness. The larger, more affirming encounter is with the holy as a word of grace that cares for and heals the relationships within the body politic and affirms the currents making for the reconciling of the world.

Conclusion: Patriotism, *Patria*, and the Context of Grace

Patriotism in the ordinary sense of the word is not a primary claim on Christians. Our primary loyalty is to God above all other things or relationships—God whom we know in Jesus Christ and the presence of the Holy Spirit and whose image we confess to recognize in all the peoples of the earth. Patriotism as a matter of political loyalty becomes a theologically grounded obligation because we are placed under responsibility to "seek the welfare of the city where I have sent you into exile, and pray to the Lord on its behalf, for in its welfare you will find your welfare"(Jer. 29:7) and because governments are invested with the task and authority to provide for order and defense and perform other necessary tasks in this world. Whatever temporal loyalties are expected of us and whatever responsibilities governments have for the use of their power are to be understood decisively only in the context of divine grace. Divine grace in its ultimate intention is redeeming grace. It is healing and reconciling. Patriotism in the context of grace never rightly can be a definer of identity that overrides loyalty to God in Christ and separates us in some final and qualitative sense from the other peoples of the world. On the other hand, the loyalty generated in the divine-human encounter does not excuse us from fulfilling the relative obligations of temporal patriotism in seeking the welfare of the city where we live.

In this essay I have redefined patriotism away from its usual reference to the loyalty of individual persons to their country and have explored its meaning as service to the *patria*. The redefinition itself allows Christians to feel more comfortable with the claims of patriotism, because *patria* embraces the diversity of the society, acknowledges the multiplicity of claims on persons and groups, and establishes rights as defenses against superior power. My main purpose in redefinition, however, is to establish the full context for legislative action with regard to the threats posed by terrorists.

This full context is a call to commit legislatively to the *patria* with its historic combination of people, institutions, customs, laws, and values. Counterterrorist legislation with this commitment is not simply *vis-à-vis* the threats of the terrorists; it is imagined and argued in a rich, inclusive, and organic social context. Responsibility to defend the society against its enemies is in no way diminished, but it is exercised with a prevenient awareness of the various dimensions and relationships of personal and social life likely to be impacted by any unusual expansion of governmental power. Consequences for rights and liberties are not afterthoughts; they are reckoned from the beginning. When actions against terrorists are thought out in this context, the legislators have—as do other branches of the government—a clear sense of responsibility for the *patria* in its totality and for intending in every deliberation and decision to strengthen all of its elements, heal the divisions of the nation, and thereby enhance its own moral authority.

In his admirable review of the various sections of the Patriot Act, Amitai Etzioni advocates a "carefully crafted balance between the two competing claims of security and freedom,"[9] and "a third way, between those who are committed to shore up our liberties but who are blind to the needs of public safety, and those who in the name of security never met a right they were not willing to curtail to give the authorities an even freer hand."[10] These proposals certainly are defensible. What I offer, however, is something more than a "carefully crafted balance" or a "third way." It is a holistic concept of political vocation that requires legislative action to hold all the values and relations of the society in view from the outset and throughout the debates, and to reflect on antiterrorist proposals in the light of their implications for all other lines of responsibility within the body politic. Nothing less than this is patriotic in the practice of legislating.

This way of thinking about politics arises out of theological wrestling with the implications of the context of divine grace, which enfolds and preserves the fallen creation and works to bring it again to wholeness. It discloses a politics that is about more than order and defense or even pursuit of the common good. It is about renewing the goods and fabric of the society in every action on its behalf, and in the process of doing so insuring that the power of government is servant and not master.

Notes

1. The Bush Administration does not, as a rule, identify "radical Islamist terrorism" as the reason for its "war on terrorism." It does not want to give credence to the claim made by Al Qaeda and others that it is conducting a crusade against Islam as such. Nevertheless, the reference is clear in context. Also, the reference is clear in the care the Patriot Act takes to protect and avoid offense to Muslims and Arabs as such.
2. Amitai Etzioni, *How Patriotic Is the Patriot Act? Freedom Versus Security in the Age of Terrorism* (New York: Routledge, 2004). Professor Etzioni's book is a very useful discussion of the elements of the act and the tensions that they generate, but the author never answers his own question, conceivably because the Patriot Act is not about patriotism.
3. *Patria,* from *pater,* the Latin word for father. Ironically, *patria* is a feminine word in Italian and Spanish.
4. For a rich and pertinent charter of governmental purpose in support of the *patria,* consider the Preamble to the U.S. Constitution: "We the People of the United States, in Order to form a more perfect Union, establish Justice, insure domestic tranquility, provide for the common defence, promote the general Welfare, and secure the Blessings of Liberty to ourselves and our Posterity, do ordain and establish this Constitution for the United States of America."
5. See Romans 13:1–7 for the full relevant text.
6. Report to Congress on Implementation of Section 1001 of the USA PATRIOT Act, January 27, 2004.
7. The U.S. Patriot Act, Sec. 502. Congressional Oversight.
8. Reinhold Niebuhr, *Moral Man and Immoral Society* (New York: Charles Scribner's Sons, c. 1932), xi–xii.
9. Etzioni, *How Patriot Is the Patriot Act?* 5.
10. Etzioni, *How Patriot Is the Patriot Act?* 8.

Part IV

The Church's Ministry

Chapter 14

Preaching Patriotism?

Alyce M. McKenzie

Bumper Stickers and Throat Lumps

For some people, patriotism is the lump in their throat when the National Anthem is sung at sporting events. For others, it is an uncritical nationalism that supports the government's policies no matter what. This outlook was expressed by the bumper stickers of the Vietnam era: "My country, right or wrong," and "My country, love it or leave it." Contrast this with the less certain sounding bumper stickers that adorn cars, trucks and SUVs in the era of the war in Iraq: "Support our troops," and "Bring our troops home." As an ordained United Methodist minister and professor of preaching, I am convinced that an important function of preaching in the United States today is to offer a definition of patriotism for Christians that goes beyond throat lumps and bumper stickers. This essay explores the deeper definition of patriotism for Christians called for by these contentious times and how Christian preaching can do its part to convey it.

On a surface level, anybody with access to a dictionary can recite an adequate definition of patriotism. Any dictionary will tell us that patriotism's etymological ancestors are the Greek word *patrios*, which means "of one's fathers," and *patris*, which means "fatherland." A patriot is one who "exerts himself to promote the well being of his country." A patriot is one who "maintains and defends his country's freedoms or rights." To be patriotic is "to be marked by devotion to the wellbeing or interests of one's country." Patriotism is "love or zealous devotion to one's country."[1] For the Christian this love of country is set in the framework of one's ultimate devotion to God as revealed in Jesus Christ.

I should say at the outset that I believe Christians should be involved in public life.[2] We need to take with us a couple of theological cautions, however. We need to go into the world fully aware of the dangers to faith of involvement in the political realm. This means never forgetting that human beings and human institutions are prone to selfishness, greed, and violence. We need to go into the world remembering that our citizenship is ultimately not of this world but rather of the kingdom of God, and that our ultimate loyalty to God trumps all other loyalties. These cautions in mind, I still think God calls Christians to regard public and political institutions and relationships as potentially positive agencies through which people in social union can serve their neighbors.[3]

Documents under Glass

School children take field trips to gaze upon the Declaration of Independence and the Constitution under glass. Those studying for the U.S. citizenship exam earnestly memorize portions of these documents. It would be a good thing, in this troubled time, if all of us paid them more attention. The Founders were not perfect. They acknowledged the full citizenship only of white males who owned property. Still, we are indebted to them for a deeper definition of patriotism than the ones we are used to. The founding documents of our nation seek to foster a society committed to the protection and encouragement of the equality of all citizens as well as individual freedoms, including the right to free exercise of religion. The Founders realized that freedom was not, as we too often define it today, freedom to be left alone or freedom from responsibility to others. Such a definition of freedom would have been, for them, the opposite of patriotic. They insisted that freedom could only be preserved when an educated citizenry actively participated in government.[4] The original portrait of the good citizen in America, going back to the late 1700s, was someone whose work ethic and goals were directed toward the good of the community. This was the Founders' democratic ideal of civic virtue. Thomas Jefferson enjoined citizens to "Love your neighbor as yourself, and your country more than yourself."[5] To that the Christian adds, "and God above all."

The values of the Founders form what sociologist Robert Bellah, drawing from the thought of the eighteenth-century French political philosopher Jean Jacques Rousseau, calls "civil religion." "Civil religion," sometimes called "public religion," is a cultural framework operating in our minds, influential and often unacknowledged. It is a conception of our nation's past, present identity, and future purpose that is heavily influenced by biblical imagery, viewing government as a covenant among people with a responsibility to God and to one another. It tells us we are a people with a mission in the world. It agrees on the importance of individual rights and dignity while acknowledging that there will be struggles over how those values will be achieved.[6] At the barest minimum, patriotism involves commitment to individual human rights and dignity and a realistic expectation of disagreement on important issues in a pluralistic democracy. Religious conservatives and liberals agree on those basics relating to patriotism.

Competing Civil Religions

Underlying that basic level of agreement, though, two different civil religions—visions of what this country is and what it ought to be—are operative. There is a conservative civil religion and a liberal civil religion. Understanding their background will shed light on the differing definitions of patriotism held by liberals and conservatives today both in politics and religion. The liberal vision is a reaction against the intense religious struggles of sixteenth- and seventeenth-century Europe and reflects the optimistic rationalism of Enlightenment political philosophy. By this view, there is a universal moral order. Individuals have a built-in, subjective sense of what living by it ought to look like. They can be trusted to make appropriate moral choices in their private lives. The United States is special in that it had the opportunity, in forming its government, to embody the universal moral sensibilities on which people of goodwill everywhere can agree.[7] Liberal civil religion believes that religious values can be brought into the secular public sphere, whether by church members or others, without having to be voiced in specific religious terms. They do not need to be mandated by a strong legislative code. Diplomacy rather than military force is preferred in dealing with foreign powers.[8]

Conservative public religion objects to the universalism and rationalism it perceives to have taken over established denominations. Religious conservatives object to the moral relativism they perceive to be gaining precedence in legal and political debates. They do not believe that individuals, generally, have a reliable moral sense built into them and believe it is necessary to have strong churches, moral instruction in schools, and legal sanctions to ensure public decency. The story of America for them is not one of gradual elevation in moral insight. Rather, it is a degeneration away from the initial values of this country brought about by the leadership of established religious and secular institutions turning away from the biblical order. America still has a mission to fulfill as far as God is concerned. Once it was fighting communism. Now it is keeping the land free of moral decay by means of a strong system of legislated morality.[9] The mission since September 11, 2001, includes, for many theological conservatives, protecting their country's way of life and future from terrorism by employing military force.

The definition of patriotism, "zealous devotion to the welfare of one's country," is complicated by these differing visions among liberals and conservatives as to what that welfare looks like and how it is best achieved. The post-9/11 context has sharpened questions regarding faith and patriotism. In this setting, sermons ought to be equipping people to raise and respond to some very complex questions with regard to the issue of war and peace. How are we as Christians who profess to love our enemies to respond to those who planned and carried out an act of aggression toward our nation? What stand are we to take on our nation's subsequent attack on Iraq? How are we to live our lives in an era when color coded alerts tell us how secure or insecure to feel on a given day? Are we to embrace the passing of the Patriot Act, welcoming it as a means to enhance national security? Or are we to criticize it as a tool that enables law enforcement to infringe upon free speech, freedom of the press, human rights, and right to privacy? How do our faith and our patriotism come into play as reports of civilian and military casualities in Iraq come in daily? How are we to think about and respond to the attacks on London subways and buses July 7, 2005, and the attempted attacks on July 21, 2005—expansions of the radius of vulnerability from America to our allies? How are we to think about Islam, a religion that fanatics are exploiting for political ends?

The relationship of preaching and patriotism would be complex enough if it were related just to issues of war and peace. It is tempting to let it go at that. But to do so would be to ignore a whole host of pertinent issues. A glance at the cases that will come before the U.S. Supreme Court in the next year offers us a sampler: abortion, assisted suicide, what constitutes discrimination against gay men and women, and standards of proof needed to establish a need for new trials. Other pressing issues include immigration, social security, public education, gay marriage, capital punishment, and stewardship of the environment.[10]

Throughout the 1980s and 1990s, I served several churches in central and eastern Pennsylvania. I currently teach homiletics, the art of preaching, at Perkins School of Theology, Southern Methodist University. My students are studying to enter the pastoral ministry, to preach weekly sermons to others who are seeking to live out their faith in the midst of their communities. This is as good a place as any to say a word about the purpose of Christian preaching. Broadly speaking, it is to invite listeners into the presence of the God revealed to us in Jesus Christ whose grace involves both justice and mercy. In service of that broad purpose, preachers are to place aspects of contemporary life in a biblical, theological context. As listeners enter into the biblical salvation story, they see themselves, their relationships with others, and their social context in light of the promises, challenges, and events of that story. In Christ's presence in the preaching moment, listeners can be equipped to live with justice and compassion in all the arenas of their daily lives.

Preaching is a form of public discourse in which God is recognized as being related to human beings not just as individuals but in the full context of their existence. The Word of God addresses us in our personal lives but also as members of the larger social world. Contemporary preaching, whether theologically liberal or conservative, seems to have no trouble speaking of God as personal, but it also needs to acknowledge God as fully social and radically present in the world.[11]

In the weeks following September 11, 2001, I both heard a number of sermons and heard about a number of sermons from students, friends, and colleagues. Some preachers opted not to address the terrorist attacks during the sermons, limiting their mention to the prayer concerns. Others focused on the heroism of those who died and empathy for their families. A few others preached that this was God's wakeup call to America to repent of our social sins. And some preached the need to apprehend and punish those who had orchestrated these events in the name of divine justice.[12] Implied in these approaches are two answers to the question of how Christian preaching ought to relate itself to the topic of patriotism—that is, devotion to the welfare of one's country. They are avoidance and endorsement. Implied in each approach is a different definition of patriotism for the Christian; withdrawal from public, political involvement and endorsement of the policies of the group(s) that holds economic, political, and social power.

Avoidance

A couple of years ago I was doing some research into how clergy viewed their role in their congregations. I interviewed about fifty clergy from various parts of the United States, from diverse ethnic and denominational backgrounds, and from a variety of theological, congregational contexts. In response to my opening question, "How would you describe your role in your congregation?" about three fourths of the white pastors I interviewed responded quickly, "I'm a pastor, not a prophet."[13] One clergywoman, when asked to elaborate, said, "I preach to a slice of George Bush's Texas. I have to be careful what I say if I want to stay here."

Most of the African-American pastors I interviewed had a different take on their role. "I am a sage. I am a community leader. I am a teacher. I am a prophet." In black faith communities the pastor is expected to speak to the dicey issues of the day. I remember one black student I taught years ago at Princeton Theological Seminary. She recalled her mother poring over the daily paper, looking at one headline after another, and saying, "I wonder what pastor is going to have to say about this. . . . Oh, he won't like that. . . . I'll bet he'll have something to say about this!"

The boldness of African-American preaching springs from their understanding of the church's role in community life. Black churches have traditionally been community centers where black self-esteem is nurtured amid a culture that erodes it. They have not been able to separate the personal from the public as easily as have whites. They have found it obvious that forces in the dominant culture undermine their personhood. Black preaching has challenged their people to see themselves as God sees them and to be a positive force in a negative world.[14]

The boldness of black preaching also springs from their understanding of the character of God. African-American preacher and professor of preaching Cleophus J. LaRue, in his recent book *The Heart of Black Preaching*, makes this comment:

> Black preaching reflects the black belief that a personal God is involved in every aspect of human existence in very concrete and tangible ways. There is little or no distinction between the sacred and the secular in black life. Consequently, there are no areas of black life that are off limits to the gospel and no avenues of human experience where black preaching fears to tread. All realms of black life are eventually exposed to the probing, searching light of the gospel.[15]

But getting back to our white clergywoman's response—"I preach to a slice of George Bush's Texas. I have to be careful what I say if I want to stay here"—I had to admire her honesty at least. To be fair to her, she was responding to the widespread attitude of many middle-class white mainline churchgoers that religion and politics do not mix. In many such congregations, though by no means all, the message is clear: "Be our chaplain, but don't rock the boat."

Conventional cocktail party wisdom tells us to avoid talking about politics and religion. Conventional pulpit wisdom counsels preachers to avoid preaching on the three hot button issues of human life: sex, power, and money. Why? Because, according to this theory, "politics don't belong in the pulpit." The proper topic for the pulpit is private spirituality.

Where did these assumptions about a division between private and public issues come from? Historian Clarke E. Cochran in his fascinating study of religion in America, *Religion in Public and Private Life*,[16] points out that modern Western liberal thought that undergirds our founding documents demanded a clear separation of church and state to protect religious freedom from established churches and from the interference of the government. Liberal political philosophy is built on a commitment to an individualistic conception of value and to the centrality of freedom conceived of as autonomy. These produce a strong commitment to separation of public and private life. While it was not the Founders' intention, religion has come to be seen as the inhabitant of the private, individualized realm while the state has come to be seen as the inhabitant of the public and secularized realm.[17]

Stephen Carter argued persuasively in *The Culture of Disbelief* that the mainline Protestant churches have played into this by allowing themselves to be sidelined from the public sphere and allowing their message to become indistinguishable from cultural values of individualism and personal achievement often measured in financial terms. In the more than ten years since his book was published the political influence of evangelicals and fundamentalists has risen dramatically.[18] If preachers in conservative evangelical churches are preaching against gay marriage and abortion and in favor of traditional family values, and if preachers in mainline denominations are keeping silent on social issues, then what can we conclude? I suspect, just for starters, that there is a shortage of sermons that help Christians deal faithfully with the issue of biblical teaching on war, the need for reform of our criminal justice system, the immorality of poverty, and the sacred responsibility to care for the environment.

This pattern of speech and silence holds true in recent political rhetoric. In the 2004 election, Republican candidates were comfortable talking about religious values and issues and promising their faith would affect their politics. Democrats, by contrast, declined to discuss issues in religious terms. Evangelical activist Jim Wallis asserts that their failure to do so was not just a political miscalculation; it showed that they do not appreciate the contributions of religion to American public life.[19] He believes that Democrats should stop suggesting that we not talk about "God." They should put their energy into arguing, on moral and even religious grounds, that all Americans should have economic security, health care, and educational opportunity and that true faith results in a compassionate concern for those on the margins.[20] Wallis points out that Catholic social teaching speaks of a "consistent ethic of life," which speaks against abortion, capital punishment, poverty, war, and a range of human rights abuses too often selectively respected by pro-life advocates. He believes that truth telling, stewardship, treatment of "the least of these," and war are deeply theological issues for which Christians should hold politicians accountable.[21]

We are used to socially progressive evangelicals like Jim Wallis, Ron Sider, and Tony Campolo advocating a broader biblical agenda in involvement in the public arena.[22] Recently a number of more conservative Christians have weighed in on issues beyond a pro-life agenda and a heterosexual definition of marriage. The National Association of Evangelicals, which represents fifty-two evangelical groups with over thirty million members, approved a sweeping document in October 2005 called *For the Health of the Nation: An Evangelical Call to Civic Responsibility*.[23] The statement lists seven priorities for conservative Christians that include not only promoting religious freedom and opposing abortion but also practicing compassion for the poor and vulnerable and protecting God's creation. The move to a broader agenda, especially on the environment, has created strains among evangelicals and between evangelicals and the Republican Party they generally support. Such tensions are welcome signs of a move from predictable, single-issue alliances to a deeper, more challenging interaction of Christian faith and public life. Only by such interaction by both liberals and conservatives can legitimate forms of religion exercise their moral grounding effect on public life and policy.

Secular humanists and liberal religionists have often agreed that religiously expressed convictions and symbols have no place in the public square out of a concern for the separation of church and state. But when church members tell a preacher that "politics don't belong in the pulpit," what I think they are really saying is, "I don't want to be challenged to think about how my religious faith ought to be influencing my involvement in public life."

When clergy give in and adopt the avoidance strategy, they violate the definition of patriotism with which we began: "a zealous devotion to the welfare of one's country." Not to preach on the public dimension of faith, issues of war and peace in the context of broader issues of justice and injustice and life and death, is to preach a half-gospel. History shows that a half-gospel can easily become worse than none. An avoidance strategy is timid faith. It is poor citizenship. It is profoundly unpatriotic.

Endorsement

Throughout the 1960s, political activism with regard to Vietnam and civil rights was associated with religious liberals. Religious conservatives began to adopt a strategy of political activism in the early 1970s as evangelical Christians began making their public voice heard on the issues of abortion and the Equal Rights Amendment. In the 1980s the Religious Right became identified with traditional "family values," pro-life, anti-gay rights, and a variety of related issues.[24]

Throughout the 1990s, politicians at the national level increasingly found that gaining the support of the country's conservative Christians was a prerequisite to gaining power. They are an important part of the political base of the Bush administration.

Robert Bellah, in an essay that still rings true almost 30 years after its authorship, analyzed the conservative, fundamentalistic preaching rising in popularity at the end of the 1970s. He points out that it is no coincidence that it makes little attempt to analyze the world in terms of its social structures. It recognizes the power of religious belief and experience. It gives great importance to the intense life of the group and the demand for personal sacrifice in the church community. But this stance, while seeming to be outwardly directed, actually represents a withdrawal into privatism. It equates the common good of the nation's peoples with the beliefs of the community. It puts a quest for certitude in place of authentic faith.[25]

The Religious Right's involvement in politics ought to embarrass church members from mainline denominations who chastise their preachers for mixing politics and religion. At least the Religious Right is motivated and active. At the same time, their activism has represented a narrowing of the biblical vision for a society of peace with justice (*shalom*) down to individual moral choices and sexual ethics on grounds of "what the Bible says." What about poverty and violence, which the Bible spends a whole lot of time condemning? What happens when religious groups ignore these broader issues, focus on personal morality and sexual issues, and give political support to the party that is willing to write their beliefs into the party platform regardless of the party stance on poverty and violence? Such religious groups align themselves with political positions that seek to help the wealthy maintain their wealth, and acquiesce to those who view war as a ready solution to the economic, social, religious complexities of conflicts among nations.

Clarke Cochran, in his study of public and private religion in the United States, identifies the dynamic I have just described as one of the primary dangers of religion's involvement in public life: that it will be absorbed into political ideologies. A particular set of political beliefs becomes identified with the expression of religious beliefs.[26] Says Cochran, "The new religious right furnishes the best illustration of ideological absorption, where religious leaders have baptized laissez-faire economics and nationalist foreign policy."[27]

Preaching Prosperity

I have said that it is unpatriotic to avoid preaching on public issues with political implications. There are two other types of preaching that are unpatriotic because, directly or indirectly, they end up endorsing the power of the economic, political status quo. The first is the preaching of the prosperity gospel. The second is preaching with unwarranted, simplistic certainty on complex, controversial topics.

The prosperity gospel is a version of the Christian message that is indistinguishable from the values of an acquisitive, radically individualistic culture. It holds that financial prosperity is a sign of God's favor and comes to those who are faithful Christians. Material prosperity is a worthy goal of and motivation for the life of faith. There are strands of this belief in the optimistic wisdom literature of the Hebrew Scriptures (Proverbs) where long life, a degree of prosperity, and many children are portrayed as the rewards of a life of wisdom. But Christian preachers ought to preach the whole biblical canon, not the perspective of single verses taken out of context. Other books, Ecclesiastes and Job among them, question the validity of the "good life-good luck formula." It is rejected by Israel's prophets, including Jesus, whose emphasis is on the need for peace with justice and the fair treatment of the vulnerable young, old, and poor in a society, if it is to be pleasing to God.[28]

The oxymoronic prosperity gospel is a corrupt identification of the Christian gospel with the cultural gospel of success. It is not patriotic in the deepest sense, because it is not communal. It is not concerned with the virtues of citizenship that work toward a peaceful, just society for everyone but with individual material consumption. The prosperity gospel crosses racial, ethnic, and economic boundaries. It is preached in upper middle-class white congregations where it congratulates listeners on the lifestyles they have achieved. It is preached in struggling communities for whom a pastor's snappy attire, luxury car, and impressive home are signs of the favor of God and worthy goals for the congregation. It is also preached in immigrant communities, holding out a vision of what "making it in America" means. Wherever it is preached, its definition of the "good life" is an insult to the Founders, not to mention to a certain first-century rabbi who, in his preaching, attacked it rather than embraced it. Wherever it is preached, in whatever century it is preached, it supports politics and economics that benefit the rich and dismiss the poor as undeserving of God's blessing.[29]

Preaching False Certainties

It is also unpatriotic to preach on complex, controversial issues simplistically and prescriptively. Why is it that some preachers preach with unwarranted certainty on a few complex moral issues the Bible does not directly address or anticipate[30] and that too many preachers fail to preach with certainty on a whole spectrum of justice issues that the Bible is quite clear about?[31] I ask this fully aware that it is a question I need continually to ask myself about my own preaching. Christian preaching ought to challenge listeners to think through the biblical and theological implications of issues for their own involvement in the institutions and decisions of public life. Rather than promising premature closure on complex issues, preaching ought to invite listeners into a process of dialogue, prayer, and positive actions despite disagreements.

Preaching on a complex, controversial social issue like war calls on the preacher to educate herself with regard to underlying causes and possible constructive responses. It ought to require the preacher to face the fact that people of sincere faith hold a view diametrically opposed to his, to acknowledge their legitimate concerns and to cultivate a spiritual posture of humility. This is not indecision or weak faith. It is respect for the mystery of God and the limitations of human knowledge. Preaching that honors the complexity of issues is not as vulnerable to the temptation to endorse groups with political, economic power on the basis of their stand on a narrow range of issues.

With regard to a complex, controversial issue with political and religious implications like war, there is surface agreement among people regardless of political affiliations. We all want an end to terrorism. None of us wants to send our young men and women into harm's way. There is the same surface agreement with regard to most chronic social problems. We all want justice in our court system. We all want an end to hunger, homelessness, child pornography, and discrimination against gay men and women.

Just beneath the surface agreement, however, lies the complexity of disagreement. People disagree on the means that need to be employed in bringing about the outcomes they all agree upon. Profound disagreements on ethical and political issues divide those who listen to sermons. Preaching on such issues needs to acknowledge the complexity of the issue and use the resources of Scripture, tradition, and contemporary knowledge to chart constructive common responses in the face of abiding differences of opinion and conviction.

When preaching on war, the preacher needs to point out that any war has multiple causes and effects. These include religious and ethnic differences, prejudices, international enmity toward our country, and our past dealings with other nations that have inevitably involved mixed motives and mishandled situations. The preacher needs to share what he has learned about the causes and background of the conflict with the congregation and also be willing to listen to their perspectives. The preacher also needs to have made a careful study of the biblical witness with regard to violence and war. The Bible's broad witness does not allow Christians easily to embrace war as a social strategy, whatever our government's policy happens to be. While parts of the Bible allude to ethical behavior in war, the social vision of the Bible, both Old and New Testaments, is one of *shalom*—peace with justice. There is no denying that Jesus' life and death witness to his own rejection of armed conflict as a means of gaining or responding to power. On the other hand, Jesus' proverbial saying about turning the other cheek should not, in my view, be generalized as an embrace of pacifism in all contexts.[32]

The preacher also needs to have made a study of the Christian traditions with regard to just war and pacifism and to offer them as resources for reflecting on this country's responses to terrorism and genocide. Just war theory is an attempt to craft a plausible moral framework for war. One of the most systematic discussions of just war is by Thomas Aquinas in his *Summa Theologicae*.[33] Just war thinking offers criteria to treat two moral dilemmas that surround war: whether to wage war (*jus ad bellum*) and how war ought to be waged (*jus in bello*). Seven *ad bellum* criteria govern why and when it is permissible to go to war: just cause, competent authority, comparative justice (the issue of whether the grievances justify killing others), right intention, last resort, probability of success, and proportionality. The *jus in bello* criteria deal with proportionality and discrimination between combatants and noncombatants as a war is conducted.[34]

The Catholic social tradition offers both the just war tradition and pacifism as gospel responses to the reality of war. It sees just war teaching and nonviolence as distinct but interdependent methods of evaluating warfare. It encourages us to see these methods not as opposed to one another, but as complementary and necessary for a full moral vision. The Catholic bishops, in a pastoral letter drafted in response to the nuclear arms race in 1983 (*The Challenge of Peace: God's Promise and Our Response*), felt the two positions shared values and served to correct and balance each other. The main difference between the two positions was not only in their conclusion on the use of force but also in how they functioned in the moral community. The nonviolent position is treated in the pastoral letter as a personal position, while the just war position is regarded as both for individuals and states.[35]

The Catholic social tradition helpfully points out that the proper context for a discussion of just war is peace. Peace is more than the absence of war. A state of peace requires justice, and a just society requires the willingness to love. Discussions of war must take place within the context of what makes for peace. Peace is reflected in a social order where human dignity is fostered and the common good sought.[36] The litmus test of faithfulness for a society, according to Israel's prophets, is its treatment of its most vulnerable citizens. Jesus the prophet holds the Roman Empire and the leadership of his own religion accountable for their treatment of the poor, the disabled and the disrespected.[37]

It is not a legitimate part of this educational component of preaching on a complex, controversial issue to identify a particular policy or political party with the gospel or to say that if listeners want to be faithful disciples they must support this or that candidate or party across the board. It is the task of preaching to witness to the gospel's vision of peace with justice and to challenge people to figure out which avenues of secular, political influence are closer to its social vision in particular instances.

In preaching on war, as with any controversial topic, it is imperative that the preacher tell where he stands on the issue without identifying his position with the gospel. She needs to indicate the struggle she has engaged in to this point with regard to the issue. If a preacher feels no struggle or conflict over a highly controversial ethical issue or if he has never thought about the legitimate concerns of those who hold a differing view then that is a very dangerous sign. It signals that we are about to hear a sermon whose purpose is to close down dialogue.

Underlying all of this is perhaps the most controversial issue of all—the interpretation of Scripture. Oftentimes a sermon that commands everyone to get in line behind a particular stand on a controversial issue does so by employing scriptural "proof-texts" with regard to issues the Bible does not directly anticipate or address. Theological liberals and conservatives disagree, of course, as to which issues those would be. Liberals would say, for example, that the Bible does not directly address the issue of committed, same sex relationships. Conservatives would say that the Bible condemns all homosexual behavior.

As a United Methodist, I come from a tradition that affirms the primacy of Scripture in theological reflection but also believes that the Holy Spirit is operative through tradition, experience, and reason as the preacher interprets difficult issues within the framework of faith. To affirm that the Bible is inspired is to express our faith that it conveys God's presence and creative power by the work of the Holy Spirit. It is not to put the Bible forward for a purpose for which it was not intended: to serve, for example, as a history book or a scientific manual.

The purpose of the Bible is to reveal the character of a just and merciful God for the shaping of the community. It is to be read as a whole, and as a whole it offers a coherent narrative through which we learn about and participate in the character of God. No portion of Scripture is excluded from usefulness, but neither are all scriptural passages of equal, direct help in showing us the character of God.[38]

The more conservative, literalistic understanding of Scripture regards every passage as of equal prescriptive value for the life of faith. It emphasizes the timeless quality of Scripture's pronouncements and believes they are equally definitive for human life.[39] There is no acknowledgement that the social sciences and scientific advances may be a source of insight for people of faith as they seek to interpret contemporary moral issues. There is a refusal to respect the identity of Scripture as a library of sacred writings that reflect the limitations and prejudices of the time of their writing. In this denial, literalist interpreters miss a powerful revelatory point: part of Scripture's sanctifying power lies in helping us identify and work against analogous limitations and prejudices in society today.

Now, here is the rub. There are preachers who feel strongly that they do have the answer because they do know God's will on a particular controversial topic not specifically addressed or anticipated in Scripture.[40] It is very difficult in this mental state of certainty to acknowledge the legitimate concerns and contributions of the position of the other side. This applies equally to those who support the war in Iraq and to those who do not. It is very difficult in this mental state of certainty to acknowledge the right for members of the faith community, much less the nation, to hold differing interpretations on a complex ethical issue. But this is just what preaching must do if it respects its biblical and social context. For the preacher, liberal or conservative, preaches in a biblical context that repeatedly remind us of human sin and limited knowledge and of divine transcendence and omniscience. We don't know everything. The preacher, liberal or conservative, preaches in the context of a pluralistic democracy. People have freedom of interpretation. And preaching that preaches false certainties is in danger of endorsing whichever political group will endorse their community's stand.

Preaching Patriotism

There are those who would say that Christians live with two sometimes conflicting loyalties, one to our nation and another to our faith. They speculate about what we do when they conflict and call it civil disobedience. I am of the opinion that we have one loyalty, to God as revealed through Jesus Christ. I believe the Christian's devotion to his country is an expression of that single loyalty to God. My best patriotic service is fulfilled when I live a life of discipleship, which by biblical definition means a public and not just a private life.

As I said at the outset, patriotism for the Christian is devotion to the welfare of one's country in the context of one's ultimate loyalty to God. It is a commitment to living out the public implications of one's Christian faith, and that means work toward a society that places a priority on protecting the vulnerable rather than creating ideal conditions under which individuals can accumulate maximum wealth and personal power.

Living out my devotion to God and to God's vision of a just society will mean that sometimes I will disagree with the laws or actions of my country and actively oppose them in acts of faithful obedience to God. Sometimes I will contest the inaction of my nation and advocate for a proactive approach to an issue or situation. My devotion to God will sometimes mean that I will work through legislative means to attempt to change the laws of the country. My devotion to God will sometimes mean that I will challenge the practices and beliefs, the actions or inactions of my own church community or denomination when I feel they are not in the interests of the common dignity and good of this nation's citizens. These actions are all expressions of the public, political dimensions of my faith. They are the ways in which I live out my devotion to this country as a Christian.

We have had enough of supporters of the war in Iraq calling nonsupporters unpatriotic and nonsupporters calling supporters un-Christian. It is high time for some genuinely patriotic preaching. It is time for preaching that reminds theological liberals and conservatives alike that it is both possible and necessary for Christians to express their convictions about public policy while still respecting the pluralism of American democracy. It is time for preaching that educates listeners to expect and even value disagreements. That means differences not only with people of other faiths but also with other Christians. It is time for prophetic preaching that confronts the acquisitiveness, radical individualism, and violence at the heart of our nation with the generosity, community spirit, and care for the vulnerable that are also at the heart of this nation and are most certainly at the heart of God.

When I taught preaching at Princeton Theological Seminary in the 1990s, the students held an annual "Theogiggle," an evening when they dressed up like their professors and put on generally good natured skits whose purpose was to mock us. The ticket money may have gone to some good cause, I can't remember. But the mockery was the main purpose. Fortunately, I wasn't present the year they roasted me. But I heard all about it. The skit was called "Jesus and Dr. McKenzie." They had a student in a shoulder-length, auburn wig, dressed in a teacher-like getup playing me and another student in a burlap robe, pasted-on beard, and sandals, playing Jesus. The skit consisted of Jesus attempting to preach his way through the Sermon on the Mount and my frequently interrupting him, offering him tips on how convey the gospel more effectively. It really ought to be the other way around.

Notes

1. *The Shorter Oxford English Dictionary*, vol. 2 (Oxford: Clarendon, 1973), 1529.
2. There are separatist traditions within Christianity that prohibit members of their community from involvement in public institutions whose goal is to maintain the

purity of their community in a corrupt world. There is also the perspective that the public realm of government is a divinely instituted authority whose purpose is the restraint of anarchy and sin to which the Christian has a duty to be obedient. There have also been liberal utopian traditions in Christian history that believe the kingdom of God can be achieved in the form of a social system in this world. Obedience to governing authorities was the position held by the Apostle Paul (Rom. 13:1–7) and, centuries later, by Martin Luther. For Paul, it was the religious institutions and customs of non-Christian society that were to be rejected. Paul and Luther sought changes in the religious institutions of their time. They mostly seemed content to let state and economic life, slavery, and social stratification continue relatively unchanged. Government existed to restrain sin and anarchy, not for a positive purpose related to God's kingdom to which the Christian could contribute. For more on this, see H. Richard Niebuhr, *Christ and Culture* (New York: Harper and Row, 1951), 187–89. For critique of Niebuhr's influential work, see Glenn H. Stassen, D.M. Yeager, and John Howard Yoder, *Authentic Transformation: A New Vision of Christ and Culture* (Nashville: Abingdon, 1996).

3. John Wesley, founder of the Methodist movement in England in the 1700s, emphasized the importance of both personal and social holiness—that is, a commitment both to the inner experience of religion and the social application of conscience. John Calvin viewed government as a positive agency through which people in social union could serve their neighbors. The Catholic social tradition affirms the importance of building societal life and institutions to foster human dignity. Judith A. Merkle, *From the Heart of the Church: The Catholic Social Tradition* (Collegeville, MN: Liturgical Press, 2004).

4. Robert N. Bellah, Richard Madsen, Williams M. Sullivan, Ann Swidler, and Steven M. Tipton, *Habits of the Heart: Individualism and Commitment in American Life* (Berkeley: University of California Press, 1985), 28–31.

5. Bellah, *Habits of the Heart*, 31. Quote from Thomas Jefferson.

6. Robert Wuthnow, *Christianity in the Twenty-first Century: Reflections on the Challenges Ahead* (New York: Oxford University Press, 1993), 145f. The political thought of the Founders represents a complex mix of influences that included both the optimistic rationalism of Enlightenment thought and biblical imagery of covenant and exodus with its more pessimistic view of human nature. Charles W. Dunn, ed., *American Political Theology: Historical Perspectives and Theoretical Analysis* (New York: Praeger, 1984), 10–19.

7. Wuthnow, *Christianity in the Twenty-first Century*, 146.

8. *Ibid.*, 146–47.

9. *Ibid.*, 147–48.

10. Daniel Eisenberg, "What's At Stake in the Fight?" *Time*, July 11, 2005, 28–30.

11. Arthur Van Seters, ed., *Preaching as a Social Act: Theology and Practice* (Nashville: Abingdon, 1988), 20.

12. For a collection of sermons from this period, see David P. Polk, ed., *Shaken Foundations: Sermons from America's Pulpits after the Terrorist Attacks* (St. Louis: Chalice Press, 2001).

13. The etymological origins of "pastor" lie in a Latin noun derived from a verb (*pascere*), meaning to feed or graze, and an Old French noun referring to a shepherd (*pastour*). See *The Shorter Oxford Dictionary*, vol. 2, 1525. The term "pastor" is used today as a general term for a minister of a congregation. When "pastoral" is used in distinction from "prophetic," it refers to that function of the ministry that focuses on

the congregation's spiritual care while "prophetic" refers to the function of challenging complacency and encouraging justice. In practice, they cannot be separated.

14. Henry H. Mitchell and Emil M. Thomas, *Preaching for Black Self-Esteem* (Nashville: Abingdon, 1994).

15. Cleophus J. LaRue, *The Heart of Black Preaching* (Louisville: Westminster/John Knox, 2000), 6.

16. Clarke E. Cochran, *Religion in Public and Private Life* (New York: Routledge, 1990).

17. *Ibid.*, 4–5.

18. "Evangelical" is a term that refers to an American brand of Protestant Christianity that has been strongly influenced by revival traditions. Evangelical Christians stress the centrality of a personal experience of conversion to Jesus Christ, being "born again," the primacy of Scriptures, and the desirability of converting those of other religions to the Christian faith. The term "fundamentalist" refers to those evangelicals who are biblical literalists. This distinction is made by Mark Noll, historian and professor of Christian thought at Wheaton College in Illinois, and I draw it from a Noll's 2004 interview with Judy Valente, April 16, 2004, http://www.pbs.org/wnet/religonandethics/week733/interview.html.

19. Jim Wallis, *God's Politics: Why the Right Gets it Wrong and the Left Doesn't Get It* (New York: HarperSanFrancisco, 2005), 58.

20. *Ibid.*, 59.

21. *Ibid.*,18.

22. Jim Wallis is a Christian activist, author, and founder of Sojourners, a nationwide network of progressive Christians working for justice and peace. Ron Sider is Professor of Theology, Holistic Ministry and Public Policy, and Director of the Sider Center on Ministry and Public Policy, at Eastern Baptist Theological Seminary. He is also President of Evangelicals for Social Action. Tony Campolo is Professor Emeritus of Sociology at Eastern University in Pennsylvania. He is the founder of the Evangelical Association for the Promotion of Education (EAPE) through which he works to create educational opportunities for "at risk" children. He is also the author of more than thirty books and a media commentator on religious, social, and political matters.

23. http://www.nae.net.

24. Richard A. Viguerie and David Franke, *America's Right Turn: How Conservatives Used New and Alternative Media to Take Power* (Chicago: Bonus Books, 2004).

25. Robert N. Bellah, "The Role of Preaching in a Corrupt Republic," *Christianity and Crisis* 38 (1978): 321–22.

26. The other danger is that religion will attempt to dominate public life, a concern I will take up later. Marci A. Hamilton, in her book *God vs. the Gavel: Religion and the Rule of Law* (New York: Cambridge University Press, 2005), points out that religious communities can pose a threat to freedoms of citizens within and beyond their communities by practices and beliefs that jeopardize their first amendment rights.

27. Cochran, *Religion in Public and Private Life*, 66. Stephen Carter also emphasizes that involvement in politics is dangerous to religion. "Politics is antithetical to religion because it generates the desire to win. The desire to win generates the willingness to do what is necessary to win, which often winds up being compromise." Stephen Carter, *God's Name in Vain: The Wrongs and Rights of Religion in Politics* (New York: Basic Books: 2000), 50–51.

28. See the recent article by Jason Byassee, "The Health and Wealth Gospel: Be Happy," *The Christian Century 122, no. 14* (July 12, 2005): 20–23, which criticizes the "your best life now" gospel of Houston preacher Joel Osteen and others.

29. See my *Preaching Biblical Wisdom in a Self-Help Society* (Nashville: Abingdon, 2004) for a broader critique of the prosperity gospel and its correction by biblical wisdom teachings of both Old and New Testaments.
30. Some examples are euthanasia, stem cell research, abortion, and same-sex marriage.
31. Some examples are poverty, justice, and care of the earth.
32. Mt 5:38–39; Lk 6:27–29.
33. An excellent contemporary work is Michael Walzer's *Just and Unjust Wars: A Moral Argument with Historical Illustrations*, 3rd. ed. (New York: Basic Books, 2000).
34. Merkle, *From the Heart of the Church*, 200.
35. *Ibid.*, 202. For a critique of both just war and pacifist positions, see two books by Mennonite theologian John Howard Yoder, *When War is Unjust: Being Honest in Just-War Thinking*, 2nd. ed. (Maryknoll, NY: Orbis, 1996); and *Nevertheless: The Varieties and Shortcomings of Religious Pacifism*, 2d ed. (Scottdale, PA: Herald Press, 1992).
36. Merkle, *From the Heart of the Church*, 200.
37. J. David Pleins, *The Social Visions of the Hebrew Bible. A Theological Introduction* (Louisville: Westminster/John Knox, 2001). For an account of Jesus' social vision, see Stephen J.Patterson's *The God of Jesus: The Historical Jesus and the Search for Meaning* (Harrisburg, PA: Trinity Press International, 1998).
38. Charles M. Wood, *The Formation of Christian Understanding: Theological Hermeneutics* (Philadelphia: Westminster, 1981); Sarah Heaner Lancaster, *Women and the Authority of Scripture: A Narrative Approach* (Harrisburg, PA: Trinity Press International, 2002).
39. A friend of mine who teaches biblical studies at an evangelical seminary admits that no one really believes this, else we would all be walking around minus eyes and hands (see Mt. 5:29–30).
40. Prohibitions of homosexuality in the Old Testament are motivated by concerns for ritual purity and by an abhorrence of the expressions of homosexuality prevalent in the experience of the ancient world: pederasty and anal rape of prisoners of war by the victors. Contemporary literalists feel confident with blanket statements that homosexuality is a choice and that committed, lifelong same sex relationships are abhorrent to God. They also feel confident that Paul's scolding of a particular group of women in a particular church can be generalized to prohibit all women from holding positions of leadership in the church that involve teaching men and boys.

Chapter 15

Patriotism Is Not Enough?

Peter J. Gomes

Thus says the Lord: "Let not the wise man glory in his wisdom, let not the mighty man glory in his might, let not the rich man glory in his riches; but let him who glories glory in this, that he understands and knows me, that I am the Lord who practices steadfast love, justice, and righteousness in the earth; for in these things I delight, says the Lord."

—Jeremiah 9:23–24

Once again I have taken as my text a passage from Scripture drawn from neither of the lessons that have been appointed for today, but one that links the two together and highlights the substance of the messages of the prophet Joshua and of the apostle Paul. I ask you to listen to this text from the book of the prophet Jeremiah as a hinge between these important lessons that we have had this morning: "'Let not the wise man glory in his wisdom, let not the mighty man glory in his might, let not the rich man glory in his riches; but let him who glories glory in this, that he understands and knows me, that I am the Lord who practices steadfast love, justice, and righteousness in the earth; for in these things I delight,' says the Lord." Those are the twenty-third and twenty-fourth verses from the ninth chapter of the book of the prophet Jeremiah.

I must begin with a confession. For the first time in more years than I can remember, my text this morning is not derived from the tranquil meditations of a summer's day in Plymouth, when I usually give final thought to the sermons that I will preach to you in the coming year—those texts and sermon titles that you have become accustomed to seeing in bold print in the *Term Book* late in August or early in September. The sermon that I had planned to preach today, entitled "The Power of the Little Things," bit the dust on Wednesday morning, and in its place has come this sermon, conceived, quite frankly, in the rising anxiety of a country surprised to find itself on the brink of war, and on the eve of the evening in which the president of the United States will attempt to justify his policies to us.

In a few weeks we will commemorate the seventieth anniversary of the building of this church, dedicated both to the war dead and to a great mission for peace. It was not just because of the remembrance of war but to ford a great hope of peace that in 1932 this church was built. Here, then, of all places on earth, and now, of all times, I, of all people, must speak of the dangers of war and our Christian mission for peace.

Last Monday I was in Kansas City, Missouri, where, as you know, everything is up-to-date. I was there giving yet another book talk, this time in a large suburban Presbyterian church, and happily for me, for my book, and for my publisher, hundreds turned out for the evening talk on *The Good Life: Truths That Last in Times of Need*. Afterward, as I signed books, I found that almost everyone in that large congregation had our present war fever on his heart and mind, and each was asking himself, and me, "How did we get here? What ought I to do? I feel so powerless, so helpless, and without a voice." Person after person said that, and I was compelled to think about it. These were not by any means your garden-variety leftists or pacifists, who form the usual list of suspects, and these were not Cambridge liberals, by any means. This was Kansas, for heaven's sake—Alf Landon and Bob Dole country—and these were Presbyterians. They love their country, and they love their God; and what do you do when your country is headed where you think your faith and your God don't want you to go?

In another instance, one of my colleagues here on the staff recently told me of a telephone call he had made to an artisan doing some work for us; in fact, he was the very man whose skills fashioned the tablet to the Radcliffe women of World War I on the north wall, which we dedicated last Armistice Day. We have a small job for him, and apparently after sorting out the details he said something of the following to my colleague, in a rough paraphrase that I now make: "What kind of place is Harvard? Is it liberal or conservative?" Now, that's a hard question, to which there really is no answer, as you know, except in the perception of the beholder. "Why do you ask?" inquired my colleague. Replied the artisan, "Because I don't hear anybody there or anywhere else talking much about this war, except those who want it; and I'm scared."

In yet another instance, let me mention that it might not surprise you to learn that over my transom passes a vast number of unsolicited church newsletters, bulletins, and pastoral communications from all over the country, and that it might surprise you to know that I read them all. Last week I was reading one from the First Parish Church in Plymouth—not from my church, but from my hometown. In his column, the minister of that old congregation remarked upon the phenomenon, new to him in Plymouth, of perfect strangers coming up to him in the street, in the supermarket, and at the gas pump, knowing him to be the minister of the First Church, and asking him what to do about this war fever. How, they ask, can we have an intelligent conversation on the most dangerous policy topic of the day without being branded traitors, self-loathing Americans, antipatriotic, or soft on democracy?

That's a good question, especially when even the president of the United States questions the patriotism of those few in the U.S. Senate who question his policy or challenge his authority to wage war at will. Must the first casualty of patriotism always be dissent, debate, and discussion? I confess to you that this is a frightening time, more so than anytime in my memory; and if one cannot speak out of Christian conscience and conviction now, come what may, then we are forever consigned to moral silence. We hear much talk of "moral clarity," but it sounds more to me like moral arrogance, and it must not be met with moral silence. At the service of Morning Prayers on Wednesday morning last, Anthony Lewis, formerly of the *New York Times*, said in his address to a very startled congregation that if the purpose of the terrorists of September 11, 2001, was to destroy our confidence in our own American values, then, he feared, they had succeeded. In the name of fighting terror both abroad and at home, our government—particularly through the Attorney General, together with a culture of patriotic intimidation—has suspended our constitutional liberties, stifled dissent, and defined a good American as one who goes along with the powers that be, in a "My way or the highway" mentality. When patriotism is defined in this narrow, partisan, opportunistic, jingoistic way, then perhaps that old cynic, Dr. Samuel Johnson, was right when he defined patriotism as the "last refuge of a scoundrel."

Frankly, I prefer his contemporary, Edmund Burke, who said, "To make us love our country, our country ought to be lovely." Our country is lovely, which is why we love it and are willing to serve it and, if necessary, to die for it. It is because we love it, and want others to love it as well, that we dare to speak to affirm the goodness and righteousness in it, the virtue and the power of its core values, and to speak against the things that would do harm to it and those core values. What is and has always been lovely about our country is our right and our duty to criticize those in power, to dissent from their policies if we think them to be wrong, and to hold our alternative vision to be as fully valid as theirs.

In 1952, a long time ago for many of you here in this congregation, but just yesterday for others, Adlai Stevenson was running for president against the patriotic and heroic Dwight D. Eisenhower, who was then, ironically, president of Columbia University. The university had said that it was trying to get Milton, but it got Ike instead, who had wanted to be president of something, and Columbia would do. Adlai Stevenson was running against Eisenhower in a run that was doomed to failure, and was asked to speak to the American League convention in New York City in the summer after his nomination. One can imagine, or even remember, the charges of eggheadism, intellectualism, of being soft on Communism and soft on patriotism—all those charges that had been leveled on the intelligent and eloquent Adlai Stevenson. Here is what he said on that very subject in a speech called "Patriotism in America," and, by implication, in response to the charges:

What do we mean by patriotism in the context of our time? I venture to suggest that what we mean is a sense of national responsibility, a patriotism which is not short, frenzied outbursts of emotion, but the tranquil and steady dedication of the lifetime.

Note the careful choice of words: ". . .national responsibility, a patriotism which is not short, frenzied outbursts of emotion, but the tranquil and steady dedication of a lifetime." How carefully, poignantly, and aptly chose are those words in comparison with some of the language we hear flashed about morning, noon, and night in recent days.

I wonder how many of you here this morning have ever seen or given much thought to the white marble statue of a British nurse standing just above Trafalgar Square and beneath Leicester Square in London, to the side of the National Gallery? Londoners and tourists, perhaps some of you, pass it in the to-and-fro of an incredibly busy thoroughfare, lingering at its island base if only to hail and elusive taxi. I have done so many times myself. It is the statue of Nurse Edith Cavell, one of whose claims to fame is that in the early morning hours of October 12, 1915, she was tied to a stake in German-occupied Belgium and shot as a traitor. Long before the war she had for many years headed a nursing home in Belgium, and even after war had broken out she had remained at her post, where, together with her nurses, she gave care to injured soldiers regardless of nationality—whether German, French, or English. Miss Cavell was arrested as a traitor by the Germans for the "crime" of assisting soldiers in their flights to neutral Holland. Determined to make an example of her, the Germans tried her under military law, under a military tribunal, and without adequate counsel she was presumed guilty, found so, and sentenced to death and executed within ten hours of the judgment: the whole episode was shrouded in vindictive haste and stealth. The debate about the exact nature of her so-called crime has gone on for years, but there has never been any debate about the heroic nature of her death, and it was this that turned her into one of the few true heroines of World War I. Some have even gone so far as to say that in her simple way, Edith Cavell was the Dietrich Bonhoeffer of that war. Her last moments, and her final words, are described as follows by an eyewitness:

> After receiving the sacrament, and within minutes of being led out to her death, she said, "Standing as I do in view of God and eternity, I realize that patriotism is not enough. I must have no hatred or bitterness toward anyone."

On the base of her London statue are carved the words "PATRIOTISM IS NOT ENOUGH." This is an impressive message from one who lost her life in the name of somebody else's patriotism.

Edith Cavell, an English vicar's daughter, lived and died a Christian, but her last words are almost too enigmatic and too simple, and they compel us to ask now, in a time of war and of rumors of war, what ought to be the proper relationship between love of God and love of country. If mere patriotism is not enough, what is it that will help us to be both conscientious citizens and faithful Christians? Are the two mutually exclusive, or is it possible, somehow, to live responsibly in the tension between those two claims? That is our business this morning, and that is always the business of any Christian who takes seriously his allegiance to Jesus Christ and his responsibility to his country and his society.

Perhaps a word from our text will help. Did you notice, in the text from Jeremiah, which is printed and available to you on the Order of Worship, that wisdom, might, and riches are set in clear opposition to love, justice, and righteousness? That is not my doing, and it is not even the translator's doing. That is what it says, and it creates for us a self-conscious biblical tension not easily resolved or explained away. Jeremiah knows that we are inclined to boast of our wisdom, particularly in the University, and that is what the Hebrew word that is translated as "glory" really means: boasting, and the thumping of our intellectual chests. We know how to do that about wisdom in the University, and we know how to boast about our might and our riches in this land of opportunity. Jeremiah knows that it is our natural penchant to seize upon and celebrate our achievements, for they define who we are, what we have, and what we do. This is the way of the world, and when we are "number one" in the world, it is "our way or the highway." How strange is it to think back on the relatively stimulating days of the cold war, when the threat of another dangerous superpower actually helped to make us behave and believe. The prophet does not deny the reality of these claims, but over and against them he sets God's claims of love, justice, and righteousness. Not only is that intellectual symmetry; it is moral symmetry. He is unambiguously clear here—would that he were not so clear. If we as God's people are to glory in anything, we must glory in—that is, we must boast of, take pride in and responsibility for—the things that God values, that God loves, and that God blesses. Why should God bless America if America does not bless the things that God delights in? What are they? Here they are, right in front of us:

> . . . but let him who glories glory in this, that he understands and knows me, that I am the Lord who practices steadfast love, justice, and righteousness in the earth; for in these things I delight, says the Lord.

If we do not delight in the things that the Lord delights in, why should the Lord delight in us? Try that one on for size. This will not fit on a bumper sticker or on a T-shirt, but you might carry it around to ponder in your hearts and minds.

The lesson we heard read from the Book of Joshua is a famous lesson about great choices. Joshua says, "Choose ye this day whom ye will serve." Will you serve the God of the Amorites, or those various other little domestic deities whom you love to serve but who don't deliver the goods? Will you serve them? Well, go right ahead, he in essence says: if that's what turns you on, lay your sacrifices before those little tin-pot gods; I understand it. Then, rising on his prophetic hind legs, Joshua says, "As for me and my house, we will serve the Lord." Well, of course they agree: "We'll serve the Lord too." Joshua, however, counters by saying, essentially, "No, you won't. You can't. Not unless you are prepared to make the significant, ultimate choice, and sacrifice. If you are really willing to choose between your culture and the God who delivered you, and you choose the God who delivered you, then you can do it, but you can't have it both ways." Again the prophet is unambiguously clear. So, after a lot of to-ing and froing for twenty-four more verses, the people come round to it and say, "Okay, okay, okay, we will serve the Lord who delivered us, and has done all these things." Joshua says, "All right, I trust you, but we're going to build a monument, and this monument, these stones, will remind you, and God, of these promises. Whenever you see this monument, remember that you have chosen the Lord and no the other, lesser deities." So they build the monument, and there it stands. Of course this doesn't really work, because if it did the Bible would end at the Book of Joshua instead of going on for another sixty books—but that's a subject for another story, and for a very good class that I'm teaching this term.

This church in which we stand, and hundreds and thousands like it across this country and around the world, reminds us of the choices we have made. "Choose ye this day whom ye will serve. . .as for me and my house, we will serve the Lord." This place has its great mission as a monument for peace, and we are reminded, on each day that we sit here or pass by these premises, that that is the choice we are required to make. It is a tension, however, and I have not easily resolved it, nor has the prophet.

That tension is even harder to avoid in the second lesson of this morning, where the apostle Paul beings by telling us—in J.B. Phillips's pungent translation—something we should listen to. You remember the Revised Standard Version translation, which we heard this morning: "I beseech you by the mercies of God." Now listen to how Phillips translates Romans 12; it is meant to grab us by our vitals:

> With eyes wide open to the mercies of God, I beg you, as an act of intelligent worship, to give him your bodies as a living sacrifice, consecrated to him and acceptable by him.

Note "With eyes wide open." Not in fake devotion or in pseudo-piety, but with eyes wide open as an act of intelligent, thoughtful worship. Your mind is engaged, and not on hold. That's what Paul says. He goes on:

> Don't let the world around you squeeze you into its own mold, but let God remold your minds from within, so that you may prove in practice that the plan of God for you is good, meets all his demands, and moves toward the goal of true maturity. (Romans 12:1–3, J.B. Phillips)

Think about that call to nonconformity. Think about that call to transformation. Think of that in the context of a choice you have made and have to make. That tension simply will not go away; it will not easily be resolved, and we, like all faithful Christians and honest citizens throughout all time, will have to live with it and through it. If we are uncomfortable in this conflict of values, we are meant to be uncomfortable. The easy syllogism, that we go to war in order to keep the peace, ought not to comfort us or our Christian president. It is that same alleged "moral clarity" that led to the infamous Vietnam logic. Perhaps you will remember it—that we had to destroy the village in order to "save" it. If that is "moral clarity," then I am Peter Rabbit.

Yet, my beloved friends, we are not without guidance or hope. Many, and perhaps some of you, will argue: who are we to challenge the moral clarity and vision of our government, of people who presumably know more than we do, and who have the awful duty not only to protect and to serve, but to anticipate and to initiate? Who are we to kibitz from the sidelines without access to secret briefings, intelligence, knowledge, and all of the apparatus of government? Well, who, indeed, are we?

First, let us remember that we are citizens. They, experts and all, work for us, not we for them. We pay their salaries through the extortion known as taxes. Let us not forget that it is our government, and not theirs. They hold our government—and, indeed, our lives—in a trust. We have a right, we have a responsibility, we have a duty to speak, and we do not have to be experts to do so. We do not require degrees from the Kennedy School or the Wharton School or the Law School to have an opinion about the moral future of our country. In fact, it has usually been the so-called experts who have managed to get us into wars in the first place. We have a duty to speak, to dissent, and to demand a better case for compromising our most fundamental principles as Christians and citizens than has thus far been made. We deserve a better case than the one that is floating around out there at the moment. As a citizen I demand a better excuse than revenge, or oil, for the prosecution of a war that is likely to do more harm than good, that will destabilize not only the region but the world for years to come, and that, worst of all, will confirm for all the world to see our country's reputation as an irrational and undisciplined bully who acts not because it ought, but because it can: we make up the rules, so it seems, as we please. I love my country too much to see it complicit in its own worst stereotype. Right after September 11, 2001, we asked in some agonizing perplexity, "Why do they hate us?" Remember that question? Well, if we persist in making war the first rather than the last option, we will soon find out. The answer will be all too terribly manifest.

Now, I know that in the mighty roar of wisdom, might, and riches, the sounds of love, justice, and righteousness—those things in which God delights, and in which God's people are meant to delight—may seem thin, feeble, and anemic. Yet my Christian conscience tells me that these "soft" values should prevail every time over the "hard," even though they often do not. If I am compelled to compromise those Christian values in the service of the state, I had better be as certain as is humanly possible that such a compromise is worth sacrificing the things I hold most precious; and I certainly won't know that, nor will you, unless there is a great deal more thoughtful discussion, debate, and dissent than there has been so far. The most terrifying indictment of Christians in modern times was the general unwillingness of German Christians, with a few notable exceptions, to challenge in any meaningful way, from a Christian point of view, the political assumptions of their government in the years leading up to World War II. They stand indicted by their moral silence, and they know it. Since we are not Nazi Germany, and because we do claim love, justice, and righteousness not only as personal values but as national values, we have all the more responsibility to make the country we love a lovely country.

It pleases me that I am not alone in this enterprise. I am not brave enough to be alone, out front on the prophetic pinnacle; I am afraid that that is a weakness of my character. It pleases me to join with other religious leaders who are beginning to speak and be heard on behalf of a thoughtful case for peace and to engage in a rigorous debate: the *New York Times* only yesterday morning noted the broad antiwar sentiment of the religious leadership across America. Religious opinion is by no means unanimous: those evangelicals who have found little fault with anything that this administration has done or proposes to do, and who seldom met a war they didn't like, lined up to be counted on the president's side. Polls show that most Americans, frustrated, alas, by the ephemeral character of the "War on Terrorism," and still angry and confused about September 11, 2001, want to do something. As we know, however, in angry, vengeful moments, the desire to do "something" is easily translated into the will to do anything, and that "anything" may very well be the wrong thing. Bombing Iraq into oblivion as payback to those who have done us injury seems to me at this moment to be the wrong thing to do. Polls do not get at the truth. Thirty years ago, most polls showed significant majorities in favor of whatever it was we were going to do in Vietnam, and eventually the majority in favor concluded that the minority opposed were, in fact, right. Polls simply tell us where we are, not where we ought to be.

The gospel, however, does tell us where we ought to be—tough, untenable, and difficult as that place may be. Wisdom, might, and riches must yield to love, justice, and righteousness. Love, justice, and righteousness are superior to wisdom, might, and riches. How often do we have to be told that? "And these are God's words," says Paul at the end of Romans 12, once again in the Phillips translation: "If thine enemy hunger, feed him; if he thirst; give him drink; for in so doing thou shalt heap coals of fire upon his head." Don't allow yourself to be overpowered with evil: take the offensive and overpower evil with good. That is what Paul is saying: take the offensive; overpower evil with good! Now, that is a radical foreign policy. That would scare the bejesus out of a lot of people, to know that with all our power we decided that we were going to overpower evil with good—and what a topsy-turvy world this would be! That should give all the hawks in Washington something to think about—that if they want us to be noticed, the world would notice us if we took seriously the idea of overpowering evil with good.

Nurse Cavell was, and is, right: "Patriotism is not enough. . . ." If we wish to be on God's side rather than making God into our own ally of American realpolitik, then we would do well to remember our text from Jeremiah. God's values are clear; so too ought ours to be.

Let not the wise man glory in his wisdom, let not the mighty glory in his might, let not the rich man glory in his riches; but let him who glories glory in this, that he understands and knows me, that I am the Lord who practices steadfast love, justice, and righteousness in the earth; for in these things I delight, says the Lord.

If you love the Lord, you will love the things the Lord loves. There is no other way around it.

Chapter 16

Resisting U.S. Empire?

Mark Lewis Taylor

I would like to reflect here on the notion of patriotism and Christian practice through a text from the Gospel of Luke (4:24–30). It is full of implications for interpreting the meaning of Christian faithfulness in relation to our loyalties to nation, to others on the boundaries of nations, and ultimately to a global humanity. Let me reproduce this text in full.

And he said, "Truly, I say to you, no prophet is acceptable in his own country. But in truth, I tell you, there were many widows in Israel in the days of Eli'jah, when the heaven was shut up three years and six months, when there came a great famine over all the land; and Eli'jah was sent to none of them but only to Zar'ephath, in the land of Sidon, to a woman who was a widow. And there were many lepers in Israel in the time of Eli'sha; and none of them was cleansed, but only Na'aman the Syrian." When they heard this, all in the synagogue were filled with wrath. And they rose up and put him out of the city, and led him to the brow of the hill on which their city was built, that they might throw him down headlong. But passing through the midst of them he went away.

Why was Jesus led to the brow of the hill? The text begins with Jesus saying: "No prophet is acceptable in his own country." Jesus was elaborating on a great passage from the prophet Isaiah that he had read in the synagogue at Nazareth to announce his entire ministry. The key verse from earlier in the chapter is familiar:

The Spirit of the Lord is upon me
Because he has anointed me to preach good news to the poor (18).

The way Jesus presented these words and handled himself in the synagogue won amazement. Such "gracious words," they said, are coming from "Joseph's son" (22).

I

It was not until he exposited further its meaning for them that he was led to the brow of the hill. Jesus drew the provocative and disturbing conclusion that the suffering of the poor takes precedence over reverence for a privileged people, a blessed nation, any genuine gender, a right race, or righteous religion.

Jesus recalls Elijah for them. When Israel's widows suffered famine by the scores, the prophet went and brought food to a widow woman outside Israel, a Syro-Phoenician woman of Sidon. And Elisha? When Israel had many lepers he, similarly, was sent to the foreigner, the Syrian Na'aman, and worked healing for him. Israel really didn't even get a traditional missionary role, taking "light to the world," famine relief, bodily healing, or liberation to these "others." God's prophetic action was one of grace; the privileged nations seem shunted aside.

This is not a repudiation of Israel by Jesus, certainly not of Judaism. Jesus spoke as a Jewish man, invoking the God of the Jews and the great Jewish prophets, and he did so to criticize all practices of chauvinism (i.e., "aggressive partisanship for one's group"). Jesus took aim not at Jews *per se*, but at all those who use narrow chauvinist notions of chosenness to substitute a religion of privilege for a global grace of liberation for the many poor of all the earth. The global poor are marked for release. God has already gone to them. The Syro-Phoenician woman matters. Syria matters. Jesus proclaims the grace of a scandalously inclusive practice of liberation.

II

Alas, many chauvinisms are alive today. They are virulent among those in the so-called U.S. Christian right who advocate United States based theocratic politics at home and abroad.[1] They are also present in other Christians and residents who live out some sense of American chosenness and so often accept or promote a role for the United States as a unilaterally operative empire.[2]

If we preach, live, and organize against the leading chauvinisms of today, especially against the drive toward a U.S. empire, we may get led to the brow of some hill. In today's climate of post-9/11 fear, a seemingly perpetual "war on terror" and hyper-patriotic public response have given opportunity to new demons of messianic nationalism and will to power. U.S. leaders have rationalized torture in their memos and then say they never commit torture. They suspend international law, break previous treaties, refuse to sign on to the International Criminal Court, announce preemptive war, and remain silent about the tens (maybe hundreds) of thousands of Iraqi civilians killed. "We don't do body counts," said celebrated U.S. general, Tommy Franks, when asked about Iraqi deaths.

These leaders then assume that our only allegiance as citizens is to secure our own nation, the United States, at whatever cost to a global humanity. The Christian gospel resists practice of that logic. It reminds that the Syro-Phoenician woman matters, the Syrian man matters, and watchfulness for release of all the earth's poor is the way to life for us and all creation. The way of the nationalist warlords (Cheney, Bush, Rumsfeld, Wolfowitz, Rice), supported by many Democrats and many others, is the erosion of world humanity. It is the strangling of God's creation. The nationalist warlords prefer that Christians worship the United States as a "city set on a hill" and hope we never dare go to the brow of that hill to expose our nation's brutal false claims.

III

Maybe today's churches and Christians fail to oppose their leader's imperial nationalism because they fear being led to that brow of the hill. No one wants to be thrown headlong. The crackdown on dissent in the United States today leads many to fear that.[3] More seriously, though, perhaps we fear being led on to that other hill, the one Jesus eventually went to, Calvary, to suffer some ultimate, torturous, ignominious abandonment and death. Maybe in the United States today we feel the screws tightening upon us like never before in our lifetime. It is no mere hyperbole; in fact, it is the warning of some of the best historians of our times: observe that political power in the United States is heading toward a crisis comparable, though not identical, to barbarities that have spawned fascism in times past.[4] There will be no exact repristination of those barbarities, and it is naïve to suggest so.

But the rise to power in the United States today of a Christian nationalism that often openly announces its theocratic intentions along with an aggressive militarist war planner elite (the "neoconservatives" of "Vulcans") both receiving unprecedented financing from wealthy corporate sources is a dangerous political brew that historically has bred forms of barbaric politics.[5] Many feel all this and are afraid. Resistance that risks the brow of the hill seems more like a rush to Calvary's hill—a vulnerability to crucifixion in today's U.S. torture state. This all can erode the courage our gospel promises for standing with the poor of other nations, even when our nation is in the wrong.

I confess to being a pessimist of the intellect these days. With my heart and my will, however, I insist on hope. Can we do otherwise? We who dare to hope might take our cue from the way the Nazareth encounter worked out for Jesus: they tried to cast him headlong over the brow of the hill, but he "passed through their midst and went away." Sounds too easy, I know, but I grasp at hope. And as gruesome as was Jesus' death at Calvary's hill, it too need not paralyze us with fear. Christian stories of resurrection can rally our courage. The empire's torture and execution is only the worst that the political warlords and religious elite can give us when we stand for life. The imperial crucifiers cannot quash life.

So, standing in the power of a resurrection faith, foolish as it may seem, why not just declare fear to be over, even the post-9/11 fear by which U.S. leaders manipulate us with their terror alerts and warnings of terrorists behind every shrub? By so doing we would deny today's leaders the fear they use as currency to fund their perpetual wars on terror. In Jesus' prophetic grace, there is Life affirmable for this time. We can say "No!" to the politics of fear. What would this look like?

IV

First, it is time for Christians to denounce in no uncertain terms the war in Iraq, the centerpiece of the Bush regime's agenda, which costs taxpayers some $170 million per day and the daily maiming and killing of Iraqis and Americans—civilians and soldiers wasted by the thousands. In so doing we would join with the best of international lawyers who point out that without having strong evidence that weapons of mass destruction were an imminent danger to the United States and allies, our assault on Iraq is exposed as a "war of aggression," one, as Michael Klare documents, that provides military bases for securing oil interests and geopolitical advantage in the Middle East and Central Asia.[6] As U.S. war planners' own documents show, Iraq was long a target for invasion and occupation with or without WMDs and with or without Saddam Hussein.[7] This war of aggression is one for which we must now make reparations and recompense, for a war of aggression, in the words of the Nuremburg trials, is "the supreme international crime differing only from other war crimes in that it contains within itself the accumulated evil of the whole."

Second, it is time for U.S. Christians to help remove their leaders from office so new leaders can begin reparations and healing for Iraq, and being what Christian faith calls a genuine "metanoia" in American foreign policy—that is, a repentant turning that works humbly and cooperatively, not unilaterally, with all the nations for a withdrawal of U.S. troops and military bases.[8] The present leadership has squandered the trust many gave it. U.S. residents must offer alternatives for our nation and for the world.

Third, it is time for Christians to hear their tortured Lord in the cries of the tortured today and then raise holy hell against our leaders' compromise with torturous confinements, interrogations, and even murders of Afghans, Iraqis and others, in the notorious U.S. detention centers of Bagram, Abu-Ghraib, and Guantánamo.[9]

Fourth, it is time for Christians to put Iraqi civilians, by name, on their prayer lists and on their action agendas. There is a stunning, inexcusable silence about the almost 100,000 Iraqi civilians killed since the U.S. illegal assault (this, according to *The Lancet Study* at Johns Hopkins University) and about the daily piling up of Iraqi civilian dead and wounded.[10] Any patriotism that leads Christians to forget these dead is betrayal of the gospel. To remember and revere only the U.S. dead and wounded soldiers and contractors and not also the innocent Iraqi civilians killed and wounded by our actions is to betray the prophetic gospel of the Jewish Jesus who preached the grace of the kingdom for the Syro-Phoenician widow and the Syrian man.

Finally, maybe then it will also be time for U.S. Christians to turn and find that the God whom Jesus proclaimed in that Nazarene Synagogue has never abandoned the poor. Their release is in the works. They are still singing, worshiping, praying, fighting, working against, and dancing down the U.S. empire.[11] Its ways will not last. Syro-Phoenicia matters. Syria matters. God's grace is springing from them, for them, inviting us to meet God in struggle with them.

In the United States, Christians may be led to the brow of a hill, but we can make life there—and on any Calvary hill, too. It's been done before. There is a grace for the courage we need. Let's go.

[These remarks, in original form, were presented in Miller Chapel of Princeton Theological Seminary, November 2006.]

Notes

1. The most careful research is by journalist Esther Kaplan, *With God on Their Side* (New York: New Press, 2004).
2. Michael Ignatiev, *Empire Lite: Nation-Building in Afghanistan, Bosnia and Kosovo* (New York: Vintage, 2003).
3. Even FOX News Legal analyst and former New Jersey judge, Andrew Napolitano, argues this vigorously and with alarm in *Constitutional Chaos: What Happens When the Government Breaks Its Own Laws* (Nashville: Nelson Current Books, 2004). For another viewpoint, see Christian Parenti, *The Soft Cage: Surveillance in America* (New York: Basic Books, 2004).
4. For one example, see Anatol Lieven, *American Right or Wrong: The Anatomy of American Nationalism* (Princeton, NJ: Princeton University Press, 2004).
5. The story of these alliances today is in my recent book, *Religion, Politics and the Christian Right: Post-9/11 Powers and American Empire* (Minneapolis, MN: Fortress, 2005).
6. Michael Klare, *Blood and Oil: The Dangers and Consequences of America's Dependency on Imported Petroleum* (New York: Metropolitan, 2005), and *Resource Wars: The New Landscape of Global Conflict* (New York: Metropolitan, 2001).
7. Thomas Donnelly, *Rebuilding America's Defenses: Strategies, Forces and Resources for a New Century* (Washington, DC: Project for a New American Century, 2000).
8. Even a retired General, William E. Odom, has now called for a withdrawal and an acknowledgment of the "strategic error" in taking on the war. He's yet to comment on any "moral error," though he implies it.
9. Karen J. Greenberg and Joshua L. Dratel, *The Torture Papers: The Road to Abu-Ghraib* (New York: Cambridge University Press, 2005).
10. Les Roberts et al., "Mortality Before and After the 2003 Invasion of Iraq: Cluster Sample Survey," *The Lancet* 364, no. 9448 (November 2004): 1, 857–64.
11. Jeremy Bracer, Tim Costello, and Brendan Smith, *Globalization from Below: The Power of Solidarity* (Boston, MA: South End Press, 2000); and Eddie Yuen et al., eds., *The Battle of Seattle: The New Challenge to Capitalist Globalization* (New York: Soft Skull, 2001).

Index